B- Boyd, Neil
Boyd, Neil
        Bles

282.092
.B789
blc
1977

B

DATE DUE

JUL 7 1986	MAR 27 2000	
JUL 1 3 1987	APR 0 2 2003	
OCT 2 8 198	DEC 2 6 2008	
DEC 2 1 1987		
FEB 4 1988		
NOV 2 8 1988		
JUN 1 1989		
AUG 2 2 1990		
FEB 2 0 1991		
APR 1 2 1991		
APR 0 4 1992		
MAY 1 4 1994		
AUG 2 6 1998		

BLESS ME,
FATHER

BLESS ME, FATHER

NEIL BOYD

St. Martin's Press
New York

For
M and F and D
with love

Copyright © 1977 by Peter De Rosa
All rights reserved. For information, write:
  St. Martin's Press
  175 Fifth Avenue
  New York, N.Y. 10010
Manufactured in the United States of America
Library of Congress Catalog Card Number: 77-9169

Library of Congress Cataloging in Publication Data

Boyd, Neil.
  Bless me, father.

  1. Boyd, Neil. 2. Catholic Church—Clergy—
Biography. 3. Clergy—England—Biography. I. Title.
BX4705.B8115A33   1978   282'.092'4   [B]   77-9169

ISBN 0-312-08379-3   B - B

CONTENTS

I   My First Confession   1
II   An Unusual Pregnancy   25
III The Bell   35
IV   The Parish Bazaar   49
V   The New Assistant   61
VI   Breaking the Seal   78
VII The Betrothal   102
VIII Crumbs   117
IX   In the Swim   127
X   Father and Mother   155
XI   The Doomsday Chair   176
XII My First Baptism   206
XIII Femme Fatale   224
XIV Father Duddleswell Drives
        Under the Influence   240
XV   The November Blues   257
XVI Hell and High Water   278
XVII One Sinner Who Will
        Not Repent   292
XVIII My First Miracle   304
XIX A Thief in the Parish   323
XX   Sex Bows Its Lovely Head   341
XXI The Season of Good Will   363

1

MY FIRST
CONFESSION

Freedom at last! Six years of seminary studies and spartan discipline were behind me. On my plate at breakfast after ordination at the Cathedral in the early 'fifties was an envelope. In it was a card with details of my first appointment and a Latin document granting me "faculties" to hear confession in the diocese.

My curacy was to be in the parish of St Jude in Fairwater, part of the Borough of Kenworthy in West London. I was told that it was not fashionable like Chelsea nor unfashionable like Poplar in the dockland district of the East End. A mixed area but mostly working class.

One bright Saturday morning in early summer, after a two-week vacation with my parents in Brighton, I alighted from the red double-decker bus in the High Street. In each hand I carried a suitcase crammed with essential belongings. My bicycle and a hundred or so books which I imagined would be of help to me in saving souls were to follow by courtesy of British Railways.

I soon left the busy High Street near the Town Hall for the quieter Chindell Road where stood the grey-brick, fifty-year-old parish church of St Jude.

Before knocking on the adjoining rectory, I entered the church to pray before the Blessed Sacrament. There, the first thing to catch my eye was a confessional at the rear bearing my name: FR NEIL BOYD.

1

I knelt down before I fell down. Worse, this, than seeing my picture in a newspaper without prior warning. I prayed fervently in the half light of the church that I would make a good curate and particularly a kind and compassionate confessor. For eighteen years, since I was six, I had been a penitent myself. I had had my share of scruples and known the embarrassment of having to accuse myself of secret sins. In the seminary I had confessed, like the other students, at the knees of the Spiritual Director every Saturday night. At least the ordinary Catholic was spared that nobbly ordeal.

When I had recovered my composure, I looked about at the statues, the baroque High Altar, and the second confessional over which was printed in yellowed lettering: FR CHARLES DUDDLESWELL. Then I genuflected and left the church.

The rectory door was flung open before I could ring the bell, and I was greeted by a large, lumpy, white-haired lady in a green dress and flowery apron on which she wiped both her hands before trying to snatch my suitcases.

"Mrs Pring," she informed me, "housekeeper."

"Neil Boyd," I said, not yet used to calling myself "Father," and resisted her efforts to help.

She insisted on grabbing the cases while calling over her right shoulder:

"Father Neil's arrived."

From a room on the right came the scratchy sound of

> None shall part us from each other,
> One in life and death are we,
> All in all to one another,
> I to thee and thou to me.

And the plump parish priest appeared in a dishevelled cassock. The top button was in the second hole and the mistake was repeated twenty times down the line. It looked as if all his ribs were dislocated.

"Hello, Father Neil. A hundred thousand welcomes. You have just saved me life, d'you know that?" I smiled modestly at having done prestigious service so soon. "I have been dying for someone with a farthing of wit and intelligence to talk to."

Fr Duddleswell pumped my hand and peered cheerfully with his big blue eyes—their roundness accentuated by round steel-rimmed spectacles—into mine.

Already Mrs Pring was struggling up the stairs with my suitcases.

"Come into me study, Father Neil," said Fr Duddleswell, and when he had ushered me in and stopped the gramophone he called aloud, "Mrs Pring, a nice hot cup of tay for Father Neil, if you please."

This pronunciation of tea was, I soon discovered, one of his ways of touching his forelock to his Irish ancestry.

"That woman," he said, indicating Mrs Pring's broad back, "came to me twenty years past. The best instance I know of the worst coming to the worst." He offered me a chair. "Bishop O'Reilly informs me he has but recently made a priest of you."

"Three weeks ago, Father."

"Well, now, since you are a holy innocent, a seminary seedling, so to speak, the Bishop has asked me, the white-whiskered one, to teach you the tricks of the trade."

He lifted his glasses on to his forehead and pushed up his sleeves a little as if he was about to do a bit of conjuring.

"First trick, Father Neil, always keep something up your sleeve."

"What sort of things, Father?"

"That," he said, pursing his lips, "I cannot tell you."

"No?"

He shook his head. "If I did that, would I not have to change what's up me sleeve?"

I said I supposed so.

"Second, Father Neil." He extended both hands in front of him, back to back, as if at any moment he was going to scoop water aside and swim out of the room. "What's this, now?" he challenged.

"Siamese twins, Father?"

He made as if to spit but checked himself bravely. "'Tis

your right hand not knowing what your left hand is doing. Keep 'em total strangers to each other and you will come to no harm." I nodded, acknowledging the undoubted wisdom of the man. "Third," he went on, "listen like a woman to parish gossip—'tis your duty to know what is not going on around you—but hold your tongue." As I nodded again, he put his tongue out, broad and pink as a pig. "Bite it, if need be, till your teeth bleed." He gave a painful demonstration of what he meant. "Finally, when speaking to the good people, make sure you do not *tell* them anything. Pull down the shutters of your mind."

With the middle finger of each hand, he closed his eyelids, gave two angry snores and opened his eyes with a start. "You are still there, Father Neil?" he enquired. "I must have dozed off. Where was I?"

"You were saying a priest has to be discreet."

"Indeed. Cards to the chest, tight lips, stony-eyed—in a word, like our Blessed Lord Himself. Now, what else must a holy priest be like?" He warmed to the subject. "Kind at all times, of course, patient, full of considerateness and love for everyone..."

Mrs Pring checked his flow by putting her head round the door. "Sugar and milk, Father Neil?"

"Herself," groaned Fr Duddleswell, "would bloody-well interrupt Jesus in the middle of a miracle."

"Both, please," I said, and Mrs Pring, smiling the smile of the just, closed the door behind her.

"Now, Father Neil, Catholic priests do not marry. And why not?"

Mrs Pring's head reappeared to provide the answer. "Because there's not enough crazy women around." Then she put her head back on and left us to chat about parish matters. Before the tea arrived we were off on an inspection of the house.

"On the ground-floor here, next to me study, is the dining room. *There* is the big committee room—we call it the parlour—and down that corridor is the kitchen."

Mrs Pring, who had just descended the stairs, said, "*My* kitchen."

Fr Duddleswell pouted amusedly. "Women," he sighed, "almost as difficult to comprehend as nuns."

He lifted the skirt of his cassock—without noticing that the buttons were awry—and proceeded to climb the stairs.

"My bedroom," he said, nodding to his left.

He led me into the middle room which was to be my study, bare of ornament but for a few potted plants; then to my bedroom, overlooking the street, in which Mrs Pring had deposited the suitcases. The bedroom was small and dark with a wash basin, brown utility wardrobe, and chest of drawers. At the head of the iron bedstead was a faded copy of Velasquez's "Crucifixion."

"Run the hot water for a minute or two," he said. "It comes eventually if you pray hard enough to St Anthony. I only hope that bed is going to be long enough for you. Why was I not warned, then, you were two yards tall?"

I muttered something about being used now to sleeping knees up in beds smaller than myself. "Good," he said, "that will save me executing your legs off as I did with me last curate."

He hurriedly concluded the tour by showing me the bathroom and pointing heavenwards up the next flight of stairs. "Mrs Pring's domain. Trepassers *will* be, I can assure you of that now. Herself does not own much, that is why she is so fiendishly possessive."

By this time the maligned Mrs Pring had brought a cup of tea, black as syrup, into my study. I noticed her matronly forearms, rough elbows and her smooth red cheeks.

"Now, Mrs Pring, leave the lad alone," said Fr Duddleswell. "Do not smother him with your maternal ministrations."

Mrs Pring tried to say something, but he stopped her with a lordly gesture.

"Let him settle down, will you not? We do not have an hour to spare, you follow?"

I was left alone to try the bed for size, tidy away my clothes, and test the efficacy of prayers to St Anthony.

I had a premonition I was going to like it at St Jude's.

A few minutes later and my few books were on the shelf

and my framed papal indulgence was hanging on the wall. There was a gentle knock on the door. Mrs Pring had come to water the fuchsias.

"Don't be put off by him," she said comfortingly. "He's really a very nice man until you get to know him. If you have any difficulties with that one, just give Churchill a ring. Winnie's been longing for a good dogfight since he finished Gerry off five years ago."

"Oh, yes," I stammered.

"Him and me are what you might call a hellish combination. I do the weeping and he does the gnashing of teeth."

Her comforting was not having the effect she was intending. "What time do you serve meals, Mrs Pring?"

"He's terribly suspicious, you know. His dad was in antiques. If you ask me, he thinks everything's a fake but himself."

"Lunch is at one, I suppose."

"It's as if," said Mrs Pring, "he's seeing things in a mirror. He don't notice because *everything* is back to front."

A sharp rap on the door startled her. She grabbed her watering can saying, "The Day of Judgement, flee the wrath to come."

"Father Neil, I was..." Fr Duddleswell's smile vanished like a T.V. picture when the set is switched off. One moment it was as wide as his face, the next it had contracted to a dot before popping out altogether. "Woman," he growled, "I do not want you walking up me curate's sleeve. Did I not tell you to go West to your kitchen for a while? I *will* be obeyed here." He stamped his foot. "I will not have you wearing the cassock in this house."

"I should think not," the housekeeper said without flinching. "That skirt went out of fashion in Queen Victoria's time."

"Ah, Father Neil," said Fr Duddleswell, the gleam in his eye showing he conceded a temporary defeat, "she is more at me throat than is me collar itself."

"What time is lunch, Father?" I asked.

Mrs Pring drove home her advantage with, "Never trust the son of a cow."

"One o'clock, Mrs Pring?" I put in with a trifle more urgency.

"Father Neil," said Fr Duddleswell, "are you to be one of those curates who is always thinking of his belly?"

"I'm not hungry, Father," I hastened to say.

"Then why in the name of Beelzebub d'you keep on asking when lunch is?"

Mrs Pring touched my shoulder. "Poor Father Neil."

"I will not have the pair of you ganging up against me," Fr Duddleswell said. "Go, Mrs Pring, before I take me tongue to you."

Mrs Pring carried on with her condolences. "I'll put lunch forward if you're peckish, Father Neil."

I attempted to bring peace by insisting that I didn't mind if she served lunch at three.

Fr Duddleswell was not pleased by my magnanimity. "He is not above one hour at St Jude's and already he is changing the times of meals." Then he dropped his shoulders and relaxed. "I repent me of me loutish behaviour," he grinned.

"I'm sorry, too," added Mrs Pring. "I don't know what came over him."

In spite of the colourful exchanges, I sensed at once that the parish priest and his housekeeper were only indulging in banter which, while heated, was neither harsh nor bruising.

" 'Tis the problem of living year by year in one another's shoulders," explained Fr Duddleswell. "I only came to tell you I am intending to give you a whistlestop tour of the parish before lunch."

I thanked him for that.

"Do you not wish to know what time lunch is?" he asked.

"Not particularly, Father."

He gave me an incredulous smile. "What a strange lad y'are surely. You keep on asking questions and have not the slightest decent interest in the answers."

First stop, the maternity-wing of the hospital. From

behind a glass partition we gazed admiringly on half a dozen newly-born.

" 'Tis an extraordinary thing, Father Neil, yet there is but one father of all these."

"A sex maniac in the parish?" Humour is not my forte but I was doing my best.

"I was speaking in a spiritual sense, if you're still with me."

"You mean God, then."

"No, Father Neil. I mean me. This is why we priests do not marry, so we can be 'father' to the whole tribe." I followed the dab of his finger. "Look at that little boy . . . or girl. 'Tis hard to puzzle which when he or she is back to front and upside down." Too true, I thought. "By the way, how would *you* tell the difference between a boy and a girl?"

I hummed for a few seconds without coming to any articulate conclusion.

"How old are you, Father Neil?" he laughed. He beckoned my ear downwards. "Boys have blue eyes and girls have pink eyes. Did your mother never tell you that?" I removed my ear from the vicinity of his lips. "And if they are asleep, what then?"

"I don't know," I said stubbornly.

"A priest must use his initiative, like. While nobody is looking, you prise their little eyes open." When he laughed this time I joined in. "Ever hear the story, Father Neil, of two families holidaying together? First morning on the beach, the little Catholic boy of four summers is playing on the sands with the little Catholic girl, both of them skinwrapped as they came into the world. Know what the Catholic boy says to his mummy?"

"Yes, Father."

He was taken aback. "You do?"

"Yes."

"What?"

Somewhat shyly I said, "Mummy, I didn't know there was that much difference between Catholics and Protestants."

Fr Duddleswell's eyes came over glazed. "What difference are you speaking of, Father Neil?"

"Um. *The* difference, Father."

"Which is?"

"The difference, um, everyone knows about."

"Excepting me, it seems." A leggy nurse chanced to walk by. "I will just ask this lovely young nurse if she knows what difference 'tis you are referring to."

"Please, *don't*," I begged.

He shrugged in acquiescence. "A further thing is perplexing me. How would seeing a little girl in the state of nature make the little lad so sure she was a Protestant?"

"It wouldn't, Father." Lamely, I added, "And that's the joke."

"The joke, you say. Would you be so kind as to explain the *joke* to me?"

"I can't, Father."

He heaved a deep sigh. "So, then, Father Neil, you have learned your first important lesson at St Jude's."

"Lesson?"

"That if you steal me best punchlines, you must expect to suffer." Without a change of pace, he pointed to a six or seven pounder, "Anyway, what would you baptize him with?"

"It's a *her*," I said beaming defiantly.

"And you pretended not to know the difference," he said. "Well, what would you baptize her with?"

"Water, Father."

"I knew you would not use pea soup but what would you pour the water from, a fire-bucket?"

"A cup, Father?" I asked, improvising.

"Even that might drown the girleen or give her pneumonia. A cupful is, to one that size, the same as a swimming pool to a Jehovah's Witness."

"A thimble, Father."

"A thimble," he echoed. "Now, where would you get one of those in a maternity unit?"

I used my initiative. "I could borrow one from Mrs Pring."

Well in the driver's seat by now, Fr Duddleswell said to himself, "The lad is wanting to use Mrs Pring's thimble for a font."

"I can't think of anything smaller, Father."

Fr Duddleswell picked up a syringe from a surgical trolley. "You would use one of these. But make sure first it has water in it and not, say, hydrochloric acid."

"Baptism isn't legal with hydrochloric acid," I said, in case he didn't know.

"Not legal," he said, "but lethal, like. So you test it out on your skin, like this." He squirted some of the syringe's contents on to the back of his hand. "If it brings up a blister, do not use it on the baby's head." He paused to rub his hand where the liquid lay and blew on it anxiously. "Oh my God," he cried. The leggy nurse had returned. "Nurse, nurse, what the divil is in this syringe?"

"Water, Father."

Fr Duddleswell licked his hand before lifting his head in relief. "Thank God for that, 'tis only tapoline. Next, an important question, Father Neil. If a child is born premature, what would you do?"

"Call a nurse quick, Father."

"Brilliant," he almost sang. "What if after the baby is born premature a nurse calls *you* to the incubator?"

"I'd baptize it—him or her, according to the difference— in case the baby died." Fr Duddleswell nodded encouragingly. "With a syringe." Another friendly nod. "Not hydrochloric acid." He slowly shook his head.

"What else would you *not* do?"

As if to give the lie to my words I said wildly, "I wouldn't panic, Father."

"You would not... light... any... candles."

"No, Father?"

"No. Because with all that oxygen around, if you struck a match the poor little mite would go unbaptized—poof!—to Limbo."

It took me second or two to recover from the explosion. "Father," I said.

He was looking down paternally on all the infants in their cribs. "Yes?"

"Is it nearly time for lunch?"

It wasn't. We stood side by side, in the treelined cemetery gazing dreamily over the grassy and concrete beds with tombstones for headboards.

"Our last restingplace, Father Neil," he whispered. "Before we go off to lunch, I am meaning."

Glad of a few moments' rest, I murmured, "It's very peaceful here."

"You would hardly expect it to be a riot," he said. "Not with all those corpses stretched out and decomposing six feet below."

I asked him if this was a special plot for deceased Catholics. He nodded gravely and gave it as his opinion that Holy Mother Church was wise not to allow mixed funerals. "At the Last Day," he proclaimed cheerfully, "St Michael will blow loud the Trumpet Blast, and winds wild as angels on horseback will blow from the four corners of heaven, and the Almighty God will start His resurrecting, like, in this sacred little plot of Catholic earth."

I was in no mood for questioning the Lord's geographical preferences on Doomsday.

"Stand up, Seamus Flynn, the Lord will cry." Fr Duddleswell's evocation made me jump to attention. "Stand up, Mary Ryan. Stand up, Micky O'Brien, if you are yet sober."

Joining in the festive mood, I chanted, "Thigh bone connected to the hip bone."

He rounded on me. "And what will God say to Paddy Reilly who had no legs to stand on in life due to a motor accident?"

"Sit down, Paddy?" I suggested.

"Where is your faith, Father Neil? At the resurrection, God will put on Mrs Pring's thimble and the legless Paddy Reilly will have new ones sewn on. A marvellous sight to behold. One thing, though."

"Yes, Father?"

As he moved on, he called over his shoulder, "I only hope I am not around to see it."

A bit further on we came to the grave of

"FR FREDERICK CONNORS, PARISH PRIEST OF ST JUDE'S, 1890-1938."

"Your predecessor, Father?"

He nodded. "I remember that day twelve years since when we buried Freddie Connors.

"Only forty-eight years old," I said, after a quick calculation.

"Surprising he lasted so long, Father Neil. Always had trouble with his internals."

"Weak heart?"

"No, his housekeeper was a really shocking cook." He became solemn again. "The whole parish of St Jude's was here, living *and* dead. Oh, 'twas a gorgeous day for a funeral. A cold, gusty, end-of-the-year, end-of-a-life sort of day. The corpses were the warmest bodies here. Trees bare. The short grass faded, almost white. And not one bird sang."

"Did *you* officiate, Father?"

He shook his head. "Fr McNally did the honours. Tall and lean. A beanpole of a man, draped in black, McNally. With a booming voice and a huge red beak on him like an eagle with 'flu." He stopped to pull up a weed and threw it casually behind him. "Same old clichés—no less true for that, mind. 'Our beloved Brother, Frederick, departed this mortal life . . . ashes to ashes, sod to sod . . . vanity of vanities . . . what I am, he was; what he is, I will be.' "

His head dropped on his left shoulder as if it was too heavy for his neck alone to support. "The pallbearers slowly lowered the coffin and frozen earth dropped like thunder on the polished wood. I stood on the edge of the gaping hole there and looked down, dizzy-like, to pay me last respects to a dear old buddy. Wailings all around me, but through me tears I just managed to whisper, 'Thank God you are dead, Freddie boy.' " A heave of his chest and a loud sniffle. " 'You would never have lived through your funeral.' "

Out of the corner of my eye I saw him looking at me out of the corner of his eye.

"And now, Father Neil," he announced breezily, "I am sure you *must* be ready for a bite to eat."

At lunch on the dot of one, Fr Duddleswell, from his presiding chair under the gaudy print of Blessed Pius X, told me that the next morning, Sunday, he had arranged for me to say the two late Masses at eleven and twelve.

"Tonight," he added, "your confessions are from five to six."

I did my best to look unconcerned.

Mrs Pring, who had just brought in the steaming cottage pie, heard what Fr Duddleswell had said and interjected:

"If he's not been in the box before, he's probably scared out of his wits, poor Father Neil."

"Rightly so," retorted the parish priest, unscrewing the top of the sauce bottle. "He is probably thinking you will come yourself and unload on him your own heinous sins." Turning to me: "'Tis better to have a fixed time for confessions because in that way you gradually build up your own clientele, you follow? The good people get to know when and where to find you."

"And how to avoid the priests they can't abide," was Mrs Pring's parting shot as she left the room.

"She beats eggs just by talking to 'em, Father Neil." Then he whispered: "Her husband chose the better part."

I was shocked. "Divorced, Father?"

"No, no. I mean he laid down his life nice and easy like, on the field of battle." The kind-hearted priest added, "God rest him," and made the sign of the cross so swift no angel would have recognized it.

Not knowing quite what to do or say, I blurted out: "Amen."

"Now," he said, coughing and adopting a brisker tone once more, "about this holy sacrament which turns the sinner's wages from death to life. First, a word of advice. Never let on you know who 'tis that is confessing to you. You must *not* say, for instance, 'You really have improved since last month, have you not, Mrs O'Kelly?' or 'Leave the door ajar after you, Mr Tracey.' Above all, you must not be querulous ever and say, 'But Mr Jones, your wife just admitted to using contraceptives *seven* times, not *five*.'"

"I promise not to be querulous, Father," I said, suspecting that one of my long legs was getting rapidly longer. "But does that sort of thing happen often?"

"Using contraceptives?"

"No, Father, lying about it."

Showing mild surprise, he asked, "Did I mention the word 'lying'? 'Tis rather like on the golf course, Father Neil. The men are such marvellous proud creatures they tend to underestimate how many strokes they take to the hole. There is no malice to it."

"Just bad addition, you mean."

"And sometimes subtraction," he responded knowingly. "At the start," he said confidentially, bowing towards me a domed head over which was slanted his thinning hair and skewering me with his eye, "at the start, I am sorry to have to tell you this, you are likely to get the more . . ." He reached for a word, missed and reached again, "hardened sinners."

"Hardened" was accentuated but softly.

My spine grew instant icicles but I tried to brave it out by joking, "Not you and Mrs Pring?"

He pointed to my plate. "Take a mound of mustard with that and you might be lucky enough not to taste the food at all." I obeyed. "Some'll think—quite mistakenly, to be sure— you are a greenhorn who's not yet heard that sin has been invented. Others'll take advantage of the fact that you cannot fix a voice to a face. But in two shakes of a black sheep's tail you will only have your fair share of *hardened* sinners."

The thought of being initially saturated with more than my fair share of trouble was to be a lemon in my mouth for the rest of the afternoon.

"Any questions, Father Neil?—apart from the time of supper."

"Tea-time, Father?" I ventured. Since it brought no reaction, I tried again. "Is it interesting?"

"Are you referring to the timetable of meals in this house or the holy sacrament? No, Father Neil, 'tis not at all interesting sitting there by the hour with harmless women and children spitting sins into your unprotected ear. 'Tis bloody

14

tedious, if you want to know, especially"—he tapped his thigh—"if you suffer from the occupational hazard. Mind you, if you have a nice juicy *murder* this very morning, that is another matter surely. Your first penitent perhaps."

I knew he was teasing me but I still gulped and said, "That's not likely, Father." When he did not reply: "Is it?"

"Oh, at a guess and on the basis of me own experience, at least four to one against. Sex, now, is another kettle of fish."

"Sex comes up more frequently?"

"Well," he tutted, "since you brought the indelicate subject up, I tell you. If an Irish girl confesses to company-keeping, be sure to investigate that thoroughly."

"By questioning?"

He looked at me as if to say, How else? "To a colleen, Father Neil, company-keeping can mean anything from holding hands in the park to multiple adulteries. And watch out for the way English people—not Americans who are decent and straightforward folk—slip their mortal sins into the middle of a pack of peccadilloes. Now, as to birth control."

To prove the adequacy of my seminary training I told him that scientists were reported to be working on a contraceptive pill.

"And no doubt," he replied scornfully, "the same Lucifer-like fellows think that one day they will fly to the moon. To practicalities. Contraception is a grievous sin because there is interference with nature to make sure that one and one do not make three." I smiled, hoping it was expected of me. "The Lord said to our first parents, 'Multiply' not 'Stultify.' And, by the way, what would have happened, like, if Adam and Eve had used contraceptives?"

"Nothing, Father."

"Indeed. For a start, you and I would not be here conversing and the whole world would be one gigantic zoo without any keepers to look after the animals. Could anything demonstrate better the evils of contraception?"

I shook my head to show his argument had convinced me.

"Father Neil, what *natural* methods of birth control are permitted by the Church?"

"Complete abstinence, Father."

"From what?" he asked. "From the drink? From flesh meat? Fish and chips? Be specific, if you would?"

"From sex."

He pursed his lips approvingly. "Complete sexual abstinence is pure. And effective, certainly. Especially if husband and wife take the precaution of sleeping in separate towns."

"The other method," I said, "is using the safe-period."

"But once the intercourse of man and woman has begun," he said, lowering his fork, "what may lawfully interrupt it?"

That was the moment Mrs Pring chose to poke her head round the door to say, "Plum pudding and custard?"

Fr Duddleswell told her with measured impoliteness that when he was ready for his plum pudding and custard he would let her know. He repeated his question about any exceptions to the general rule of not interrupting intercourses—"apart from Mrs Pring's dessert."

I played for time. "You do mean married couples?"

"If they're unmarried, boy, they should interrupt it before they start."

I had never asked myself such an intimate question before and so I enquired distractedly if an earthquake would do.

"Surely, Father Neil, but do you mean that as cause or effect?" When he saw I had finished guessing he put it to me, "Suppose the children come unannounced into their parents' bedroom."

"During..."

"Yes."

"For a drink of water, Father?"

"For any reason whatsoever, whether to drink water or to pass it."

"Ah," I exclaimed, as my memory came into focus, "it's all right to stop sex—in the middle—if the bed breaks, Father."

"Correct!" He slapped his knee in applause. "Provided of course their intention is not to prevent conception but only to restore a semblance of order to the room."

When lunch was over, Fr Duddleswell led me into the church. After a prayer he showed me my confessional at close quarters.

"You will notice," he said, "I have seen to it there is a blackout curtain over the grill. The good people like to think you cannot tell them from Adam and Eve."

"And *can* you, Father?"

"The priest in the confessional, Father Neil, is like a blind man: all ears. Consequently, his hearing becomes very acute, if you're still with me. In a while you will recognize every voice in the parish. More," he spoke with a certain professional pride, "before they even open their mouths, you will know who is there from their footsteps, from how they open the confessional door, from the squeaks they make when they kneel down on the prie-dieu—even from the way they breathe."

My breath caught in my throat on hearing of Fr Duddleswell's remarkable talent for detection.

"Often, Father Neil, you will know their sins before they confess them."

"Even the mortal, Father?"

"*Especially* the mortal."

I guessed he was finding me an audience very much to his liking.

"Sometimes you will smell it on them like booze and garlic. But most horrible of all..."—I waited, my mind boggling at the prospect of what was to come—"you will know which of them should visit their dentist. The sins themselves are odious enough, but bad breath! Phew. Now, finally," he seemed relieved he had got that off his chest, "deaf-mutes."

Disconsolate, I could only repeat the latest source of my troubles.

"There are two problems with them," he said briskly. "They cannot hear you and..."

"You cannot hear them." He was pleased I was so quick on the uptake. "How do you hear their confessions, then?"

"Unless you can work a miracle, you cannot. See here." He entered the confessional and showed me a drawer under the grill which he pulled out. "It opens two ways. The deaf-mute writes his sins on a piece of paper and sends it to you. You then write his penance underneath, return it to him and give him absolution. If it says on the paper, 'A pound of sausages and two lamb chops,' you know the butcher has just received a very interesting order."

"What," I objected, "if the deaf-mute can't read or write?"

He looked at me a little wearily. "Father Neil, must you be ever manufacturing difficulties for yourself. Whoever heard of a deaf-mute going to confession if he cannot read or write."

"But suppose one does."

"Oh," he concluded, as if no solution could be more obvious, "You pull down the curtain, lad, and use sign language."

Mrs Pring served tea at four, and it lasted a quarter of an hour. I did not take in much of what was said to me. Immediately afterward, I went to my room to prepare myself for the impending ordeal. I was quivering as, I imagined, a surgeon is before his first operation—except I knew the harm I could do was far worse since it was harm to *souls*.

I put on my cassock, recently purchased from Van Haigh's, the clerical tailors for my ordination. My parents, though not well-off, insisted I have it. There were no soupstains down the front. It had all its buttons. My hand trembled so that I had difficulty in fastening them up.

Fr Duddleswell came to my study to lead me, as he said, "through the milling crowds" to my confessional.

I expressed gratitude for his support.

"I only hope, Father Neil, that your dear knees are not knocking their heads together."

We descended the stairs and passed through the door connecting house and sacristy. Thence, apprehensively, into the church.

It was empty.

I had expected to find benchfuls of sinners waiting to make their confession. For some reason, the emptiness had a more damaging effect upon my constitution than if the place had been crowded. It made me feel more isolated than Moses on the mountain top.

"God heavens, Father Neil, there is not an individual here. I should have placed an ad in the paper."

I genuflected with a wobble and walked down the side aisle to the confessional with my name on it, our footfalls echoing as in a museum. There he shook my hand with emotion and left.

I opened up the priest's side of the box and put on the purple stole that was draped across the chair, closed the door, and sat down. At least I was privately alone there and not publicly alone as in the church.

The door of the box had a top section of smoky glass. Through it, I saw amorphous shadows dancing in the flickering light of candles. The irreverent thought came to me that this was like sitting on an ancient lavatory.

I had almost succeeded in pulling myself together when I became aware that I was not alone after all. There were *noises*.

I imagined someone had either tiptoed into the penitents' side of the box or been hiding there all along. I listened. I said, "Yes?" in case there was a penitent waiting to begin. No speech, only noises.

I felt some *thing* brush against the bottom of my cassock.

With a yell, I pushed open the confessional door and jumped out of my seat with an almighty crash. It was a mouse—rodents always give me the creeps—a mother mouse followed crazily by two smaller mice. They must have been nesting since spring behind the radiator. They scuttled away into the gloom.

I could not follow their course because I saw another spectre. An elderly lady in a flowerpot hat had entered the church at the very moment I burst out of the box. Unaccustomed to such a wild display from an unknown clergyman, she screamed and ran from the church.

There goes my first penitent, I reflected. I hoped she would not report me to the police.

I returned warily to the box and saw that in my haste to escape I had kicked the chair from under me and smashed one of its legs. It hung on by a sliver of wood.

I would have fixed it on the spot if I had been a practical man. But it so happens I'm what my father calls "maladroit."

Even my right foot is left-handed, so to speak. Guiltily, I crossed to Fr Duddleswell's box carrying my chair and exchanged it for his.

Back in my own box, I switched on the naked bulb above my head. Having assured myself there was no daddy mouse lurking in a corner waiting to pounce, I opened my breviary. This was a grotesque piece of self-deception. Prayer was impossible, and I had already recited my office for that day in any case. But the black leather-bound book gave me a much needed feeling of warmth and security.

In the seminary, Canon Flynn had advised us to copy out the Latin formula for confession in case we should forget it in a moment of crisis. I had written it out in capitals on a sheet of paper. When the penitent came in, the custom was to extinguish the light which meant the letters had to be large if I was to read them.

I was grateful for Canon Flynn's advice. By then I would have found it difficult to recite even the Lord's prayer without a prompter.

Ages seemed to pass. My watch, which never panicked, told me it was eight minutes past the hour. Then came the sound of feet brushing hard on the rough mat at the entrance to the church. Someone knelt noisily and with a sigh near my confessional box but beyond my range of vision. I wondered if the lady with the flowerpot hat had summoned enough courage to return and, if so, what would I say to her? And what would she say to me?

"Bless me, Father, for I am a sin."

In my relief, I could have given my invisible young penitent a big hug for making such a shambles of the opening formula.

"*Dominus sit in corde* ... May the Lord be in thy heart and on thy lips that thou mayest truly and humbly confess thy sins, in the name of the Father and of the Son and of the Holy Ghost." I made the sign of the cross.

The child's voice went on:

"Father ..."

20

"Yes?"

"This is my *second* confession."

My first, I thought. I said: "And when was your first confession?"

There was a pause before the voice answered. "Just before my first Communion."

"When was that?"

"Two weeks ago. Everybody knows that."

"Well," I explained, "I'm new to the parish, you see."

"Oh," the voice said, not very convinced.

Another silence which the voice broke by asking: "Are you still there, Father?"

"Yes," I said, grateful for some sign that my penitent hadn't abandoned me. "What are your sins, dear?"

I was pleased with that. "Dear" was a good indefinite English word with which to address a child whose age and sex were undetermined. Of course, Fr Duddleswell would have had the edge. . . .

"I called the grocer a pig."

So it wasn't only the Yanks who were frank about their faults. "Yes," I murmured noncommittally. I didn't want to appear either to condone the offence or to be shocked by it.

"Two times, Father."

"Why did you call him that?"

"'Cos he deserved it. He *was* a pig. He wouldn't give me a chocolate marshmallow when I asked him to."

Another pause, so I said: "Was there something else?"

After a silence broken only by the rocking on the prie-dieu, the voice whispered:

"I committed adultery three times."

I blinked in the darkness. Was I dealing with an older person, after all—say, a dwarf with a high-pitched voice? I managed to get out a question Canon Flynn had advised us never to put: "What exactly did you do?"

"I took three pennies out of mummy's purse." Then the voice corrected the mistake: "No, that's the next commandment isn't it, the funny one? I know what it was, I stoled three times."

"Mummy trusts you, dear," I said, gently rather than reproachfully, "and you shouldn't let her down, should you?"

"She don't," returned the voice.

"Doesn't what?"

"She don't *trust* me, not further'n she can throw me."

"Anything else?" I asked, ready for a change of subject.

"She owed me it for washing up."

"Anything else?" I repeated.

"She did, too."

No comment.

"I committed a mortal sin."

"How?" I bit my tongue. Another prohibited question.

"I didn't go to Mass last Sunday."

"Why was that? Were you ill or something?"

"No," replied the voice, sighing and blowing on the bottom of the confessional veil so it billowed and touched my ear. "Marge wouldn't come with me."

"Is Marge your sister?"

"No, Marge is my mum. Everybody knows that."

"I'm new...," I began but gave up. "Doesn't your father go to church?"

"My dad, you mean?"

"Yes, your dad."

"He came to my first Communion."

"Not otherwise?"

"He says next time he comes it'll be in a bleedin' box, Father."

I quieted my soul with the reflection that the child was only quoting.

"Is he a Catholic?"

"No, Father."

"Is he a believer, then?"

"No, he's a bus-driver."

"Well," I said, having sat in judgement long enough on my first penitent, "for your penance I want you to go to Our Lady's altar and say one Our Father and one Hail Mary for your mummy and daddy. Now make a good act of contrition while I give you absolution."

I spread out my sheet of paper on my knee and started to quietly read the absolution. I tried to be conscious of the solemnity of the occasion in spite of having to do my balancing act on the chair. For the first time in my priestly life I was forgiving sins in Christ's name.

"*Misereatur tui, omnipotens Deus...*"

I had gone some way and still no sound of the act of contrition from the penitent. I halted and said encouragingly:

"Oh my God, because Thou art so good..."

The voice repeated, "O my God," and, satisfied it would continue under its own steam, I finished off the absolution.

At the end, I said:

"Go in peace, dear, and pray for me."

There was a creak and a shuffle before the voice said: "I forgot my penance, Father."

"One Our Father and one Hail Mary."

The other side of the box banged open. I saw a pint-sized shadow flitter by and heard the clip-clip of a child's feet going through the church.

Someone else had entered the box with a heavy sigh and creaking of the prie-dieu. I suspected I wasn't going to be let off so lightly this time. I gave the blessing. I listened. No sound.

"How long is it?" I asked. Since there was still no sound I repeated my question, only louder.

The clip-clip in advance of a shadow was already on the way back past the confessional. There was a light tap on my window and my first penitent said, "Bye-bye, Father."

"Goodbye, dear," I said, as tiny footsteps were swallowed up in the open air, and the voice went home to Marge. Now I could concentrate on my second penitent. "How long is it since your last confession?" I could hear heavy breathing continuing so I banged nervously on the box to get some reaction.

Then the situation became painfully clear. A deaf-mute? Must be a deaf-mute.

I opened up the drawer. Nothing there. Frantically I wrote on the back of my sheet of paper: "WHAT ARE YOUR SINS?" and put it in the drawer. I waited for a few seconds until the sound of scribbling on the other side of the grill had ceased, then pulled the drawer out again. Underneath my question, written in the clearest hand, was the answer: "MIND YOUR OWN BUSINESS."

Angrily I pulled aside the curtain to see Fr Duddleswell's cherubic face beaming at me through the grill like a fish in a net. "Do not forget to replace me chair when you have finished with it."

"No, Father."

"And, Father Neil."

"Yes, Father?"

"May your stay at St Jude's continue as happily as it has begun."

2

AN UNUSUAL
PREGNANCY

My earliest impression of my parish priest was that, notwithstanding his bland exterior, he was a wily old bird. This impression was soon to be confirmed.

We were standing side by side outside the church one Sunday morning. He was still wearing his vestments because it was his custom, immediately after he had celebrated the late Mass, to leave the sanctuary while the choir was still busy chanting the prayer for the King and race down the aisle like a rabbit to greet the parishioners as they filed out.

"We priests have got to be as sociable as sun and rain," he'd said to me, and as the "good people" emerged blinking into the daylight, he shook their hands, spoke to each of them, and wished them "God's blessing on you and yours."

Fr Duddleswell introduced me to any number of the congregation, mentioning their names and addresses. It was like expecting me to memorize the telephone directory. But towards the end of the line, he introduced me to a couple whose name had a familiar ring.

"Father Neil, I'd have you meet Mr and Mrs Macaulay, stalwarts of the parish."

They beamed at the compliment and shook my hand with Irish *bonhomie*.

"And this," added Fr Duddleswell, "is their married daughter, Mary Frost."

I exchanged greetings with Mary Frost, a little alarmed as celibates tend to be, at the fact that she was so advanced in pregnancy.

"Father Neil," said the obviously dominant Mrs Macaulay, "our Tim has often spoken of you."

Then I was certain I was being introduced to the family of Tim Macaulay who'd been my best pal in the seminary.

"Our Tim's turn next, Father," Mr Macaulay softly said to me.

"And a grand priest he'll make, too," said Fr Duddleswell.

"It so happens," said Mrs Macaulay, telling me what she must have realized I knew as well as she, "our Tim is a subdeacon, but this time next year he'll be celebrating his first holy Mass in St Jude's."

"God willing," added the quiet Mr Macaulay.

"And how is Mary?" asked Fr Duddleswell, turning to the round and lovely daughter whose features reminded me very much of her brother.

Mary said blushingly, "As well as could be expected, considering, Father."

"Delighted to hear it," responded Fr Duddleswell.

"Father married Mary and Patrick in St Jude's a little over nine months ago," Mrs Macaulay announced to me in a volume more appropriate to a loudspeaker.

"A great occasion," said the parish priest. "Will I ever forget it? I never will."

"And the power of Fr Duddleswell's blessing will soon be made manifest to all the world," said the eloquent Mrs Macaulay.

I thought the world had a grandstand view already.

Next to me, Mr Macaulay shuffled his feet and whispered, "We're very much looking forward to the happy event, Father."

"In a couple of weeks," said his wife, "Mary is going to present us with our very first grandson. Isn't that so, now, Mary?"

Mary blushed a deeper hue. "God willing," she murmured.

Sharing Mary's discomfort, I attempted to put her at her ease, "And how is your husband, Mrs Frost?"

"Very well, Father, thanking you. He's in Birmingham. I'm just down for the weekend."

"Mary," said Fr Duddleswell, "I think you are a very brave girl coming all this way from the Midlands on your own at this time."

"I'll be all right, Father, and Pat's going to pick me up at Birmingham New Street tonight."

Mrs Macaulay put in: "So it'll mean another baptism for you not too long hence."

"I look forward to every christening," said the parish priest. "Now run along with you and do not keep poor Mary on her feet one second longer than she needs."

As the happy family group departed, Fr Duddleswell was repeating mostly to himself: "A lovely girl, a lovely girl that Mary, lovely girl."

At lunch, I remarked on the striking likeness between Mary and her brother, Tim.

"Provided she does not take after her mother, she can count herself blessed among women."

"Her mother is a strong character, I could tell."

"Strong as Gorgonzola cheese and proud as a paycock."

I thought his tone uncharacteristically acid. "She seemed a pious sort of person," I ventured.

As he flicked over the pages of *The News Of The World*, he said: "Oh, she is pious all right. A Pharisee of Pharisees, if you ask me."

"She's looking forward to a little grandson, Father."

"Not this time round."

I was silent for a moment, wondering whether he were a prophet or gynecologists were at last able to determine a child's sex before birth.

"Are you sure, Father?" I said.

"Quite sure."

Fr Duddleswell suddenly closed his newspaper with a swish, raised his spectacles onto his forehead and said:

"Promise me you will not let on."

I promised, not knowing what this was all about.

"*Sub sigillo*, I mean it," he continued. "Treat this as a confessional secret. The truth of the matter is: Mary Frost is not pregnant at all. At least, I hope to God she isn't."

It was on the tip of my tongue to ask him if he might be mistaken. Each time he opened his mouth I was becoming more confused.

"Father," I managed to say, "she *looks* pregnant."

"She is supposed to look *very* pregnant. But, in fact, Mary Frost had her baby a couple of months ago." He must have seen my look of disbelief, for he added, "And 'twas a girl, not a boy. Mrs Macaulay has a grand-daughter, and that is more than she deserves."

"And why, Father, does Mary look pregnant, when she isn't?"

"An old trick. Cushions, Father Neil, cushions."

Grudgingly, he explained. "Mary Macaulay was made pregnant by Paddy Frost two months before they married. Mary is no whore, let me assure you of that. The first and only time she went company-keeping, Paddy got her in the family way. Their proficiency was entirely due to inexperience, you follow?"

"A popgun wedding?" I asked.

"A *shot*gun wedding is the more common phrase," he said, smiling faintly, "but I reckon, Father Neil, that your description is the more apt."

"I meant they had to get married."

"In a manner of speaking, but they loved each other, mind. Paddy is your typical Irishman, not disposed towards marriage unless there is sufficient reason for it. His unexpected talent for paternity supplied the precipitating reason, and they were wed without argument. Nothing like a child, as they say, to bring a couple together."

Fr Duddleswell went on to say he'd had to resort to subterfuge on account of Mrs Macaulay's excessive pride.

"Mary knew well enough the kind of mother she had

inherited. If she had owned up to her condition, Mrs Macaulay would have shown her the door and used her timid little man for a doorstopper."

"Would she *really*?"

"Not a doubt about it, Father Neil. Remember the woman comes from the heart of bogland. Did she not name her daughter after the Blessed Virgin herself? 'Tis a marvel to me she let her darlin' Mary enter the lustful condition of matrimony at all. Anyway, the real light of her life is Tim, who is destined to be a priest and thus guarantee a place in heaven for all the family. Mrs Macaulay could not bear the thought of it being whispered abroad that her holy son has a harlot for a sister."

"I know the kind of thing you mean, Father. There was an Irishman entered the seminary with me who gave up after six months and..."

"And he could not return to his native Dublin on account of him being 'a spoiled praste' and a disgrace to his bloody family."

"It was Galway, actually."

"What *can* you do with people of that mentality, Father Neil? Two months after the ceremony, before anything showed, I parcelled the newly-weds off to Birmingham. Paddy is only a bricklayer, and he can lay one brick on t'other as well in Birmingham as anywhere else. They rented a room on the edge of town. They are finding it tough financially, you know how 'tis, starting with two mouths and two salaries and now three mouths and one salary. But they manage. They are content just being away from Mother Macaulay."

I worked my way through most of my first course before daring to say, "One small question, Father. How do you manage to...?" I hesitated.

"To square it with me conscience?"

"What I meant was..." I couldn't delicately express what I meant but he seemed to understand.

"'Tis like this, Father Neil: Mary's not saying she's pregnant. Neither am I."

"Everybody else is, Father."

"'Tis true. But that is their look-out, is it not?"

"And you don't feel in any way responsible for their misunderstanding?"

"Father Neil, Mary is making a justifiable mental reservation. You know what a mental reservation is?"

I thought, "Putting a cushion up your jumper and letting folk believe you're pregnant when you're not." But I only dared say, "It's the art of letting people deceive themselves without actually telling them lies."

"A definition worthy of St Thomas Aquinas," he exclaimed appreciatively. "There are times, believe you me, when to lie would be a sin and to tell the truth would be a disaster."

"And silence?"

"Silence...silence can be very...pregnant, if you will forgive the expression. Silence can arouse the very suspicions you are aiming to eliminate."

"I suppose so, Father."

"Father Neil, a priest has to become a good poker player. He has so many secrets, confessional and otherwise, he cannot reveal that he has to be a skilled practitioner of the mental reservation."

To change the subject, I asked, "When have you decided the baby's going to be...born?"

"In a day or so, Mary's hubby, Paddy, is due to send a telegram to Grannie Macaulay. Here, I'll show you."

He took two pieces of notepaper out of his wallet.

"This first is the telegram. It reads: 'Mother and baby doing well. It's a girl. Love Pat.' I'm not sure Paddy can write, so I have to put words on the lips of his pen, like. And this here," he said, waving the second sheet, "is a letter from Mary to be sent a couple of days later. In it, Mary explains that the baby having been born premature..."

I looked up. "Premature, Father?"

"Two months premature, in fact. Due to this, shall we say, early delivery, a priest in Birmingham baptized the baby, naming her Kathleen after her grandmother." He gritted his teeth at the reference to a lady whose excessive pride, he considered, was causing him much inconvenience.

"*Is* the baby baptized, Father?"

"Of course. You do not think I would ask Mary to tell a lie on my behalf, do you? I baptized little Kathleen three days after her birth in Paddy's flat."

"*You're* the Birmingham Priest?"

"The priest *in Birmingham*," he corrected me.

"But, Father"—I spoke as politely as I could—"I was taught you can only baptize a baby in private when there's danger of death."

"Quite right, Father Neil. And was there not an imminent danger of death when Kathleen came into the world?"

"You mean she really *was* premature?"

"Not at all. She was born nine months to the second after she was conceived. I mean there was danger of spiritual death, you follow? Now don't you try telling me that is not what canon law intends. 'Tis what the Almighty intends that matters."

"Spiritual death?" I echoed, hoping for some sort of explanation.

"Would there not be slaughter of souls all round, Father Neil, were the truth to be broadcast? Mrs Macaulay would disown her daughter and die like the Pharisee she is, Mary and baby Kathleen would be deprived respectively of mother and grandmother—no great loss from an outsider's point of view but distressing perhaps from theirs."

At this juncture, Mrs Pring came in to remove the remains of the first course and supply us with strawberries and custard.

Pointing to the bowl of strawberries, Fr Duddleswell said, "Sacred Hearts again, Mrs Pring?"

"Yes, your irreverence. There's a glut of 'em in the market, so the price has fallen faster'n Lucifer himself. If they go down much more I can see you having 'em for breakfast besides."

"And *custard*?"

"I know you likes it, so why shouldn't I pamper you?"

As Mrs Pring prepared to depart in a clatter of cutlery and dirty dishes, Fr Duddleswell said for her benefit, "We had an American priest supplying here last summer, Father Neil, and he suggested that in England the taps should be marked Hot, Cold, and Custard."

Mrs Pring snorted like a cow on a cold morning and lifted her nose in disdain.

"Oh, and by the way, Mrs Pring," Fr Duddleswell said, before she could screen herself with the door.

"I know. Midwifery again tonight."

"Mary will come to the side at eight o'clock as usual, and I'll run the both of you to Euston Station."

"This'll be the third time I've delivered that bairn."

"And the last, Mrs Pring."

"I'm pleased for Mary's sake you've finally agreed to let Kathleen come into the world. Must be the longest pregnancy on record."

When she had gone, Fr Duddleswell's comment was: "She has her uses, does Mrs Pring. *Très formidable*. Arms like Moses. Should have been a windowcleaner."

He went on to explain that Mary was currently carrying Mrs Pring's kitchen cushion. He and Mrs Pring were meeting Mary at Euston on Fridays, where the foetus was implanted in the Ladies room and the miscarriage took place on the Sunday evenings following.

"There is only the christening to think of now," said Fr Duddleswell. "Kathleen has been baptized; all that remains is to supply the rest of the ceremonies in St Jude's."

"When will that be?"

"No hurry. We will wait awhile so 'tis not so easy to judge how old the child is. Everyone will say that Kathleen is very advanced for her age, and this will make her old granny prouder and fitter for the Fire than ever."

To stir things up a little, I put forward a hypothesis of my own: "What if Mary really is pregnant again and another child turns up too soon after the first? Won't you have to go through all this trouble again?"

"Not on your life, I won't. I won't. No. I won't. I would not care now if the next babe were born two days after its conception. That would be a miracle, no doubt, but no aspersions would be cast on its legitimacy. So!"

"Aren't you afraid," I asked finally, "that Mary and Patrick will give you away?"

"Not a chance, Father Neil. They are terrified of that old harpy, can you not see that? And," he added less convincingly, "they are terrified of me, too. I have warned 'em that if they let the cat out of the bag, I'll whip 'em to a pulp with me rosary."

"It seems safe enough, then."

"Of course," he added, "I put the fear of God into them for good measure. Told 'em I considered the whole matter is under the seal of confession. They will not breathe a word of it now, even to their guardian angel."

A few weeks later, I went to the reception at the Macaulays' after Kathleen's christening. There I made the acquaintance of Paddy, an incoherent lad with freckles who had originated the whole train of events, and I said "Hello again" to Mary, now a trim, relaxed young woman.

Across the room, I could see Fr Duddleswell listening with growing agitation to something Mrs Macaulay was whispering in his ear. He was becoming redder and redder, and he kept raising his spectacles and lowering them on his nose, a gesture I interpreted to mean he was furious about something.

After a couple of minutes, he suddenly broke away from the conversation, proclaiming with masterly self-control, "Charming little grand-daughter, you have, Mrs Macaulay, to be sure, charming." But as he grazed past me to get to the door, he was muttering so only I heard: "The bitch. The bloody bitch. Deceiving me all this time."

He left in an almighty hurry.

Mrs Macaulay, for her part, followed Fr Duddleswell with a beatific smile. Then she came across to me and led me to where Kathleen was lying asleep in her cradle.

"Fr Duddleswell..." she began.

"Yes?"

"He's a real saint is that darlin' man and innocent as a newborn babe. As the saying is in the Emerald Isle, may he be in heaven half an hour before the devil knows he's dead."

"I'm glad you think so highly of him," I said, saddened that her kindly sentiments towards my parish priest were not reciprocal.

"Yes," said Mrs Macaulay. "I can tell *you*, Father, because you're a praste. It was Fr Duddleswell himself saw to it that our Kathleen was born legitimate, like."

3

THE BELL

"How'd you like a bell, Padre?"

We had just finished my first meeting of the board of school governors when Major Timmins, a retired army officer, addressed this question to Fr Duddleswell.

"What sort of a bell, Major?"

"Cast-iron . . . bell-shaped . . . you know what a bell's like."

Fr Duddleswell had previously told me the Major was a rich, kindly gentleman of few words, and he certainly lived up to this non-description.

"How large might it be, now?" asked Fr Duddleswell.

"Couple of hundred pounds. Bought it in my village in Wiltshire."

Apparently, it really was the Major's village. His family had owned most of the farmland in the area for generations.

"Is it very old, Major?"

"Victorian. Perfect condition. Taken from the Anglican church at the end of the war. Meant to boost the war-effort—cannons, shells, that sort of thing."

"And they did not put it back for some reason?" asked Fr Duddleswell, almost standing to attention.

"Couldn't. The tower was tumbling down. Nitwits rebuilt it on economy lines, and now the damn bell won't fit."

"That's very generous of you, Major."

"Not at all," said the Major, blustering at the compliment. "Only cost me £50. Thought of you immediately, Padre."

"I will ask our architect to look into the matter straight away. If the tower's foundations will take it, we would be delighted to accept your kind offer."

"Let me know, then," coughed the Major, as his chauffeur stepped smartly forward to open the rear door of his Daimler. "Glad to see, by the way, you've got a new recruit."

"What a marvellous slice of luck," Fr Duddleswell said to me when the Major had floated out of sight. "I have been desiring a bell for years and now the fairies have offered me one for free."

"Why did St Jude's never have one before?"

"It did. But ours, too, was commandeered with the railings for the war-effort and it never came back. Since then, all we have had in the tower are Billy Buzzle's blasted pigeons."

Mr Buzzle, who lived beside the church, had his back yard next to ours. I often saw him whiling away the afternoon hours among the flowers. He always looked the same: mottled face, square jaw, bushy eyebrows, a wisp of hair curled by tongs jutting over his right eyebrow. He invariably wore a smart pin-striped suit, from the sleeves of which emerged large, stiff, white cuffs with diamond links which made it seem as if both his arms were in splints from the elbows down.

Billy was a bookie, but he wasn't on good terms with Fr Duddleswell for a number of reasons. Firstly, Billy's business interests, according to Fr Duddleswell, were mostly illegal. Apart from his Nightclub, The Blue Star, which had a shady reputation in the district, Billy also employed several "runners" who accepted bets on his behalf at street corners, in pubs, factories, cafés, and on building sites where many Irish laborers worked. These runners were occasionally picked up by the police and fined. Billy paid the fines with the money he saved on income tax.

But what incensed Fr Duddleswell most was the fact that Mr Buzzle, a pigeon-fancier, kept in his garden a hundred racing pigeons, a great number of which nested by preference in our church tower.

From my study window I had seen and heard Fr Duddleswell several times chiding Mr Buzzle over the garden fence for "the unseemly behavior of your blankety-blank birds billeted without leave on our premises."

Whenever Fr Duddleswell complained about the noise, the stench, and the mess in the tower, Billy said, "Aren't they *holy* birds, now, Father? And isn't your God Himself a pigeon-fancier, using one to tell the world the Flood was over? And wasn't there another pigeon crowning Jesus the Christ when he got himself baptized?"

To this Fr Duddleswell replied with a warmth I now knew he reserved for his special friends. "Nothing of the sort, you heathen, you. It was not Jesus but Jehovah that soaked the world with a Flood. And never was a scraggly pigeon used in the Bible period, d'you hear? It was a dove, I say, a beautiful, snow-white dove."

"What's the difference, Father?"

And Fr Duddleswell promptly withdrew from the conversation, his irritability heightened by the fact that he didn't exactly know what the difference was.

On the day the Major spoke to us, Fr Duddleswell's mood was effervescent. "Just think, Father Neil," he chortled, "from now on we will be able to toll the bell at funerals and weddings and christenings."

"And at the consecration of the Mass?"

"Indeed, yes. Oh, yes, indeed. I can just hear that beautiful bell sounding now on Sundays and feast days, calling the good people to Holy Mass. 'Twill be like the old times before the war."

"What about the Angelus, Father?"

"Father Neil, you plucked the sacred word right out of me mouth. We will have the Angelus ringing out morning, noon, and night. 'Twill sound all the sweeter, believe you me, for having been rescued from a Protestant temple. 'Twill remind the whole Borough of Kenworthy of the time when the Angel Gabriel announced to the Blessed Virgin she was to be the Mother of God, won't it just?"

He was looking forward to the bell as excitedly as a child looks forward to Christmas.

The architect reported back in four days and confirmed that the tower had not been weakened by the German bombs which had fallen nearby. It could easily accommodate a bell of moderate size.

Fr Duddleswell was delighted with the news. "D'you hear that, Father Neil?" he exulted. "We will get it installed as soon as I can fix things with Major Timmins. Ah," he reflected nostalgically, "'twill take me back to me student days in the Venerable English College in Rome. The Holy City was as full of bells as a Suffolk garden is full of roses in the month of June; and on Sundays and festas, they'd be a-ringing and a-singing, dong, dong, dong."

Even when expenses such as he'd never envisaged began to mount, he didn't complain. There was first the cost of transporting the bell from the depths of Wiltshire to the metropolis. It would need three men, apart from the driver, and a considerable amount of equipment to move the bell from Major Timmins' barn to our parish church. Then the architect told us he'd have to hire a contractor to put in an electrical time-switch and automated ringing device which would amount to another £200. The installation alone would account for £100, and all this apart from the expense of entertaining the Bishop and the clergy on the day the bell was consecrated.

"The parish funds will run to it, Father Neil. Besides, where is the sense in letting our money deteriorate in the bank?"

Our "free" bell was going to cost us something in the region of £450. So intense was Fr Duddleswell's desire for it that never at any point in the negotiations did he demur.

"We will economize in other ways," he said in the hearing of Mrs Pring.

"Like on tea and sugar, Father?" she asked him.

"Perhaps," said Fr Duddleswell, contracting himself like a concertina.

"Another of your spectaculars, eh, Father D? We *could* pass the basin round the parish, I suppose. Need to, to make up that tidy little sum."

She elicited no comment.

Mrs Pring went on, sailing as close to the wind as she dared: "You still haven't replaced the stained-glass windows and now..."

"Mrs...Pring."

"Hold your row, Father D. It's only a walking funeral, *you'll* have."

"Mrs Pring!"

"That's all *you* deserve."

Before he opened wide his concertina, she'd left.

The bell arrived on a truck one Tuesday morning. This impressive, shiny black object caused Fr Duddleswell to tap his chest with both hands and exclaim good-naturedly, "'Tis indeed exceedingly bell-like and no mistake, *exceedingly* bell-like."

A wooden frame, five feet high, had been built and placed in anticipation in the centre of the sanctuary. The bell was hung from the roof of the frame. Fr Duddleswell, in an access of high spirits, pulled back the tongue of the bell and released it with a bong that made the air vibrate with ear-tingling sound for nearly thirty seconds.

The ladies of the parish clucked away, busily decorating the frame with roses, lilies, and brightly colored ribbons. And the next day, outshining even the decorations in his purple robes, the Bishop appeared.

I hadn't seen Bishop O'Reilly since the day of my ordination. It is hard to recapture, still harder to convey, the feelings a young priest has for the Bishop who has shared with him the inestimable gift of the priesthood, given him *ex gratia* the power to celebrate Holy Mass and the sacraments.

The Bishop was a small, distinguished-looking, simple-minded man and very Catholic. I mean he understood, as so many of his detractors did not, the Catholic mystique: the emphasis on pageantry and hierarchy and obedience. I felt doubly indebted to him for first accepting me as a junior seminarist, since his general policy was to refuse any candidate who wasn't first or second generation Irish. He used to say privately—or so it was rumored—that the Irish and Italians are the nations dearest to God's own heart. Looking at the calendar of the saints, bursting with Celts and Latins, I thought this to be an opinion beyond dispute.

Bishop O'Reilly had given us deacons—there were six of

us—a short homily in his private chapel at Bishop's House the night before he ordained us. I admit that in my naïvete I was expecting a fiery sermon on the high office and onerous, but rewarding, duties of the priesthood. Instead, he contented himself with warning us off the twin dangers of "Punch and Judy," the clergy's term for "drink and dames." I could only assume he had his reasons, based on two decades of episcopal experience, for concentrating our minds on these earthly topics.

In the sacristy before the service of consecration, I heard the Bishop say to his private secretary, Monsignor O'Connell, "Now, remember, Pat me boy, lead me very slowly around the church so the congregation gets a generous view of me. They love it, so they do. It's not every day of the year, they get a chance to cast eyes on their beloved Bishop."

Non-Catholics may laugh, but I really admired Bishop O'Reilly's concern for our parishioners who had made a sacrifice to be there that evening on his account.

As the Monsignor dressed the Bishop like a doll, he kept promising him a suitably slow gyration. He made him put on three chasubles and two pairs of gloves—only *then* the ring—and large shuffly buckskin slippers. Next, he pressed the tall golden mitre down on his head, keeping the second, the Precious Mitre, in reserve for solemn moments in the ceremony, finally handing him a silver crozier almost as big as the Bishop himself.

I would have hated to have to sit there meekly and passively as Bishop O'Reilly did and be clothed by a breathless, sweating Monsignor. The burden the Bishop had to bear and his humility came home to me as never before.

In the opening, tortoise-like procession, I walked alongside Fr Duddleswell and only two yards in front of the Bishop. I imagined I could feel upon my back the unswerving episcopal smile and the ringed right hand raised in countless benedictions. I confess it gave me a *frisson* of distress to hear a six-year-old, standing at the end of a bench, say in a loud voice to his mother, "Mummy, why is she wearing that funny hat?"

No doubt, Bishop O'Reilly was used to being thought a fool for Christ's sake. Fr Duddleswell's comment to me as we genuflected together seemed discourteous. "Out of the mouths of babes and sucklings," he whispered.

The choir struck up *Ecce Sacerdos Magnus*, Behold Our Great High Priest, and the hour-long service began. My memory of it is fuzzed by the innumerable anointings and blessings of the bell which the Bishop made with exemplary patience. There were also lots of prayers and stirring hymns, after which all thirteen clergy present on the sanctuary were permitted like schoolboys to ring the bell after the Bishop. I have to admit I enjoyed that part of the ceremony the most.

The one harrowing incident occurred when we were sitting while the choir sang a Latin motet. Because of the intense heat and the crowded church, the west door had been left wide open to let some fresh air blow through the building.

It wasn't until he was half-way down the central aisle that I was aware of the entry of Billy Buzzle's big black labrador named Pontius. Pontius came on sniffing to right and left, surprised that for all his friendly sniffles and energetic wagging of his hindquarters, no one in that huge crowd paid him any attention. He had a quizzical look on his dignified face as if he couldn't understand the sudden waning of his popularity. Those of the congregation who saw Pontius didn't want to know.

On he marched until it became clear to me he was heading for the sanctuary. Maybe the clergy were drugged by the heat or lost in the music but, whatever the reason, not one of them stirred either. Fear made *me* sit as blind and still as a pepper pot.

Fr Duddleswell was the first to admit to the foreign presence on the sanctuary. Slowly, and with as much dignity as was possible in the circumstances, he rose, bowed to his fellow-clergy, and went across to try to grasp Pontius' collar. Pontius swerved, eluded Fr Duddleswell's outstretched hands, and made towards the Bishop as being the most interesting figure there.

The Bishop, seeing the black menace, sat back as far as he could on his pontifical throne, cowering. The benign Pontius, drooling and undeterred, approached him and with a jump laid

41

his forelegs on the Bishop's lap.

Bishop O'Reilly tried pushing the panting dog away with his crozier but only succeeded in dislodging his mitre so it fell over his eyes, temporarily blinding him.

All this time, the choir, who had a grandstand view of events from the choir-loft, were gradually slowing down like Fr Duddleswell's old gramophone badly in need of a rewind. Then they gave up the ghost and ceased altogether.

In the uncanny silence that ensued, Bishop O'Reilly's voice could be heard screeching, "Do something, Pat! Why aren't you *doing* something?"

Perhaps the Monsignor had a phobia about dogs, for in this dire episcopal emergency, he seemed singularly lacking in obedience.

By now, Fr Duddleswell had made his way on tiptoe to the Bishop's throne. Uttering friendly clucking noises, he succeeded in grabbing Pontius' collar. But when Pontius went sharply into reverse, Fr Duddleswell was taken by surprise and dragged, off balance, by the great labrador half-way across the sanctuary on his back.

I had no difficulty in guessing what would happen next. Pontius, losing his sense of direction in the fray, bumped into the scaffolding and the considerable weight of man and dog made the bell give out one enormous bong followed by several lesser bongs.

Pontius was so shaken by the noise, he tore himself free, barked stupendously, and fled unopposed from the church like the Wind of Pentecost.

I rushed forward to help Fr Duddleswell to his feet and removed a lily that had become wedged in the frame of his spectacles. He was muttering something about Billy Buzzle which, I am sure, he afterwards repented and confessed.

The Monsignor rearranged the Bishop, the choir resumed their motet, and the rest of the ceremony passed without incident.

At the end, still seated on the sanctuary, the Bishop cleansed the oil from his fingers with segments of lemon and breadcrumbs—a medieval method in harmony with the intended elegance of the ceremony, and always very much appreciated by the faithful. Then we all processed slowly round the church again so that the congregation could have a final filial look at their father in God.

In the sacristy, even as we were unvesting, the Bishop took me aside, asked me how I was liking St Jude's, and let me kneel for his blessing. I kissed his ring and gained thereby, I think, a hundred days' indulgence.

In view of the gallant efforts made to save him, I thought the Bishop somewhat less liberal in his indulgences when he icily addressed Fr Duddleswell in front of everyone, including the lay servers. "For the future, Father," he said, "I trust you'll see to it that no wild animals gain admittance."

Commenting later on the public character of this dressing down, Fr Duddleswell said to me in his best Gilbertian manner, "At least, Father Neil, I was 'beheaded handsomely.'"

Next day, I heard Fr Duddleswell, after his siesta, tackling Mr Buzzle with the "disgraceful behaviour of that blankety-blank beast."

Mr Buzzle replied indignantly: "My Pontius is a gentleman. He didn't do no damage, did he?"

"He trespassed into *my* church."

"He's house-trained," said Mr Buzzle.

At this, Fr Duddleswell walked into the rectory, slamming the door while Mr Buzzle called out after him, "A regular St Francis and no mistake!"

On the morning of August 14th, the eve of the Feast of the Assumption, Fr Duddleswell personally supervised the hoisting of the bell into the tower. He was standing there, getting in the workmen's way and reciting his breviary.

"*Deus in adjutorium meum intende*," I heard him mutter, "O God, come to my aid."

I suspect that even then he was planning reprisals against Billy Buzzle.

The following morning, I was awakened early by the bell in the tower ringing out the Angelus. Thrice three strokes, followed by a series of nine, all at solemn intervals.

I tried to recite the prayers laid down by the Church for this devotion, but before completing the third Hail Mary, I had drifted back into the Land of Nod.

Mr Buzzle, it seemed, had not been so fortunate. Just before midday, from my study, I heard him bitterly attacking Fr Duddleswell for violation of his privacy.

"Pray, what *are* you talking about?" asked Fr Duddleswell sweetly.

"You *know*," fumed Billy. "That noise, that, that infernal racket, early this morning."

"Are you referring to our new bell, Mr Buzzle? That was proclaiming the Assumption of the Blessed Virgin Mary to the good people of St Jude's."

"That bell nearly bloody-well blasted me out of bed. Don't you know I sleep on the back of the house and that bell let rip like Big Ben only a few feet from my head?"

"I *am* sorry," said Fr Duddleswell without a spark of repentance.

"And why so early, may I ask?"

"Six o'clock. Is that early, would you say?"

"Yes, I bloody well would, especially as I only get back from The Blue Star at three."

"I said I was sorry."

"Okay," said Billy in a milder tone of voice. "But make sure it don't happen no more."

"I cannot promise you that Mr Buzzle. In fact, 'tis me religious duty to assure you of the exact opposite. The Angelus will ring out three times every day, at six A.M., midday and six in the evening, the hours which Holy Mother Church has always observed."

One of these hours was even then upon us, for the bell began to chime with amazing vigor. From the pigeon lofts in Billy's garden, there was a frightful clatter of wings as a hundred startled birds careered into the air.

While Fr Duddleswell knelt ostentatiously—head bowed, eyes closed—on the lawn to say his prayers, Billy Buzzle kept up a stream of abuse mercifully deadened by the sound of the Angelus. Only in between the chimes did I make out the occasional profanity.

"Father," pleaded Mr Buzzle, as his adversary got to his feet, "Fr O'Duddleswell, can't you see what your bell is doing to my poor pigeons?"

"Could you not see what they *were* doing to my poor tower?"

"Once I wake up of a night," said Mr Buzzle pitifully, "I can't get back to sleep again."

"In that case, I suggest," retorted Fr Duddleswell, before returning to the house, "you go to your bed at a civilized hour. Then you will be able to rise at six. As I do."

When I spoke tentatively to Fr Duddleswell about his apparently harsh treatment of Billy Buzzle, he was adamant that he was acting from the highest motives. Paganism must not be allowed to run rampant. From this time forward, the Blessed Virgin had to be honored publicly at the liturgical hours; the good people of the parish were to be summoned to church on Sundays by the Lord's own voice.

"Won't Mr Buzzle be entitled to take legal action against us for disturbing the peace?" I asked.

"He dare not," answered Fr Duddleswell. "'Tis not in his interests to antagonize respectable church-folk, nor does he desire to get embroiled with the police. His business dealings are far too shifty for that."

On another occasion, I witnessed a further episode in the feud. Billy was complaining across the fence about his insomnia and the poor health of his pigeons. Three of them had flown away never to return, which he interpreted to be a form of pigeon suicide.

"Can't we come to some arrangement?" pleaded Billy.

"I would have you know, *I* do not take bribes."

"Can't you give me a fair chance?" Billy said, taking a coin out of his pocket. "I'll toss you for it."

"I am not a betting man."

Billy went on regardless. "Heads you don't start your bell till ten o'clock in the morning."

"What is that, a two-headed penny?"

"I thought," shouted Billy, "you were bloody well supposed to love your neighbour as yourself."

"I care for you far more than that," replied Fr Duddleswell smugly.

"Religious people!" said Billy in a scornful voice.

"Mr Buzzle," said Fr Duddleswell, "I love you as a Christian but that is as far as I'm prepared to go." Then he softened to say, "I really do hope you start sleeping better very soon."

Next day, through the letter box came a letter from Mr Buzzle's solicitor advising us that his client was taking action against the church for erecting a bell in contravention of the borough's bye-laws. These bye-laws stated categorically that prior to the introduction of a bell in any public building, the consent of the local taxpayers was needed. Mr Buzzle, the inhabitant most likely to suffer from the aforesaid bell, had not been consulted nor was he willing to give retrospective consent. Failure to consult meant that the Council's officers were empowered to remove the said offending instrument. The defendant was granted ten days' grace before official legal action was taken.

Fr Duddleswell's immediate response was to rush into the church shouting "Bluff, bluff!" and start the bell tolling as for a funeral. Next, he called on his own solicitor and sought advice. This he found most satisfying.

The solicitor wrote Billy a letter by return to the effect that the prohibition of bells applied only to *new* bells. St Jude's was a replacement for an old one, hence no prior consultation was required by law.

I thought that Billy Buzzle was stymied now. His only hope was that Fr Duddleswell would relent and ring the bell at reasonable hours. Otherwise, he'd have to move house. But I had reckoned without the resourcefulness of a man accustomed to earning his living by guile.

One day, six rolls of wire-netting were delivered to Billy Buzzle's back garden. An hour later, two men appeared and started to erect wire enclosures over the whole area. In the afternoon, several big crates appeared and from the bird-noises coming from them I guessed that Billy was increasing his supply of pigeons. The crates turned out to contain about fifty chickens.

It wasn't until the next day that Billy's plan was fully

revealed, for ten smaller crates were deposited in his garden. When Billy, wearing protective leather gloves, gingerly removed the lids with an iron bar, my eyes were drawn to the ten wickedest looking cockerels in England. Each was placed in a roofed-in wire pen of its own, adjacent to the large enclosure where the hens were left free-ranging. The noise of frustrated love was wretched enough, but when the midday Angelus rang out, the conjoined sound of pealing bell, madly fluttering pigeons and trumpeting cocks was indescribable.

When Fr Duddleswell retired to his bedroom to take his siesta, I knew he wasn't likely to be blessed with much repose. I heard him restlessly pacing up and down his room, and, from time to time, opening and closing his window with a bang. Once I heard him open his window and yell, "Do you not know that cock-fighting is against the law, you gambler, you?" Then he slammed his window shut with a clonk that broke the cord and smashed one of the panes. Before evening, the whole window frame was double glazed, but it didn't seem to help.

Fortunately for me, my bedroom, like Mrs Pring's above, was on the front of the house. During the hours of sleep, I didn't catch the full blast of the bell or the ravenous excitement of the cocks. Poor Fr Duddleswell was in the cocks' direct line of fire twice a day.

Within a week, he was but a shadow of his former self. He'd lost weight, and there were large bags under his red-rimmed, blood-shot eyes. Clearly, he, like Billy Buzzle, was becoming an insomniac.

Mrs Pring fetched him tranquillizers from the doctor and filled him to the brim with hot Ovaltine at night. He never went to his bedroom even in the afternoon without his Thermos-flask full of what Mrs Pring called "soporificking fluid." All to no avail. "I have a famous appetite," he said pathetically, "for a large loaf of sleep."

After that, I didn't see Billy around for about ten days and suggested to Fr Duddleswell that he had probably taken to sleeping at The Blue Star.

"The divil," was his only reply.

I think it was this piece of news that finally persuaded Fr Duddleswell to call a halt to hostilities. At lunch, he said to me:

"I've a job for you, lad. I have come to the conclusion that I have not been acting in a very priestly way towards Billy Buzzle."

"Really," I replied, refusing to take sides.

"'Tis true, so very true. I did not think for one moment he would take the matter so hard. I never intended, God help me, to drive him away from house and home."

"No?"

"No," he said. "An Englishman's home is ... Those cocks."

"Yes?"

"They've stirred me conscience as they did the conscience of the Prince of the apostles. So, I would like you to pop along to The Blue Star and take with you this letter"—he drew it from his cassock pocket—"to Billy Buzzle."

He didn't tell me the contents of the letter, but when I visited Billy in his office—decorated with pictures of horses, dogs, and ladies just as scantily clad—he seemed pleased with what he read.

"Tell your boss-man, messenger boy, that Billy Buzzle agrees terms."

And so ended a feud which threatened the peace and quiet of the entire neighborhood. From that time on, the bell was never rung before ten in the morning, not even for the Angelus, and the tempestuous cocks and their female friends were transferred doubtless to a calmer, more permissive setting.

4

THE PARISH BAZAAR

Though the annual bazaar was scheduled for the first Saturday of September, preparations were well under way by the middle of June.

"Now, me dear people," urged Fr Duddleswell from the pulpit, "I want you, for the love of Almighty God, to make a supreme sacrifice this year. The church committee has set us a target of £600 which is to go to the building of our new hall. Since the Hun demolished our last ten years since, we have been deprived of a fitting place to conduct our parish business. I beg Christ's Holy Spirit to inspire you to heroic feats of generosity. Above all, *pray* mightily for the success of our Bazaar. Sometimes the Lord is hard of hearing, so use a hammer."

He then outlined his plan of campaign: posters all over town; a raffle every week ("Overcome your diffidence and natural timidity. Tickets for the raffle should be purchased with avidity."); programs sold in advance at threepence a time, reduced to tuppence for the under sevens and the over sixty-fives. At the back of the church each Sunday, there would be wicker-baskets to hold the commodity requested for that particular week.

The first Sunday, I remember, the church was inundated with tinned food: peaches, pears, baked beans, curry, mustard, salmon, herring. Even during the sermon, tins were still being dropped with a clunk by latecomers; and afterward the church looked like a deserted delicatessen.

The second Sunday: toys. Toys in wood and tin and plastic; Meccano sets and games of Monopoly and snakes and ladders. That week the children wouldn't sit still but constantly evaded their parents' watchful eyes to wander down the aisles to gaze at this Aladdin's cave full of all the things they'd ever wanted.

Another time it was books.

"Books of a helpful and edifying character, you follow?" preached Fr Duddleswell. "No lurid, titillating paper-covers, if you please. No naked ladies or seducing gentlemen. No *Gone With The Storm* sort of thing on our Catholic bookstall. Not, me dear people, that I am exactly asking you to bring only the Holy Bible or *The Imitation Of Christ* either."

Perhaps the parishioners didn't grasp Fr Duddleswell's meaning, or they had no books of the kind he seemed to want. Whatever the reason, the yield that week was pitifully small.

Knitted goods brought a better response, as did the mechanical goods the following week. I remember seeing a lawn-mower that somehow found its way into the rectory garden on Monday afternoon. Fr Duddleswell, I felt sure, had paid adequate compensation into the Bazaar fund.

The lawn mower apart, all the articles were stored in the huge, dark cellar under the church. Those were still post-war days of rationing and austerity; and each week when Fr Duddleswell surveyed the piles of new and secondhand items the faithful had brought, he couldn't help nodding his head and repeating: "What lovely people. What generous, lovely people."

On the final Sunday before the bazaar, Fr Duddleswell, now sleeping better then he'd slept for weeks, made an impassioned appeal at all Masses for the ladies of the parish to bake cakes and pastries and bring them directly to the Argos playing fields on Saturday morning. Argos was a chemical factory which, to foster good public relations, was letting us use their playing fields free of charge.

Lately, the weather had been impeccable, but Fr

Duddleswell, drawing attention to the exposed nature of the bazaar site, pleaded for prayers for "a sky of heavenly blue." Pray, pray, pray—that was his message—so that St Jude's would reach its customary target of £600.

"And I have put me total trust in the Almighty," he said, "that we will make not one penny less."

On Monday, I tentatively put it to Fr Duddleswell that though we had been experiencing a heat wave for three weeks, this already constituted an abnormally lengthy summer for England. It couldn't possibly last much longer, especially as September had begun.

"Out with it, Father Neil, what sort of a riot is going on inside that curly head of yours?"

"I thought it might be worth hiring a big tent so that at least perishable goods can be kept under cover."

"Have you no faith in the protection of the Almighty, Father Neil?"

I remarked that I *had* known instances of believers being rained on.

"You cannot mean real believers, *true* believers," he said, with fluttering eyes.

"Catholics, Father."

"In name only. I have never known in me long life any project entered into by *true* believers that foundered."

I marvelled at this Old Testament faith of his.

"Besides, Father Neil," he added, "I looked into the possibility of hiring a tent, and d'you know what the cost of it would be? Fifty pounds."

"If it rains, you might think it was worth it."

Fr Duddleswell retorted whimsically, "Did y'ever hear the story of the drought in Ireland, Father Neil?"

Having been on the receiving end of so many, I took the easy way out and said I couldn't remember.

"Well, it was in County Donegal; there was this drought which lasted ... Come to think of it, now, it was County Cork. Anyway, it lasted for eight weeks, like, and the potato crop was in peril of ... Correction, Father Neil, I'm quite sure it was County Cavan. Perhaps you remember the tale now?"

I assured him that now I remembered it even less well than before.

"Whenever there was a drought, you see, the parishioners of the Church of the Annunciation processed with their statue of Our Lady into the tater field and begged her to rend the heavens and favor them with a shower or two. 'Rain, O Blessed Virgin, rain,' they cried and they chanted and they sang.

"Well, now, on this occasion—after eight weeks of intense drought, you recall—they prayed aloud: 'Rain, O Blessed Virgin, rain.' And what d'you think came to pass, Father Neil?"

"It poured."

He looked at me suspiciously. "You *have* heard it."

"An inspired guess," I said humbly, "but please go on with your story, Father."

"There was this cloudburst of apocalyptic proportions, a veritable avalanche of rain, y'might say, and all the faithful people of County Cork or wherever the bloody county was, sang and chanted and cried, '*Stop*, O Blessed Virgin, *stop*.'"

He laughed merrily, and I laughed with him.

"You are sure you never heard it before?" he stopped to inquire.

"Not in that precise form. But what's the moral of it, Father?"

"Moral? Does every humorous tale have to have a moral to it? What a funny English feller y'are, to be sure."

"There are signs, Father, that the fine weather's breaking up. The Meteorology Office says that perhaps by the weekend..."

"Prophets of doom have beguiled thy faint heart, Father Neil. I repeat to you, I have run ten bazaars since I came to St Jude's and many prior to that. And have I had one of them fail me yet? Indeed, I have not. Each year, we have exceeded our target. And this year will be no exception."

I had already admitted defeat and needed no reminding of Christ's words, "Ask and you shall receive," and "If you have faith, you can move mountains."

"Come along with me to the school, Father Neil."

It was the third lesson of the morning. Fr Duddleswell's

custom was to knock abruptly on each classroom door, steam in, and take charge of a class for a few minutes at a time.

The children stood up at his behest to pray for the success of the bazaar and sat down to hear his homily about gloom-mongers who prophesied we'd never make £600 on account of bad weather. The boys and girls, sweating in the humid heat of that blazing summer, thought this a sick joke.

"Father Neil," I was asked afterwards, "tell me, now, are you not ashamed when you see the faith these youngsters have? If only we could become as little children."

The children got littler and littler because, after we left the school, Fr Duddleswell drove me to the orphanage. Any child old enough to walk and kneel on his own was rounded up to pray for the success of Saturday's bazaar.

"Father Neil, d'you think that the Lord who loves little children can refuse the petitions of his darlin' little ones?"

Mentally, I buried my head in my hands. What reply can you make to Biblical blackmail?

Cloudless days followed throughout the week. Nonetheless, the temperature was falling slightly and faint winds stirred the topmost branches of the apple trees in the garden. On Friday night, I couldn't see the stars.

Saturday morning dawned, dull and grey. Mrs Pring said, "Don't you worry, Father Neil. His Reverence has special arrangements with the Devil himself."

But I did worry throughout Mass and breakfast and afterwards as I cycled towards the Argos playing fields to help organize preparations for the bazaar.

I stopped on the way at a public phone booth to call the Met. Office and find out the day's forecast. I didn't want to use the rectory telephone in case I should be overheard and my infidelity broadcast. The prospect, I was told, was bleak in the extreme: "Showers everywhere, heavy in places."

As I cycled on under a mackerel sky, I imagined I could already smell rain in the air.

Though it was only nine o'clock, the playing fields were a hive of activity. Stalls were being erected by shirt-sleeved parishioners on the perimeter of the cricket pitch. Two huge trucks arrived packed to the roof with tinned foodstuffs and toys from the church cellar. Vans chugged up in convoys to the entrance of the car-park, bedecked with bunting and Union Jacks. There were two station wagons bearing household pets: rabbits, hamsters, and lots of white mice still odious to me in spite of their pink eyes. Then came a large truck out of which trotted half a dozen shaggy donkeys: and two men with pitchforks heaved out big bales of straw to supply their needs for the afternoon.

A loudspeaker system was being set up all over the field— it was on loan free of charge from Pimms and Sons, the electrical shop in the High Street. Coconut shies and an amusement arcade were soon erected. And over and above all this, there was a constant stream of Fr Duddleswell's "good ladies of the parish" bearing the most delicious-looking and odoriferous products of their ovens: cakes, buns, doughnuts, pies, biscuits.

Fr Duddleswell himself was here, there, and everywhere at once, greeting, thanking, cajolling, chastising, encouraging and, no doubt, praying. A few drops of rain pattered on my head, and he caught me looking skywards apprehensively.

"Father Neil," he tutted, "Father Neil."

No further remonstrance was required. I too prayed that, despite the auguries, all would be well. God love little children, I begged.

At 12:30, having assured ourselves that everything was under control, Fr Duddleswell drove us home for a bite to eat. His confidence in his mountain-moving God was undiminished.

On our return at 1:30, we saw the gaily decorated entrance to the playing fields. Over it, a huge banner proclaimed: ST JUDE'S BAZAAR—TODAY 2-6 P.M.

The bazaar was to be opened by T.V. personality Frosty Jones, a local boy with a dead-pan face who was the straight man in a popular comedy doubles act. He put in an appearance at ten minutes to two and remarked at once on the ominous signs of rain.

"If it pours, where do we take cover?" he asked.

"Under the umbrella of the Almighty," joked Fr Duddleswell, evoking no response on Frosty's professionally frigid face.

Twelve minutes later, with only half a dozen customers added to the fifty or so helpers, Frosty Jones declared the Bazaar open with a speech "notable," as Fr Duddleswell was to put it, "for its audacious economy."

Frosty kept looking anxiously at the black-jowelled clouds racing overhead, and, having said his piece, shook the parish priest and me by the hand before making a dash for his Jaguar.

The wind had freshened considerably by this time and was threatening to become a gale. We almost needed a torch to find our way out.

Then at precisely eight minutes past two, the heavens opened. No Hollywood Bible epic ever caught a downpour such as this on celluloid. Orange lightning dazzled us, and the thunder accompanying it deafened us. I have never seen such a skyquake. I expected Moses to appear and unburden himself of twin tablets of stone. Instead, there was only this huge, grey scroll of tumbling water.

"Four inches of rain fell in fifteen minutes," the local press claimed afterwards. An exaggeration, but for those of us who lived through it a pardonable one.

The gallant helpers scattered to their stalls to try to keep them intact against the screeching wind and blinding rain. All the books were soaked immediately. Almost all the tins lost their labels so it was impossible to decide afterwards whether the contents were rice pudding or baked beans. The donkeys went wild and kicked over everything in sight including the wire-fronted hutches containing the rabbits, hamsters and white mice. I watched two assistants squelching in the mud on hands and knees attempting futilely to domesticate the animals again. Cakes, biscuits, and doughnuts floated by, downstream.

I felt a tug on my jacket and looked down to find a drenched six-year-old tearfully asking for his tuppence back.

The parish priest was all this time running round with gay

frenzy, crying again and again, "Stop, O Blessed Virgin, stop."

It took too long for his message to reach the Holy Mother.

By the time she heard and answered his prayer, the playing fields were a disaster area. When the rain ceased completely at three o'clock, there was nothing to do except clear up the mess and go home.

Fr Duddleswell knocked into me. "It's me spectacles," he said apologetically. "They keep misting up on me. Nothing dry enough to wipe 'em with."

"Mind you don't catch cold, Father," I said without caring very much at the moment what happened to the stubborn old boy.

He must have read my thoughts. "Good job we didn't hire that tent, Father Neil," he remarked, peering over the top of his blurred spectacles.

"Tell me more," I said with what I took to be ferocious irony.

"Would have blown down in that gale as sure as sure, and somebody, a child for example, might have been killed."

I pondered this as the local authority dustmen came to shovel all the cakes and books and most of the toys into their cart; I pondered it as the R.S.P.C.A. came in response to a phone call to claim the tinier pets and calm the donkeys before removing them, still braying in protest, in a lorry.

The sun came out. Over the west, I saw a double rainbow.

"What," I asked Fr Duddleswell, "does the Bible promise about there never being another Flood?"

"Father Neil," he said, "do you not consider that the Almighty can bring good from evil?"

I showed him the takings for the afternoon: one shilling and ninepence.

"There's an awful lot of evil here, Father, for him to draw good from."

That evening at supper, Fr Duddleswell was—how shall I put it?—sober, self-contained. Mrs Pring failed to rile him with her indelicate comments on the day's proceedings.

"No tent needed, eh?" she said, but his ears were double-glazed. "What about always reaching your target now?" He held his peace.

Later, when I heard him ask Mrs Pring for a hot water bottle, a couple of aspirins, and a hot lemon drink, I regretted my cruel irony at the bazaar.

Next morning, Fr Duddleswell rose for the early Mass but said from the sanctuary he couldn't preach because he'd caught a chill. The tinned food and the toys that could be salvaged, he explained, had been sent to the orphanage. He thanked from his heart all who had contributed to the Bazaar and said he did not doubt but that the takings, when they were counted, would show we had, as usual, reached our target.

After this amazing pronouncement, he retired to bed, delirious I was convinced, and with a temperature of 102.

In the next couple of days, the phone never ceased ringing with people commiserating and promising financial support to help redeem the disaster.

All this time, no sound came from Fr Duddleswell's bedroom. I relied on his nurse, Mrs Pring, to provide me with a rundown on the course of his illness.

"It's not pneumonia as he deserves, God be praised, only a 48-hour 'flu," she said, and was proven correct.

On Wednesday morning, Fr Duddleswell rose, celebrated a private Mass and afterwards joined me in the dining room wearing one of his most sheepish smiles. On his side plate was an enormous pile of letters.

"There's another two bundles in your study," Mrs Pring said, as she ferried in our breakfast.

Fr Duddleswell, in between mouthfuls of toast, was slitting open the envelopes with a butter knife and giving me a running commentary on "this unexampled generosity of our good people."

"Here is a note from an old-age pensioner, Mrs Wright, and her postal order for two pounds ten shillings. What d'you think of that, Father Neil?" he asked as his spectacles steamed up from emotion. "And here's a letter from Colonel Sir John Tophall wishing me a speedy recovery and sending me a cheque for a pound."

While I was not unappreciative of this beneficence, I couldn't help reflecting that the other two "bundles" in his study would have to reach the ceiling if we were to reach our target of £600. Again, he must have seen through me, for he whispered:

"Father Neil, will we ever make a *true* Christian of you?"

I swigged a cup of coffee to prevent myself becoming ironical again.

Just then, Fr Duddleswell came across a long envelope that caused him to release an exultant cry:

"*That's* the bit of charity I've been waiting for."

He slit the letter open and admired the contents for a moment before holding up a cheque before my eyes. It was from the Moonlight Insurance Company to the tune of £600. My eyes had never settled on such a valuable piece of paper.

"You mean," I gasped, "you insured the bazaar against a downpour?"

"I do the same every year, Father Neil. In fact, since I have never had so much as a shower fall on it in the last eight years, the premium this time was only £10."

"Cheaper than a tent, you mean?"

"Mind you, Father Neil, we only received £600 because the bazaar was completely washed out."

"Rain, O Blessed Virgin, rain."

"The Holy Mother can always be relied on, can she not, Father Neil?"

At this precise moment, there came the sound of something heavy being dropped through the letter box. A few seconds later, Mrs Pring entered bearing a big brown envelope.

"Another offering from the faithful, I suppose, Father," she said as he was just about to rise from table.

She continued standing there, wondering as I did, what the envelope contained.

"Off with you, now, Mrs Pring," he urged. "I am sure you have lots of things to attend to."

"No hurry," she said, obstinately holding her ground.

Fr Duddleswell snorted before slitting open the envelope and tipping the contents onto the table. Once more, my previous financial standards of comparison were overturned, for there, spread out before my eyes, were more fivers than I'd ever seen.

"A very charitable parishioner," said Mrs Pring, biting her tremulous lower lip.

"You know as well as I, woman, where it came from," said Fr Duddleswell.

"Where?" I asked naïvely.

"From Billy Buzzle," he said.

"That's his winnings," put in Mrs Pring, before retiring and slamming the door.

"How much, Father, six hundred?"

"And thirty. I get me stake money back as well, you follow?"

"You laid out thirty on a downpour?"

"I was desperate to show Billy there was no ill will between us."

"There probably is now."

"Not at all. His respect for me will have rocketed sky-high."

"Thirty pounds," I whistled.

"It seemed good odds at 20-1."

"*Very* good."

"Mind you, Billy thought he'd got me over a barrel. After all, it had not rained for nearly four weeks."

I tried to absorb this new piece of information. "So altogether you've made a profit of £1,200 on the bazaar."

"More," he said reluctantly. "There's all these contributions of the faithful to be added to that."

"*Faith*-ful?"

He missed my point, I suppose, for he added, "The good people will be *so* pleased we reached our target after all their efforts and prayers. Had we failed, it might have weakened their trust in the Almighty no end."

"But, Father," I protested, dropping irony as a weapon, "how can you talk about 'faith in God' when all the time you've been making deals behind the scenes with an Insurance Company and laying on bets with an unscrupulous bookie?"

"Does not God help those who...?" He stopped in midstream. "Of course," he admitted, "gambling is a heinous sin. You are quite right." And he thumped his breast. "*Mea culpa, mea culpa, mea maxima culpa.*"

"And these, Father, are the wages of sin."

"Father Neil, I will not try to hide from you the fact that your parish priest is a *terrible* sinner. I will undeniably end up in hell like the chappie in *The Mikado* who cheated at billiards."

"How was he punished?"

"Oh, he was condemned to a fiercely guarded dungeon,"—here he began to recite while making the appropriate gestures over the table cloth:

> And there he plays extravagant matches
> In fitless finger stalls
> On a cloth untrue
> With a twisted cue
> And elliptical billiard-balls.

"D'you know, Father Neil?" he said, with a twinkle of unrepentance in his blue eyes, "sometimes I ask meself if I have any faith at all."

5

THE NEW ASSISTANT

"Tony Marlowe's the name, Father."

"Pleased to meet you, Mr Marlowe."

"This is my wife, Rena, and our two girls. Mary's eight and Joanna's five."

It was early Friday evening. I had been standing alone, smiling inanely at no one in particular from the back of Tipton Hall. We hired it out once a week for family get-togethers. I was wanting to be sociable, and it came as a relief to have a friendly group come up and speak to me.

"You're our parishioners, I take it, Tony?"

"Been here all my life. Rena's the foreigner. From Glasgow. The girls have picked up the accent. You'd hear it if only their tongues weren't tied in knots."

The girls, clinging to their mother, twisted their legs and giggled.

Tony said, "Why don't you pop in and see us some time, Father?"

"Yes, and join us for a cup of tea," said Rena in a strong Glaswegian accent. "We'd be pleased to see you at *any* time."

"I'd like to do that. Where do you live?"

"Our flat's over our shop, the grocer's shop on the corner of Calvert Street."

"I know it," I said. "And how's business?"

"Too busy at the moment, Father," Tony replied. "My

chief assistant has just come down with an attack of chronic bronchitis, and I can't get a replacement for love nor money. The job's tough, and if that weren't enough, nobody wants to work Saturday afternoons any more."

I remembered that chance conversation when, after the midday Mass on the Sunday following, a broad, squat, venomous-looking character appeared, cap in hand, in the sacristy.

"Archie Lee," he announced, as I was taking off the green chasuble.

I thought I'd better give him the benefit of the doubt and shook his hand. A very gnarled hand it was, too, like the branch of an oak.

"What can I do for you, Mr Lee?"

As I was saying it, I felt he was mentally picking my pocket. He was in his fifties, unshaven, poorly dressed.

"I need a bit of 'elp, Father."

"Well, Mr Lee..."

"*Archie*."

"Archie. In this parish, we have a very well organized conference of the St Vincent de Paul Society. If you have any genuine needs, I'm sure..."

"It's not money I'm after, Father."

"Not money?"

"Not money," he said.

"What then?"

"I need a job."

"Is that so hard to find?" I asked, as if *I* managed to get a new one every week. "What's wrong with the Labour Exchange?"

"No use, Father. Even when they get me a job, which ain't often, I can't seem to keep it for long."

"Been 'inside' have you, Archie?" I asked knowingly.

Archie bowed his head. "You won't tell no one, will you, Father?"

"Wouldn't dream of it."

"In strictest confidence, yeah?"

"Word of honor. I'll treat it," I said, taking a leaf out of Fr Duddleswell's book, "as if it were a confessional secret."

Archie positively purred with pleasure. "This is 'ow it is, Father," he confessed. "I've been inside many a time in me life. More inside than out, if you grasp my meaning?"

I nodded.

"But 'onest to Gawd, Father," Archie said, signing himself, "six months past, I promised meself I'd go straight and I 'ave, I really 'ave."

"I'm glad to hear it," I said, as I removed the last of my Mass vestments. I was intrigued by Archie; he was the first convicted criminal I'd ever come across. I hoped the encounter would prove beneficial to my ministry.

"Been a bit of a challenge, Father, I can tell yer. When people 'ear you've got a record, they don't wanner know. Grasp my meaning? And I get shot out in the snow on me . . . on me back, time and again."

"People inform on you, do they Archie?"

Archie pursed his lips and sighed as if the situation was often desperate. "I struggle on, Father, because . . . well, it ain't fitting to be crooked all yer life, is it? But you wouldn't know about that sort o' thing, I s'pose."

I hastened to assure Archie that understanding was my *métier*.

"What about 'elping me get a job, Father?"

It was then I remembered Tony Marlowe's words about being short-staffed in his grocery shop.

"How strong are you, Archie?"

"I once lifted a safe weighing near three 'undred pounds on me own."

"Did you have to do that Archie?" I asked, displeased at the example he had chosen to illustrate his strength.

"Yeah. Yer see I couldn't break the bloody . . . the thing, Father. Shall I give you a demo'? See that safe there"—he pointed to our parish safe in which we stored the chalices and the Sunday collections—"tell me where yer want it put, and I'll oblige."

"No need, I assure you, Archie," I said, as I moved over to the safe, heaved it to and turned the key.

"You don't 'ave to lock up on my account, Father. I could open it with a toothbrush if I chose, but as I told yer, these days, I'm straighter'n a corpse on the end of a rope."

"I'm sure you are," I said ashamedly. "One more question, Archie."

"Fire away, Father."

"Do you mind working on Saturday afternoons?"

"Never done it, not since I left jail. But I'll try anything if it's gonna keep the wolf from the door."

"All right, Archie, I'll see what I can do. I know a grocer who's looking for an assistant in his store. If you'd care to come to the rectory at three o'clock, I'll tell you if he'll take you on."

"That's real Christly of you," was Archie's parting remark.

After lunch I phoned Tony Marlowe and told him I had a prospective assistant for him who could start whenever he liked and who didn't mind working on Saturday afternoons.

"What's he like, Father? Give it to me straight."

"Seems honest enough," I hedged.

"Is he sharp at figures?"

"I know he's handled a lot of money in his time," I said. "And you can take it from me he's as strong as a carthorse and as willing."

"I tell you what, Father. I take your word for it he's okay. I'll give him a week's trial. He can start tomorrow morning at eight o'clock."

"Thanks a lot, Tony."

"My pleasure. But do stress that to begin with it's only for the week."

I promised to do that. When I spoke to Archie later that afternoon, he was overjoyed at the opportunity of proving himself.

"And yer didn't let on about my record, Father?" Before I could chastise him for doubting me, he said, "'Course you didn't. I won't let yer down. What's past is over an' done, ain't that right? You can rely on Archie."

Next morning, I took it into my head to visit the Marlowe family and at the same time check on whether Archie was behaving himself.

It was about 11:30 when I set foot in the shop. Archie was busy filling two tall shelves with cans of Heinz Baked Beans. When he saw me, far from looking apprehensive, he greeted me with a big trusting smile.

"Nice to see yer, Father."

"You, too, Archie. I've come on a parish visitation to see the Marlowes."

"Mr Marlowe!" called out Archie.

Tony had a small private office at the back where he kept his accounts and dealt with travelling salesmen.

"Hello, Father," he said. "I've got a traveller with me at the moment. I'll tell Rena you're here."

Rena came to collect me. "Come upstairs, Father, and I'll get you a cup of coffee."

In the sitting-room, Rena told me that Tony's impressions of Archie were so far very favorable.

"He works hard, he's friendly with the customers, and what's more, he seems to be an honest bloke."

"That's fine," I said.

"Yes, there's this old lady—always in here and a real pest she is—well, she was picking and prodding our tomatoes when she dropped her purse without noticing it. Archie saw what happened and gave it back to her. She had £15 in it, she said."

We chatted on for about twenty minutes while sipping coffee, when suddenly there was the sound of someone charging up the stairs and Tony burst into the room.

"Fr Boyd," he blurted out, "there's someone on the telephone. I think you ought to hear what he's got to say. I've switched over the extension so you can listen in."

With that, Tony rushed down the stairs again.

Wondering what this was all about, I picked up the phone as I'd seen private eyes pick it up in films. Through the earpiece I heard a door slam and Tony's breathless voice, "I've just seen a salesman off the premises, sir. Now we can talk in peace and quiet. Perhaps you wouldn't mind repeating what you said before."

"Nobody can overhear us, I take it?"

"Nobody," said Tony, obviously not thinking it worthwhile to mention me.

"First my name," came from a very cultured voice at the end of the line. "I'm Peregrine Worsley, and I'm a retired accountant."

"Yes, Mr Worsley."

"I hope you don't think I'm prying into your personal affairs, but I couldn't help noticing as I chanced to be strolling past your place an hour ago that there was a fellow, seemingly in your employ, whom I have come across before."

"That was probably my new assistant."

"Would he answer, by any chance, to the name of Archie Lee?"

"He would."

The caller sighed aristocratically. "I didn't think I'd made a mistake. You see, Mr Marlowe, it is my unpleasant civic duty to apprise you of the fact that Archie Lee has a criminal record."

I was glad I'd taken the precaution of putting my handkerchief over the mouthpiece, otherwise *two* gasps of horror would have assailed Mr Worsley's ear.

"A *long* criminal record," the caller emphasized.

"Anything really serious?" Tony managed to get out.

"Theft."

Tony said almost to himself: "I'll have to make sure he keeps away from the cash desk."

"I'm afraid that's not all, by any manner of means. Archie Lee has been incarcerated thirteen times and four of them for robbery with violence."

"Oh my God!" exclaimed Tony as if he was about to make an act of contrition on my behalf. "G.B.H."

"I beg your pardon?" questioned the imperturbable Mr Worsley.

"Nothing, sir. Grievous bodily harm. That's quite another matter, isn't it?"

"'Fraid so," drawled Mr Worsley. "I'd rather not say any more about this frightful business over the telephone. But, Mr Marlowe, if it'll put your mind at rest and dispel any suspicion that I'm just a nasty anonymous caller intent on blackening a man's character, I'll willingly come and see you face to face."

"Perhaps that would be better, sir."

"More *honorable*, I feel. What time might your assistant be going to lunch?"

"Mondays we close from one till two."

"May I come along, then, say, about 1:15?"

"Certainly, Mr Worsley, sir. I'll make sure the coast is clear."

After the call, I prepared myself for Tony's justifiable annoyance.

"How *could* you do this to me, Father? If news of this got out, don't you know what this would do to business? Imagine, having a violent criminal working in my store!"

I expressed heartfelt sorrow for my fault but in general terms.

"I suppose," he said, softening, "you didn't realize Archie had a long record."

"I did," I admitted.

"Then how *could* you, Father?" said Tony, stamping his foot and puffing furiously at his cigarette.

"I knew, and I didn't know, Tony."

Rena came to my rescue. "The seal of confession, Father?"

"Something like that."

"I'm sorry, Father," said Tony, gentle again. "The problem is what to do."

Rena reminded Tony of the time he'd become drunk after a Cup Final at Wembley and thrown an empty quart-sized beer bottle at a pal. It missed and went through the big plate-glass window of Woolworth's.

"Yes," admitted Tony, "I was 'interned' for a while for that."

"You were lucky you didn't hit him, Tony," Rena added, "otherwise you'd have been doing porridge for six months or more."

Turning to me, Tony said, "What Rena's trying to say is that I turned violent once and was given a second chance."

"This isn't quite the same thing, is it?" I said, siding with Tony. I felt I owed him something. "That was an isolated incident when Tony'd had too much to drink."

"I agree, Father," Tony said, glad of support. "Archie Lee's been bent all of his life, so it seems."

"Once a crook..." Rena said.

"I'm not his fairy godmother, love, am I? Suppose Archie snatches an old lady's handbag and clouts her on the head, the magistrate'll say to me: 'Did you know the accused had a prison record?' I couldn't take refuge in the seal of confession, could I?"

I turned my head away at the unintended rebuke.

"Think," continued Tony, "how my reputation and the business would suffer. There'd be a headline in the local rag. I can just see it: 'Grocer Employs Violent Ex-Con,' And, hell," he contributed as an afterthought, "some nosey reporter's bound to dig up the fact that I've been in the clink myself."

"That settles it," Rena said with a trace of sarcasm, "he'll have to go."

"Let's wait till Mr Worsley arrives," I proposed. "He may be able to advise us what's the best course for all concerned."

At one o'clock Tony dismissed Archie for lunch, and soon Mr Peregrine Worsley put in an appearance. He was a stately figure, indeed: polished black shoes; well-creased, pin-striped trousers; black herring-bone jacket with grey silk tie; and a rolled umbrella despite the perfect summer's day. When he removed his bowler on entering the room he revealed a bald head as shiny as his shoes.

I took an instant dislike to him. Archie, for all his rugged ways, was much more to my taste.

On seeing me, Mr Worsley turned to Tony. "Called in the

strong arm of the Church, eh? Good show. I presume you have told the vicar the state of the game."

Tony assured him I was well briefed.

The visitor hitched up his trousers as he sat down and said, "A most distressing visit, what, distressing to me and much more so to you."

"We're grateful to you for taking the time and trouble to come," said Tony.

"My card," he said, flourishing a visiting card on which I read at a glance, Peregrine A Worsley, C.A. and an address which ended Chambers. "You may care to look at my credentials."

"No need, sir," said Tony, waving the card aside so that Mr Worsley returned it to his well-stacked wallet. He stroked his neatly trimmed moustache and adjusted his horn-rimmed spectacles with their very thick lenses.

"I assure you," Mr Worsley said, returning to the point, "it's no trouble. I've retired altogether from accountancy. If, in any minute particular, I can ameliorate this wicked world one whit, my life will be complete."

"To go back to Archie Lee," began Tony in his blunt way.

"In the presence of your gracious lady and the local vicar, I'm not at leave to catalogue all the misdemeanours of the said Archie Lee. All I can prudently remark on at this moment is his cold-blooded brutality."

"He seems so gentle," I said.

"Your kind-heartedness, sir," replied Mr Worsley, "is a credit to your cloth. Is it not right that you, a professional humanitarian, should defend the criminal?"

"I only meant," I added, "that every one of God's creatures is entitled to a chance."

"You are enhancing, sir," said Mr Worsley, "my opinion of the Church you represent with every utterance. *A* chance, I grant. *Several* chances, that too I will allow. But how many chances? That is the question."

"Seventy times seven," I proposed.

"Sir, I feel altogether humbled in the presence of such

magnanimity. But, I beg, can the Almighty Himself pardon an unrepentant sinner?"

I thought, "This Mr Worsley has theological insight as well as expertise in accountancy."

"No, He cannot," I conceded.

Mr Worsley now proceeded without interruption. "Do believe me when I say I am not judging Archie Lee. Many others are employed for *that* purpose by His Majesty's Government. These unsocial habits he has acquired are traceable no doubt to upbringing, environment, or personal misfortune. Which of us ought not to bow the head and say: 'There for the grace of God...?' But I must not trespass on your territory, Vicar, must I?"

I begged him to continue his admirable discourse. He was perfectly willing to oblige.

"We should attempt to reform the individual criminal, that is true. But must not our chief priority be to protect the interests of the great innocent British public?"

"Exactly what I think," said Tony.

"Now," Mr Worsley said confidentially, "let me come clean, as the saying goes, and confess to you my indubitable bias. I happened once to be in a bank in Sunbury, drawing out some money, when in charged the energetic Archie Lee. I was able to witness at first hand the man's barbaric behavior. He hit one of the customers over the head with a...sandbag."

Tony winced.

"I remonstrated with him," said Mr Worsley, "and he threatened to 'cosh' me too if I didn't 'shut my something trap.'"

We all exhibited, in varying ways, our disapproval.

Mr Worsley went on: "As you may imagine, my lips were straightaway sealed, but not by any means forever. The police, naturally, caught up with the miscreant; and that I followed the case very closely I have no need to assure you. I went to court myself in order to 'open my trap' and give evidence. Indeed, I was in court the very day that Archie Lee was sentenced."

"What did he get?" asked Tony.

70

"Nine months that time. In my opinion, far too humble a sentence for the iniquitous crime I'd seen him commit."

"What to do now?" asked Tony despairingly.

"Can there be any dispute?" said Mr Worsley, who seemed to know his way around such cases. "Surely you should dispense with his services forthwith."

"But on what grounds?" said Tony. "And what if he decides to turn on me?"

Mr Worsley appealed to me: "Couldn't you lend a hand, Vicar?"

"I'd like to," I said, "but he might think I was the one who betrayed his confidence and lose faith in religion altogether."

"A sound argument," conceded Mr Worsley, to my considerable relief. "You are, reverend sir, if I may put it thus, so wise for a gentleman of such tender years."

"I've got an idea," said Tony, snapping his fingers, "if only you'll give me a bit of help, Father."

Back at the rectory, I waited for signs of movement in Fr Duddleswell's bedroom. As soon as he emerged puffy-eyed from his siesta, I invited him into my study to discuss the problem of Archie's sacking. I omitted to say I had been the one to recommend Archie to Tony Marlowe.

After he had heard me out, Fr Duddleswell gave his opinion: "There is something very fishy about this Peregrine Worsley."

I hadn't liked the man, I granted, with his archaic use of language and ingratiating compliments. But he seemed trustworthy enough.

"Not at all, Father Neil. In the first place, he gave his address as something 'Chambers.' Now, there's places aplenty in Kensington and Chelsea and Victoria with that kind of high falutin' name but none such in Fairwater."

"Which means?"

"It means he's an outsider. He did not just 'chance' to be strolling past Tony's store. He must have come of set purpose. Second point: Mr Worsley claims to have seen Archie Lee working in a grocer's shop on the very first morning he takes up his employment. First morning, mark you! What a coincidence, Father Neil! And why, in heaven's name was an accountant interested in what is going on in a grocer's shop? And, for good measure, what splendid eyesight our conscientious gentleman must have."

"In fact," I contributed, "he wears bi-focals."

"And he claims he saw Archie working in Tony Marlowe's but did not ring for a whole hour. Did he take that length of time to look up Tony's number in the telephone directory, or was he perhaps hoping Archie would disgrace himself in the meanwhile? Mr Worsley does not tell a very plausible tale, d'you reckon?"

"What can he be up to then?"

"In my view, he's shadowing Archie everywhere or perhaps employing a private detective to do it for him. What his motive is, I cannot tell for sure. Could it be he was frightened out of his wits when Archie threatened to cosh him, and he has had it in for Archie ever since?"

"And now he won't let Archie hold down a steady job?"

"Seems so, but 'tis only an educated guess. 'Tis something out of the ordinary, I'll be bound."

"But Mr Worsley did take the trouble to come in person, Father."

"Even that might only be his way of exerting moral pressure. Tony's a nice lad but easily swayed, you follow? He might be disposed by nature to give Archie a chance to make good but not when a respectable, establishment figure like Mr Worsley starts prying and showing disapproval. No, I feel Mr Worsley was pulling out all the stops to get Archie Lee dismissed."

"And he succeeded."

As Fr Duddleswell got up to go, he said, "Father Neil?"

"Yes?"

"It was not you by any chance who found Archie that job?"

"It was."

Fr Duddleswell slumped down again. "You did not tell me that," he said uncomplainingly.

"You didn't ask, Father."

"A mental reservation?"

I swallowed hard but didn't reply.

"You have one disadvantage, Father Neil, you know that? You have a nut made of glass." And he recited a verse from *The Mikado*, altering the words, as he sometimes did, to suit himself:

> I know you well,
> You cannot tell
> A false or groundless tale—
> You always try
> To tell a lie
> And every time you fail.

When he had finished, I said, "I knew he was an ex-con, but not that he had a record of violence."

"'Twas too risky anyway, lad."

I thought for a moment before declaring stubbornly, "But if we take that attitude, how are we any different from Mr Worsley?"

"Do you not see, Father Neil, that *because* a priest recommends a man for a job, the prospective employer does not vet him as he's entitled to. *We* can employ an ex-con if we like but we ought not to foist him on another."

"That's true," I said. "Chaps like Archie then'll have to go on following falling stars. But I'm sorry, I made a mistake. You wouldn't have done anything so stupid."

"I probably would at that," he said, slowly nodding his head.

"You would?"

"I was only telling you what I *shouldn't* do, not what I *would*."

"You'd have gone against your better judgement?"

"'Tis often, Father Neil, the only decent way to behave.

Seeing what a lot of Pharisees we are, what great confidence can we put in our better judgement?"

"So I did right, after all?"

"No, young man, you did abysmal wrong."

"Like you would've?"

"Correct. You asked me advice, and I have to say, as any older and wiser mortal should: 'For God Almighty's sake, never follow *my* example.'" He shook his head in despair of himself. "Tea in ten minutes."

Then he upped and went.

I felt slightly better after that. Except that, for Tony's sake, I had committed myself to aid and abet Mr Worsley in his campaign of victimization. How I disliked that bald-headed accountant with his immaculate attire and fat wallet. Why did he have to pursue Archie so ruthlessly, making him pay ten times over for his misdeeds and provoking him to a life of crime?

In my mind I went over Christ's parable of the Pharisee and the publican. The Pharisee was named Peregrine and it was Archie who kept banging his breast with a crowbar and muttering, "Lord, be merciful to me, a sinner."

At 4:30 precisely, I phoned Tony. He had arranged to have Archie in his office at that time.

"Fairwater 2321," said Tony, when he picked up the receiver.

"Hello, Tony, it's me, Fr Boyd."

"*Hello*, Jim," said Tony breezily. "Nice to hear your voice again. And so *soon*. I thought your bronchitis would last a month or more."

I grimly held on to the receiver, wondering whether this fractured conversation was morally permissible.

"That's mighty good news, Jim. You mean the doctor said, he actually said, you can come back to work tomorrow? Great! I look forward to seeing you at eight o'clock. And, Jim, give my love to the wife and kids."

Then Tony hung up on me and my family.

At 6:30, Tony rang me again. "Thanks for your help, Father."

"How did it go?"

"Like a charm. He took it without a murmur when I explained he wouldn't be needed any more."

"I'm so glad. I feel I was mostly to blame."

"Never you mind, Father. Do you know, I think he suspected someone had ratted on him. Didn't complain but looked real crestfallen, he did, as if this has happened to him before."

"Poor Archie," I said, for I had a curious fondness for the crook.

"I felt really sorry for him myself. As the wife says, you can't help being a wee bit on his side."

"You couldn't have done anything else, Tony. Too much of a risk."

"Sure, Father, but I'm only saying I felt Archie really has turned over a new leaf, that's the sad part. There was the purse he gave back, and another thing..."

"Yes?"

"Well, when I paid him his wages—£10 as we'd agreed—I said, 'Look here, Archie, I'm awfully sorry to put you to this inconvenience, you having to find another job in midweek and all, here's an extra couple of quid to make up,' you know what he said?"

"What?"

"'No deal, Mr Marlowe. We agreed £10 and not an extra farthing will I take.' And he *wouldn't*. Ever known a crook turn down two quid when it's been handed to him on a plate?"

"Thanks for ringing me, Tony," I said in conclusion. "All's well that ends well."

Naturally, things hadn't all ended as far as I was concerned. I was troubled lest Archie thought I'd given him away. The day before, I'd taken his address in Begnall Street, and I was sorely tempted to call on him and enquire how he was. But I was frightened he might throw me out or, worse, ask

75

me to find him another job 'under the seal,' as it were. On balance, it seemed better to let matters rest. But three days later, I was walking in the High Street when I ran into Archie. My feelings were mixed. I didn't know whether to flee or commiserate with him for losing his job or accuse him of not telling me the truth about his record of violence.

Archie was all smiles. "Come and join me in a cup o' char, Father?"

I agreed and we sat down in a little café in a side street. I offered to pay but he wouldn't hear of it.

"Be my guest," he said.

Seeing his pacific mood, I decided to get something off my chest. "Why didn't you tell me you had convictions for G.B.H.?"

"Why should I, Father? I'm not violent no more. I'm not a thief no more. Why should I tell all and sundry I've got me a record of crime?"

"I'm not exactly all and sundry, Archie."

"True, Father, but you couldn't 'ave put me in for a job if you knew, could you?"

"No."

"There y'are then. You weren't to know I'm now gentle as a lamb."

"One thing, Archie," I said, conceding the force of his argument.

"Yes, Father?"

"*I* didn't inform on you."

"I know that, Father. It was a bloke called Peregrine Worsley."

"Has he informed on you before, then?"

"Father," replied Archie, "'e's doing it all the time."

"I *am* sorry," I said, my hackles rising again at the thought of Peregrine Worsley, Pharisee.

"Nothin' to be sorry about, Father. 'E's my best pal. We're confederates, always working 'and in glove."

"You mean this was all a con trick?"

"Nothin' like *that*," said Archie, horrified. "Let me

explain, Father. Perry used to be an accountant earning five or six grand a year. But 'e got 'isself into 'ot water, embezzling a few thousand more, see? So 'e joins me in a job at a bank in Sunbury. 'E was only trying to straighten 'isself out so 'e wouldn't 'ave to lead a life o' crime. 'E was supposed to be my decoy, only he opened 'is big gob when 'e shouldn't 'ave and nearly ruined everythin'. In the end, we got nabbed, thanks be to Gawd, and put away together." He looked up from his tea cup. "'E told you all that, I suppose."

"Not exactly in those terms," I said with understandable annoyance.

"Anyways, Father. This is 'ow we earns our keep now. I reg'larly get a week's wage for one day's work, sometimes with luck, for 'alf a day."

"But, Archie," I cried, very vexed, "I resent being *used* like this. Don't you realize you've implicated me in your crime?"

"Crime, Father?" asked Archie, aghast. "But where's the crime? We didn't even tell lies."

6

BREAKING THE SEAL

"Did you enjoy the roast beef, Fr Duddleswell?" the busty young waitress asked.

"Indeed, I did, Nelly. Me compliments to the cook. If he is in today."

I was lunching with my parish priest in the restaurant of The Clinton Hotel, a small place with a few tables and a bar, which had something of the atmosphere of a village pub. It was a little luxury we indulged in from time to time to give Mrs Pring "a holiday from the kitchen sink and ourselves a respite from her stirabout," as Fr Duddleswell put it.

I was dimly aware of Fr Duddleswell asking Nelly if she had managed to buy the house she was after but I was examining the Menu for a dessert and failed to pick up Nelly's reply.

"Father Neil." I jerked my nose out of the Menu. "Did y'hear what Nelly said?" I shook my head. "Nelly's got a flat."

At this moment Nelly was leaning over the table sweeping up the crumbs with a silver brush and pan. Her capacious bust was but a few challenging inches from my eyes, monopolizing the whole horizon, so to speak. Mesmerized, I could only repeat stupidly, "Flat? Flat? I don't know what Nelly was shaped like before, Father."

Nelly gave me the stony eye, straightened up and asked, "Anything to follow, Fr Duddleswell?"

"'Twould be difficult to follow that, Nelly," he replied with a grin. "The roast, I mean." He looked across at me. "How about you, now? Something exotic, Father Neil. Like, say, a hot cup of coffee."

I closed the Menu and handed it to the waitress. "Thank you, Father."

"The cream is extra, Father Neil."

"Black will be fine," I said.

Fr Duddleswell touched Nelly's wrist. "Fetch me curate a black coffee and one with cream for me, Nelly, if you would." As Nelly was adding his Menu to mine under her arm, he said, "I think Fr Boyd would appreciate a bowl of strawberries."

I gave a grateful gurgle which he acknowledged before touching Nelly's wrist again. "Without cream."

"Strawberries for you, too, Fr Duddleswell?"

"For me, no."

"I thought you liked them," Nelly said.

"I do, Nelly, indeed I do. But the price has risen alarmingly of late and they are far too expensive for the both of us to be eating them."

As Nelly went on her way, Fr Duddleswell held up what was left of our bottle of Nuits St Georges. "More wine for yourself?"

"Just a little, Father," I said, not expecting the fraction of an inch which was all I received.

"Just a little," breathed Fr Duddleswell, "for your stomach's sake, as St Paul counselled Timothy." He then filled his glass with the remainder. "Cannot have you abstaining altogether," he said, "else Nelly will suspect you of being a Methodist preacher."

He glanced sideways before putting his left hand to his mouth in what he took to be a surreptitious movement. From behind the barricade, he muttered like a gangster, "Over there, lad." He indicated two elderly ladies coming to the end of their meal at an adjoining table. "The two Miss Flanagans."

"Catholics, I presume."

"They turn up more regularly at Mass than Jesus Himself."

The ladies must have caught his eye because he smiled courteously and acknowledged them. "Miss Flanagan, Miss Flanagan." I half-rose and joined in with "Misses Flanagan."

Nelly brought my strawberries. "Coffee coming up, gentlemen."

Fr Duddleswell, in one of his more mischievous moods, remarked, "I do not for the life of me know how someone shaped like Nelly will fit into a flat."

If this was some sort of a game, I wasn't playing. I dug into my dessert.

"'Tis a strange thing, Father Neil, the association of ideas. Some are good, and some of 'em are bad."

A meticulous observation, I thought.

"A good association of ideas, now." Plucking a strawberry from my dish before I could rap his knuckles with my spoon, he held it aloft by the stalk. "'Tis when you look at a strawberry and it reminds you of the Sacred Heart of Jesus." He swallowed it.

I had heard him crack that one before. To humour the likeable old chap I asked, "And a bad association of ideas?"

As if he had prepared and rehearsed it well in advance, he drew from his inside pocket the relevant gaudy "holy" picture and held it up for me to see. "'Tis when you see a picture of the Sacred Heart and it reminds you of a strawberry."

Poised to bite such a hallowed object, I set it down slowly on the dish. Right, so it was war.

"I was thinking, Father."

"Very daring of you, Father Neil."

"What did you do with the money from the bazaar?"

"The money from the bazaar?" he echoed, as if it were news to him there'd been a bazaar. "Why, of course, 'twent into the fund for the church hall."

"All of it?"

"All of it?" he said in a kind of minor key. I nodded. "All that was donated by the insurance company, that is."

"And the rest?"

"Oh, the offerings of the faithful, too, naturally."

"Naturally. And Billy Buzzle's contribution?"

"The faithful were very generous in our hour of need, wouldn't you say?"

I looked at him without blinking.

"Billy Buzzle's contribution? Well, I could not advertise that, could I?"

"I'm not suggesting you stashed it away in a private account in Zurich," I said. The red wine was making me belligerent.

"There is no *secret* about it, Father Neil. 'Tis gone into the Wallington Building Society, where it brings us in a good three percent per annum. The interest goes towards the expenses of the church."

"Precisely, and in my view we ought to spend some of that money."

Fr Duddleswell who, as Mrs Pring observed, was tight as a reefknot with parish funds, his bell apart, looked agitated. "What on?" he asked.

"You know the mikes in our church."

"Mike O'Leary, Mike O'Donnel, Mike..." It was a brave attempt.

"The microphone mikes," I said.

He was very much aware he was being got at. "Ah, yes? Polish off those strawberries, now, and do not be wasting parish funds."

I refused the hint. "I think you need a new loudspeaker system. The one we've got gives off a terrible hum. The congregation can't hear you. Not even your appeals for money." The last part registered, at any rate.

As Nelly arrived with the coffee, I added, "You also need new confessionals, Father."

"Nelly," he said, "what did you lace those strawberries with?"

With a puzzled expression, poor Nelly went back to her work.

"Father Neil, what is wrong with the confessionals we have?"

"They're made of cardboard. Not soundproof. I read in an old parish magazine that they were put up during the First World War."

"Things were better made in the old days." He spoke with a dreamy nostalgia.

"In war-time, Father, there are always economy measures and the confessionals must have been one of them."

"Have they not served the parish well these last forty years?"

I paused dramatically.

"Well, have they *not*?"

"Someone who shall be nameless, Father, walked past your confessional and heard a penitent confess to . . . adultery."

Fr Duddleswell nearly choked on his wine. "'Tis not possible."

"You mean there's no adultery in your parish?" I asked with a kind of tipsy irony.

"Keep your voice *down*, Father Neil." He caught the eyes of the ladies again and smiled sickly. "Miss Flanagan. Miss Flanagan." From behind his hand again: "I mean nobody, but *nobody* could possibly hear what is being said in my confessional."

"Father, with respect," I said, "could it be that your hearing isn't as good as it was?" Before he could object, I added, "And to be honest, Father, mine isn't all it should be, either. I'm going to Dr Daley's soon to have my ears syringed. I'm finding difficulty in hearing what penitents say to me these days. I keep having to tell them to speak up."

"'Tis hard to credit that what is said in . . ."

"Mrs Conroy, Father."

"What about Mrs Conroy?" he snapped.

"Mrs Conroy, the butcher's wife, and the undertaker."

"The undertaker is Mr Bottesford," he said, reduced to a whisper.

"Rumour has it that Mrs Conroy and the undertaker are . . . you know."

"Father Neil, you are talking in riddles like the prophet Daniel. Know *what*?"

I swallowed a strawberry with a gulp. "Having an affair."

"'Tis news to me," said Fr Duddleswell, biting his lip and tapping with his foot.

"If you *have* heard of it in confession your lips are sealed, I know. You can't say they're committing adultery..."

"Keep your voice *down*," he interrupted me angrily. Another polite nod and smile to the ladies. "Miss Flanagan. Miss Flanagan."

I insisted on completing my sentence. "And you can't say they're not."

"I *am* saying they are *not*."

"Father," I said in a hoarse whisper, "I'm not asking you to pass judgement on allegations of a parish scandal. I realize I'll never know if what you're saying now is a mental reservation or the plain, unvarnished truth." Before he could edge in, I continued, "Even if you say it's the plain unvarnished truth, that too may be another quite legitimate mental reservation to defend the seal of confession as best you can."

"What is the point of all this?"

"It's this. The scandal, justified or not, has gained ground because parishioners suspect that the walls of our confessionals have ears."

Fr Duddleswell missed the last bit. He was distracted by two men who had come in through the back door and were making a bee-line for the bar. As they brushed our table, they said in unison, "Afternoon, Fathers."

Fr Duddleswell recovered quickly from what must have been a nasty surprise. "Fr Boyd, this is Bottesford, the undertaker." I shook hands with the big, burly man who wore a black tail-coat and carried a topper. "And this," Fr Duddleswell went on, "is Mr Conroy, husband of Mrs Conroy." Realizing the inappropriateness of such an introduction he tried to cover it up with, "And the best black-market butcher in the business."

Mr Conroy, smiling at the compliment, tipped his straw hat and took my hand. "Liking the parish, Father?"

"It's more interesting," I replied, "than I can possibly tell you, Mr Conroy."

Mr Bottesford took advantage of the chance meeting to criticize one aspect of my parochial performance so far. "You've not put any custom my way as yet, Fr Boyd." He handed me a black-edged card. "My motto is: 'Go to the Lord, With Bottesford.' Ten percent reduction for deceased Catholics, as you'd expect."

"Do not let us keep you gentlemen," hinted Fr Duddleswell, and the butcher and the burier went to the bar for a quick jar.

"They seem good pals," I said guiltily.

"The best, Father Neil. They are both in the meat trade, in a manner of speaking. The butcher would surely know if he was drinking with a man who undressed his prime joint."

I acknowledged the force of that.

"Mrs Conroy," he went on, "is very silly even as women go but she must realize that if she went into the undertaker's parlour she would suffer a fate far worse than death."

"I'll have to tell Mrs Pring there's..."

He cut across me. "I knew it was she."

Anxious for a change of topic, I asked, "Is Mr Bottesford married?"

"He is. But his two children left home long ago and his wife just ran off with a commercial traveller." He drained his glass. "So he has a lot to be thankful for."

He jerked his chin at the last of my strawberries. "Did you by any chance intend to eat that?"

"I don't think so, Father."

He grabbed and swallowed it. "We will motor back to the church to experiment, like."

He rose, said a quick grace and pointed to Winston Churchill's picture hanging on the wall a few yards from our table. "Astonishing man, Father Neil."

I drained my cup and got to my feet. "Yes, Father."

"He has brains," said Fr Duddleswell, shaking his head with incredulity, "to lick the Hun and still not enough to become a Catholic."

"Time for the news, Father Neil."

84

It was ten minutes later and he had me standing in the pulpit with the heavy old-fashioned mike round my neck.

I looked down the church at him. "My dear brother in Christ," I began in as muffled a manner as I could manage.

"Get on with you, lad."

"My text is: 'Father Noah hogged the wine and became drunk and lay naked in his tent.'" The church's emptiness made my voice echo and re-echo. The indistinctiveness of my contribution was beyond question.

Fr Duddleswell was scratching his head. "'Tis right what you say, Father Neil."

I cupped my hand to my ear. "What did you say, Father?"

He beckoned me to leave the pulpit. When I joined him, he was muttering, "It sounds as mixed up as a woman's motives or an Irish stew, and no mistake." He enlisted my help once more. "Now, into me box and confess your sins." Seeing my unwillingness, he said, "I promise to keep whatever you confess under the seal." As I entered, he called after me, "And do not forget to admit you gobbled up all those strawberries when there are millions starving in India."

I knelt down and fairly bellowed in my clearest accents, "Bless me Father, for I have sinned." Since he didn't tell me to stop, I shouted on, "It's twenty years since my last confession. I stole the sweet rations of children in the orphanage. I didn't wash my feet last month. I committed adultery."

Fr Duddleswell gave a sharp tap on the box.

Lingering lovingly on each loud syllable, I cried, "Did you hear my A-DUL-TER-Y?"

Another tap and a crisp command. "That is enough, Father Neil. 'Tis quite enough, d'you hear me speak to you?"

I emerged from the confessional with a sense of a job well done. The smile vanished immediately from my face when I saw who was kneeling piously in the rear bench.

Fr Duddleswell said, "Miss Flanagan. Miss Flanagan." And this time, I thought it polite to add, "Miss Flanagan. Miss Flanagan," on my own account.

In a soft voice, Fr Duddleswell said, "Your sins are a deal more entertaining than your sermons."

One of the ladies stood up. In a loud stage-whisper: "Would you mind hearing our confession, Fr Duddleswell?"

"Delighted, Miss Flanagan, delighted." To me, he said, "God forgive me for being such a hypocrite. Into the house with you. Cannot have you hovering in the vicinity of me confessional. These two old dears may have been handing round more elderberry wine."

He entered his box and turned about to face me. "If I am not out by supper time, fetch me me nose-bag here."

He gave the gentle whinny of a horse and slammed the top half of his box.

Back in the presbytery, I told Mrs Pring about my ears. Immediately she came to my room armed with a spirit lamp, a spoon and a bottle of olive oil.

She sat me down and draped a towel round my neck. "I'll spoon-feed your ears with olive oil to loosen the wax that's blocking them," she said.

As she went about her work, I apologized for letting her down. I admitted mentioning her name in connection with Mr Bottesford and Mrs Conroy. She shrugged it off as of no consequence. Fr D had to learn somehow.

"You did actually hear what Mrs Conroy said in confession, Mrs P?"

"No."

"*No*?"

"Mrs Davis, my friend who's an assistant in Woolworth's, she heard."

I was shaken to discover that what I had relayed to Fr Duddleswell in good faith was only an unsubstantiated rumour. When I told Mrs Pring that only a few minutes earlier we had seen the butcher and the undertaker having a friendly pint together she uttered a dire warning about what she would do to "that hussy Mrs Davis" next time they met. I agreed it would be kind to put the record right.

"I went to Fr D for confession," said Mrs Pring dreamily. "Only once."

"So did I," I said. "But that was brave of you, Mrs P."

"Not really. I told him exactly what I thought of him. That's the only time he's ever forgiven me." She broke off. "Hold your head to one side, please." I obliged. "Don't forget your convert is coming for her first instruction this afternoon."

"What's she like?"

Mrs Rollings, she explained, was married to the baker. Wilf was a cradle-Catholic and they had twin boys aged eight. As to Mrs Rollings herself, Mrs Pring suggested, "Fr D's handed her over to you because he considers her unteachable. And for once in his life, he may be right."

"Any idea why she wants to become a Catholic?"

"Strictly between you and me, Father Neil?" I nodded. She bowed her head conspiratorially. "I think she wants to become Pope."

A last scalding of my ear with olive oil, a plug of cotton wool and she was done just as Fr Duddleswell appeared.

He eyed her with disfavour. "If 'tisn't Saint Joan of Arc herself with her heavenly voices. Our very own furtive fly on the confessional wall."

"I only tried to help."

"Woman," he said, "if you milked a cow 'twould come out curdled."

"I said," repeated Mrs Pring, "I was only trying..."

"Indeed," broke in Fr Duddleswell, "you are *very* trying, but I am not here to discuss the secrets of the confessional with the likes of you." And he started shooing her out.

Mrs Pring pouted, picked up her equipment and exited with a sigh.

When I apologized for having spoken too hastily, he replied:

"Not at all. I heard every wicked thing you uttered in the blackness. Tell me, now."

I had already done some research and drew a pamphlet out of my pocket which he snatched from me.

"There's a firm near Westminster Abbey," I said, which sells neck mikes that work off a battery. They're light and you only need one. You can wear it all through Mass, whether you're at the altar, in the pulpit or moving along the altar rails distributing Communion."

"The price?"

"A hundred pounds," I said, adding quickly, "but the congregation will hear your appeals to pay for it."

"I will think on it. And the confessionals, like?"

"Sixty pounds."

"Each?"

I nodded. "Soundproof and installed in a week."

"Sixty pounds each," he mused.

I could see he was impressed by the relative modesty of the outlay. "Not much is it, Father, to safeguard the seal of confession?"

"Mind you," I seemed to hear him say, "we will have to make stringent economies to pay for them. No more living riotously like the Prodigal Son on Nelly's strawberries."

What with my plugged ears, once we got off the topic of mikes and confessionals I found difficulty in understanding him. I gathered it was something to do with strawberries. Recalling his stress on economy at The Clinton Hotel I said innocently, "Nelly's strawberries? Without cream, Father."

I saw his shocked look and lip-read him saying, "What d'you mean by that?"

"What did you mean, Father?" What could he have seen in such a harmless remark?

"*I* meant strawberries, Father Neil."

"And *I* meant cream."

"You did?"

"I did."

"Then there is no quarrel between us."

If there had been I would not have known what it was about.

He held the pamphlet up. "I will keep this and peruse it at me leisure. And remember, Mrs Rollings is visiting you this afternoon. She is a very good woman and that really is her only fault. Since she is your very first convert, I will be on hand, this once, to offer you me . . . condolences."

Mrs Rollings, eager, inquisitive, highly-strung, perched on the edge of her chair as she made ready to interrogate me.

I explained to her the difference between mortal and venial sin; how mortal sins like murder and rape ruptured communion with God, whereas venial sins like white lies or stealing sixpence diminished friendship with God but didn't demolish it altogether. Next, I told her that in this sacrament the penitent is obliged to tell the priest all his mortal sins, their number and species."

"What's that mean?" she asked in a quavering voice.

I explained that the penitent has to say exactly what sort of mortal sin he's committed—murder, abortion, large-scale theft—and how many times he's committed it.

"Catholics have to keep a strict count of things like that?"

"Pardon?" I said, taking the cotton wool out of one ear.

"A strict count?"

"Yes." And I put the plug back in.

"If a murderer or a raper or a crook confess their sins, are they forgiven?" I nodded. "And if they die they go to heaven?"

I was pleased to tell her that God is very merciful.

"Maybe," came back Mrs Rollings, "but Heaven don't sound very safe for children. Catholics have to confess regular, I suppose, because of all those rules to break. Sunday Mass, no meat on Fridays, et cetera. They must find mortal sins easier than normal people."

I made no comment on that.

"Tell me about yourself, Father."

"Myself?" I repeated, slightly panicky.

"Yes, do *you* go to confession?"

"All priests go to confession every two weeks."

"Nuns, too?"

"Every eight days."

"Go on," she said. "What *do* they get up to, locked in behind them high walls? More often than priests. Those nuns must have very strong urges."

"Even the Pope confesses regularly," I said in the nuns' defense.

"Really," she whistled. "But *you*, Father, do you prefer

going to confession or hearing them?"

"It all depends," I hedged.

"On?"

I refused to be drawn. "It all depends."

She had too many lines of enquiry to pursue to bother about one cul de sac. "If I became a Catholic, Father, would I have to confess all my sins to you?"

"All your *mortal* sins." I added hurriedly, "That's if you have committed any, of course, Mrs Rollings."

"Will you settle something for me, Father?"

"If I can."

"The other day, I heard one of mine arguing with the other about this: if an altar boy puts poison in the priest's wine and tells him so in confession just before Mass, has the priest got to drink that wine?"

It was an old chestnut. "I've heard of that case," I said.

"What's your answer?"

"There are several opinions," I said professorially. "One solution is to say the priest mustn't break the seal of confession for any purpose whatsoever."

"So he drinks it and dies?"

"Yes. Another suggestion is that since the altar boy has poisoned the wine and refused to tip it away, he's not going to confession with the right intention. He's going not to confess his sins but simply to gloat over the terrible trouble he's causing the priest."

"So?"

"Since he's not making a real confession, so this argument goes, the priest could either denounce the self-confessed altar boy assassin or secretly empty the wine down the drain and refill the cruet."

"But what do *you* think, Father?"

"I think a priest should always choose to uphold the secrecy of the confessional."

"Then you'd drink the poisoned wine?"

"It'd be safer," I said.

"Safer?"

"For the sacrament, I mean. Above all else, we must

protect the seal of confession."

Mrs Rollings seemed enthusiastic about the whole thing. "I'm very interested in this confession business." That pleased me until she dipped down to the personal level again. "Have you been a priest long?"

"Two or three months."

"How old are you, then?"

Reluctantly I admitted I was getting on for twenty-four.

"And you're not married?"

"Catholic priests," I told her, "aren't allowed to marry." I hoped that might impress her.

"What use are *you* in confession, then?"

I took out an earplug to make sure I had heard her correctly.

"How can you say people mustn't use birth control," she asked, "when you're...well, when you don't practice marriage?"

There was a knock on the door and Fr Duddleswell, bleary-eyed from his siesta, appeared. He sized up the situation in an instant.

"I thought you were free, Father Neil, but I see you are a prisoner."

"Come in, Father. *Please* come in. Mrs Rollings was just asking about contraception."

"'Tis forbidden."

"I know," she said, "but why?"

"Because 'tis a grievous sin, that's why."

"I see," said a cowed Mrs Rollings.

"Another thing, Mrs Rollings," said Fr Duddleswell. "Do not use that word 'why?' too often, like."

That word was on the tip of Mrs Rollings' tongue when she bit it off and said, "No, Father."

"'Why' is a nasty little Protestant word, you follow? Catholics, now, say, '*Credo*, I Believe,' to whatever the Pope says. If you want to ask 'Why?' go ask the Anglican vicar to instruct you in unbelief and he will let you 'Why-why-why?' to your heart's content."

Poor Mrs Rollings was like a flat dose of salts after that.

All she could say was, "But you *are* bound to keep secret what you hear in confession?"

"Mrs Rollings," replied Fr Duddleswell, softening towards her, "a priest has to protect the seal at all costs. Suppose you come to me in confession. Am I permitted to tell your husband who is next in line what you have revealed to me? Or may I tell Father Neil here? Indeed, I may not." He pursed his lips for emphasis. "Not even if you have confessed to squandering your whole week's housekeeping money on a bowlful of strawberries."

A week later, Fr Duddleswell and I were standing in church in front of a new, solid-looking confessional bearing the name FR CHARLES DUDDLESWELL. It had two lights, red and green, for engaged and free.

"There, now, Father Neil, what d'you think of her?" I drew in my breath in the manner expected of me. "Inside with you and put her to the test."

He said that or something like it. I couldn't be sure because a combination of wax, olive oil and cotton wool had qualified me for a hearing-aid on the National Health.

I spoke some less reprehensible sins this time and considerably softer. Still he banged on the box. I just made out the word "Louder." I tried to give value for money. I only stopped when he opened the door and yelled, "The all-clear has sounded. Lazarus, come forth." Plainly, he had ordered me more than once to dry up.

Outside, he said something which I made him repeat. "Father Neil, I am mighty glad you have mended your ways." I smiled and he mouthed slowly, "WHAT THE HELL IS THE MATTER WITH YOU?"

I outlined my predicament.

"Deaf?"

"I couldn't hear my own confession, Father."

To that I think he said, "Saved you scandalizing yourself, at any rate." He mouthed again, "GO SEE DR DALEY AND HAVE YOUR EARS SYRINGED."

I nodded. "What about buying the new mike, Father?"

He cupped his hand to his ear. "Pardon?"

"The new mike, Father."

"SPEAK UP, LAD," he enunciated clearly, "I AM HARD OF HEARING, YOU FOLLOW?" He relaxed to tell me, I guessed, that he *had* decided to purchase the new mike.

To make sure, I said, "Pardon, Father?"

His final remarks were unmistakable. "Bloody heavens, Father Neil, go see Dr Daley about those ears straight away. Talking to you is almost as ruinous as talking to Mrs Pring."

Dr Daley, portly and bald, was as Irish as a sprig of shamrock. On his shelf, that Saturday afternoon, was a bottle of whiskey, the worse for wear, and an empty glass. A lighted cigarette was wedged in the corner of his mouth.

"The first ear done," he said, as he surveyed the yellow debris floating in the small enamel bowl he held in his left hand. In his right was an enormous brass syringe. "Enough wax there to build three tall beehives in Connemara."

He was speaking in a kind of monologue, apparently under the impression that I couldn't hear a thing. This wasn't so. I was only completely deaf in spasms now. Some of what he said got through to me, including:

"You are deaf as an adder for the moment, Fr Boyd, which is why I'm going to make my confession to you." He gestured to the bottle. "A drink of poteen, Father? Of course, not. Mind if I do? The drought is upon me, you see."

He poured himself another treble and raised his glass to me. "Cheers, Father." He drained his glass, without removing his cigarette, in one gulp. He put the glass down with a crash and took up the syringe in a trembling hand.

"Without the hard stuff, I'd be a bundle of nerves." At this, he launched the brass torpedo into my other ear. "The ears of my soul are deaf to the Almighty's entreaties to give up the drink. Sweet Jesus, but it is impossible—keep yourself still, Father—to straighten the twist in an old stick, and that's the truth. Charles, our revered parish priest, has sounded the fire-alarm at me often enough and raised the ladder to the burning building. But it's no good, you see. I will surely end up with flames licking all round me and not so much as a friendly spark to light my fag with." He shone his torch in my ear. "In a minute or two, the bubbles will burst."

Then nothing. But I had heard enough already. I was sad for old Dr Daley and his unavailing efforts after his wife died to give up the booze. I was worried about my hearing, too. The doctor had rid me of half a dozen large pellets of wax. What was the meaning of this uncanny, inner wall of silence? I wondered whether he had shot right through my eardrums and deafened me for life.

Then followed two small explosions in quick succession, one in each ear. It was as if a sound-proof door had suddenly been thrown open onto Piccadilly Circus at the rush hour.

"They've popped, have they?" roared Dr Daley.

I nodded and rubbed both ears in amazement. Every sound was considerably magnified with electrical clarity.

"Try combing your hair," he suggested.

I put my comb through my hair and it made a noise like giants crawling through a field of straw.

Dr Daley proceeded to reward himself by filling his glass to the brim.

"For a day or two, Father, before you adjust, your electric razor will scream at you like a pneumatic drill." He paused to steady his glass. "I have it on prescription, you see," was his explanation. "And you'll be able to hear the circulation of your blood, as well as everyone else's in a three mile radius."

Dr Daley knelt with a wobble, signing himself and making sure he didn't spill a drop.

"Now, give me your blessing, Father."

I felt he had earned spiritual rewards of every sort. As I stood over him, gratefully, he bowed his broad, flat, wrinkled head.

That evening, as Fr Duddleswell was serving supper, there was a small, elegant box on the table beside his plate.

"Before I waste me precious breath," he said behind his hand, "tell me if you are still deaf or no."

"I hear you painfully well," I said.

He wanted to know where I had been that afternoon. The men had come to fix the loudspeaker system in the church. I told him of my visit to Dr Daley's.

"Well oiled?" he asked.

"He was."

"I know *he* was," he said. "I was referring to the wax in your ears."

He proudly opened up the box to reveal the new, miniature mike.

"There she is, Father Neil. Light as a feather, clear as a bell." He lifted it up and fitted it round his neck. "It works like a charm. Audible to the deaf and the dead." That rang a bell. "Where is Mrs Pring?"

I listened for a moment and enlightened him. "At the back door, having words with Mrs Davis from Woolworth's. Mrs Pring is giving her a piece of her mind."

"Which she can ill afford," said Fr Duddleswell, absorbed in the microphone's beauty. He awoke from his reverie to strain his own ears. "How did you know that, Father Neil?"

Without waiting for my reply he went to the door and called, "Mrs Pring!" As the lady of the house came running, he growled, "'Tis the Charge of the Heavy Brigade."

"Speak, Lord," said a breathless Mrs Pring, "for thy servant heareth."

"Father Neil, there is nothing like a dutiful woman to cheerfullize the place. Now, Mrs Pring, I have decided in view of the vile thieves abounding round here to keep this new microphone on me mantelshelf instead of in the sacristy. You may go."

Mrs Pring stood there amazed. "Where to?"

"Do not tempt me, woman," he replied.

Mrs Pring almost intoned, "May God in His mercy stretch out His hand to you, Fr Duddleswell, and strike you down."

"I am more determined than ever," he returned, "to save up and send you to America." As Mrs Pring made to leave for a destination of her own choosing, he called after her:

"Oh, and, Mrs Pring. I will be saying the two early Masses tomorrow morning. I do not want Father Neil to oversleep himself. When you get up, would you mind tapping on his door with your tongue?"

Next morning, I rushed downstairs and almost collided with Mrs Pring as she returned from the eight o'clock Mass.

"How did the new mike sound, Mrs P?"

"Terrible."

"Terrible?"

"For the first time in years I could hear every word of his sermon." As I bent down to do up the last few buttons of my cassock, she reflected ruefully, "It's a good job that man doesn't practice what he preaches. I couldn't stand it."

I opened my arms wide in the ritual gesture. "I could hear his *Dominus Vobiscum*," I said, "even through the roar of my razor."

In church, the benches were beginning to fill up. I was relieved to see I wasn't late. No one was waiting outside my confessional. I entered, sat, removed the cotton wool from my ears which I still wore as a protection against noise, and started to recite my breviary.

"Bless me, Father, for I have sinned." It was a woman's voice. I was surprised because I hadn't heard a penitent come in. I raised my right hand and was about to give the blessing when another gave it: Fr Duddleswell. "*Dominus sit in corde...in nomine Patris et Filii et Spiritus Sancti. Amen.* And how long is it since your last confession?"

I knew my hearing had improved within the last few hours but I wasn't prepared for anything like this. I could distinctly hear what was going on in Fr Duddleswell's allegedly soundproof box forty-five feet away.

The penitent said, "Two weeks, Father, and these are my sins. I told a few white lies."

"No such thing," said Fr Duddleswell, "all lies are black, as well you know."

"I told a few little black lies."

It was impressed on her that lies of whatever hue are never *little*, either. I stuffed the cotton wool back in my ears but it made no difference. While it was instructive to witness the master at work, I could hardly listen in good conscience to the penitent's confession when I was in no position to grant her absolution.

"I gave short change in the shop, Father," the lady said.

"How long is short?"

"Only the odd threepence and sixpence on a joint, Father."

That was when it hit me that the penitent was Mrs Conroy, the butcher's wife. Having identified her, I was entitled even less to sit there listening to confidences not meant for me. I pushed open the door of my box, intending to return to the house. Immediately I did so, I became aware of the electric atmosphere in the church.

Fr Duddleswell was still wearing the portable mike and had forgotten to switch the thing off. Either that or the whole congregation was also graced with super-sensitive hearing.

Fr Duddleswell was saying, "'Only' is the divil's own word, me dear. You will have to make restitution, will you not? Let me ponder, now."

While he pondered, the congregation started turning with varying emotions towards Fr Duddleswell's box. Some laughed and some frowned. One lady had her handkerchief over her mouth while her rosary was dangling from her hand, another pressed her fingers in her ears. A child was standing on a bench holding a toy train and pointing in Fr Duddleswell's direction.

"The best thing for you to do, I'm thinking," decided Fr Duddleswell, "is to undercharge a few customers this week. That way you will make up for what you overcharged them last week. Will you do that for me, now?"

I spied Mr Conroy outside Fr Duddleswell's box, still as stone, his jaw almost to his chest, while from within came Mrs Conroy's voice:

"I promise you, I'll do that."

"Anything else?" asked Fr Duddleswell, with the slight world-weariness of the skilled confessor.

By this time, I was creeping on tiptoe round the back of the congregation, heading for Fr Duddleswell's confessional. I was careful to genuflect slowly at the center aisle. Apart from anything else, it gave me a few more precious seconds to reflect on what I ought to do.

"I added three pounds to my housekeeping from my husband's takings, Father."

Mr Conroy's face registered annoyance at that but he recovered somewhat when Fr Duddleswell told his wife she must give that back, too.

"Anything else bothering you, me dear?"

"Yes, Father. I thought Thursday was Friday."

"Where is the sin in that?"

"Well, I ate meat thinking it was Friday, so I don't know if that was a sin or not."

Fr Duddleswell was subject to no such uncertainty. "If you intended to sin, you sinned."

I had reached Mr Conroy. I gripped his arm and told him to accompany me. "We'll turn the switch of the loudspeaker off," I told him. "That way, we won't interfere with the confession."

Out of the corner of my eye, I saw Mr Bottesford the undertaker, higher up the aisle, first sidling and then positively scuttling towards us. He almost knocked me and Mr Conroy flat.

"Morning, Father," he said to me in passing, and to Mr Conroy, "Sorry, Bill."

As we advanced up the aisle, Mrs Conroy was saying, "It was only a ounce or two. And it *was* chicken."

"So?" asked Fr Duddleswell.

"Chicken's not really meat, is it, Father?"

"It is so," Fr Duddleswell insisted, as I began to examine the loudspeaker by the side of the pulpit. I only wished I had been present when the system was installed.

"But chickens come from eggs, Father."

"I am long aware that chickens come from eggs, me dear, even though the Church has not yet defined which of 'em came first. Is there some point to all this?"

When I told Mr Conroy there wasn't a switch on the loudspeaker he begged me to pull the wire out. I saw there was no alternative. I pulled and pulled. Instead of snapping, the wire kept coming.

"Chickens come from eggs," argued Mrs Conroy, "and you can eat eggs on Fridays."

"If fish laid meat balls you still could not eat meat balls on Fridays."

In desperation I asked Mr Conroy if he had a knife. No. I asked a lady in the front row if she had any scissors and she fished me a pair out of her handbag. As I held it aloft in triumph for Mr Conroy to see, Mrs Conroy, unaware of our efforts to preserve what was left of her honour, was still insisting that chicken isn't meat.

"Look," said an exasperated Fr Duddleswell, "d'you sell chicken in your shop?"

"Yes."

"Then chicken is meat."

"But we sell eggs, too, Father."

"For the purposes of confession," said Fr Duddleswell, coming on like a heavy, "the Pope has decreed infallibly that chicken is meat."

Mrs Conroy capitulated. "Then bless me, Father, for I have sinned."

"Was there something else?"

I thanked God we would never know, for at that moment I cut the wire. Mr Conroy and I sighed with the sense of a job well done. We had caused some material damage but that was easily reparable. The main thing was we had not meddled with the sacrament of Christ's forgiveness. As I instinctively held out the hand of comradeship to Mr Conroy, Mrs Conroy said:

"I'm still thinking, Father."

My comrade and I looked at each other aghast, then at the *second* loudspeaker. We genuflected to the Blessed Sacrament at the center and stood beneath the speaker. It was much higher up than the first, with no wires visible from below. If I stood on the butcher's shoulders I might just about reach it. Contrariwise, I might fall and break a leg.

"Get a chair, quick," I said, and he started desperately looking round for one.

Then, the crushing blow. In a voice which dipped with self-consciousness but was still perfectly audible all over the church, Mrs Conroy said, "I committed adultery again last week, Father."

"With a gentleman," Fr Duddleswell put it discreetly, "you say, not your husband?"

This was too bad. I gave up any idea of looking for chairs and wires and set off, running on tiptoe, in the direction of Fr Duddleswell's box.

"With the undertaker, Father," said Mrs Conroy.

"I do not wish to know what your accomplice does for a living."

"I didn't mean to do it."

"Not mean to?"

"He induced me," whimpered Mrs Conroy. "In the cemetery, Father. Didn't seem quite right somehow, Father, under the yew tree with all those gravestones looking on."

Fr Duddleswell was not put off his task by the beautiful outlook. "How many times?"

"Twice times twice, Father." She paused before adding, "And once, almost, Father."

"Which means?" asked a puzzled Fr Duddleswell.

"They started to shut the cemetery gates, Father."

"I see."

I was now outside Fr Duddleswell's box, well aware it was far too late to mar his model interrogation. Even then it cost me an effort to intrude on someone's confession. I plucked up the necessary courage as Mrs Conroy had her final word:

"He said he didn't want to stay in all night as well as all day, Father."

I flung the door open. There was Fr Duddleswell sitting, wearing a long white alb, purple stole and the new mike. I was met by two large eyes quite horse-like in their astonishment.

I went for the microphone cord round his neck, but since I still had the scissors in one hand, he could not make out whether I intended to strangle him or cut his throat.

"Are you out of your *mind*, Father Neil?"

I snatched the cord from him without a word.

Shall I ever forget Fr Duddleswell's look of horror as it dawned on him that for the first time in his long and venerable priestly career he had broken the seal of confession?

7

THE BETROTHAL

"'Twill be a bit of a farce, I am warning you in advance," said Fr Duddleswell. "But, as you will discover, there are times when charity demands we go along with the whims and fancies of the faithful."

The reason for this caution was the betrothal of a young Sicilian couple who came from the families Bianchi and Christini. The Bianchis lived on Fr Duddleswell's side of the parish, the Christinis lived on mine.

"I'm glad it's a joint effort," I said. "I don't speak a word of Italian."

"Neither do they," Fr Duddleswell said. "When they are together, they speak an impossible dialect but they will probably take pity on me and converse in half-English and half-Italian."

It was such a fine summer's morning, we chose to walk; and first to go to the Bianchis, who were providing the bride.

"This," said Fr. Duddleswell, "will be an occasion the like of which you have never seen. Sicilians are marvellous Christians but impossible Catholics, except for important celebrations."

"Christenings, weddings, funerals?" I suggested.

"*And* the big feasts like Christmas, Epiphany, Easter. For the rest, churchgoing is left entirely to the ladies. Do you know, Father Neil, when I once said to old Bianchi, the head of the family, 'Why do you not come to Mass every Sunday?' he replied, 'We is *Cattolici non fanatici.*'"

I smiled hoping I'd understood the joke.

"'Tis a strange thing, Father Neil, but some Italians who never go to Mass in their lives leave pots of money in their will for Masses to be said for them when they die."

"Illogical," I said.

"There was one chap I knew, name of Zeffirelli, who left £1,000 for Requiems, all at the lowest rate of five shillings a time. Kept an African missionary in stipends for over a decade."

"Ten years of black Masses!" I said sympathetically.

"The poor fellow probably needed every single one of 'em, Father Neil. Otherwise he would have been locked up in Purgatory, like, till the place shuts. Now back to this betrothal business. Tomfoolery or no, 'tis important to them. The Sicilians came to England from Messina in 1908, or the original stock did. Survivors of the earthquake. The eldest, Signor Bianchi, was only a lad when he last saw his native land. The same goes for old Christini. But you would never guess it. They speak but pigeon-English and keep to customs which most likely died out in Sicily before the First World War."

I was enjoying the walk. The sun was climbing the blue sky, and its golden glow made me feel it was good to live in our part of London. I loved the red buses; the plane trees dotted about in surprising places; the quiet, mysterious mews in which tiny houses nestled—no more than stables really but very expensive—with red, yellow or green doors and bright brass knockers; the old, tall, gas-lighted lamp-posts; the patient road sweepers with their wide, black, bristly brooms.

From out of a kind of happy mental mist, I heard Fr Duddleswell expanding on the subject of the Sicilian betrothal.

Gelsomina Bianchi and Mario Christini had been to the same primary and secondary school. We were to witness the "arranging" of their marriage. The pretence was they had never set eyes on each other. It would certainly be thought a '*scandalo*' if they had gone out together or held hands. The planning was left entirely to the heads of the family.

"I will try and explain things as we go along," Fr Duddleswell said. "Remember 'va bene' means 'okay.' You can travel all over Italy with that if you keep varying the intonation. Two other phrases, perhaps: 'Grazie tante' means 'thanks' and you respond to that with 'prego' meaning 'don't mention it.'"

We were met at the door of a large mansion-type house by Mrs Angelina Bianchi, a distinguished greying lady with a parchment-like face.

She greeted Fr Duddleswell with "Buon giorno, padre" and knelt to kiss his hand.

Without another word, Signora Bianchi conducted us to a large inner room where the male Bianchis were assembled. All five of them, seated around a table, rose to their feet.

Signor Bianchi, seeing me, exclaimed: "Ah, due preti, two priesters" (he translated after a fashion for my benefit). "O what a beautiful augurio!"

As head of the family he introduced us to his sons who came forward in turn to bow and kiss our hand: Giorgio, Letterío, Domenico, and Peppino. To each of them I gave a smile and said "va bene." Afterwards, I felt as though I'd been flavored all over with garlic.

"And this," said Fr Duddleswell introducing me, "is Padre Neil Boyd."

Signor Bianchi responded with, "Gli amici dei nostri amici sono i nostri."

"The Signor says," interpreted Fr Duddleswell, "Our friends' friends are our friends."

That put my head in a whirl, but I took it as a compliment and bowed politely and said, "Grazie tante, signor."

"Prego," exclaimed Signor Bianchi delightedly, "parla bene Italiano il Padre Boyd."

"No speak Italian," I said in a panic. "No va bene."

"You is English Englishman?" asked our host.

"Yes," said my interpreter, jumping to my rescue. "I Irish Englishman not Padre Neil."

The Sicilians looked at me wonderingly as if they didn't

know the Pope allowed English Englishmen to be ordained as priests.

"Padre Neil," said Fr Duddleswell, "is almost twenty-four years old. Of good parents, *buoni Cattolici.* He has three brothers and two sisters."

"Ah, *buoni Cattolici*," emphasized Signor Bianchi, showing his big yellow teeth in approval. "And now *una preghiera, per piacere, Padre.*"

I gathered we were expected to open the proceedings with a prayer. Everyone turned towards the wall where I saw what I took to be a pair of horns and, nearby, a shelf with a red votive lamp alight under an old print of the Madonna and Child. The Virgin was bejewelled and smiling against a rural background and wearing a golden crown. The Child was at her breast, also crowned, and in his hand were three ears of corn symbolizing, I supposed, fertility. In the ornamented silver picture frame were sprigs of lavender.

Fr Duddleswell intoned the *Pater Noster* and *Ave Maria* which all present rattled off in Latin. And then, "*Nostra Signora di Custonaci.*"

"*Prega per noi*," all responded. I said, "Pray for us."

As we sat down, Fr Duddleswell explained to me that Our Lady of Custonaci was the patron saint of Sicilians.

"That peecture ... over the sea come ... from Alesandria," said Signor Bianchi.

Giorgio, the eldest son, a real *mafioso*-type if ever I saw one, fat, greasy, and black, added, "It was pain'ed by San Luke *evangelista*, but the faces is pain'ed by the Gabriel Archange-lo."

Letterío took up the story: "*La Madonna di Custonac' preserva* us from drought and *pestilenze and terremoto*, 'ow you say? earfquike, and from the *milioni* of locusts."

When Domenico contributed his piece, I realized I was listening in on a Sicilian saga, like the Jewish Passover, in which all the males had a traditional part to play.

"On the *festa* of *la Madonna*," said Domenico, "nobodies swears on the island."

"A truly *grand' miracolo*," put in Fr Duddleswell without a smile.

"*Davvero, Padre*," said Domenico. "No stealings, also, and even thieves are *buoni Cattolici* for one only *die*."

Finally, the youngest, Peppino, a fine-looking young man, took his turn: "This is why the wedding has been fixed a year ahead for next 25th August, the *festa* of the *Madonna di Custonaci*."

Peppino's English was easily the best of the five, which I presumed was due to the fact that, having lived all his life in London, he couldn't escape English influences altogether. But for some reason his brothers seemed not to approve of what he'd said. They glowered at him. I wondered if he had spoken out of turn when it was old Signor Bianchi's privilege to name the wedding date.

The patriarchal Signor Bianchi then clapped his hands and in came his wife smartly, carrying a tray with a flask of red wine and seven beakers.

"Please," said Signor Bianchi, holding the tips of his fingers together in prayer, "please to take to drink a cup of marsala. It do mucha good to the spireets and the *stomaco*."

After a few swigs, the bargaining began.

Signor Bianchi asked with ample gestures:

"*Quanto*, 'ow mucha for the *compana*?"

Fr Duddleswell said, "The bell? It costa five shilling."

Signor Bianchi thought about that for a bit before nodding.

"*Va be'*," he said, and signalled to Giorgio to write it down, "*Scrive, Giorgio*," which he did in a big leather-bound family album. "And the *organo*, padre?"

"One pound ten shilling."

"*Misericordia! Troppo*, padre."

"*Not* too much," Fr Duddleswell insisted, waving the palm of his right hand from side to side.

"A li'l bit *troppo*," pleaded Signor Bianchi.

"*Va bene*," conceded Fr Duddleswell, "one pound only."

I had never witnessed simony at such close quarters before. I confess I was too fascinated by the whole mercenary process to be as scandalized as I should have been.

"Flowers for the *sanctuario*, padre, *e confetti?*"

"Confetti?" exclaimed Fr Duddleswell in a shocked tone. "*Dio mio! Impossibillissimo!* Flowers, *sí,* confetti, *non.*"

"Padre, padre," said Signor Bianchi in a perfect whimper, his joined hands stretched out before him in imprecation.

Fr Duddleswell sipped his wine, pouted and said:

"*Un po' di confetti.*"

"*Grazie*, padre."

"*Prego*," said Fr Duddleswell, and, holding his left finger and thumb together to make a circle, repeated, "*Un po*, only a leetle beet."

Signor Bianchi turned to Giorgio, "*Scrive* a li'l beet," and then to Fr Duddleswell, "'Ow mucha?"

"Two shilling."

"*Scrive*, Giorgio, two sheeling."

So the bargaining went on to the accompaniment of gestures so magnificent I could follow most of what was said without difficulty. Each time agreement was reached, the glasses were clinked in salute and a toast drunk.

Then came the momentous question of the cope Fr Duddleswell was to wear at the wedding.

Domenico said, "The golda cop, padre, we musta haf the golda cop. This is what says our *adorata mamma*."

Fr Duddleswell slowly shook his head discouragingly.

There was alarm in Signor Bianchi's eyes. "For Gelsomina, padre. For our *carissima* Gelsomina."

Fr Duddleswell maintained his stubborn stance.

"'Ow mucha, padre?" Our host's shoulders slanted forward as if, should the need arise, he would part with all he possessed for such a favor.

"Too much, Signor Bianchi."

"Plen'y mucha money?"

"*Sí, signor.*"

"Fiva pounds? I expect with anxiousness your *responso*."

"*Va bene*," said Fr Duddleswell grudgingly.

"Three pounds, will that be enough?" asked Peppino hopefully, and, for no reason I could fathom, aroused again the silent wrath of the fraternity.

"Three pounds?" mused Fr Duddleswell. "*Va bene*."

"*Scrive, scrive,* Giorgio, t'ree poun's for the golda cop." Signor Bianchi was triumphant. "All feeneeshed."

And all the brothers cried out, "*Evviva*."

Giorgio, on his own behalf, said, "Padre, you pay the seesters in the *convento* to pray for our Gelsomina?"

"*Certamente*," replied Fr Duddleswell.

"We give our Gelsomina," Giorgio said, "lots of indulgénces, t'ousands of days of indulgénces."

He made it sound as if the Church's system of indulgences was a protection racket invented by the Mafia.

Another clap of the hands from our host and his wife, right on cue, brought in biscuits and sugared almonds and a huge decorated flask of chianti.

For the next half an hour, it was all "*grazie*" and "*prego*," as they filled my glass whenever, like a fool, I drained it.

I remember Signor Bianchi saying in exultant mood, "Ah, Padre Duddleswell, the *matrimonio*, is it not the only vendetta blessèd by the Church?"

"The only *vendetta benedetta*," said Fr Duddleswell with an uncustomary giggle.

"*Sì*" said Giorgio, "when I marry my Teresa, my *mamma* she say to me, 'Giorgino, why you wanna marry tha' *signorina*? If you be married, you will not love any more tha' lady.'"

The *mamma* smiled like the Mona Lisa, but tradition forced her to hold her peace.

"Women," Giorgio went on, "don't be thinking of nothing but the *bambini*."

"The *matrimonio*," Letterío said, "is like what is called in Sicilia, '*una tassa sull'ignoranza*,'" and, translating for my benefit, "'a taxes on the *stupidità*.' But, Padre Neil," he said, looking at me fixedly, "I advertise you not to never pay in your 'ole life this taxes."

At this everybody laughed and I said a trifle unsoberly: "I no pay *no* taxes."

"It is mucha better," Domenico said, "to be free as the salt."

"*Grazie, cara,*" Signor Bianchi said pointedly to his wife, motioning her to leave. "You are too much busy to remine."

I inferred from this the talk might become too indelicate for women's ears.

"I wanna you," said Signor Bianchi confidentially to Fr Duddleswell after his wife had departed, "I wanna you to be telling Signor Christini my Gelsomina is very gooda girl for 'is boy."

Fr Duddleswell nodded agreement.

Signor Bianchi went on: "My Gelsomina is pura as the Madonna but not pregnanted in the slightest, *capisc'*?"

"*Capisco.* I understand," said Fr. Duddleswell.

"*Scrive*, padre," insisted the proud father, "*scrive*," so that Fr Duddleswell had to take out his diary and write in big letters: "Gelsomina is not pregnanted."

"In the slightest," said Signor Bianchi, concluding his dictation, and he made Fr Duddleswell write that down too.

"But *after* the *matrimonio*," said Fr Duddleswell with a wink.

"Then," Signor Bianchi said, "plen'y pregnanted." This seemed to jog his memory for he added: "The benediction at the *matrimonio*."

"Yes?" asked Fr Duddleswell.

"In Italiano, yes? If you don't bless in Italian, per'aps no *bambini*."

"To make sure, the *benedizione* will be in *Italiano*."

Signor Bianchi sighed with the pleasures of grandpaternity to come.

"Now to see the bride," he said.

He clapped his hands and this time his wife led in Gelsomina. The shy young woman was about nineteen, with long black hair and dark lashes. Blinking to clear my vision of a pink haze, I saw she was pretty, though she moved in a slightly lame fashion and had a definite cast in her left eye.

"Padre Duddleswell," urged our host, "you tella Signor Christini our Gelsomina is *bella* also *pura*. She worth all the mucha money I you pay for the *matrimonio*. I no wanna 'im to robba me of my Gelsomina for nuttin'. *Capisc'*?"

"*Sì*," Fr Duddleswell assured him, "and I tella that to Signor Christini."

"Now, padre, *un fervorino* for Gelsomina."

I gathered Fr Duddleswell was expected to preach a little sermon to the future bride.

"Gelsomina," said Fr Duddleswell, sipping his chianti, "Gelsomina..."

"*Un fervorino, per piacere*," repeated our host.

"Gelsomina," said Fr Duddleswell, "do not quarrel the first time."

Everybody applauded, and Fr Duddleswell expanded his thought thus: "Do not quarrel the first time with your *marito*, your husband. If you do, it will never end. If you do not, it will never begin."

Such priestly wisdom brought a gasp of appreciation from all the male Sicilians present and a plum-like blush to the face of the bride.

Signor Bianchi drove home the point. "Gelsomina, Padre Duddleswell is to you telling to don't be quarrelling."

Fr Duddleswell blessed Gelsomina and she left, limping a little, with her mother.

Our business at the Bianchis was nearing its end. It was agreed that Giorgio would represent the family and come to the rectory at eight o'clock to seal the contract with the representative of the Christinis. With many exchanges of *addio, arriverderci*, and "'appy days," we staggered to the door.

When we made the fresh, scented summer air, I began to sober up.

"Lovely people," enthused Fr Duddleswell, "even their religion does not seem to do them any harm. They *liked* you, Father Neil." And ignoring the passers-by, he proceeded to sing:

> For you might have been a Roosian
> A French or Turk or Proosian
> Or perhaps Sicili-an.

But in spite of all temptations
To belong to other nations
You remain an Englishman
You remain an Englishman.

There were many questions I wanted to ask him, "What about those horns on the wall?" I said for a start.

"Their religion does not much interfere with their superstitions either, I'm afraid, Father Neil. They are first and foremost *Siciliani*, are you with me? Those horns are on the wall to ward off the Evil Eye." Seeing I had only the vaguest notion of the Evil Eye, he explained: "'Tis a subtle, malign influence which they break up by hanging horns on their walls or wearing them on their persons. Made of coral or mother of pearl."

"Where is this evil influence supposed to come from?"

"Ah, Father Neil, many Italians think that Pius IX himself, their beloved *Pio Nono*, had the Evil Eye."

"Really!" I exclaimed in horror.

"Yes, indeed, even some cardinals, when they had an audience with His Holiness, used to make horns at him with their fingers under their robes."

"That's true?" I asked incredulously.

"True as true. I would not joke on so serious a matter. And do you know how the Sicilians account for Britain's victory over the Nazis in the war? 'Twas due, they say, to Winston Churchill foiling Hitler's Evil Eye with his Victory sign."

It took me some time to recover from the insult to the Holy Father. When I did, I said, "I didn't like that bargaining over holy things."

"Father Neil," tut-tutted Fr Duddleswell, "what a puritan y'are."

I accepted the rebuke as meekly as a Christian should.

"Father Neil, if only you had troubled to add up all the 'charges,' you would realize they come to £10 exactly, which is the standard fee for all weddings of this sort."

"But the indignity of it."

"Indignity, my eye!" he said, still doubtless the worse for

drink. "'Twas to save the old man's dignity I dealt with him in the way I did, the traditional Sicilian way, you follow? He needed to assure the Christinis that he paid a notable price for the wedding and his own family that he struck a good bargain. I saved his lovely old Sicilian face on both scores."

"And the gold cope?" I spoke more diffidently this time.

"I wear it at all weddings without exception."

"Do *they* know that?"

"Of course they know it. They are not fools."

"I'm not sure anyway that I approve of arranged weddings, Father. It might be all right for Asians and Sicilians on their medieval island, but here, in the middle of the twentieth century..." I broke off in a chianti-induced scorn.

"I will talk to you about that later," he sighed, as if I'd never learn. "For the present, let us conclude the pact with the Christinis, shall we?"

The Christinis lived in a semi-detached house on Eastside.

"We was expecting you intensely," said the petite Signora Christini at the door.

Here we go again, I thought.

Signor Christini, though in his sixties, had a full head of black hair and an enormous brush for a moustache. He looked like a benign bandit. After seeing me, he promoted Fr Duddleswell to Monsignore as a mark of distinction.

The Signore had only two sons present—Mario, the groom, was kept out of sight—one was Enrico, the other Umberto.

Once more, a litre of marsala was produced, and I regretted I had drunk so much on our first port of call.

Fr Duddleswell extolled the beauty and innocence of Gelsomina in the kind of terms usually reserved for the Blessed Virgin in her litany.

"Gelsomina is as *pura* as a pine tree," he almost sang, "*innocente* like the spring, and the eyes...the eyes are the eyes of Dante's Beatrice."

"And she walks with *dignità*?" inquired the eldest son, Enrico.

"She walkas," responded Fr Duddleswell, with a touch of sibilance, "soft-foot like the stars in the skies of night."

"She no walka under them stars with other men, Monsignore?"

"*Fedele sempre*, always faithful she 'as been and willa be," said Fr Duddleswell, becoming more and more ample in tone and gestures, "*fedele* to Mario, 'er 'usband."

"*Va be'*," said Signor Christini, much relieved. "*Scrive*, padre, '*sempre fedele*.'"

Fr Duddleswell wrote this in Enrico's big ledger, and it reminded him to take out his diary and read: "Gelsomina is not pregnanted in the slightest."

Signor Christini was fully satisfied, especially when Fr Duddleswell said: "He paid plen'y much money."

In came Signora Christini with biscuits, sugared almonds and chianti, and, in time, we were allowed to see Mario, a nice, quiet, ordinary-looking lad a few years my junior.

To him, Fr Duddleswell was made to repeat his injunction, to equal acclaim, about not quarrelling.

When we left, Enrico promised to be at the rectory at eight o'clock. For my part, I couldn't get home soon enough to rest my fiercely pumping head on a pillow.

That evening, Giorgio Bianchi and Enrico Christini arrived at the rectory together. Now almost recovered, I was awaiting them in Fr Duddleswell's study.

"Come in George, you too, Henry," he said.

I was pleased that this time the Sicilians shook my hand and didn't lick it all over.

Giorgio said: "It really was frightfully good of you, Fr Duddleswell, to help us out again as you did this morning. Splendid show."

Instead of being knocked sideways by the extraordinary change in Giorgio's accent, Fr Duddleswell answered calmly, "Not at all, George, pleased to be of help."

"I don't know how you manage it, Father," put in Enrico in the same cultured tones, "but be sure your efforts on our behalf are highly appreciated by the entire family."

Once again, Fr Duddleswell shook off the praises being showered on him. "I have made out two identical documents in Italian, if you would both sign and countersign them, I'm sure your fathers' minds will be put at rest."

After the signing, Fr Duddleswell added his own name, stamped the parish seal on the papers, shook hands with the young men—they each gave him £10—and walked them to the door. I remained behind scratching my head.

When Fr Duddleswell returned, I thought it about time I stood up to him. "So it was another game, was it?"

"Game. Not at all. Serious business."

"But what about that nonsense in their homes, all of them talking like Italian organ-grinders."

"Respect makes them adopt the language of their fathers. Remember, with Sicilians the family is the only country they recognize, and they are usually very loving families."

"The Bianchi boys didn't look too lovingly on Peppino."

"That," said Fr Duddleswell, "was because Peppino was getting careless. His bad English was not nearly as good as his brothers. They feared their father might become suspicious."

"And all that writing down of the bargains, that too..."

"That too was for their father's sake. You see, neither Signor Bianchi nor Signor Christini can read or write. They are both what Italians call '*analfabeti*.'"

"Why, then, was everything written down?"

"Ah, well, Father Neil, the Sicilians do not trust the spoken word, not even that of a priest. Words pass without trace, you follow? Like the wind. Only when they are written down do they have faces; the fathers can see them, even if they cannot read them."

"And all that sickly stuff about Gelsomina's beauty."

"I thank God she is not a deaf-mute," he said. "At least she has the qualities of the best Italian *campagna*, warm, soft, and fertile."

"And her virtue?" I droned on.

"That was genuine enough, Father Neil, believe you me. If Gelsomina were found to have gone with another man, the Christini boys would have to attempt to murder her."

114

"Murder her?" I cried. "How horrible!"

"Father Neil, I did not say they *would* murder her, only *attempt* to murder her, which is the exact opposite. Sicilians attempt murder as often as Englishmen attempt suicide. It is of the essence that they fail."

I put my hands over my eyes and pressed hard.

"I've drunk too much red wine," I said, meaning it as a criticism of my mentor. He did not appear to notice any rebuke.

"You see, Father Neil," he continued unperturbed, "the Sicilians are true *mafiosi*, like."

"You can say that again," I said, opening my eyes.

"You evidently do not understand that term as the Sicilians do. For them, *mafiosità* is equivalent to being a real Christian, you follow? They have another equivalent term, *omertà*, manliness. I once came across a young Sicilian chappie who slit the throat of his young wife from ear to ear because he suspected her of infidelity. *Omertà* demanded it of him. If he had not done it, his wife would have lost all respect for him, even though *she* knew she was guiltless. Well, now, the police, who fail to understand such things, called me in as interpreter, and do you know what the young man said? No? He said, 'I did not meana to kill 'er, only to mortally wound 'er for a few seasons.' Which is what he did. The young lady survived and they are very happy together as far as I am aware. Honour was preserved all round."

My suspicions were roused so much by now, I asked, "And *was this* an arranged marriage?"

"In a sense 'twas, Father Neil, and in a sense..."

"'*Twasn't.*"

He was reluctant to continue till I spurred him on.

"Well, Father Neil, even the sons are not cognizant of this. But Mario and Gelsomina have been going out together for the past eighteen months."

"You don't say!"

"Tuesdays and Thursdays, when all the menfolk go greyhound racing, Gelsomina's mamma was supposed to take *her* to a dancing class and Mario's mamma should have accompanied *him* to singing lessons so he could learn to sing like Caruso."

"That was no good?"

"Terrible. I tried Mario in the choir. Sings like a frog."

"No, Father, I mean the women didn't do what their husbands expected them to do?"

"What an original idea, Father Neil. No Sicilian does what he is expected to do, otherwise they'd never be able to trust each other. No, the mothers made a twosome at bingo, and Mario took his Gelsomina to the Picture Palace."

Again, I covered my eyes with my hands, feeling I was aging far too quickly. Then I stood up shakily to take my leave.

"It seems to me," I said, "we have been engaging, you and I, in a piece of gross deceit."

Fr Duddleswell firmly but kindly raised his hand and, with a sigh, laid it on my shoulder. "Remember this, Father Neil, the whole of life is a farce and a deceit." Before I could interrupt, he said, "How else could we be content, now? The women deceive the men..."

"And," I contributed, "the men deceive the women."

"They lika to thinka so," said Fr Duddleswell, with an impish smile. "Mosta times, they are happy enough to deceiva themselves."

8

CRUMBS

When I tried to explain to Mrs Rollings the sublime Catholic teaching on the Eucharist, she showed scant interest.

"The bread becomes the body of Christ," I said.

"Can you tell me somethin', Father?"

"I'll try."

"At Mass, why do you make a circle with your index fingers and thumbs?"

"After the consecration," I explained, "the bread is not bread any more but every particle of it is the body of Christ. That's why we have to handle it with the utmost reverence and make sure no fragment falls on the ground." I spoke quietly in order to convey the Catholic's awe at the Eucharist.

"Now I know," she put in, revelling in the flawless logic of Catholic practice, "why you always sweep up all the crumbs afterwards and swallow them."

When my ordeal was nearly over and she was going out the front door, Mrs Rollings turned to me. "One last question, Father."

"Yes?" It was to be agony to the end.

"You know all that sweeping up of the crumbs. D'you think Jesus did that at the Last Supper?"

"Shall we talk about that next week, Mrs Rollings?"

"What a good idea," she said. "You don't mind me asking questions, do you?"

I assured her that I found all her queries very stimulating. "It makes one examine the roots of one's own beliefs," I said.

The following morning, soon after seven, the phone rang. Fr Duddleswell was in church making his meditation before Mass, so Mrs Pring yelled out to me to take the call.

"A priest on the line."

I interrupted my ablutions and picked up the receiver in my study. "Fr Boyd, Fr Duddleswell's assistant. Can I help you, Father?"

"Hugo, O.P."

"O.P.?" I asked, not yet fully awake.

"Order of Preachers. A Dominican. It's like this. I'm leading a pilgrimage from Tonwell, south of the river, to the shrine of Our Lady of Walsingham. What I want to know is, can we celebrate Mass at your place?"

"Of course, Father."

"There're only a dozen of us. My party's made up of university students who, for reasons beyond me, are keen on carrying a big wooden cross on their pilgrimage."

"What time will you be here, Father?"

"About eleven, but it might be later."

"I'll be expecting you, Father."

Since it was Fr Duddleswell's day off, I caught him as soon as his Mass was over and told him about the call. He wasn't pleased.

"Dominicans," he snorted, removing his alb with a scowl. "Unsound to a man—apart from St Dominic himself who popularized the rosary and Thomas Aquinas. They are grubby. They often do not wear their habit or the clerical collar. Some of 'em do not even say their beads any more."

"Well, Father," I said, struggling to put the alb over my head, "it's nice to know that one of them, this Father Hugo, is going on a pilgrimage to Walsingham."

"In atonement, I should not wonder. Anyway, Father Neil," he said brightening up, "I will be off in half an hour, and Mrs Pring's about to visit her daughter in Siddenhall this afternoon. So keep an eye on things while I am away. And a sharp lookout for that Dominican. Don't want any of his hanky-panky in St Jude's."

Now fully vested, I promised to protect the premises. As he rang the bell to warn the congregation that Mass was about to begin, he whispered loudly: "I am picking up Mrs Pring at her daughter's place tonight. Back sometime before curfew."

My duty that day was to stay in the rectory, answer the phone and the door bell. I was also "on call" in case any parishioner was taken seriously ill and needed the last rites.

The morning passed off uneventfully. Around eleven o'clock I was expecting the arrival of Father Hugo and his students, but they didn't turn up.

Mrs Pring served me lunch before setting off for Siddenhall by bus, and I retired to my room to read *The Life Of Christ* by Riccioti.

At tea time, still no sign of the pilgrims. But at five, the door bell rang. Standing there fronting a dishevelled group of young men was a Dominican.

"Hugo, O.P."

I just had time to glimpse his white stained habit with rolled-up sleeves, his rosary dangling from a leather belt and his big brown boots. On his back was a large grey knapsack.

He pushed past me uninvited. "Sorry," he said over his broad shoulder, "we're a bit late."

"I expected you before midday, Father."

"Got held up. A couple of the lads had trouble with blisters." He removed his knapsack and turned round to face me. He had ruddy cheeks and, though not yet middle-aged, a shock of steely grey hair. "Aren't you going to invite them in? They're Catholics."

"Of course," I said. "Please come in."

About ten university students, mostly bearded, trooped in, leaving a large wooden cross leaning against the lintel of the door.

"You don't *still* want to say Mass, do you, Father?"

"Why not?"

"It's five o'clock." My protest didn't seem to register. I said, "We're not allowed to say Mass in the evening unless..."

Father Hugo raised his right hand and made a dusting movement to silence me. "We'd like to start without delay if it's all the same to you. We've a long way to travel before nightfall."

"The church..." I stammered. "I'll come with you and show you where the vestments are and the chalice and..."

"No need for all that palaver, Father. Haven't you a room here where we can celebrate together in a family way?"

He was opening the door of Fr Duddleswell's study. I raced to stop him. "You can't go in there. That's the parish priest's..."

Already Father Hugo was trying the door of the parlour. He threw it open. "Just the job."

He looked approvingly at the large, polished mahogany table planted centrally on a threadbare Wilton carpet.

The students followed him like a bearded tide and proceeded to move the chairs from the sides of the room towards the table.

If only Mrs Pring were here! "Father Hugo," I objected, "you can't possibly..."

He obviously could. "Like the Last Supper, don't you think?"

Breathing heavily, I decided to make the best of a bad job. "I'll go into the church and get you vestments and an altar stone. Fr Duddleswell keeps one in the sacristy."

"We've got everything we need, thank you, Father."

Father Hugo was drawing an old tin mug out of his knapsack. Could *that* be his chalice? One of the students pulled a small brown loaf from a paper bag. Could *that* be the altar bread?

"What about vestments, Father?" I whimpered.

My last hazy impression of the parlour was of the Dominican seated squarely at the head of the table surrounded by a group of medieval peasants.

I almost crawled upstairs to my room. How could I explain *this* to Fr Duddleswell? Below, a guitar struck up and I

120

heard the strains of a popular folk song. What a din for only a dozen people! I hoped the neighbours wouldn't complain. I contemplated phoning the Vicar General and asking his advice, but I feared he might insist I put a stop to it. For all my size I didn't feel equal to that.

After forty-five minutes of music punctuated by long silences, there was a clatter of chairs and footsteps. The celebration was at an end. I rose from prayer and raced down the stairs in time to see the students leaving. They were picking up their belongings and four of them were struggling with the cross.

Father Hugo stretched out a large, firm hand with "Thanks for your hospitality, Father," and I shook it without enthusiasm. "We'll pray for you at Walsingham."

"Thank you," I said, "thank you very much."

But he was already on his way, his knapsack bumping up and down on his back like a grey-clad child. I'll need all the prayers I can get, I thought.

I closed the door and went with trepidation into the parlour. The students had left the room as they found it. Except that all over the mahogany table were strewn the remains of their sacred repast. The bright evening sun, shining through the garden window, turned the polished surface into a huge golden paten and everywhere, particularly where Father Hugo had been sitting, were little piles of crumbs from the Hovis loaf.

I had never been in such a panic. The body of my Lord and God was scattered all over the table.

Heretic! No other word was ugly enough to describe my loathing of that Dominican who had left me to cope with this wretched situation. I closed my eyes and sank to the ground to implore God's guidance. He did not forsake me. I soon jumped up and went to the sacristy where I rounded up a couple of candles, a clean linen purificator, and an empty ciborium from the safe.

Back in the parlour, I lit the candles at each end of the table, put on a white stole and proceeded, with the purificator, to brush the sacred particles into the ciborium. It took me some while because, in the bright sunshine, every speck of dust became visible on the polished table-top, and it was difficult to distinguish it from the body of the Lord.

I had completed my task and stepped back to survey the table when it entered my head to look down at the carpet. Horror of horrors. Sacred particles everywhere. Already I must have ground Christ underfoot any number of times. I stood petrified from fear and devotion.

I couldn't, in all reverence, use Mrs Pring's old brush and pan with which she cleaned out the kitchen grate. Then I remembered that only a few days before, Mrs Pring had acquired a new vacuum cleaner, a Hoover. This would suck up all the sacred particles, and then I only needed to take out the paper bag and make a sacred bonfire of it in the garden. After that, no traces of the Dominican's infamy would remain.

I took off my shoes, walked gingerly out of the parlour, and returned with the Hoover. I plugged it in and, starting from the door, proceeded to vacuum the carpet. In ten minutes the task was complete. Even with the lamp from my bicycle, I couldn't find any more particles on the floor or the soles of my shoes.

Not being in the slightest bit mechanical, I had never examined a Hoover; but it occurred to me that I ought to turn it upside down. When I did, I received the sharpest shock of all. Why hadn't I realized there were *brushes* underneath? There, caught in the bristles, were countless holy crumbs. It would take me hours to remove them and even then I couldn't be sure of complete success.

Once more I sank down desolately on my knees. It was 6:30. Fr Duddleswell was bound to return by 10:30 because diocesan regulations said all priests had to be indoors by eleven, and he was always on the safe side. There seemed nothing I could do but keep lone vigil by the Hoover—a most unorthodox tabernacle—until he returned and sorted out the mess.

In my misery, I acknowledged I had brought this calamity upon myself. Fr Duddleswell had warned me forcefully enough about the hanky-panky Dominicans get up to. In conscience, he would be forced to write to the Vicar General, requesting him to remove me from St Jude's and suspend me from priestly office. The Vicar General would inform Bishop O'Reilly who would haul me over the coals for an unexampled act of folly: allowing the body of Christ to become inextricably enmeshed in the brushes of a Hoover. I could just see my old Professor of moral theology being summoned to propose "the more probable" moral solution to this improbable dilemma.

I began to wish I'd never been ordained.

Kneeling there in sunlight and candlelight, I suddenly saw red. Why should I be victimized for the blasphemous behavior of a brother priest? Why should my career be nipped in the bud for no fault of my own? Why should I have to endure ridicule for the rest of my priestly life for attempting to rectify a grievous wrong?

I made my decision. I'd wait until the sun had declined further, then bury the Hoover in the garden.

There was, I had noted, a tool shed in the garden containing a fork and a spade; there was also plenty of space beyond the far hedge for digging in. The hedge would protect me from prying eyes, especially when dusk fell.

In the meanwhile, I remained kneeling beside the Hoover which I both hated and revered. I kept promising God that I would pay back over the months the price of the Hoover—Mrs Pring said it cost £12 with all the attachments—by putting money in the Poor Box.

In the dining room, the clock struck 8:30. Time for me to remove my jacket and start digging.

In the garden, beyond the hedge, it was darker than I had expected. After several days of unblemished sunshine, a storm was brewing and dark clouds were scudding overhead. I planned to dig a trench two feet deep, two feet wide and just over four feet long to accommodate the Hoover; and time was short. As I perspired, mosquitoes came in waves to pester me, and the rain lashed down. It must have been about 9:45 before the hole was big enough. All the time I was praying that Fr Duddleswell wouldn't return before my task was done.

I went back indoors, put on my white stole of office, and

covered it with my jacket. I grabbed the Hoover in one hand and the ciborium in the other.

At the scene of operations, I used the purificator to sweep the particles from the ciborium into the hole before gently laying down the gleaming Hoover on its side. The waste of such a grand piece of equipment hurt me deeply, but what choice had I? I piled on the fresh earth until it looked like a newly dug grave. Now all that remained was to cover up my traces.

I put the tools back in the garden shed, and replaced the ciborium, the stole, and the candles in the sacristy. Then I ran upstairs to get out of my drenched clothes.

I was running the bath when I heard Fr Duddleswell's car drive up ten minutes ahead of schedule. I stepped into the tub with a sigh of relief.

A couple of minutes later, I heard a loud and now familiar tread on the stairs. Surely Fr Duddleswell wasn't going to bed so soon? Why wasn't he finishing his breviary in his study as he usually did? Why was he, yes, making straight for the bathroom door?

Was there some incriminating evidence I had overlooked? I started to splash and hum loudly "I'll Sing A Hymn To Mary" as nonchalantly as I could. I pitched it far too high and sounded falsetto.

There was a loud rap on the bathroom door, and Fr Duddleswell called out, "Is there something wrong, Father Neil?"

"No," I returned. "Why do you ask? I'm only having a bath."

My racing mind told me he couldn't possibly have seen "the grave" so soon, especially as it was raining and dark. Perhaps the neighbour, Mr Buzzle, had informed him there was a suspicious character digging at the end of his garden or Mrs Pring had noticed her Hoover was gone. Must be important for him to interrupt my bath.

"That is all right, then," said Fr Duddleswell. "'Tis only that Mrs Pring said you had not eaten the supper she left you. We were asking ourselves if you were unwell, like."

"Never felt better, Father," I lied brazenly. "I had an

enormous lunch, and I thought I'd leave myself with a snack before I turn in."

I heard Fr Duddleswell walk away mumbling to himself:

A tenor, all singers above
(This doesn't admit of a question)
Should keep himself quiet,
Attend to his diet
And carefully nurse his digestion.

I sighed so heavily with relief the water rose and fell in the bath. Then his footsteps approached again.

Hell, what now? I thought.

"By the way, Father Neil. Did that foreign priest turn up for Mass this morning?"

I thought swiftly and made a couple of "monumental" reservations.

"He came, Father, but he didn't celebrate Mass this morning, after all."

I was right not to call that evening charade a Mass.

"Highly delighted, so I am. You never can tell what antics those Dominicans are likely to get up to."

It wasn't until the next day that Mrs Pring reported that her Hoover was missing. Fr Duddleswell had just said, "Father Neil, I repent me of what I said yesterday. About the Dominicans. Must not judge the whole crew by one or two mutineers."

His U-turn on the question of clemency failed to impress me.

Then in came Mrs Pring. "Strange," she said, as she was plying us with coffee and toast. "I've searched even the mice holes for my new Hoover and not a sign of it. I do believe someone's pinched it."

"Poppycock," said Fr Duddleswell, "how could anyone have pinched it?"

"The latch wasn't on the side-door yesterday. P'raps a beggar looked through my kitchen window..."

"The latch *should* have been on, Mrs Pring. 'Tis your business to *see* that 'tis on." Turning to me: "You did not notice, I suppose, any shady-looking characters hanging around the house yesterday."

"No one," I replied, sad that Mrs Pring was being blamed for my misdeeds. "It can't have walked far."

She said, "There's thieves around here as could steal the milk out of your tea."

Fr Duddleswell had a more amusing hypothesis. "I should not be at all surprised, Father Neil, if that Dominican had something to do with it."

"Very likely," I said.

Later that morning, while Fr Duddleswell was out on his rounds, Mrs Pring told me, "That Dominican is on the line again." My big chance. I thought, I'm really going to give him hell.

Before I could unburden myself of bile, Father Hugo apologized for having to leave in one unholy rush to keep up with his schedule. He had meant to say he was sorry for leaving the parlour in such a frightful mess.

"I should think so," I said, gathering myself for a prodigious outburst.

"The lads hadn't eaten for hours and they insisted on finishing their sandwiches before they started up again."

"Sandwiches," I gasped. "Is that all?"

"Yes," he said, "but what else could there be?"

I didn't elaborate. Instead, I put the phone down in a daze.

9

IN THE SWIM

"'Tis complaint-time, Father Neil."

Fr Duddleswell had invited me to his study and settled me in comfortably before giving me this information.

"Complaint-time, Father?"

"Indeed. You have been some time with us at St Jude's now. And have you any complaints?"

"About you, Father?"

"Well, I was thinking more...Complaints about anything. Meself included, I suppose."

I was brief and to the point. "No, Father."

"That is *nice* of you," he said smiling, as if he was surprised at me giving him a clean bill of health. "Of course, if at any time in the future you find anything even slightly complainable in me behaviour you will be sure to..."

"Tell you."

"I would be gratified. How about Mrs Pring, like?"

"She hasn't complained about you either, Father."

"Then she must have worn her tongue threadbare an' all. No, Father Neil, I was meaning, have you noticed anything strange about *her*?"

I reflected for a moment to show I was trying. "Not really."

"Come, come, Father Neil, have you been blindfolding your ears altogether? You must have remarked her speech-defect."

I had to confess I hadn't.

"Surely?" he said, with a twinkle that characterized him when he spoke of Mrs Pring. "She cannot stop. She has a tongue on her the size of Southend Pier. Many a time have I beseeched her to take up the bagpipes so I can get a few inches of peace and quiet around here."

"She works very hard, Father," I said weakly in Mrs Pring's defence.

"She has a strong snout on her for digging, I grant, but after twenty years of her I realize that however hard you scrub a crow 'twill never turn into a dove."

I could hardly say I had realized that before I even thought of it.

"Well," he went on, "I cannot tempt you or twist your arm into a complaint? No? A pity since..."

I anticipated him. Biting my nail, I asked, "You have a complaint against *me*?"

"Do not bite your thumbnail, lad," he said hurriedly, "you may need it for the boiled potatoes, as me father used to say. No, 'tis not so much a complaint against you as against your preaching. D'you know the words of the famous song about Fr O'Flynn,

> Powerfullest preacher, and
> Tinderest teacher, and
> Kindliest creature in ould Donegal.

"No, Father."

"I have just told them you. Now what is wrong with your preaching."

I hazarded a guess. "Everything?"

"You *could* put it like that," he said, bowing once or twice. "Why, tell me, do you *read* your sermon?"

I explained the obvious: nerves, inexperience, fear of forgetting what I want to say.

"The trouble is, Father Neil, when the good people see you reading in the pulpit, they think 'tis a pastoral letter from

Bishop O'Reilly and promptly fall into a dead faint in the pews."

I agreed that my sermons did seem to have that sort of effect.

"Another thing," he said, laying it on with a trowel, "you mumble." Involuntarily, I gave him a demonstration of my talent then and there. "You should open your mouth." He showed me—and it was like the opening of a farmyard gate. "Wide, Father Neil, so the congregation can see the darns on the inside of your socks."

I started chewing imaginary gum to show willingness.

"And, remember, Father Neil, should they snore you in the face, give 'em hell. Like the old Irish preacher, 'The lions will roar at yez, the serpents will hiss at yez, the owls will hoot at yez, and the hyenas will laugh you to scorn.' 'Tis such a wonderful consoling doctrine," he murmured, "'twould awaken the dead from the long sleep. Finally,"—I had been thinking that, like hell, this would never end—"why do you preach so short?"

I explained, reasonably it seemed to me, that I stopped when I had nothing more to say.

He was a mixture of the amused and amazed. "You do not need to have something to say to go on preaching, Father Neil. That is the art of it, surely. Besides, if you run out of words, take a dictionary with you into the pulpit."

"Is three minutes too short, Father?" In the seminary, we were told *that* was the attention-span of most congregations today.

"Not only too short," he said, despising modern theorizing, "'tis terribly dangerous. The good people who come in late, which is the most of them, will miss Mass altogether. And worse, they will miss the collection."

The prospect of losing two or three pounds sterling every time I preached the words of God had staggered him.

He asked me what I intended preaching about next Sunday. I told him.

"Jesus walking on the water? Beautiful theme. Make it plain to the doubters below you, mind, that He was not using water skis, a surf board or a raft. Nor was He treading water or merely walking in the shallows." He paused to offer an apology. "But you would have said that anyway, I am thinking."

"I'm not sure, Father."

"'Twas a great miracle to prove our Blessed Lord was God and gravitation had no pull over him, you follow? The rest of us mortals have to swim like St Peter. When *he* tried to walk on water, did he not sink like a rock?" He laughed at that. "Our Lord's own pun, you recognize? 'Peter,' 'Rock.'" I nodded. "Why did he not swim, now?"

"Jesus? Perhaps he couldn't."

"Do not speak heresy in me presence, Father Neil, even in fun. In any case, I was referring to St Peter. Even I have been known to do the hundred yards when pressed."

"Thank you very much for all your help," I said, straightfaced.

"Think nothing of it, Father Neil. I like to give encouragement when I can. Oh, and by the way, we have Councillor Albert Appleby coming to tay this afternoon."

Mrs Pring had already told me that Mr Appleby, a Catholic, was the Mayor-designate of the Borough of Kenworthy.

"Great honour for the parish," I said.

"Indeed, 'tis so. I have only one or two little bumps to iron out with him."

I volunteered to absent myself from tea if he preferred to talk to the Councillor privately.

"Not at all, Father Neil," he said. "You will have to deal with Mayors yourself some day, so you might as well have a lesson in the best way to go about it."

At a quarter to four the next afternoon, the front door bell rang. Mrs Pring answered it, and I heard her knocking on Fr Duddleswell's study.

"Mr Appleby's arrived, Father."

"'Ello, Farver."

I was struck immediately by the cockney voice.

"Hello, Bert. Welcome and heartiest congratulations."

The words of the two men tailed off as they went into a huddle before tea.

When Mrs Pring rang the bell, I was already stationed in the dining-room, waiting. For about five minutes, I heard muffled voices coming from the study before Fr Duddleswell led in the Mayor-elect, grey-suited, medium height, with white crew-cut hair. He looked about fifty-five.

"This is my assistant Father Neil. Mr Albert Appleby."

We shook hands. The Mayor-elect had a firm grip.

When we were seated before a bright assortment of bread and jam and iced cream cakes, Fr Duddleswell began to pour.

"I will do the honours. Father Neil takes milk first, Bert, how about you?"

"As it comes, Farver."

It seemed to me that beneath the tranquil exterior, there was an unmistakable tension building up. After an exchange of compliments and some good-natured surprise at what Mr Appleby referred to as "all those mounds of edibles," the serious stuff began.

"You have done us proud, you know that, Bert, getting yourself elected Mayor."

"Quite undeserved, I can assure you."

"Not at all, not at all, I tell you. You have worked hard for years and earned it."

The Mayor-elect bit into a slice of bread and jam so as not to have to reply.

"All the more glory for St Jude's, Bert, because everyone knows your family's such staunch Catholics. *Roman* Catholics first and foremost."

That was the first shot in a fierce campaign. After a few more pleasantries, Fr Duddleswell asked, "And what might your duties consist of, Bert?"

"Opening garden-fêtes, bazaars, dances, schools, et cetera. A regular bottle-opener, you might say."

I smiled appreciatively at the modest witticism, but Fr Duddleswell swiftly rejoined, "And nothing else, Bert?"

"Well... attending the odd religious service."

"Yes, Bert, tell me more."

"Only in an honorary capacity, of course."

"Ah, Bert," sighed Fr Duddleswell. "Even Anglican services?"

"The Church of England *is* the established Church, Farver."

"So they tell me. Established by Good Queen Bess nearly four centuries ago."

"Oh?"

"Yes, excommunicated by the Pope for so doing. But do go on, Bert."

"The inaugural ceremony is always 'eld..."

"Not in St Luke's Anglican church?"

"You know it always is, Farver."

"But, Bert, we have never had a *Catholic* Mayor before. We have no precedent for it, have we, now? Why in an Anglican church with an Anglican minister presiding and prayers being said in *English* so God Himself cannot follow a word?"

"I've already said 'cause the Anglican Church is by law established."

"I thought you, Bert, as a Roman, an *Appleby*, might have given precedence to the law of Almighty God."

To avoid taking sides, having consumed four slices of bread and jam, I turned my attention to the cream cakes.

Bert Appleby, who wasn't a war veteran for nothing, was about to group his forces for a counter-attack.

"Did I or did I not read in *The Catholic Herald* that under canon law mayors and bridesmaids *can* attend non-Catholic ceremonies...?"

"Under certain circumstances," said Fr Duddleswell grudgingly.

"Could one such circumstance be that the Mayor is actin' in 'is official capacity?"

"Other conditions, too."

"Such as," continued Mr Appleby, who had clearly done his homework, "that 'e don't give interior assent to what's going on? I know as well as the next man it's wrong to say so much as the Our Father with nonbelievers." Getting no further response, he said, "In fact, I'll be a-fingerin' my rosary in my pocket."

"Praying for the conversion of the Vicar."

"That, too," Mr Appleby answered, wisely riding high on the wave of sarcasm.

"You see, Bert," urged Fr Duddleswell, "Anglicans are outside the one, true Fold and so in peril. Good people, I know that. God loves 'em for sure. But they are too much like us, you follow? Do not they have Holy Communion even, so it looks no different from the true body of Christ?"

"But," argued Mr Appleby, "they receive their Eucharist with bread *and* wine like at the Last Supper. They don't fool no one."

"*You* may not be deceived by all this, Bert, but think of the simple faithful. Do you want them to stray from the straight and narrow because of you?"

The last argument obviously proved decisive. After a moment's thought, Mr Appleby, disconsolate, said: "I'll 'ave to make the sacrifice, won't I?"

"All Catholics have to make sacrifices, Bert," said Fr Duddleswell, softening, "especially professional people, the likes of you and me. After all, Catholic chemists and barbers are not allowed to sell contraceptives, and that cannot be good for business, can it?"

"I'll 'ave to resign then since I don't want the rest of the Councillors ridiculing me."

Fr Duddleswell only appeared to have heard the second half of Mr Appleby's remark and, to counter it, launched his final offensive.

"Was not Jesus Christ Himself ridiculed and crucified because He was a Catholic? You cannot imagine *Him* attending an Anglican Church, now."

Then he paused, as if the reference to resignation had only just sunk in. "Who said anything about *resigning*? You have not even taken office yet."

"I know, Farver, but I can't take an oath to serve the Borough if I can't fulfil my duties, can I?"

"But..." began Fr Duddleswell.

"It's no good, Farver. I told you, even the inaugural service is in St Luke's. I'll just 'ave to inform the Council it's not possible to 'ave a Catholic Mayor in this Borough. Councillor Biggins will gloat, o' course. 'E always says Catholics 'as to do what their priest says."

Apart from the chink of crockery and my munching and gulping, there was no sound for fully two minutes.

"Bert," said Fr Duddleswell appealingly, as if confessing he'd overplayed his hand.

"Yes, Farver?"

"I *could* give you a dispensation."

"Thank you kindly, Farver. But Catholic Mayors, too, 'ave to make sacrifices."

"By not becoming Mayors?"

"I don't want to scandalize the faithful any more'n you do, Farver."

"I could do my best to explain it to the good people at Mass. After all, the Earl Marshal of England is a Catholic and he is in charge of the Coronation Service in Westminster Abbey when the King is crowned Head of the Anglican Church."

"Ah," said Mr Appleby, shaking his head, "I can't pin my conscience on another man's back."

The silence was painful until Albert Appleby, who, I felt, wasn't mentioned twice in despatches for nothing, raised his eyes from his empty cup to say: "*You* can't be married; *I* can't be Mayor."

"Bert," said Fr Duddleswell, acknowledging defeat, "cannot we work out a compromise?"

"A drop more tea, please?" asked his victor, pleasantly holding out his cup. "A compromise? Not with my faith, surely?"

"No."

"Nor with my conscience?"

"No."

"Well," went on Mr Appleby, "—a nice cup of tea, this—I

dare say I *could* prevail on the Council to 'old the inaugural service in St Jude's…" Fr Duddleswell began to smile with relief. "But at a small cost, mind."

"Yes," said Fr Duddleswell keenly, "how much?"

"Not in money, you understand."

"So?"

"I'd 'ave to persuade the Councillors, especially Mr Biggins that you 'aven't got me in your cassock pocket."

"And how do you propose to do that?"

Mr Appleby put down his cup before replying. "By getting you to take part in the swimming gala."

"I could hand out the prizes, you mean?" asked Fr Duddleswell apprehensively.

"That's *my* job."

"Not by swimming in the Clergy Race against the Anglicans and Methodists?" The very prospect pained him.

"Not the Methodists," said Mr Appleby. "They've pulled out because one of their ministers was recently attacked by the Word of God."

Fr Duddleswell asked what he meant.

"He dropped the Bible on his toe, Farver, and broke it. So without you, no race."

"Impossible!" cried Fr Duddleswell. "I would sink faster than the Rock of Ages. D'you want me to get my death?"

"You can't swim, Farver?"

"He *can*, Mr Appleby," I said, "he told me so this morning."

Fr Duddleswell pointed accusingly at the food on the table. "Jesus Himself would sink in the waters if He had to eat *that*. No, I am not able for it. I am out of shape. I have got too much shape, if y'like."

"He's being modest as usual, Mr Mayor," I said.

Fr Duddleswell looked at me blackly. "Thank you, Father Neil," he said most ungratefully.

"It's nothing, Father. I like to give encouragement when I can."

Mr Appleby asked me if I could swim and I told him it was

my only accomplishment. "Good," he exclaimed, and proceeded to tell me that the Clergy Race was a medley with three ministers to a team.

"There we are," put in Fr Duddleswell. "I only have one assistant."

"I've a friend at the Cathedral," I volunteered. "He swam for Reading before he went to the seminary. Fr Tom Fleming."

"Bert," sighed Fr Duddleswell, "I may be a bit old-fashioned..."

"Yes, you may be, Father," I said in his support.

"But," he continued, "you cannot expect me to expose me..."

"Your what?" asked Mr Appleby quickly.

"Me soul and belly. Me cloven hoof." More irritably, "Me nipples and things."

"What things?" asked Mr Appleby, expecting an answer.

"Don't you know, Bert, I bulge in all the wrong places. Well, *almost* all the wrong places. Besides, d'you want me to put sinful thoughts in damsel's heads?"

"I'm sure Mrs Pring won't even notice," Mr Appleby said soothingly. "There, there, Farver. Only a couple of lengths from you, and St Jude's will 'ave its first Catholic Mayor." He smiled broadly. "One of them small sacrifices us professional Catholics 'ave to make from time to time."

Later that evening, I was drinking a cup of cocoa in Mrs Pring's kitchen. She was horrified to hear that Fr Duddleswell had agreed to swim in the Gala. She remarked, "If you ask me, His Reverence will have a heart attack."

The subject of her solicitude bellowed from the other end of the corridor, "I'd be much obliged if you would be keeping to yourself your untutored opinion on me state of health."

"And who'll lay you out if you cop it, tell me that?" Mrs Pring yelled in return.

"You should humour him, Mrs Pring," I whispered.

"Let his back go on itching, I say."

Another outburst: "Father Neil, will you leave that

unfortunate ear-chewing woman forthwith and come to me study, if you please."

Mrs Pring said half-aloud to me, "He was made on a conveyor belt, and he thinks he was hand-carved. Ah, if only I could buy him for what he's worth and sell him for what he thinks he's worth I'd make a fortune."

"Father *Neil*!"

"Trot along little doggie," said Mrs Pring kindly.

In his study, Fr Duddleswell was at leisure to tell me more about the forthcoming race.

Each member of the team had to swim two lengths, the first swimmer free-style, the second backstroke and the third breaststroke. The senior curate of St Luke's—a late vocation, now nearing fifty—was a stylist and a force to be reckoned with in spite of his years. As an undergraduate he had swum for Oxford. The new second curate was listed to swim the backstroke. He was such a fat fellow and he smoked so much, Fr Duddleswell reckoned he would float better than he would swim. The Vicar, Percival Probble, D.D., rather fancied himself at the breaststroke.

"Now, Father Neil, I am morally obliged to take on Probble. Besides, which 'tis the only stroke I can manage. What will you opt for yourself?"

"Backstroke, I think, Father. Tom Fleming will gladly swim the first leg. He's a whizz at the crawl."

"My problem is how to get in trim in time for the race."

He had made enquiries and discovered that Bollington Hall, the local swimming baths in Trickle Way, could be hired to private persons out of hours for a modest fee. "Ten shillings per hour, in fact," he said. "The mere price of a good Mass stipend."

"What time might 'out of hours' be, Father?" I inquired, relishing the idea of a late-night swim.

"Six to seven in the morning. It means getting up a little earlier than usual, Father Neil, so as to be back by 7:30 for the first Mass. But, remember, the morning hour has gold in its mouth."

Seeing a shadow of reluctance flit across my face, he said, "You do want to accompany me, I suppose?"

"Certainly, Father," I responded hastily.

"Must practice so the Protestants do not get the better of us."

"I agree," I said.

Bollington Hall was an old grey brick, glass-topped building which the school children frequented after classes and at weekends.

Inside, the baths, with narrow paved sides, ghostly light, and twenty-five by ten yards of still, glassy water smelling strongly of chlorine, echoed with our early morning footsteps.

Mrs Hetty Gale, the cleaner, showed us to our specially appointed changing rooms. After getting into my tartan trunks, I stood shivering on the brink awaiting the advent of Fr Duddleswell. I wanted to allow him the privilege of first dip.

After fully five minutes, Fr Duddleswell emerged in a huge white woolly bath robe, his head squeezed into a silver bathing hat. Hetty Gale, leaning on her mop, a cigarette dripping from the corner of her left upper lip, looked on in disbelief.

Making his way to the shallow end of the pool, Fr Duddleswell dipped a big white toe into the water and snorted at the cold belligerence of it before dropping his robe in a single lordly gesture.

Mrs Gale's mouth was agape, the cigarette dripping from her upper lip. "O my gawd," she said, "'e's changed into a bleedin' seal!"

From the side, I saw him clad in a one-piece glossy black costume of Victorian dimensions. He resembled a friendly ageing seal. There was a silver crucifix about his neck and what I took to be a miraculous medal pinned to his chest.

The whole pool recoiled as he jumped in. He swam laboriously with much imbibing and swooshing out of water; but he *could* swim. I dived in dutifully to keep him company, and it wasn't many seconds before I was pleased I'd come. The early reveille to defend the honour of Holy Mother Church had its compensations, after all.

It wasn't until the following Monday morning when I saw Fr Duddleswell was feeling chirpy about his progress that I dared to broach the subject of his bathing costume. We were walking home in the bright morning sunshine when I said, "Have you had your costume long, Father?"

"Yes."

"Are you thinking of getting a new one?"

"They do not make 'em like this any more."

I was well aware of the reason for their rarity. I said, "Why not buy one of the...new sort?"

"Why *should* I make concessions to the permissive society?"

I waited before replying. "It's actually easier in bathing trunks. More freedom of movement for the shoulders."

"Father Neil, to be frank, I feel 'tis improper for a priest to appear naked as a frog before the grinning populace." Noticing my discomfiture, he added, "When he is no longer young, I mean."

"But Mr Probble, the Vicar. I presume..."

"I was talking about a *real* priest, you follow? Not about a doubtfully baptized layman of the so-called Church of England. Besides, where would you obtain a pair of bathing trunks sizeable enough to cover my rotundity?"

I seized the opportunity to ask, "What's your waist measurement?"

"Forty-four at the last count."

"They do stretch, I know, Father."

He looked hurt. "The same will happen to you, Father Neil, when you are my age."

"Oh, Father, I was referring to bathing trunks not to your..." I couldn't find the proper word and wasn't taking any risks.

My embarrassment brought out the gentleman in him. "Are there big *black* ones?"

"Big black *what*, Father?" Once bitten, twice shy.

"Big black bathing trunks. Not tartan or rainbow ones. Black ones or clerical grey."

I nodded. "I would not need to be fitted for 'em in a shipyard?"

I took out the tape-measure which I had borrowed from Mrs Pring. "I'll just check your size," I said. "You wouldn't care to remove your cassock?"

"No."

"Not for a few seconds?"

"I *will* not be defrocked, like, even for a few seconds." As I put my arms round him, he said, "This is rather like being swallowed by a benevolent octopus."

Mrs Pring was wrong in her assessment that the five-foot tape measure wouldn't "reach." Even so, I did not frighten him by revealing the result.

As I was leaving, he said, "To be perfectly honest with you, Father Neil, the old costume *was* beginning to feel a bit too tight under the arms of me legs."

That afternoon, at Fr Duddleswell's invitation, I joined him in his study. I had purchased a pair of pure wool, black bathing trunks in Piccadily and wanted to know what his reaction was.

Having told me to shut the door on myself he slowly raised his cassock to his hips. Above the shoes, socks, suspenders and broad white legs was the new costume.

"What d'you think?"

I accepted the challenge as best I could. "Breathtaking, Father." No other response was possible to such a sight.

"Do you not think I am sort of...um...underdressed."

"On the contrary, Father."

"*Over*dressed?"

"Just right," I assured him.

Fr Duddleswell pointed to his legs. "Me Betty Grables are a bit on the anemic side, wouldn't you say?"

"A trifle pale. Perhaps."

"Not surprising, Father Neil, seeing they have lived in the shadow since I was long-trousered at the age of twelve." Still looking down, he said, "But it is very obvious in this costume, is it not?"

"What?"

"Me rotundity, me misplaced halo."

I was firm with him. "Father, I couldn't disagree with you more if you made me."

"Nice of you," he said, "but in the last three days before this contest, I propose to live off nettles and dandelions, as a treat, like, *and* to take the edges off me circles."

I explained that since the "new" variety of bathing trunks had no shoulder straps I had chosen one with a belt. He appreciated the added safety device and only curdled a bit when I told him the price.

"Thirty bloody bob," he said, paying up with three crumpled ten shilling notes. "They used to be much cheaper."

"Inflation," I said, hastily adding, "the cost of living, I mean."

"And there used to be five times the material in 'em. Oh for the good old days, Father Neil."

Mrs Pring happened to barge in. Fr Duddleswell immediately dropped his cassock. I couldn't be sure whether she had seen his lily-white legs or not.

"Trying on a new set of vestments for low Mass, Fr D?"

"Hold your tongue, woman," he said reddening, "and even a wise man will not know you are a fool."

"What every well-dressed clergyman is wearing this season," she said sarcastically. She turned to me. "Oh well, at least you've saved him from one piece of ignom'y. Him appearing in the local paper in his old suit along with pictures of bathing belles."

"Sorry?"

"The Clergy Race," she explained, "comes straight after the Beauty Contest." *That* was why he had parted with his thirty bob. "If his Reverence strays into the Beauty Contest," went on Mrs Pring, "he could come in First, Second and Third."

"Mrs Pring," he said darkly, "would you mind going fast ahead of your heels before I take me best right arm to you out of the mothballs."

"Okay, Fr D, I only came to ask about the sherry party after the inaugurals."

"Two bottles of sweet and four of dry," he said.

"I didn't expect a floor show in 3-D."

He raised his hand, whether to Mrs Pring or the deity I could not tell. "Go, before I send hornets upon you."

"Don't," she warned. "You know it's against the law for nudes to move on stage."

The inaugural ceremony was held at six o'clock on the Saturday evening. Mr Appleby looked neat and distinguished as he walked behind the mace-bearer, wearing his nineteenth-century gilded chain of office.

All the local dignitaries attended. There was the acid-tongued, anti-Catholic Mr Biggins with the rest of the Councillors; the local clergy—with wives—including all three Anglicans, the Congregationalist, and the bearded Methodist minister.

Looking from afar through the spy-hole in the sacristy, Fr Duddleswell whispered to me above the choir an impertinent greeting for each of them in turn as they processed up the center aisle. For all his gentle mockery, Fr Duddleswell was proud St Jude's was hosting that distinguished company.

The prayers Fr Duddleswell had chosen were mostly of a nondenominational sort so as not to cause offence. But not being one to compromise his (or the Mayor's) most cherished convictions, he followed the prayer for the good estate of his Sovereign Majesty with a ponderous prayer for his Holiness, Pope Pius XII.

The service ended with Fr Duddleswell walking down the sanctuary steps to where the new Mayor was kneeling at a special purple prie-dieu usually reserved for the Bishop. There he made an almighty sign of the cross over him in benediction as if to say, "Both of us know who's boss."

After the service, a sherry party was held in the presbytery parlour.

Dr Daley immediately grabbed my arm. He held up his thin glass filled with "that doleful liquid" and said, "There is not as much here as would relieve the faintness of a cat. There is nothing stronger, I suppose."

"Sorry, Doctor," I said, "only the landlord's language."

142

"It's a poor house, Father, that will not hold another still. D'you drink yourself?" When I said very little, he smacked his lips. "A wise lad. Better to lay your head where you will find it in the morning. Ah, but me darlin' sin is the drink, all right." He showed me, if not the darns in his socks, at least his tonsils. "I have this wicked wide throat on me." He put his head on my shoulder. "I took a urine test of myself only the other week."

"Oh, yes," I said, as if it were a piece of information I received regularly from all my friends.

"Forty proof," he said proudly.

I asked him, half-seriously, if he ever asked God to help him give it up.

"The drink? I only have the courage to pray for sobriety, d'you know, when I'm drunk."

"Then I'll pray for you, Doctor."

"No, no, *no*, Father. If you were successful, would I not have to ditch the drink?"

I was separated from Dr Daley and pitched into a conversation between the Probbles and my parish priest. The Vicar was saying:

"Thank you so much, Father, for that *beautiful* service of inauguration. And the *angelic* choir."

"Kind of you to admit it, Mr Probble," said his opposite number.

"It is so good to know," said Mrs Probble, "that today Catholics and Anglicans are at last learning to pray together."

"Madam," interrupted Fr Duddleswell, "we were not praying together. I was in charge. You were praying with us but we were not praying with you. 'Tis forbidden to us."

"That is a very fine distinction," objected Mr Probble.

"I am glad you appreciate it," said Fr Duddleswell.

"What Mr Probble is suggesting," said Mrs Probble, "is that your attitude appears to be a trifle narrow."

"Indeed, Madam. Like the road that leads to salvation. But be sure that though I may not pray *with* you, I pray *for* you in season and out of season."

Mrs Probble said, "you make us sound like plums and damsons, Fr Duddleswell." Then even more haughtily, "But we badly need your prayers, I suppose, being such sinners."

"May God bless you, Madam," Fr Duddleswell retorted, "for your insight and humility."

"But, my dear fellow..." began Mr Probble.

Fr Duddleswell naughtily looked over his shoulder before facing the Vicar again. "Oh, you mean *me*," he said.

"Of course, we prayed together," the Vicar insisted. "If you and I play soccer together, does it matter who is *in charge* of the football?"

The Mayor, doing the rounds, came in at that point. "After the swim, are you two Reverends planning a game of soccer, then?"

"If 'tis *my* football, Bert," Fr Duddleswell said with a grin.

The Probbles moved into quieter waters as the Mayor introduced Fr Duddleswell and me to Mr Biggins.

"The Mayor has been telling me about you, Mr Biggins," Fr Duddleswell said as he shook hands.

"Nice things, I hope."

"The truth, like," Fr Duddleswell replied ambiguously. "The Mayor was saying, Mr Biggins, you are an unbeliever."

"I'm a free-thinker."

"Oh," whistled Fr Duddleswell, "free-thinking can be a very expensive thing if by it you lose your soul."

"Better that than losing my reason," Mr Biggins said. "But tell you what, if I'm wrong and there is a God, I'll apologize and stand you a drink on the other side."

Fr Duddleswell, who seemed to be revelling in the battle of wits, said, "'Tis you, I am thinking, who will be needing the drink on the other side, Mr Biggins."

"Do you still believe in hell, then?"

Fr Duddleswell drew himself to his full height and looked up. "Mr Biggins, everybody who meets me believes in hell— *after*, if not *before*."

A few seconds later I found myself confronted by a salmon-faced gentleman. His eyes were screwed up to keep out the smoke from the cigarette which he appeared to be devouring rather than puffing.

He stretched out a hand. "Pinkerton's the name. John

144

Pinkerton. I say, that Duddleswell's a rum 'un, eh?"

"You think so," I said.

"Whenever I see him," Pinkerton coughed, peering through his slits, "I thank the Lord for making me a Protestant."

"You do." I pointedly fanned away a part of his smoke-screen.

"Don't you?"

"Yes, Mr Pinkerton," I grinned, "I too thank God for making you a Protestant."

He stopped chewing his cigarette and drew in a couple of chins. "Aren't you Tinsy the new Methodist minister?"

"No, I'm Boyd, Fr Duddleswell's new curate."

A kind of incantation struggled out of his throat. "O *my* God, *your* God and *everybody's* God."

We were saved further embarrassment as Fr Duddleswell clapped his hands for silence.

"Mr Mayor," he began, "ladies and gentlemen. What a grand occasion is this." Some said "Hear, hear," and others, less reverent but thankful nonetheless for the Amontillado sherry, said, "'Ear, 'Ear."

Above appreciative murmurs, foot-stampings and tapping of the table, Fr Duddleswell continued, "Fairwater now, at last, has had the good sense to choose a *Catholic* Mayor." A polite titter greeted this intentionally partizan remark. "You will be delighted to know that I wrote a letter to this effect to the Palace, Buckingham not Crystal, you follow?" That put things on an even keel for a moment and someone said "Good show." "No reply," said Fr Duddleswell, "and none was expected.

"I wrote also to Rome and only this morning I received the following message from the Secretary of State to Pope Pius XII." The boat was definitely rocking as he unrolled and read from a yellow scroll. "'The Holy Father sends to His beloved son, Councillor Albert Appleby, and the entire district under his charge His Apostolic Blessing.' And now, ladies and gentlemen all, I give you a toast."

We raised our glasses muttering, "A toast, a toast," before

the ship finally went down. Fr Duddleswell lifted his own glass and said:

"To His Holiness the Pope."

There was some hesitation and a certain amount of unfeigned distress among the company but I am sure I saw Fr Duddleswell and Mr Appleby wink knowingly at each other.

After "For 'e's a jolly good fellow," the Mayor left in his chauffeur-driven Rolls, and the party broke up in a haze of cigarette smoke, conscious that a fair start had been made to the Borough's week of celebrations.

"Charming, charming," purred Mr Percival Probble, the Vicar, as he languidly took his host's hand. "Till we meet again. Celebrations in water next time, not sherry, what?"

Referring to that tender adieu, Fr Duddleswell said to me later, "God's me witness, 'twas like shaking hands with a tired sausage."

Mrs Pring, who had begun to sweep up the ashes and rearrange the parlour after what she called alternatively the "binge" and the "debauch," complained, "They've killed eleven bottles and"—here we heard the crunch and tinkle of glass—"they've gone and bleedin' well broke—broke your Reverences' pardon—five of my best sherry glasses."

"The wives of the clergy did it, Mrs Pring," said Fr Duddleswell. "Out of pique."

"Oh," said Mrs Pring disgustedly, marshalling her epithets for a combined attack. "What a binge! What a debauch!"

On the Saturday of the race, I was allowed to sleep in until seven o'clock. When I woke, the sun was already bright and everywhere was steaming.

The Gala was to be held in the grand open-air municipal baths in the town centre. I had arranged to meet Tom Fleming at the main turnstiles at 1:45 because we were keen to see the earlier races.

Fr Duddleswell caught up with us at three o'clock in the hot and crowded arena. He was flustered and a bit edgy after a curtailed siesta. Mrs Pring had insisted on joining him and he could not see why "except out of a prurient curiosity." He was even beginning to call the race "an unlucky job" and to waver in his resolve to swim in it until I told him how proud Tom and I were to be with him in this "straightforward contest between the one, true Church and the usurpers."

At 3:30 the bathing beauty competition commenced, so we decided it was time to make ourselves scarce and prepare ourselves for the race. We three moved as a body towards the changing rooms. One of the stewards of the meeting was standing by with a list of competitors and the rooms assigned to them.

Fr Duddleswell made himself known. The steward said, "Yes, sir," immediately betraying by this mode of address he was no member of the one, true fold, "your room is the big one at the end, Number 23."

"Neil Boyd," I said, checking in.

Before Fr Duddleswell had trotted out of earshot, the steward said, "Same room, sir. All the clergy change in Number 23."

Fr Duddleswell turned back on his tracks. "That cannot be," he protested.

"I'm afraid it is, sir. As you can see, there's over a hundred contestants in the swimming gala and thirty entrants in the Bathing Beauty Competition. Number 23 is a very large changing room, I do assure you, sir."

"For *all* the clergy?" asked Fr Duddleswell.

The steward nodded affirmatively. "There's a Rev. Probble there now, sir, who has the key to lock up all your valuables."

Fr Duddleswell, his tail up, said, "Catholic clergy, *sir*, have *no* valuables."

With that he led off his small black brood towards Number 23. At the door, he halted, drew a deep breath, and signalled to me to knock.

"Come in," said a high-pitched voice (that of Fatty Pinkerton).

When we entered, we saw the three Anglicans already changed and sitting in brightly coloured beach robes. The

Vicar was flanked by his two curates. On the right, with military moustache and greying temples, was the former Oxford blue, and on the left, Pinkerton was puffing voraciously on a cigarette.

Mr Probble stood up and extended his languid hand to Fr Duddleswell. He glanced at his watch, and said, "Cutting it fine again, what?"

We three newcomers proceeded slowly to undress in front of the Anglican clergy.

Mr Probble said, "This race is the highlight of the Gala."

Fr Duddleswell, removing his large linen collar, muttered something about not being in the least surprised.

"The locals find it even more intoxicating than the Beauty Contest," Pinkerton said.

"Yes," continued Mr Probble, "they only see us normally in clerical garb, collars back to front, lurid vestments, and that sort of thing. They're delighted and amused to find that underneath it all we're organically no different from themselves."

Everyone laughed except Fr Duddleswell who was still trying, improbably, to balance his linen collar on a peg.

Mr Probble, being a gentleman if nothing else, as Fr Duddleswell put it afterwards, sensed that the tardiness with which his Catholic counterpart was removing his plumage had something to do with the presence of the Anglican Church. He handed over the key and suggested to his team that they leave.

Fr Duddleswell, in his relief, went across and shook each of them by the hand promising to see them soon.

With the usurpers out of the way, Fr Duddleswell put a towel round his waist and said, "I suppose you two lads did not bring your breviaries with you."

Tom Fleming took the hint. "Would you prefer us to leave as well, Father?"

"Not at all," Fr Duddleswell said unconvincingly.

"We will if you like," I said.

"Very well, Father Neil, if the pair of you have something more important to do, you can wait for me outside."

There, I explained to Tom that Fr Duddleswell was only

making a pretense at clinging to proprieties. At lunch he had told me he would be wearing his costume to the Gala under his trousers, "just to be on the safe side, like."

A few minutes later, Fr Duddleswell appeared, locked the door and pocketed the key. As a group we followed our opponents into the open air. Once out of the shadows, we felt the burning tiles under our bare feet.

"My godfathers!" exclaimed Fr Duddleswell. "I am going to get blisters underneath the arches."

A roar of applause accompanied our arrival on the scene. Fortunately, it was only for the last five girls to reach the final of the Beauty contest. I was surprised and far from displeased to find that one of the five was Nurse Owen, a Catholic nurse I had met on my occasional visits to Kenworthy General Hospital. Her red hair had been let down for the occasion, and I wondered how she managed to cram it all beneath her nurse's cap. She was even shaplier than I would have imagined, had I dared to imagine.

The crowd was hushed as the jury made their decision in reverse order. Nurse Owen was declared the winner. "The Catholics," Fr Duddleswell said, "out in front again." It was, I thought, an aptly descriptive phrase.

After the mayor's crowning of the Beauty Queen and the photographs, the loudspeaker announced the climax of the afternoon: the medley race between the clergy of St Luke's (cheers) and St Jude's (bigger cheers).

"The English always like an underdog," said Fr Duddleswell through gritted teeth.

I suspected his silver bathing hat had something to do with our being the darlings of the crowd.

Mrs Pring appeared, ready to hold our towels and robes.

"Are you a water-nymph," Fr Duddleswell said to her, "that you are waiting to wash me shroud on the edge of death's lake?"

Mrs Pring took no notice.

Fr Fleming was to start against Mr d'Arcy. Then me against Pinkerton. The anchor men were Fr Duddleswell and the Vicar.

The opening leg proved to be a surprise for onlookers and contestants. In spite of his superb style, the Rev. d'Arcy lacked stamina. After two lengths, he was down fifteen yards. Soon it was clear that Fr Fleming would give us a lead of nearly twenty-five yards. Fr Duddleswell was ecstatic.

I disrobed and was followed by the fat Rev. Pinkerton. He stood beside me sporting a pair of bathing trunks colored red, white, and blue. The crowd cheered a churchman who was patriotic enough to carry the Union Jack on his backside. I thought it was in dubious taste, and it made me all the more determined to beat the daylights out of him.

On the backstroke, I saw the Rev. Pinkerton all the way. I gradually increased our lead. By the time I finished the second leg, the Catholic clergy were nearly a length in front. Fr Duddleswell had only to stay afloat for us to win.

A deafening cheer heralded his entry into the water. I clambered out to find Mr Probble perched on the side of the pool hoarsely urging on his patriotic but overripe colleague. By the time the Rev. Pinkerton had touched and the Vicar had plunged in to the accompaniment of further cheers, Fr Duddleswell, in a flurry of water, had nearly reached the forty-yard mark. He turned well, and it was then I began to detect a drop in his stroke-rate.

Fr Duddleswell was almost on a level with Mr Probble going in the opposite direction when he ceased moving forward altogether and started bobbing up and down. Oblivious of the crowd, I raced down the side of the pool until I was in line with him. Above the cheers, I could just make out his cry:

"Help me, Mother of God. Help!"

Mr Probble either heard Fr Duddleswell's yell of anguish or divined why it was the gap between them was not being narrowed by his opponent. Before I could dive in, he had moved sideways and grabbed Fr Duddleswell round the neck and proceeded to swim with him to the side of the pool. I reached down and dragged Fr Duddleswell from the water. He lay there on his back, spluttering and gasping.

Nurse Owen, still clad in her bikini, was pushing her way through the crowd. I heard her say, "I'm a nurse. He needs artificial respiration."

Next moment, she was by my side. She was about to begin her ministrations when I caught her arm.

"I'll do it, Nurse, thank you."

I hadn't the slightest doubt that the local press would be onto this literally in a flash. I didn't want my revered parish priest, after one calamity, to be photographed half-naked as he received the kiss of life from the newly crowned Beauty Queen.

"You're crazy," Nurse Owen cried, "the poor man needs help urgently."

Not heeding her remonstrances, I lowered myself next to Fr Duddleswell. It was like kneeling next to a landed whale. As I dipped my head, Fr Duddleswell squealed in agony, "Get off me belly, boy," and rolled over onto the offended part of his anatomy.

To add to the confusion, Mrs Pring arrived. I'd never seen her so agitated. She pulled the bathing hat from Fr Duddleswell's head and handed me a little silver phial.

"What's this?" I asked.

"Holy oil. For the anointing. I knew this would be the death of him."

"Mrs *Pring*. It's not a heart attack. He's swallowed too much water, that's all."

As I knelt down again beside the writhing figure—the top of his white bottom showing above the slipping bathing trunks—I realized my diagnosis needed amending. Fr Duddleswell was moaning: "Me left leg. The back of it. Cramp. Oh, 'tis agony, agony."

I massaged where the pain was: a big, stiff ball of muscle behind the left leg at the top. After a few minutes—I lost count of the bulbs flashing in the meanwhile—he was sufficiently restored to stand on his feet to the sympathetic cheers of the crowd. Fr Duddleswell held both hands high like a defeated boxer who had just picked himself up off the canvas. I looked about me for Mr Probble to thank him for helping but he had modestly melted into the crowd.

Mayor Appleby insisted that Fr Duddleswell, Mrs Pring, and I should be transported home in his Rolls. Mrs Pring was so concerned about Fr Duddleswell's health she made us leave immediately. I only had time to gather up our belongings from the changing room before jumping into the Rolls.

No sadder or stranger little group, even at a funeral, ever travelled in more majesty. In the streets, some passers-by, seeing the car with its armorial standard on the front, showed a marked respect for it until they glimpsed the occupants. Fr Duddleswell promptly draped a towel over his head.

Back at the rectory, Mrs Pring ordered him straight to bed. When I had changed I went to his bedroom to offer him my sympathy. He was not there. I found him in his study clad in a clean pair of pyjamas and a dressing gown with a thermometer sticking in the corner of his mouth.

"I am *not* staying in bed, Mrs Pring." It was obviously not the first time he had said it.

"Keep that thermometer in your mouth," she commanded, "and don't bite *that* thing's head off."

"What is the point of it," he grumbled, "the very vision of you raises me temperature fifteen degrees."

The front doorbell rang and Mrs Pring said she was going to let Dr Daley in.

Fr Duddleswell started to say, "You didn't call..." but he interrupted himself with the first sounds and stiffening motions of a sneeze. He held it in check as long as he could but it finally overwhelmed him just as Dr Daley made his entrance.

The doctor did not seem to mind the cloudburst. "Bless me, Father," he said, "for you have sneezed. Now what is this I hear of you, Charles, that you have been at the swimming pool, drinking it dry?"

"Leave us, Mrs Pring," bade Fr Duddleswell, "and see to it we are not disturbed." Then to Dr Daley: "There is nothing much amiss with me, Donal. I am not killed completely."

"Take your gown off, Charles, anyway." He obeyed. "Sit your softy down on the desk there."

"Do not ask me to go any further with removals, Donal. I have had enough of the striptease."

"It's all right, Charles," said Dr Daley, trying to soothe his tattered nerves, "I have seen worse sights before. In motor accidents mainly, and on marble slabs in the fish shop. But you are about as bashful as a virgin on her wedding night. Put your collar back on if it makes you feel any better."

Once more Fr Duddleswell protested his rude health.

"Charles, my dear friend, water in the bladder is bad enough but in the lungs it can be terrible destructive. Oh, but I *hate* the water, Charles. It is all I can do to make myself dip the tip of my middle finger in the holy water stoup." He looked about him for the whereabouts of important things. "You wouldn't have a dram of the hard stuff locked away anywhere, I suppose?" Fr Duddleswell shook his head. "Oh, *Charles*, for the sake of many good, hard-working times we've had together joining hands round the beds of the departing."

Fr Duddleswell relented. He pointed to the cupboard by the door. "Help yourself to the mischief, Donal."

"God bless and keep you, Charles, anyway. If I hadn't been baptized when I was three days old I would have refused the honour because of my fear of the water." He knelt down by the cupboard. "But you *are* in the dolours today, Charles."

"And who would not be?"

"It is not every day a man is frightened out of the husk of his heart by the drowning." He filled his glass. "Can I pour a Paraclete for yourself, Charles?"

Fr Duddleswell declined the offer. "True for you. I thought I was about to leave this country for a better. And beneath the airless water me soul shrank within me like a pair of socks in Mrs Pring's washtub."

"What could be worse than that?" said Dr Daley, growing strangely melancholy as he took his first relieving sip.

"Worse by far is the humiliation, Donal. Will I ever get the better of me shame? I will not."

"What is your shame, Charles?"

"To start with, them photographers hurling their lightnings at me and taking pictures of me posterity. And now I am smarting until the crack of doom from the indecency of having me life saved by an Anglican Vicar." He tut-tutted more than a few times. "He was even too little of a Christian to stand still for me to thank him. And that, mind, after I let him half strangle me in the water to make a hero of him."

At this point, I left them for my study which I had offered to Tom Fleming as a changing room. We took tea and chatted together for about an hour.

As I was showing him out, Mr Probble, Mr d'Arcy and Pinkerton appeared. They were on a flying visit to see if the incumbent had recovered from his dipping.

It never occurred to me that Dr Daley was still there. I knocked on Fr Duddleswell's door and went in, followed by the Anglican clergy. "Father," I announced, "these gentlemen just dropped in to see if..."

Fr Duddleswell was still perched in patient misery on his desk with his belly bared to the elements. Dr Daley had interrupted his examination to knock back another drink.

My parish priest made a leap for his dressing gown, and, drowning me from afar with one wave of his wrath, he called out, "Donal!"

"Yes, Charles."

"Would you hurry up fast and pour me, too, a double flagon of whiskey."

10

FATHER AND MOTHER

One day when Mrs Pring was dusting my room, she informed me that Fr Duddleswell's parents had emigrated from Cork soon after they were married. The family had lived for a few years in Bath where Fr Duddleswell was born and eventually settled down in London's famous Portobello Road. His father had owned an antique shop there.

According to Mrs Pring, Fr Duddleswell's upbringing accounted for his "craftiness" and his refusal to take anything at its face value. For my part, I had noticed his tendency to collect "little items of value" and to smuggle in pieces of furniture which he hoarded in the loft, usually when Mrs Pring was out shopping.

One morning, Fr Duddleswell decided I needed another bookcase for my study and generously agreed to let me borrow one of his precious *"objets d'art"* now growing cobwebs "upstairs."

I was holding the ladder for him as he slowly ascended, torch in hand, and raised the trap door into the loft. That was when Mrs Pring appeared.

"Come down this minute, Tarzan, do you hear me?" she cried.

Fr Duddleswell, his round face already smudged, silently glowered down from the loft like an angry cherub.

"You'll tumble and break your stubborn neck, that's what you'll do," Mrs Pring persisted.

"Mrs Pring," said Fr Duddleswell menacingly, "d'you not think I would have wed had I thirsted for the advice of a woman? And *are* we man and wife?"

"No, Father D, folly has its limits."

Fr Duddleswell looked down on her for a moment like an admiring deity. "Pure Jack Point," he said. "Now, Mrs Pring, stand there if you would be so kind and help Father Neil take a hold of the bookcase when I lower it."

In an echoing voice, he warned us he'd have to hand us down an old picture so as to give himself room in the crowded loft to get at the bookcase. I only glanced at the gilt-framed picture. It was ugly and over-laid with dust.

"Mother Foundress again," sniffed Mrs Pring, before placing the picture diagonally against the landing wall.

By now, Fr Duddleswell was ready to lower the heavy mahogany bookcase. When it came to the test, Mrs Pring didn't have Mosaic muscles, after all, and she impeded me from applying mine. Fr Duddleswell himself had to take most of the weight as he gingerly stepped down the ladder.

He had only two more rungs to go when the picture began to slide down the wall. With his last little sideways jump, he put both feet clean through the canvas.

Not that he was in the least distressed by the accident. "*O felix culpa*, I have been wanting to do that for years," he laughed, "and never found the courage."

He paused for a moment, gazed quizzically at the picture as though he *had* regretted the damage he'd caused, and promptly forgot about my bookcase altogether.

"Something strange about this picture," he said, carrying it effortlessly past me down the stairs. "I am wanting to see it in a better light."

When Mrs Pring and I reached his study, I found he had turned his table lamp like a spotlight onto the ancient portrait of a nun.

"It certainly *is* strange," I commented on entering. "Never seen a ghastlier picture in my life."

The picture represented an elderly haloed nun in the black habit of an earlier era. She was kneeling in front of the Virgin's statue, placidly holding a skull in the palm of her right hand.

Fr Duddleswell, crouching on the floor, said, "By 'strange' I meant something quite other, Father Neil. I do feel this portrait has been painted on top of something else."

"I'll give this the once over," Mrs Pring said, pointing towards the picture which was about five feet by three.

While Mrs Pring went about her dusting, he explained that the good sisters who ran the local orphanage had donated their precious portrait of Mother Foundress to St Jude's in the person of his predecessor. That was over twenty years ago when the present Superior, Mother Stephen was first appointed.

"Well, Father Neil, as you will realize, when I took charge of St Jude's, I was in a dilemma. The picture is so awful, I could not leave it there to frighten the women and children, but had I removed it without cause, I would have offended the good sisters or, at any rate, Mother Stephen."

"Who frightens *him*," contributed Mrs Pring.

Fr Duddleswell did not deny it.

"So?" I asked.

"The Lord draws good out of evil, does He not? As soon as the Blitz began, I made the excuse to Mother Stephen that I would have to remove the portrait of her Foundress to a safer place."

Mrs Pring contributed, "In this area, Father Neil, nearly all the churches were bombed out during the war."

"Thank you, Mrs Pring," said Fr Duddleswell, hoping she would go.

"Don't mention it, Father," Mrs Pring said, continuing unabashed with her dusting.

"The long and short of it is, Father Neil, that I put the portrait up in the loft."

"With the other rubbish," said Mrs Pring, who had paused to shake her duster out of the window.

"What about *after* the war?" I asked.

"Well, now, in the last few years, Mother Stephen has asked me a hundred times when I am going to adorn the church with it again."

"And you reply?"

"Whatever enters my head. I have said that the copy of the Leonardo which replaced Mother Foundress is much loved by the people. I have said, God forgive me, that an original oil painting is a target for vandalism; some ruffian might come along and daub it all over with dye or slash it with a knife."

"Or put his feet through it," added Mrs Pring who had by now reached the bottom of the portrait.

"Do these explanations satisfy Mother Stephen?"

"Not at all, Father Neil. She is a very intelligent woman."

"There *are* some, then," muttered Mrs Pring.

"Mother Stephen," said Fr Duddleswell, "has never forgiven me."

Mrs Pring was about to leave the room. "Lunch in ten minutes," she said.

Fr Duddleswell used the interval to tell me of the running battle he had waged over the years with Mother Stephen.

"She is very holy, Father Neil, and so 'tis very difficult to get near her."

I recognized the type.

"Mother Stephen," he went on, "believes she is in the place of Christ, that is why she demands absolute obedience. The nuns are not even allowed to pray for fine weather without her consent."

"Really!"

"'Tis a question for nuns, Father Neil, of following their rules to the death. And the rules of their order, alas, were drawn up by the foundress, Mère Magdalène who came from Aix-en-Provence. You would never believe this..."

"Try me," I said.

"She was a married woman with a husband and two children when she left home to found an orphanage."

"God moves in mysterious ways His wonders..." It

struck me I wouldn't have spoken like this a couple of months before.

"Anyway," continued Fr Duddleswell, "she took the veil."

"Judging from this picture, she should have kept it over her head."

"To continue with the present Superior. One of the battles I fought and lost was over dear Sister Perpetua. When Sister Perpetua's father died, Mother Stephen told her she had to make a choice: she could go either to her father's funeral *or* her mother's when the time came, but not to both."

"Is that really written in the rules?" I said, spewing like a whale.

He nodded, saying, "Mère Magdalène."

"For heaven's sake, why?"

"To show that her nuns, having put their hands to the plough, were not to turn back; to prove they had left father and mother for the sake of the kingdom."

"Then why not be consistent and let *all* the dead bury the dead? Why present poor Sister Perpetua with such a dreadful alternative? You say you lost the battle."

"That I did, Father Neil. I suggested in the end she go to her father's funeral to console her mother."

"And when her mother dies?"

"We will leave that to the angels, like."

Seeing my disgust, he went on, "'Tis an old saying but true: 'You can drive out nature with a pitchfork and she will slink in the back door.' The fact of the matter is that in spite of their inhuman rules, most of these sisters are lovely people."

I said I needed some convincing.

"But, Father Neil, you must have seen 'em with the kiddies. Was there ever a happier orphanage than ours? The sisters are devoted to the little ones, so they are."

I conceded the point. "But no thanks to that witch," I said, pointing to the picture of Mère Magdalène.

After lunch, we drove off with Mother Foundress to the Portobello Road. We parked and knocked loudly on the bolted door of *Duddleswell's*. Eventually we managed to rouse the new proprietor, Fred Dobie, from his slumbers.

Seeing our picture, Mr Dobie said, "For old times' sake, Fr Duddleswell, I'll give you five shillings for the frame."

"'Tis not the frame I've come about," said Fr Duddleswell.

"It can't be about the portrait," responded Fred, twirling his big waxed moustaches in disbelief. "You must be joking."

Fr Duddleswell explained his hunch. After a microscopic inspection of the canvas at the place where it was torn, Fred confirmed that there was indeed another painting underneath.

"What makes you think that what's below is any better than what's on top?" Fred asked.

"It couldn't be worse," I said.

"Feelings, Fred, feelings."

"I've known your feelings before," Fred said respectfully.

"I want it X-rayed, Fred. Can you do that for me, now?"

"That requires expensive equipment, and you know I'm not in the big league."

"I realize that. I want you to take it to one of your contacts, a real expert, and get an opinion. I will pay all the dues."

"Okay, Father. Give me three or four days."

Fred phoned the next day begging us to come round immediately.

"Well, Fred?" asked Fr Duddleswell breathlessly on our arrival.

"Mate!" said Fred excitedly. "Are you in luck!"

"Come on, Fred, out with it, tell us more."

"I took the picture along to James J. Brockaway. He wouldn't touch it at first till I told him who'd dropped it in."

"He was a friend of me father's," explained Fr Duddleswell.

Fred continued, "Brockaway put it under his lamp and inside five minutes he could tell me that underneath that muck is an original by Jean-Paul Tichat."

"Never heard of him," confessed Fr Duddleswell.

"Tichat was a friend or at least an associate of van Gogh and Gauguin."

"The divil," roared Fr Duddleswell. "*Now* I place him. He came from... Holy Jesus, from Aix-en-Provence!"

Fred Dobie was beaming. "Jean-Paul was one of the leading lights in the Impressionist movement. He visited van Gogh when he was put in the asylum at Saint-Rémy in 1889."

"A few months after van Gogh did those self-portraits with a bandaged ear."

"Yes, and Tichat went to see him. And, in the view of James J. Brockaway, Tichat was in fact the sitter for van Gogh's painting which is usually entitled 'The Peasant.'"

"Know it well," said Fr Duddleswell, "lovely picture with cornfield and orchard in the background. But why does Brockaway think the peasant was Tichat?"

"Because of the dating, the established timing of Tichat's visit to Saint-Rémy and also because of the consumptive appearance of the peasant."

"Explain that last bit, if you would be so kind," said Fr Duddleswell wiping the mist from his spectacles.

"Well, Father, Tichat died of T.B. in 1890."

"So he did, now, God rest his soul, so he did. Only twenty-six or twenty-seven years of age."

"And," continued Fred Dobie, "he left behind him at least a hundred canvases. But they didn't have the good fortune to survive like van Gogh's."

"But this one has."

"This one has," echoed Fred excitedly. "There are only three others in existence as far as we know. One is in private hands somewhere, one is in New York, and the third is in the Pitti Gallery in Florence."

"I am mystified to know how..." began Fr Duddleswell.

"How Brockaway could know so soon that it's a Tichat?"

"Yes," said Fr Duddleswell. "*No*," he suddenly exploded in understanding. "'Tis the cat."

"Dead right, it's the cat. Ti*chat* always signed his portrait, not with his autograph, but with a cat, *chat* in French"—that was for my benefit. "That alone would make the picture invaluable. But there's more."

"More? Get on with it, then, man," urged Fr Duddleswell.

"It's the subject of the painting that's so fascinating. It's of a wheatfield with crows."

"The absolute divil," cried Fr Duddleswell.

"The composition shows it's very like van Gogh's picture of July 1890."

"And Tichat died when?"

"On 18th June 1890."

Fr Duddleswell could scarcely breathe for excitement. "So 'tis possible van Gogh painted his picture as a kind of memorial to his friend."

"Entirely different styles, of course," said Fred. "Tichat's is all light and the other sombre and heavy."

"Naturally, but..." Fr Duddleswell was lost for words.

Delighted at causing such joyous consternation, Fred said, "Aren't you going to ask me what it's worth?"

"No," said Fr Duddleswell flatly.

"*I* am," I said. "How much?"

"Brockaway tells me someone's been gilding a real lily. It's worth upwards of £6,000."

"But," I objected, "Father's put his footograph on it."

"No matter," said Fred. "It'll take a couple of thousand quid to get rid of that muck on top and restore the original, but even so."

"Even so," I took up, "it'll bring in a profit of £4,000?"

"That," said Fred, "depends on whether Brockaway is right and the picture underneath is in good condition *and* whether there's a ready market for it."

"And," added Fr Duddleswell quietly, "whether the owner is disposed to sell."

"Say the word, Fr Duddleswell," said Fred, "and I'll take a risk. I'll write you out a cheque here and now for three and a half thousand quid."

"Cannot be much of a risk, then, Fred."

"To tell the truth, it isn't. In my view, even if the picture is severely damaged, the least it's worth is what I'm offering. But I'm prepared to draw up a contract so that anything earned on the sale of it in the next two years, over and above five and a half thousand, is divided between us equally."

"That is very generous of you," Fr Duddleswell said reflectively. "But I really am not sure who owns it."

"It's not yours?"

"'Tis and 'tisn't, if you follow me. 'Twas donated by the good sisters to the parish. I do not know at all whether I have the right to sell. You see, the nuns are rather fond of what you call 'that muck' overlaying the Tichat."

"But, Fr Duddleswell," Fred Dobie objected strongly, "you can't possibly let that ... that nun stay for ever on top of what is probably a masterpiece. Wipe her off and give the sisters a share in the proceeds. There'll be enough in the sale to divide three ways."

"Thank you, Fred," said Fr Duddleswell, offering him his hand in farewell. "How much do I owe you for ..."

"Forget it, Father. It's peanuts. Brockaway wouldn't charge *you* for an opinion, anyway."

"Grateful." And with that, Fr Duddleswell gathered me to him, and we beat a hasty retreat.

In the car, my mentor moaned, "Ah, what 'tis like to have divided loyalties, Father Neil."

I asked him to explain the reason for his lamentation.

"To be torn twixt love and beauty."

"That's no clearer," I said.

"I do not want to upset the sisters whom I dearly love, but if I leave their Mother Foundress undisturbed what becomes of that exquisite beauty hidden underneath?"

"If you ask me," I said, "Mother Foundress has been hiding too much beauty for too long already. It's about time the old witch was knocked off her perch."

"Father Neil, Father Neil," he groaned, "you are so wicked and so right."

"Tay time, Father Neil."

Seldom can Fr Duddleswell have been so glum at the prospect of tea. The reason was that we were to partake of it at the Convent. He had telephoned Mother Stephen asking for an interview, and in her sisterly charity she'd invited him to sit down at table.

At the convent, a Sister Frederick greeted us silently with a bow, and we followed her swishing skirts along a gleaming parquet corridor to the parlor. We were shown into a cold, dust-free room stuffed with silence and there abandoned. A bloody statue of the Sacred Heart was its only ornament. There we awaited the Superior.

"A cheerless place," I whispered conspiratorially, "specially reserved for visitors?"

"I breakfasted here once," Fr Duddleswell whispered in return. "'Twas the first time in me life I saw egg-cosies. And somethin' else: they not only gave me two boiled eggs, but also two spoons to eat 'em with."

"Very hygienic," I laughed softly, as though we were in a graveyard and didn't want to scandalize the dead.

"'Twas a cold morning, Father Neil, around Christmas time. They had kindly lit a fire for me. The table was over there"—he pointed to the centre of the room—"and the cutlery was in front of the fire *warming*."

There was a knock on the door so slight it could have been made by a sponge, and Fr Duddleswell called out, "Come in, please."

Mother Stephen's long, narrow head appeared round the door and intoned, "*Laudetur Jesus Christus*." She gave the impression of a hungry crow.

"*Semper laudetur*," replied Fr Duddleswell, "may Christ be always praised."

The Superior followed her head and was followed in turn by Sister Gemma, an elderly nun who acted as the Convent Bursar.

"A companion must be present," explained Mother Stephen. "It is written in our holy rules."

"Of course," said Fr Duddleswell who had evidently made treaties with nuns before.

"Are you ready for your tea, Fathers?" asked the Superior.

I noted Mother Stephen's sentence-form was often

interrogative when the tone was unmistakably affirmative.

"Indeed, Mother," said Fr Duddleswell, and I seconded him.

It occurred to me—and the thought nearly made me giggle—that I had been invited as his chaperon.

Sister Bursar opened the door, smartly clapped her hands, and two pretty nuns with down-cast eyes entered bearing a table set for two. They put the table down in the centre of the room and, bowing, retired.

As a spectacle it was nothing short of oriental.

Chairs were set at table for us by Sister Bursar, and we were admonished to sit and eat.

"You will not join us, Mother?" asked Fr Duddleswell, purely out of politeness.

"Our rules, Father."

"Of course."

I poured out the tea. In that enormous silence, it sounded like an old-fashioned lavatory cistern; munching the delicate cucumber sandwiches made a churning sound noisier than a cement mixer.

"October is round the corner, Mother," said Fr Duddleswell, directing his words at the Superior with some difficulty, for she had stationed herself like October just out of his sight, by the window. He was at a disadvantage, and he knew it.

"October? So it is, Father." She spoke as if she entirely approved the regularity with which the days and months succeeded one another.

"I was wondering if you would like Father Neil to come here to give Benediction on Friday evenings in October. With the rosary, of course."

"Thank you, Father."

"Does that mean yes?"

"No, it means no."

"Ah," said Fr Duddleswell, "I thought it might be convenient for you."

"No, Father." Her timing was perfect. She waited before explaining: "Our rules prescribe special devotions, the litany of

Mary, prayer to St Joseph, and the stations of the cross, throughout October."

"'Twas only a thought," murmured Fr Duddleswell, and went back to mixing cement.

Out of the corner of my eyes, I could see Mother Stephen fingering her rosary beads as if wanting our visit to interfere as little as possible with her supplications for a happy death.

Fr Duddleswell put down his tea-cup on the saucer with a cymbal-like clash and said, "I have been seeking an opportunity to talk to you, Mother, about the picture of Mother Foundress."

"We want it back, Father," said Mother Stephen, quiet but assertive.

"I beg your holy pardon, Mother?"

"We want it back. You see, an eminent Jesuit in Rome, Fr Giuseppe Orselli, has agreed to take up the cause of our Foundress with a view to having her beatified by the Sovereign Pontiff in 1955."

"But why the picture, Mother, 'tis not miraculous?"

"Something far more important. It's the only one there is."

"That," wheezed Fr Duddleswell, with masterly understatement, "is inconvenient."

"How 'inconvenient'? Has it not been stored away from view for several years?"

"I always intended, Mother . . ." Fr Duddleswell began but braked suddenly when he recalled what he'd said to me a few days earlier.

"As St Francis de Sales put it," said the Superior, "God does not count our good intentions; He weighs them."

I thought that Fr Duddleswell's good intentions in this respect would hardly trouble the scales.

"The Leonardo, Mother . . . a masterpiece."

"Does God concern Himself so much with masterpieces, Father? Can He not make and unmake masterpieces when He wills? Surely God's heart is moved much more by sincere and simple things?"

"Is not a masterpiece, Mother, God's gift to man given through man?"

166

"Ah, Fr Duddleswell, do you not agree with Thomas à Kempis when he writes, 'God does not so much regard the gift of the lover as the lover of the giver'?"

"I do, Mother. I do. Indeed, I do. 'Tis why all these years I have treasured the portrait of Mère Magdalène, not for its intrinsic worth but because of the love with which you gave it."

He emphasized the word "gave."

"*Gave*, Father?"

"Mother, *gave*."

"But, Father, does not giving imply acceptance?"

"Mother, does not God give His grace even when we refuse it?"

"No, Father, He does not. He offers it but does not give it, otherwise the sinful soul would be in a state of grace which, by definition, it is not. God does not give in this instance because He cannot."

"D'you compare your Foundress's portrait to the gift of grace?"

"It was meant, Father, as God's blessing on the whole parish."

"And so it shall be," said Fr Duddleswell, completely vanquished at theology. "But I am obliged to tell you a painful fact I would rather have kept from you."

"Yes, Father," said Mother Stephen, suddenly starching her habit.

"The picture..."

"It's been stolen!" cried Mother Stephen.

"No, Mother. It has been in a slight... accident."

"Tell me!" The tone was magisterial.

"I...I...I put me feet through it."

"*Miserere mei, Deus*," moaned Mother Superior. "More than ever must we have it back."

"'Tis too precious, Mother," said Fr Duddleswell.

"*Now* you tell me, Father! You lock up our Order's most treasured possession in a dungeon"—wrong end of the house, I thought—"stab it with your feet, and then you tell me it has become precious to you. What would you not have done to it had you hated it? Do you not know that our humble Foundress always wore a veil so that throughout her years in the Convent her features were unknown? The face is on that portrait providentially. It was painted from life by one of our founding sisters less than an hour after Mère Magdalène had expired."

"Really!" I cried, unable to contain myself. It explained why the portrait made my flesh creep.

Mother Stephen looked at me disapprovingly as though I were one of her nuns who had broken the *magnum silentium*, the great silence, of the night hours.

At this point, Fr Duddleswell felt it incumbent on him to tell the Superior how he was using the term "precious" when he applied it to the picture.

"You mean," said Mother Stephen, after hearing the whole story, "that our Foundress is to be erased from memory..."

"We have no portrait of Jesus," put in Fr Duddleswell.

"The Holy Shroud of Turin, Father," I said.

"With that one exception," Fr Duddleswell added black with rage, realizing I had inadvertently demolished his strongest argument.

"Our Foundress is to be erased from memory so that you can make a few pounds profit."

"Mother Superior," exclaimed her protagonist, "you do me dishonor. I am not doing this for money. 'Tis for the sake of art."

"Our Foundress is to be erased from memory," repeated Mother Stephen inexorably, "so that pagans may gape at a secular landscape."

Put like that, Fr Duddleswell's aim sounded decidedly heathen: "I have no choice, then, Mother," he said.

"None whatsoever."

"I mean, Mother, since we cannot agree on who owns the picture, nor on what to do with it..."

"*You* cannot agree," interrupted Mother Stephen.

"But *you can*?" asked Fr Duddleswell, puzzled.

"I agree with what Christ has spoken through me."

Fr Duddleswell preferred to ignore Christ's intervention

on this occasion. "As I was saying, Mother, I have no choice but to submit the case to the highest authority."

"To God?"

"To the Bishop."

"Then, Fr Duddleswell, I give you ample warning. I intend to inform the sisters and orphans of your irreligious purposes. I will tell them you have, like a pagan, thrust both feet through the portrait of Mother Foundress. And I shall put them under obedience to bombard heaven with their entreaties until we have restored unto us our most treasured possession."

As we left, full of undigested food, Fr Duddleswell belched and said to me, "Talk about bringing in the big battalions."

"D'you think," I asked, "that the Lord who loves little children can refuse the petitions of his darlin' little ones?"

A week later, the four of us reassembled at Bishop's House. This time we were mercifully spared tea.

"Dear Father and Mother," said Bishop O'Reilly, as if he were beginning a letter to his parents. "I have read very carefully the submissions both of you have sent to me. And now, with all the authority of office invested in me by Christ"—I was interested to know whether Christ was about to contradict Himself—"I have come to this prayerful and irrevocable decision. That picture—so dear to all of us for diverse reasons—must be accounted the heritage of the whole diocese. I, as Christ's representative, will do with it as He Himself would wish. And now, if you would care to kneel, I will give you all my apostolic blessing."

The interview lasted approximately thirty seconds. Never before had I been so vividly aware that the imparting of information is a minor function of language. Stripped of its theological finery, the Bishop's contribution amounted to this: "Hello. A curse on both your houses. I'm the boss. The picture's mine. I will do what the hell I like with it. Good riddance and the devil go with you."

All of us, the Bishop included, knew that's what he meant;

but obedience forbade us to voice any objection.

As we prepared to leave, the Mother Superior asked the Bishop for "a word in private, my Lord," which he granted.

Outside in the street, Fr Duddleswell was fuming. "She broke the rules," he complained.

"Not of her Order?"

"The rules of common decency," he said. "Now I have to figure out for meself what she is up to."

But he didn't succeed in that. He consoled himself by venting his feelings about the Bishop by means of a loud rendering of the song of the King of the Penzance Pirates:

> Many a king on a first-class throne,
> If he wants to call his throne his own,
> Must manage somehow to get through
> More dirty work than ever *I* do.

It was barely four weeks later when Fr Duddleswell came tearing up to my study. "Fred Dobie's just phoned," he said. "He told me to look in today's *Times*. I went out and bought it. *See*."

He spread out an inner page of *The Times* on my desk, and there was a large reproduction of "A Recently Discovered Tichat." Underneath, there was a learned article about Tichat's influence on van Gogh and the early Impressionists. Finally, a note that the picture, put up by a private dealer (name unknown), was to be auctioned at Ritzie's the following day.

Fr Duddleswell was ecstatic with relief and joy. "So the Bishop did not listen to old Sourpuss, after all."

I needed no persuasion to go along with Fr Duddleswell to Ritzie's for the auction. I must confess that the picture disappointed me. The restoration was masterly; it was hard to tell where the canvas had been rent. But the picture itself seemed to me to be swathed in mist; not at all precise and photographic in the way I liked.

"'Tis a beaut," sighed Fr Duddleswell, ogling it, "'tis a gem, a masterpiece."

"And," said Fred Dobie, resting his chin on Fr Duddleswell's shoulder, "in five minutes it'll be mine."

I was astonished at the speed with which the bidding rose from its reserved starting price of 4,000 guineas to 9,000. Then, in no more time than it took the Bishop to send us packing, the bidding ended. Fred, with barely a twitch of a moustache, had purchased the Tichat.

"It's not all mine," he said modestly. "I'm buying for a consortium in which I've got a stake. Shouldn't be surprised if, in three years time, we sell it for double or treble."

I realized later that it was this last phrase that wriggled into Fr Duddleswell's conscience like a worm into an apple.

"A cheque for 2,000 guineas!" exclaimed Fr Duddleswell. He flagged it in front of my eyes at breakfast.

"This is becoming quite a habit, Father," I said. "From the Bishop?" I had noticed the envelope bore the Bishop's crest, "*In Medio Semper.*"

He nodded. "'Tis a token gift from the proceeds of the auction."

"It'll help in the rebuilding of the church hall."

Fr Duddleswell didn't reply at once, but at length he said, "I will have to hand it over to the good sisters."

"Must you?"

"It struck me at the auction that there was more than a granule of veracity in what Mother Stephen said. The sisters would have revered the portrait of their Foundress. Instead, 'tis disappeared for ever, and mercenaries like Fred Dobie and his associates have acquired the Tichat. *They* only appreciate it for the profit 'twill bring. There would have been far more beauty in the sisters' eyes than ever these dealers will find in Tichat. I am afraid, Father Neil, I have allowed me aesthetic sense to overcome me love of our holy religion."

"How can you say that, Father? As a good priest should, you left the decision to the Bishop; and he chose to give the work of art to the nation, to posterity."

"Perhaps Bishop O'Reilly is short on faith, too, Father

Neil. Could it be that he, like Fred Dobie, was only out to make a pretty penny? He sold the Tichat for 9,000 guineas. What if he had it restored for two thousand and gave me another two? By my reckoning, he has picked up a cool 5,000 guineas merely by talking to a dealer on the telephone."

"Could be."

"The least we can do, Father Neil, is to hand over this cheque to Mother Stephen. 'Twill console her to know that, though Mother Foundress died fifty years ago, she is still working overtime in heaven raising money to support an orphanage."

After telephoning the convent, he told me the bad tidings: it was to be a tea again in the nuns' parlor that very afternoon.

Once more we were bowed into the spotless reception room. The first thing to greet us was the portrait of Mother Foundress in the place of honor above the fireplace.

"It's impossible!" I gasped. "Look, Father, there's where your feet went through it."

"I have heard of experts removing icons *in toto* when one has been painted on top of another but..." he smiled knowingly, "I have never known 'em transfer a rip in the canvas before."

Just then Mother Stephen knocked and entered, followed by two young sisters who carried in the tea table set for two. This time, as the sisters left, they bowed reverently towards the portrait of Mère Magdalène.

"No Sister Bursar today, Mother?" asked Fr Duddleswell archly.

"Not disposed, Father."

"Does that mean 'unwell' or 'told not to come'?"

"I thought, Father, it *might* make her unwell if she came."

"Mother," said Fr Duddleswell, as we all took our places, "I was wanting to hand you this cheque the Bishop sent me to atone, in so far as I can, for the loss of your beloved portrait."

My head was in a whirl. The portrait was patently hanging in its gilded frame above the fireplace.

"I have signed the cheque on the back, Mother, so you can

put it straight into the convent's account."

"No, Father."

"I assure you, Mother, my one aim in all this was to preserve an art treasure for the world. But I am thinking now that perhaps you were right and I was wrong." Holding out the cheque to her, he said, "Please, take it, Mother."

"No need, Father."

From the folds of her habit she produced a cheque for the same amount.

"Snap!" I said involuntarily.

"I think, Mother," said Fr Duddleswell apologizing for me, "we are making Fr Boyd indisposed." Mother Stephen actually smiled, wolfishly. "May I tell him, Mother?"

Mother Stephen gave her consent with a nod.

"That portrait up there is a copy, you follow?"

"The only copy of the original in existence," put in Mother Stephen.

"'Tis exact down to every detail," went on Fr Duddleswell, "even to showing signs of me pagan footprints. But," turning to Mother Stephen, "why did you ask the Bishop to have *them* included?"

"Not to perpetuate your crime, Father, I assure you. But, you see, I did carry out my threat to tell the sisters and the children what happened...."

"That tear is the authentic touch, you mean, Mother."

"Exactly. Things were made easier for me because the older sisters haven't seen the original for years, and their memories are none too good. The younger sisters have never seen it at all. But all of them, the children too, are convinced that their prayers brought Mother Foundress back to us."

"And her face," I ventured to say, "is still preserved for all posterity."

"You express yourself so nicely, Father," said Mother Stephen, not reprimanding me this time for opening my mouth. "Further, Fr Duddleswell, our 2,000 guineas are going towards the beatification process of Mère Magdalène. With that amount of backing, God's grace can hardly fail."

"A very good investment," I said, hovering on the brink of sarcasm. I was thinking that for 2000 guineas I could get Fr Duddleswell canonized while he was still alive.

"A very good investment," I said, hovering on the brink of sarcasm.

"It is, Father," replied Mother Stephen. "It'll mean more vocations for our Order and more sisters to look after orphans all over the world."

I felt properly put in my place.

Fr Duddleswell said, "If the Bishop paid 1,000 guineas for this copy..."

"It's the most expensive fake in the business," I said.

"And 2,000 guineas apiece to Mother Stephen and me," Fr Duddleswell continued, "then after the fee for restoration he only left 2,000 for himself. I have maligned him."

"He is less than half the scoundrel you took him for," I said.

"Now, Fathers," interrupted Mother Stephen, assertively, "shall we take tea?"

She drew up a chair for herself and, carefully seated with her back to Mother Foundress, she produced from the labyrinthine folds of her habit an enormous tea cup.

Back at the presbytery, Fr Duddleswell coaxed me into his study. "Delightful, sensitive lady, that Mother Superior." A burp brought him to his senses.

I said, "No need to swear, Father," just as I noticed a large brown-paper parcel on his desk.

Mrs Pring entered with her broom. As Fr Duddleswell cut the string and began to remove the wrapping, she told us, "It came by Post Office van."

Fr Duddleswell, snowy-faced, held up a second portrait of Mère Magdalène, indistinguishable from the first.

"A present from the Bishop?" I cried.

Fr Duddleswell shook his head and proceeded slowly to read the attached letter. "Monsier le Curé... Dear Father... It's from the Mother General in Aix-en-Provence. She thanks me cordially for all the help I am giving her Order and the orphans and...she states there were in fact five portraits done of the dead Mère Magdalène at the one 'sitting'—and...and would I like another?" He looked up, his mouth agape. "D'you reckon that old crow at the convent knew all along her picture was not the only original in existence?"

He handed the picture to me while he picked up the phone and dialled a number. For a moment I thought he was going to have words immediately with Mother Stephen.

"Fred? Fr Duddleswell here. Just to let you know I think we may have acquired another Tichat...You heard me. Another Tichat."

In her curiosity, Mrs Pring came closer to examine the picture in detail. She tripped on the carpet and her broom went through the canvas. She herself ended flat on the floor like a plate of porridge.

Fr Duddleswell raised his eyes to heaven but his mind and heart were in the other place. "Hell!" he yelled before he could contain himself. "Forgive me, Fred, I was just saying safe home to a fallen woman...Yes, Fred, by the most ugly of coincidences this one, too, has a whopping great hole in it."

11

THE DOOMSDAY CHAIR .

It was a chance remark of mine that turned the breakfast conversation to the topic of superstition.

"It says in today's paper, Father, that a Church of England vicar doesn't believe in the fires of Hell."

"Then," said Fr Duddleswell, slitting open a letter as though it were an infidel's throat, "I hope he has made provision in his will to be buried in asbestos underwear." He nodded to Mrs Pring at the end of the table. "A cut of bread, if you would be so kind. Ah, yes, Father Neil, 'tis always the absence of faith that leads to superstition."

Mrs Pring, her bread knife poised, said, "The Irish are superstitious enough."

"Incredible as it may seem, there is something in what the lady says. In me parents' home-town in County Cork..."

"Will one slice do?" interrupted Mrs Pring.

"Two," and he proceeded to direct her hand with his wagging index finger. "Thicker, please. That way the butter ration goes further." He signified approval of her efforts. "Yes," he went on. "In County Cork, now there was a superstition among some that if a dog bit you, you should take a hair from his tail and 'twould heal the wound forthwith."

Mrs Pring was putting the bread on his plate. She touched his head, pretended to claim a hair and gave me a wink.

"Insurance against an attack of rabies," she said.

"A feebleminded feller, name of Seamus Crowe," Fr Duddleswell proceeded, "was one day accidentally scratched by a huge, thin mongrel. A *gentle* dog was Rover," he emphasized, "but something of a cross between a Great Dane and the Eiffel Tower. 'Twas but a wee scratch on the leg. Even so, Seamus pulled a hair from Rover's tail."

Instead of continuing his story, Fr Duddleswell crammed his mouth with toast. "So much for *that* superstition," he concluded.

"It didn't heal the scratch?" I asked.

"I have no idea. But I do know that afterwards, Seamus Crowe had to make do with four fingers on his right hand."

"I don't suppose there's much superstition round here, Father."

"The usual dependence of the weak-minded, Father Neil," he replied with a glance at Mrs Pring, "women mostly, on mascots, mediums and fortunetelling."

"There's one gentleman not far from here," growled Mrs Pring, "who thinks he's God."

Fr Duddleswell took no notice. "Many who would not dream of coming to church decorate the dashboards and windscreens of their cars with St Christopher medals."

"Don't you?" challenged Mrs Pring.

"Of course, woman. But I believe in St Christopher."

"And they don't, I suppose."

"Certainly they do not. They expect a little bit of unconsecrated metal to assist them," he said, starting to shake the salt shaker over his fried egg. "Whereas I rely on the intercession of the saint himself with . . . God Almighty!" The last words were more an expostulation than the conclusion of a sentence. The top of the salt shaker had come off and there on his plate was a pillar of salt as big as Lot's wife. "Woman," he exclaimed, "I have told you a thousand times to well screw the top of that salt shaker."

"You're not superstitious, I suppose," said Mrs Pring unperturbed.

Fr Duddleswell took a pinch of salt with his right hand and threw it over his left shoulder where Mrs Pring happened to be standing. "Indeed, I am not."

Mrs Pring dusted the white crystals from her dress and apron. "You read your horoscope every day, you can't deny it."

"Only to find out how marvellously mistaken 'tis. You, now, get St Vitus's Dance if even a stray black cat enters the house lest death should enter with it."

I went on munching, not very involved, until Mrs Pring, obviously riled, said, "What about The Doomsday Chair, then?"

Fr Duddleswell put down his fork and leaned on his elbow. "The age of persecution is not over by any means, Father Neil."

Mrs Pring explained for my benefit that The Doomsday Chair was a chair in the local public house, The Pig And Whistle. Legend had it that whoever sat on it would die very shortly thereafter.

The parish priest sighed and shifted to his other elbow for support.

"Is there anything in it?" I asked.

"As much," said Fr Duddleswell, "as you would find with a microscope inside that lady's head. 'Tis all dreamed up by the publican, Fred Bowlby. His wife Eileen is a darlin'. She always appreciates a visit, by the way. But Fred is another who would do well to invest in a fireproof shroud." With that satisfying observation he resumed eating.

"I thought," sniffed Mrs Pring, "that Jesus was the friend of publicans."

Out of the corner of a crammed mouth, Fr Duddleswell managed to joke, "The friend of tight men and loose women, eh?"

Mrs Pring didn't let go. "Last Saint Patrick's Day, Father Neil, Fred Bowlby issued a public invitation. Any Irishman who wanted to, was free to sit on his Chair. Including Fr D."

Fr Duddleswell didn't care much for my asking whether he had accepted or not. "I would not be seen dead in Bowlby's pub, you follow?"

"That's the truth of it," jumped in Mrs Pring. "He was afraid he'd die. So everyone said, 'If the Catholic priest at St Jude's is scared out of his wits, there must be something to that Doomsday Chair.' The legend grew because of his Reverence's superstition."

Once more, Fr Duddleswell put down his knife and fork. His voice was soft but there was menace in it. "I...am...not...superstitious."

Mrs Pring turned to address me. "Do you know, every time he sees a ladder he *has* to walk under it."

The tiger broke loose in him. "Woman," he roared, banging the table, "I am not superstitious, I tell you!"

The shock wave was considerable. Lot's wife jumped a foot in the air with most of what was on the table. A mirror fell from its nail on the wall and smashed into a thousand pieces on the sideboard.

A stunned silence ensued.

Mrs Pring, without stirring, whispered, "Fr D, you broke that mirror without even looking in it."

"Seven years bad luck," he retorted in the same reverential tone, "after herself has been with me twenty years already."

At ten o'clock that same morning I was banging the black, brass-knockered side door of The Pig And Whistle.

A tense, red-eyed, middle-aged lady, smartly dressed, opened up. She no sooner saw me than she relaxed into a smile. "The new assistant. I've seen you at Mass, Father."

Soon we were seated at a small table in the well-kept public bar, sipping tea and nibbling biscuits. Several tables were already set out for lunch. I had an over-all impression of large bow-windows, gleaming mahogany, polished brass, hundreds of upturned glasses, coloured bottles of spirits hanging downwards like so many udders from the shelving behind the bar. The air was heavy, smelling slightly stale and sour.

"My Fred's still in bed, Father," Mrs Bowlby said apologetically. "The Pig And Whistle keeps us up very late at nights."

I smiled understandingly.

"Another cup of tea, Father?"

I pointed to my collar. "I'm full up to here, Mrs Bowlby."

"And so am I, Father," she said in a choking voice, as she reached for her handkerchief.

"Have I said something to upset you, Mrs Bowlby?"

"No, no, Father." She dried her eyes. "Forgive me. It's just that I'm fed up to the teeth with... with that Doomsday Chair."

Without looking, she thumbed across the floor of the bar. Between the piano and dartboard was a cane chair. It had a gold cushion on it and was chained and padlocked to a fixture on the wall. On the cross-section of the back-rest was a silver plaque inscribed with the words: THE DOOMSDAY CHAIR.

"Time and again," said Mrs Bowlby, "I've asked my Fred to get rid of it. He even sells models of it. Look." There were a dozen wooden models on the bar counter. "Five shillings each. He says the Chair is good for business."

"Is it?"

"It does draw in hundreds of tourists a year," she conceded. "Americans mostly. They come to see the Crown Jewels and *that*."

She was in such a highly-strung state I tried to comfort her. "Is there any harm in that?"

"Precisely my sentiments."

The voice belonged to the publican who had made his way, very quietly for such a burly man, into the bar. He was wearing a loose pink shirt and baggy tweed trousers. The trousers were supported by a broad leather belt studded with badges and from the belt dangled a large bunch of keys. He was holding his tea mug. "Fred Bowlby," he said in introduction, "you must be..."

"The new curate at St Jude's, Fr Boyd."

"Eileen's told me about you. Made quite a hit with the ladies, so I believe."

"Take no notice, Father," said Mrs Bowlby, "he has no respect for the cloth."

Fred started to pour himself a mug of tea. "Come to see The Doomsday Chair, have you, Father?"

Mrs Bowlby rose immediately and hurried out clutching her handkerchief. Her back was shaking as if she were in tears.

"Are you off, then, love?" But she was already out of hearing. Fred turned to me. "She takes it hard, Father. But you Catholics are a superstitious lot, aren't you? What with your medals and statues and incense and dressing up like Masons and kneeling in front of bits of bread."

"Mr Bowlby," I said, raising my fist, "we are *not* superstitious." Remembering only too well the effect of Fr Duddleswell's fist on the breakfast table, I brought mine down soundlessly beside the teapot.

"You do realize, Fr Boyd," Fred said, testing the warmth and texture of the tea on his tongue, "Catholic superstition well nigh ruined the beginning of my marriage. Know what my wife made me do all through our honeymoon?"

That question revealed at once Fred's talent for and delight in double-meanings.

"No," I gulped.

"I thought it was odd at the time, mind, but"—he gave me a knowing wink—"well, you're a man of the world, when you're newly wed you'll go to any lengths to please the little woman. That's why Eileen and me spent all our time in...churches." The last word, beautifully timed, brought a self-satisfied smirk to his flabby face.

"Rome," he went on, when he had recovered from his own joke. "The Holy Year it was. And in St Peter's Basilica was this big, black, horrible-looking statue of St Peter. The foot was worn smooth by kisses."

"Italians are very passionate," I told him, determined to hold my own.

"Eileen said, 'For my sake, Fred, give it a kiss.'" Fred nodded amusedly several times. "Like a coalman's boot. 'Give it a kiss, Fred,' she says. A bleeding funny honeymoon, I can tell you."

"*I'm* laughing," I replied with a Stan Laurel face.

"As I bent down to kiss it, I slipped and my tooth went

181

clean through my bottom lip." He pulled the pink rim of it down to show me the actual site of the wound. "After that, Eileen had to do without. Kisses, I mean. It's all right, love, I said, I'm off to Lourdes next week for a cure."

"About this Chair."

"Come and see." As we walked across, he asked, "Care for something stronger?" I shook my head. "A glass of Holy Water?" He apologized before pointing to the Chair. "There she is, Father."

Above this harmless-looking Chair was a notice board on which were posted yellow newspaper photographs and press cuttings. I spied headlines like THE KILLER CHAIR and DEATH CHAIR'S LATEST VICTIM.

"When we took this pub over three years ago I found *her* in the cellar. Newspaper cuttings, too, which spoke of a Doomsday Chair. Anyone who sat on it died *inside the week*."

"Week?" I packed the word with scorn. "How childish. And that's the Chair, I presume?"

His answer surprised me. "Dunno, to be honest. Maybe it is, maybe it isn't. In the beginning, it never occurred to me there was anything haunted about that Chair because," he said sarcastically, "I'm not that way inclined. I even threw the cuttings in the fire. Then to jog business along in a slack period I got the Chair out, gave it a lick and a polish, and stuck it in the public bar where you see it today."

He broke off from his story. "Sure you won't have a snifter?" When I shook my head, "You might need it." I let him see he wasn't impressing me any.

"Well, then, Father, for fun I called it The Doomsday Chair. The locals came in, eyed it suspiciously and asked me why I called it that. I told them whoever sits on it dies inside a week and, hell—begging your pardon, Father—not one of them dared sit on the flaming thing. 'A free drink,' I said, 'to any chap who plonks himself down on my old cane chair.' And know what?"

"Surprise me."

"No one would."

"You said you threw away the press cuttings."

"Oh, those," Fred said, pointing to the notice board, "those are new ones. I tell you. A year or so ago, a posh, redfaced city gent came in here. Six o'clock of a thirsty evening, the whole place bursting at the seams. 'I'm not afraid of that nonsense,' he said. And he sat down *there*."

Good for him, I wanted to say, but didn't.

"'Called your bluff, he has, Fred,' all my clients laughed. 'Give the brave bloke a pint.' 'Why not?' I said. 'He'll be stiffer'n his rolled umbrella inside a week.' *Well*."

"Well?"

"One sip of his pint of best bitter, he puts his glass carefully on the table. And drops dead on the spot. Right where you're standing."

"A heart attack," I suggested, moving slightly to one side.

"No sign of one before, mind."

"From Beer To Eternity, so to speak."

That took Fred off his guard. "Very jovial," was all he could manage.

"Came to a bitter end," I said.

"Ha, ha, Father. Must store up these little witticisms for my grandchildren. But," he turned solemn, "such a waste."

"Married with kids, you mean?"

"No, I was thinking of the rest of his beer. No one would finish it for him. Next," he went on, "a Jehovah's Witness. Came in screeching 'Godlessness, Superstition!'"

I said I agreed with him.

"But so do I," said Fred, touching his heart. "He sat down on it and wouldn't even take a pint for his pains."

"And that didn't put a stop to it?"

"Nah, well, it wouldn't, would it? He caught a plane to a big Witnesses' Convention in Miami six days later and it sort of...crashed."

"All killed."

Fred nodded delightedly. "It never made the headlines, though, till the third victim."

I could feel my Adam's apple rise and fall quite painfully.

"Charlie Skinner, a regular, should have known better. Folks used to say, if ever Charlie has a post-mortem they won't find a trace of blood in his alcohol. So, there was Charlie soaking his back teeth for two hours, one double Scotch chasing another down the tunnel, and, I suppose, he sat down without realizing."

I swallowed hard.

"After that, not one of his mates would lend him a hand. Charlie staggered to his feet, went out to his car and drove straight in the river. Only three feet deep and Charlie six feet two." Fred Bowlby wiped his eyes with the back of a hairy hand. "Drowned."

"Ironic," I said.

"*Very*," returned Fred, cheerful all of a sudden. "Normally, he didn't take water with his whiskey. His car was a write-off."

"So was Charlie," I said.

"And the Coroner's verdict?"

"Dead drunk."

The smartness of my reply made Fred say admiringly, "You beat me to it."

He leaned over the plaque of the Chair, breathed on it and polished it with his sleeve. "My pride and joy, Father." He touched his belt. "I had a special silver lock made for it. Keep the key in my belt here, day and night. Unnecessary, really. No thief is going to break into this pub. Not with the Chair there."

When I asked for an explanation of the unusual events, Fred feigned surprise. As far as he was concerned there was nothing to explain. A matter of a weak heart, a faulty airplane engine and a crowd of idiots too superstitious to help a drunk home because of what might happen to him—and so it did. After that, The Pig And Whistle did rather well. There were newspaper articles, the B.B.C. did a television feature. Orders for the model chairs came from as far afield as Japan, Tibet and places Fred had never heard of.

I tentatively put it to Fred that he was trading on people's credulity.

"Course I am," he agreed. "It's up to religious experts like you and your chief to get rid of credulity, isn't it? And you don't seem to be having much success, if my wife is anything to go by."

His mercenary and cocky attitude so roused me I responded with what he took to be a trial of strength. "Mr Bowlby, have *you* ever sat on it?"

"No." He saw me chuckle drily. "Not what you're thinking, Father. Cross my heart, the Chair doesn't scare me. But if I did sit on it, I'd have to admit it to my customers, wouldn't I? And I'd be living proof my Doomsday Chair is a dud. Bad for pounds, shillings and pints."

I nodded, only half convinced.

"I challenged your Fr Duddleswell to sit on it. Offered him a hundred quid." I started at that and he noticed. "Oh, he didn't tell you that, then? But he was too superstitious."

Once more I was obliged to defend Fr Duddleswell's honour.

"Okay," said Fred. "Tell him, I repeat my offer. A hundred quid. Any old time. More, if he sits on it—and survives—I'll sit on it myself." This tickled his fancy. "Safest bet I ever made," he laughed.

It was getting to me that I had bitten off more than I could chew. I glanced at my watch. "I'll have to be going."

"Before you vanish, Fr Boyd."

I turned back. "Yes?"

"Care to try it out yourself?"

"I'm sorry," I stuttered, "I don't know what you mean."

"Have I said something clever?" he leered. "You're not superstitious, you said. Besides, I bet old Duddleswell would bury you for free."

I was still searching desperately for some slender theological reason for not availing myself of his hospitality when Mrs Bowlby's voice pierced the silence.

"Fred! What *are* you up to? You're not trying to get our nice Fr Boyd to sit on that dreadful thing. You're not to, do you hear? *Not* to."

She stamped her foot and fled from the bar in tears.

"Catholics!" Fred said, winking at me. "My offer's still on." He gestured to the Chair. "Be my guest."

I returned to the rectory too shaken to continue my rounds. Why was I so scared to sit on an innocuous cane chair? What was I scared of? As a Christian and a priest I shouldn't be afraid of martyrdom, but what possible danger was involved in the case of The Doomsday Chair? Perhaps it was my duty to go straight back and sit on it. Perhaps it wasn't.

Fr Duddleswell was in his study. "You visited The Pig And Whistle, you say, Father Neil. You saw it, then."

I nodded casually. "A load of codswollop," I said. "Didn't believe a word of it."

"In *my* parish," Fr Duddleswell snorted. "Under this"—he tapped the offended organ—"very nose. Eileen, Fred's wife, has not had a decent night's sleep in months for worry."

As nonchalantly as I could, I volunteered the news that Fred Bowlby had offered to let me sit on the Chair.

"He *what*?" exploded Fr Duddleswell. "Were I not a man of God I would give him a thick lip." He clenched his right fist in front of his face to show the instrument he would do it with.

"I think St Peter feels the same way about him, Father."

"Well, did you, Father Neil?" I answered his look of concern with a shy shake of the head. After a moment, he asked, "As a point of interest, *why* didn't you?"

I cleared my throat and pointed to my chest. "I forgot to pin on my St Christopher medal this morning."

Instead of splitting his sides with laughter, Fr Duddleswell slowly raised and lowered his large head. "Very wise of you, Father Neil. *Very* wise."

I was so embarrassed I gave him a piece of information I had resolved to keep to myself. "He repeated the challenge he made *you*, Father."

Fr Duddleswell clasped his hands together as if in prayer and closed his eyes. He came out of his trance to say determinedly:

"The elastic of me patience has just snapped. I am resolved

to put a stop to Fred Bowlby's caper once and for all. 'Tis me duty as parish priest, you follow?" I pursed my lips in encouragement. "Very soon, Father Neil, I will have that proud turkey cock going down on his benders and kissing me feet."

Breakfast time, a few days later. I asked Mrs Pring why she wasn't serving bacon and eggs, the usual Saturday morning fare.

"No point in frying up for one," she replied. "I don't eat it and his Unholiness has been off his food for a whole week."

Just then, Fr Duddleswell entered, grunted, said his grace and sank down in his chair. He looked very tired, I thought, as though he had spent the whole night praying. Three tufts of cotton wool on his face covered the spots where his razor had slipped.

If he had prayed a lot, it hadn't done anything for his mood. "Where to God," he asked, "is me blessèd bacon and eggs?"

"Ran out of eggs," said Mrs Pring.

"Ran out of eggs," he said. "Any one would think she lays the perishing things."

As Mrs Pring left, clucking like a hen, he followed her with the words, "That woman is about as useful as a bicycle without wheels."

Then he turned his attention to what was on offer. He sipped his coffee. "Stone cold! What sort of a breakfast is this, then, dead coffee and"—pointing to the toast—"cremated bread?" He sighed deeply and composed himself. "Me humble apologies, Father Neil. This morning I'm feeling miserable as sin."

"Not sleep well, Father?"

"Had some difficulty slippin' over the border, that's all."

I grunted in sympathy.

Suddenly he put his cup down with a crash and looked at me solemnly. "Keep after supper free this evening, lad." I nodded. "Prepare tomorrow's sermon early."

I waited for further enlightenment.

"I have thought and prayed for a whole week now. 'Tis about time I rooted out this wretched superstition of The Doomsday Chair." He crammed his mouth with toast. Then, dramatically: "Even if it kills me."

During evening confessions, my mind kept returning to The Doomsday Chair and wondering what Fr Duddleswell was up to. After an unusually quiet and strained meal he told me to get ready for the road.

I stepped out of my cassock, put on my jacket and coat and went to join him in his study. The door was open. I found him kneeling on his prie-dieu, which faced the wall, gazing at a crucifix.

"Father," he whispered, "not my will but Thine be done. But do not let it hurt, Lord, do not let it . . ."

Glimpsing me over his shoulder, he coughed and rose. I apologized for interrupting his devotions. "I was just putting in a good word for meself," he said. As I held out his jacket for him, he was saying, "I am expecting your full support, Father Neil."

"The Pig And Whistle, Father?"

"Aye. You are no yellow-belly." I smiled at the thought. "You are not one of those priests who are all words and have no faith at all." Another wan smile. "You do want to come, of course?"

I was afraid. I desperately wanted to say "No," but I hadn't the courage to be a coward. "Yes," I said, "I'm coming."

"Friend of me inmost heart," he said with relief. "I knew I had only to drop the slightest hint and you would follow me to the death."

It was almost eight o'clock. The High Street, after a heavy day's trading, was carpeted with refuse: cardboard, orange peel, empty cigarette cartons. News vendors were still calling out, "*Star, News* and *Standard*, paper-late," and red buses were charging angrily up and down like armourplated cavalry.

Without a moment's hesitation, Fr Duddleswell pushed

open the pub door. There were not too many patrons in at the time. A pianist was dreamily playing "Galway Bay."

Fr Duddleswell nudged me. "'Tis a most beautiful hymn, Father Neil, but beseech the organist to rest his fingers awhile till I'm done." Fortunately, the pianist stopped of his own accord.

Gradually word went round the pub that they had company. Even the hardened pub-crawlers must have sensed that something unusual was in the air if two parsons were breathing it; and the chatter and clinking of glasses abated until only Fred's voice was audible.

The landlord was standing, arms akimbo, facing The Doomsday Chair and explaining its history to a man who was wearing a kind of stetson.

"Straight up," Fred insisted. "The Governor of California wrote me only last week to ask if he could borrow it. To execute criminals, I believe."

"Gosh, is that so?"

"Cheaper in the long run than electricity."

"Guess it is."

"Make me an offer, go on," said Fred. "Nothing less than half a million. Pounds, naturally."

Fr Duddleswell and I threaded through the silent throng to the bar behind which Mrs Bowlby and a well-built platinum blonde were operating. Fr Duddleswell picked up one of the model chairs from the counter.

"That'll be five shilling, please, sir," said the blonde innocently.

My parish priest withered her with a glance, grabbed a bar chair and walked to where Fred Bowlby was standing, frowning now, beside the American tourist. There he set the chair down, stood on it rather shakily and turned, white-faced and trembling, towards the crowd. He clapped his hands, unnecessarily, for silence.

"Me dear Brethr..." He corrected himself. "Gentlemen...and ladies. Ladies and gentlemen. Your attention, please."

At this, Paddy, one of our more notable parishioners,

stepped forward, none too steady on his feet. He wore a three-piece suit and a trilby so far back on his head it looked as if it was trying to escape. Each time he said "Father" he touched his forelock.

"Can I buy ye a drink, Father?"

"Not now, Paddy," said Fr Duddleswell. Then a thought struck him. "And why have I not seen you at Mass these last few Sundays?"

"You didn't notice me because probably I was praying with my eyes closed, Father."

Fr Duddleswell straightened himself and addressed the crowd. "Now, why should I, a Catholic priest, dare cross the sacred threshold of The Pig And Whistle?"

Paddy craned his neck. "Father, what're ye doin' here for heaven's sake?"

"'Tis because," called out Fr Duddleswell, "I am concerned for the pagan practice being perpetrated in this pub. He who sows the wind"—here Paddy burped loudly on cue—"shall reap the whirlwind."

"I'll be communicating tomorrow for sure, Father," said Paddy.

Fred Bowlby attempted to intervene with "Couldn't we talk this over, Father, in the back room?"

"I refer of course, ladies and gentlemen, to The Doomsday Chair, so-called. In lieu of anyone better qualified, 'tis up to me, the Lord's unworthy servant, to undertake this task meself."

Fred tried again. "Fr Duddleswell..."

"The very same," said Fr Duddleswell mischievously, as if he had just been formally introduced to Fred's customers.

"Father, Father," said Paddy, twice touching his forelock. "Keep away from that Chair, else tomorrow you'll be saying a Requiem Mass for the repose of your own soul."

Fr Duddleswell lifted his voice again. "Fred Bowlby has generously offered me one hundred pounds if I dare sit on this miserable Chair."

"I'm upping the offer," Fred proclaimed out of the blue.

"Two hundred pounds." That really impressed his regulars. "Provided," he added, "that you *don't* sit on it."

When the murmurs of the crowd subsided, Paddy was heard to mutter, "That'd buy me enough of the hard stuff to retire on," and Fr Duddleswell announced gleefully, "Fred is afraid, y'see, that I will prove the curse of this Chair is but a confidence trick and 'twill ruin his trade."

"Never!" cried Fred. "I don't want you to die, that's all."

"I am about to sit on it, all the same. This very hour. And at the same hour each evening till one week from now."

I had called out "Hear, hear," before I realized how silly it sounded.

"At the end of the week," Fr Duddleswell said, "I will claim the Chair for me very own. Agreed. Fred Bowlby?"

Fred said that if Fr Duddleswell were alive in a week's time the Chair wouldn't be any good to him, so he didn't care who owned it.

Just then, the clock struck eight and Fr Duddleswell stepped down from his temporary pulpit. The patrons of the pub, having retreated to a safe distance, could all see him as he—rather dramatically for my taste—made a huge, wind-sweeping sign of the cross and hovered over the Chair before dropping down into it.

There were a few loud sighs, a slight shuffling of feet but no other sound until Fr Duddleswell, in his lordliest sanctuary manner, called out:

"A drink, Eileen, if you would be so kind."

"What'll it be, Father?" Mrs Bowlby's hoarse voice returned.

"What have you got?"

A few sniggers greeted this innocent query but, for the most part, the customers were aware of being in the presence of greatness.

Mrs Bowlby said, "Will a pint of dark ale do, Father?"

"Make it a half." He didn't drink beer normally. "A *small* half."

As Mrs Bowlby brought him his drink, a bulb flashed as a

local press photographer—forewarned, I had no doubt—took a picture, then five more of Fr Duddleswell enthroned on The Doomsday Chair, serenely partaking of a small half of ale.

He drained his glass in silence. As he rose he must have slipped in a puddle of beer because he landed flat on his back with a thud. Strangely, the crowd in the bar shuffled backwards like startled horses instead of forward, as was natural in view of the plight of a fellow human being. Only Paddy stood his ground, his faith sorely tried. "Jesus, Mary and Joseph," he said, "one half of ale and the holy Father is fallen over drunk. Call a priest to hear his confession."

With real concern I rushed to Fr Duddleswell's assistance. "You all right, Father?"

He rose to his feet and adjusted his hat. "'Tis only the divil doin' his darndest." And he handed me the fractured remains of the model chair. Next, he put his hand inside his jacket. When he withdrew it, I saw the palm was bright red.

"You're bleeding badly, Father," I cried out, much to the consternation of the bystanders.

Fr Duddleswell took my arm and whispered in my ear. "Get me out of here quick, Father Neil, I have broken something vital to me."

"What, Father?"

He winked broadly. "Me red felt pen."

I supported him as he walked to the door, bidding everyone adieu. "Until the same time tomorrow," he said.

"A good dose of absolution, Father," advised Paddy, "and sleep it off."

"Good night to you, gentlemen *and* ladies."

Outside the pub, his first words to me were, "I hope to God I have not fatally bruised me spine, like, or spiked me lungs with a couple of broken ribs."

"You were superb."

"Wasn't I, just?" After a couple of minutes walking in silence, he slanted his head towards me and said, "D'you know, that was one of the greatest ordeals of me life. I really *detest* dark ale."

True to his word, Fr Duddleswell returned Sunday night and Monday. Nothing seemed to disturb his peace of mind. I had never seen such tranquillity in a man who was, in the general estimation, destined to leave us soon. I was more than proud to be under the tutelage of this man of faith who could laugh in the teeth of death.

Walking the streets with him was like striding alongside Elijah who defeated the prophets of Baal, or Christ who drove the money-changers out of the Temple, or St Paul who stopped the trafficking in idols at the temple of Diana of Ephesus, or even dear old St Patrick himself who drove all the snakes out of Ireland into England.

Mrs Pring knew no such serenity. She blamed herself for initiating the whole horrible course of events. "Father Neil," she confided, "only two days and nights of this and I'm a nervous wreck. Even if Fr D survives, I won't. Can't you at least keep him indoors?"

"Not a hope," I said. Nor was there. I had offered to take Communion to the sick on his beat and to do his hospital rounds for him. All these offers he sweetly refused as if he couldn't see any reason for me to put myself out.

I tried by many ingenious means to keep him in, in case he should be knocked down by an infidel lorry driver or assaulted by some lunatic set on notoriety. But I noticed no change at all in his demeanor or in any of his daily habits.

To console Mrs Pring I told her I was accompanying him everywhere. "Not," I insisted, "that he seems to have a care in the world."

"His face is buttercupped and daisied all right," she said, and we both spoke in admiration of "the faith of the man."

Mrs Pring held up a large rosary. "I'm knitting the rosary for his Reverence three times a day."

Just then Fr Duddleswell came in. He immediately went across to her. "Me dear old friend," he murmured. "What's this?" he said, holding up her hand which was still holding the rosary. "Saying your beads. Truly wonderful. But promise me one thing, dear Mrs Pring."

"Anything, Father."

"Promise you will not pray for me." He smiled ever so tenderly. "Things are bad enough already."

On Wednesday evening at The Pig And Whistle, Fr Duddleswell was vested in cassock, cotta and biretta. To a piano accompaniment, he conducted the growing crowd in singing "Faith of our Fathers."

With the final duplication of "We will be true to thee till death," Paddy almost collapsed in tears. "I never thought," he moaned, "to hear such a beautiful tune in a pub."

Fr Duddleswell, aloft, said:

"I have been holding a holy service here for four evenings already." He paused to thank Mrs Bowlby for handing him his pint. "And now," he went on. "'tis about time I introduced you to the most Catholic thing there is."

Paddy held up his froth-topped glass. "Guiness, Father."

"No irreverence from you, Paddy Shea. Not Guiness, neither is it the shamrock, nor the Blessed Virgin, nor even the Pope of Rome himself. While I risk me life once more, me devoted assistant will show you"—here he removed the green wrapping—"a Catholic collecting plate."

He sat down to drink while I was forced to move among the customers like a soldier in the Salvation Army.

Friday was a day of sparkling sunshine. Fr Duddleswell insisted on going for his morning constitutional. He stopped at the end of a line of sycamore trees to watch the sun twinkling through the leaves and stippling the grey pavement with burnished gold.

"Such beauty, Father Neil," he sighed, "such intolerable beauty. There are but two ways to look at the things of this world: as if 'twere the first time and . . . as if 'twere the last." But his face wore no obituary blackness when he said it.

Further on, he stopped in his tracks to ask, "D'you find me a very attractive person, Father Neil."

"I do, Father," I affirmed. "But what do you mean?"

"You seem to enjoy me company more than most." He had obviously twigged as to why I never let him out of my sight.

Throughout the walk, as was now customary, people greeted him with, "Pleased to see you, Father," and "Glad to know you're in the pink." Even from inhabitants not normally concerned for the welfare of the clergy came, "All the best, mate."

One dear old lady said, "Keeping well, Father?" "Fit as a circus flea." "Stay well-wrapped up, Father," she urged, though the temperature was in the eighties. When we were out of earshot, he said, "Anyone would think I was a kiddy's Christmas present."

A most unsavoury character drifted into view: a tramp. "'Ello, mate," he croaked, grasping Fr Duddleswell's hand. "May I shake your 'and?"

Since he had no choice, Fr Duddleswell said, "Yes, mate."

The encounter lasted but a few seconds, then the tramp broke it off with a fervent, "Best wishes to you, mate." He had obviously got wind of the risks my parish priest was running.

"That was the very first time," Fr Duddleswell whispered, "that I have ever *touched* a tramp."

"Unhygienic," I said. "I only hope he hasn't given you anything."

"Ah, but he has." Fr Duddleswell opened his palm to reveal a half crown.

Then he did the most foolish thing I ever saw. Without looking, he stepped off the curb in the path of oncoming traffic. The tramp's generosity must have dulled his senses. Three or four vehicles screeched to a violent halt. A small red van in particular stopped within three inches of him. Only the driver's superb reflexes prevented a fatal accident.

The van driver put his head out and yelled, "You bleedin' fool. What d'ya think...?" He had recognized the man who had almost upped his insurance premium for the rest of his life. "Fr Duddleswell?"

Fr Duddleswell, as unconcerned as if he had just watched a leaf fall from a tree, walked to the side of the cabin. "Yes, mate? This is a strange place for you to ask for me autograph, in the middle of a busy thoroughfare."

The driver, quietly and in a different tone of voice, said "Bleedin' fool" again, wound up his window and drove off.

I ran to Fr Duddleswell to escort him safely across the road. On the other side, he said:

"When I have bought the Friday fish for Mrs Pring, we shall go to the church, Father Neil, to thank God for that driver's narrow escape."

"*His* escape?"

"Indeed. He will probably never know how close I came to punching his bloody nose."

It was then that the awful truth dawned on me. So great was his faith that sitting on The Doomsday Chair, far from making him fear for his life, had made him feel invulnerable. Now I was really worried.

Mrs Pring had reached the limits of anxiety long before. She was testing all the food she laid before him lest it be poisoned and regularly checking the gas appliances in case death, in its hunger for the parish priest, should devour two more victims.

"I can't go on," Mrs Pring confessed on Friday evening. "I can't eat or sleep. I can't even cook." She promised she would never again accuse Fr D of being superstitious if only I got him to stop.

The consolation I gave was immediately taken away by Fr Duddleswell himself. He came in carrying in his arms and stroking a black cat.

"I just found this little feller wandering around the garden like a lost soul. D'you think, Mrs Pring, you could spare him a saucerful of milk?"

It was a remarkable week and, speaking for myself, a sleepless one. On Tuesday, *The Kenworthy Gazette* brought out a special edition to cover the story. By Wednesday, the telephone was ringing nonstop and, next day, it was national news. Pictures of Fr Duddleswell seated on The Doomsday Chair appeared in the tabloids.

On Saturday morning, Fr Duddleswell's Mass was better attended than if the Sovereign Pontiff had been celebrating it. Even the Sicilians were there. Spying them from the sacristy, he said to me, as he plunged his head in his chasuble. "*Dio mio*, Almighty God works in mysterious wayses."

It was probably on the spur of this Sicilian moment that he announced after Mass:

"Tomorrow, holy Mass at nine will be a Requiem for the repose of the souls of three good citizens who died a natural death after parking their backsides on a perfectly harmless Chair."

Before lunch, I was in his study. There was a tremendous bustle and a sense of excitement in the air. I heard him answer the phone.

"*The Express*, you say? Yes, the finale is at The Pig And Whistle this evening at eight. Of course you can send a photographer along." He smarted up his hair and eyebrows as if in readiness. "God bless, now."

"Another batch of newspaper cuttings and telegrams," I said, holding them up.

"Not too many with black edges, I'm hoping, Father Neil."

Mrs Pring came in to announce, "Three more reporters at the front."

"Not now, Mrs Pring. Tell 'em I will be holding a press conference tomorrow afternoon, even if I have to rise from the dead for it."

Mrs Pring checked a tear and went out as the phone rang again.

"Fr Duddleswell. And who the divil is it this time?... Bishop O'Reilly? Yes, me Lord... No, me Lord. I assure your Lordship there is no need to send an exorcist. 'Tis just a trivial instance of local superstition which I will deal with in the normal course of duty..."

When his hour of confessions was up that evening, there were still fifty or sixty penitents outside his box waiting to be shrived. I told them to go home because Father had to fortify himself with a meal.

At this point, he emerged from his confessional to say, "I will be here next week for sure," he went, head high, via the sacristy into the house.

A quiet meal. Neither of us was keen to speak. At the end, only: "Pray for me, Father Neil. And tell Mrs Pring to have faith for once in her miserable life and leave the holy oils in their rightful box."

Near the dining room door, Mrs Pring, already clad in her outdoor clothes, made it plain she wasn't going to wash up the dishes now or maybe *ever*. She was shaking like a leaf but determined to see this thing through.

The streets were lined as for a carnival. There were cheers and jeers and scattered applause, which he acknowledged as if he were "royalty or higher," as he put it. Tradesmen were selling gigantic balloons with Fr Duddleswell's face on them; there were three hot-dog stalls and, in a glance, I took in five ice-creams vans, probably with a new specialty: "Duddleswell's Delight." Policemen were controlling the traffic. Fr Duddleswell stopped to sign a dozen autographs.

At the entrance of the pub, the crowd parted respectfully to allow the two priests, with Mrs Pring in close attendance, to get through.

The bar was packed with customers, reporters and photographers. The pianist was giving a lively rendering of "Bless 'em all." While Fr Duddleswell was putting on his alb, stole and biretta I held Mrs Pring's hand for mutual comfort.

Fr Duddleswell was ready at last. He stood on a specially prepared platform and blew into the mike. A thoughtful patron, anticipating that the crowd would be of soccer proportions, had installed a loudspeaker system so that the overspill in the street could keep in touch with the proceedings.

Tongue-in-cheek, Fr Duddleswell thanked the publican for his generosity and the assembly for their patronage and prayers, without which he could not have endured the rigours of the week.

"But, as you perceive, ladies, gentlemen—and all you

kiddies outside"—there were cheers—"the superstition has not killed me. And I am about to kill *it*, through me absolute faith in Almighty God." More cheers. "First, though, a surprise for you. I have me own challenge to deliver the publican here."

Fred stepped forward. "Oh, yeah?"

"You promised, Fred Bowlby, that if I sat on that Chair, you would."

"Did I? Okay, after you."

Fr Duddleswell's mocking laughter, echoing like thunder, was much appreciated by the crowd. "He is still hoping I will die before me week is complete. Perhaps a sudden hemorrhage." Laughter. Or lightning from heaven." More laughter. "Or I will fall from this chair and break"—he staggered. "Whoops!"—he righted himself. "Break me neck." Cheers. "More likely I will die laughing." This brought the loudest laugh of all. "Fred Bowlby, I will give *you* a hundred pounds if you sit on that Chair *before* me week is up."

Fred squared his jaw. "Think I'm scared, do you?"

"I do."

"You're on." And without a moment's hesitation, Fred sat down on The Doomsday Chair. There was a ripple of applause before a dazed Fr Duddleswell said:

"You are braver, Fred Bowlby, than I gave you credit for."

"It's easy for me," replied Fred, "cos I'm not superstitious, see. Now we're evens."

"And I," sighed Fr Duddleswell, "who have borne the burden of the heat and the day do not even get the consolation of a hundred pounds. Only that blessèd Chair."

The clock struck eight. As he got down: "Eileen, fetch me me pint of ale."

Eileen was already on hand.

Fr Duddleswell blew on the froth and scattered it on the bystanders like holy water, so that Paddy and other Catholics present made the sign of the cross. With the microphone in one hand, the pint glass in the other, he sat down for the last time in The Doomsday Chair.

The applause was deafening. When it subsided, Fr

Duddleswell drank his brown ale into the mike as noisily as a cow. Then he stood up and shouted so the loudspeaker nearly burst the eardrums:

"Behold me name is Lazarus AND I LIVE!"

Spontaneously the crowd sang, "For he's a jolly good fellow," and afterwards there was more applause. When there was a semblance of silence, Fr Duddleswell turned to me and in a whisper magnified by the speaker said, "Now 'tis your turn, Father Neil."

I was shattered by this unexpected turn of events. "But, Father, I've no stomach for beer."

"You do not have to drink, lad. Just park your bum there like a good Christian."

Seeing the strength of my reluctance, he turned disgustedly to the publican's wife. "Come on, Eileen, if your husband has no objections.

"None at all," said Fred with a grin. "Never had any objections."

With a flourish, Eileen drew herself a short brandy from the bar and went to sit on the Chair which had caused her so many sleepless nights. More cheers.

And then Mrs Pring.

"What's yours?" asked Mrs Bowlby.

"A pink gin."

"There is no sin hidden," muttered Fr Duddleswell, "that will not be revealed."

Mrs Pring sat down and drained her glass in a gulp.

Shamed by the courage of the weaker sex, I belatedly took my life in my hands and sat down. Diluted applause was all I deserved.

"That's me boy," Fr Duddleswell said with a trace of irony. "Eileen, pull me curate a glass of orange juice, if you please. He will need it if he is soon to carry that Chair home for me."

Everybody seemed happy that evening except me. In the moment of his greatest need, after pledging my support, I had failed a man of God. As we walked home together, Fr Duddleswell, noticing my mood, said, "Pick your chin up off the ground and show a dimple, Father Neil. Your instincts were absolutely right."

"But the women," I began. "Mrs Pring..."

"Bone to the tips of their ears. You cannot blame 'em. Ever since Eve ate the apple, they have had no theological appreciation of the mystery of iniquity, if you're still with me."

"I'm a coward," I said, grovelling.

"It takes a brave man to admit it, Father Neil. But please take it from me, in my estimation, you are both manly *and* prudent."

He obviously couldn't see me shaking as I held The Doomsday Chair at arms' length.

I was only too relieved to reach his study and put the Chair down.

"'Tis all right, Father Neil," he said, "'tis defused." We sat opposite each other. "And now a wee confession."

I wasn't interested.

"'Tis a temptation that comes to us all."

"What is?"

"First of all, drink. A week past, I loathed the filthy stuff. And now." He licked his lips.

"What else, Father?"

"Pride without foundation."

"Father, let's stop sparring, shall we? You're brave and I'm not. You're a man of faith and I'm more of a heathen than Fred Bowlby will ever be."

Fr Duddleswell coughed with embarrassment. "Not at all, at all. I tell you this, now, to show how much more manly you are than I." I waited with growing curiosity. "I could not tell anyone before because, y'see, secrecy was of the essence."

I wasn't helping him any.

"Me little secret is, I never sat on The Doomsday Chair at all."

I blinked. Recalling how, in the Junior Seminary, we had coped with masters who used to paste our posterior, I asked,

"Do you mean you put the Holy Bible in the seat of your pants?"

"No, I mean I destroyed The Doomsday Chair before I sat on it."

This was his story. He had gone down the Portobello Road to look for a duplicate of The Doomsday Chair. He knew it wouldn't be difficult because he was quite an expert on furniture and the Chair was very ordinary. His task proved even easier than he had expected. He came across one straight away, in Tompkins. Only two pounds. He hid it in his garage till early last Saturday morning—"You will remember, Father Neil, how I was miserable as sin." He had entered into league with Mrs Bowlby, so on that Saturday morning at three o'clock, according to a pre-arranged plan, she had let him into The Pig and Whistle. She had borrowed the key to the padlock from the belt of her snoring spouse. She and Fr Duddleswell substituted the new chair, screwed the silver plaque onto the back-rest and replaced the gold cushion.

"It was all over in half an hour," he said.

My admiration for him—undiluted, if a fraction altered—made me enquire further: "But what did you do with the real Chair?"

He reddened. "I am not superstitious, mind, but I could not take any chances, like."

"Go on," I said, rising from the chair I was sitting in and settling myself comfortably in the replica of The Doomsday Chair.

"I took it to the bombsite in Ordnance Road."

"Then?"

He was reluctant to finish his story.

"First of all, I sprinkled it with holy water and spoke over it the exorcism from the Roman Ritual."

"To be on the safe side, like," I mimicked. He nodded. "But what did you *do* with it?"

"Broke it up. I could not burn it, you follow? It might have attracted attention at that hour of the morning."

"So?"

202

"I was intending to leave it among the rubble but I thought some kiddies from the district might be using that site as a playground and I did not want to risk them..." His voice had run into the sand.

Again I urged him to continue.

He coughed. "In the end, what could I do but take the full responsibility on meself? I brought it back here." He saw my look of alarm. "Take it easy, Father Neil. 'Tis quite safe, I tell you. By that time, it was after four, so knowing that you and Mrs Pring could sleep through the Last Trump, I went out into the garden." I'm sure there was a peculiar kind of terror in each of my bulging eyes. "And there," he went on, "I buried it in the soft earth beyond the distant hedge."

"I can see Mrs Pring having to do all the gardening in future," I managed to say.

He nodded. "Then on that awful, awful Saturday morning, I really felt more strongly than ever before there was something spooky about that Chair."

I knew what he was going to say.

"I uncovered Mrs Pring's Hoover."

My gasp of horror was genuine enough.

"What crank, d'you reckon, Father Neil, would want to bury a brand new Hoover at the bottom of our yard?"

A knock on the door relieved me of the necessity of hazarding a guess. In came Mrs Pring. "Your humble servant, Fr Duddleswell," she said, curtseying by the door. Beneath the gentle surface mockery, the admiration showed. "Shouldn't be surprised if you see the century out, God help us. But you *are* marvellous."

"Have I ever denied it?" he replied. He indicated the Chair. "For you, Mrs Pring."

I vacated it and made a gesture of offering it to her.

"Really, Father? For my kitchen?" He nodded. "Oh, thank you. By the way, I nearly forgot. A visitor for you. He walked me home."

From behind her, Fred appeared. His whole demeanor was altered. He looked humble.

"Come to kiss me feet, Fred Bowlby?"

"In a manner of speaking, Fr Duddleswell."

When Mrs Pring had left to wash up, Fr Duddleswell said curtly, "No, you cannot have it back. I have just given it to Madame Tussaud for her chamber of horrors."

Fred said, "That's not The Doomsday Chair."

"How did you..." began Fr Duddleswell. "I mean, what d'you mean?"

Fred went as red as a poppy. "Well, Father, as you know I'm not..."

"Superstitious," I said in anticipation.

Fred nodded. "But after Charlie Skinner got drowned three months back I decided to get rid of it. In case somebody else—you, for instance—accidentally died on it and I was had up for manslaughter."

"So?" encouraged Fr Duddleswell.

"So I found another just like it."

"In the Portobello Road." Fr Duddleswell wasn't asking but telling.

"How did you know?"

"The obvious place to look."

"Only cost me a couple of quid," said Fred.

"In Tompkins," I said.

"Yeah." Fred was more mystified than ever.

"Where else?" I said, pleased to regain a bit of self-respect.

"I put it in place of the real one," Fred continued. "Didn't even tell the wife. Too proud to, I suppose."

Fr Duddleswell's brain was working faster than mine. "What did you do with the 'real' one, Fred?"

"I would have preferred to bury it in the garden but Eileen's a keen gardener." He blushed again. "So I took it back."

"To Tompkins?" I gasped, edging away from the Chair.

"Yeah. Told 'em it didn't suit the decor of my place. Sold it back to 'em for one pound ten." He shuffled his feet. "I only came to say, Fr Duddleswell, that though you didn't sit on my Doomsday Chair, you thought you did. That's the main thing, isn't it?"

Fr Duddleswell was muttering, "I don't know, I don't know."

"You're the brave one, not me, Father. Well, I didn't mean to, but I stole your thunder a bit tonight and I hadn't the heart to steal your hundred quid as well. So *here*." He handed over a thick wad of notes. "Now I'll leave you in peace." He turned to go and since neither of us stirred, he said, "Don't bother. I'll let myself out."

Fr Duddleswell collapsed in his armchair, ashen-faced. "Leave me in peace? he says. I nearly bloody-well massacre meself six or seven times over and that dirty double-crosser says he will leave me in peace."

"What shall we do with that *thing*, now?" I asked. "Take it back to Tompkins?"

"And do the cowardly thing like Fred Bowlby? Never! I will coax herself to let me have it back from her kitchen for fifty pounds. Meanwhile, Father Neil, grab a spade and start digging another bloody great hole in the garden."

12

MY FIRST
BAPTISM

"That uproarious wretch, that blighted black-eyed potato of a woman." Fr Duddleswell was performing on the landing.

"What's up?" I said, poking my head round my study door.

"Me keys," he snapped, his blue eyes frothing behind his steel-rimmed spectacles. "Can I find me keys? Indeed I cannot. Mrs Pring has filched them from me dresser, and neither she nor the blessed St Anthony has any idea where she has deposited them."

I took one look at him and said, "You've tried your pockets, Father?"

"Is it an idiot you think I...?" He was busy scratching the smooth outer skin of his cassock like an itchy monkey. "In me pockets?" he asked now only half in scorn. "Me pockets, you say?" His hand had settled around a bulky something in his bottom left pocket. He slowly brought the keys into the light of day. "That accursèd daughter of Eve," he muttered, "has she not hidden 'em in the recesses of me very own pocket?" He suddenly yelled down the staircase. "Mrs Pring!"

Unhurriedly our plump, white-haired Mrs Pring appeared at the foot of the stairs, clasping a broom like a crosier. "You've found them, then," she said. "I'll get the choir to sing the *Te Deum* in thanksgiving."

"'Twas not meself that found them," came thundering back at her, "but Father Neil."

"And *where* did he find them?"

"Does it at all matter, woman, where he found them, seeing as he found them?"

Mrs Pring suggested none too politely that they had never been missing.

"Woman," he cried, "I will not have you coming at me with a full udder of incivility. Now, I am asking you, could Father Neil have found them if they were never lost? Father Neil," he bellowed in my direction, "would you be so kind as to inform this lady who is astray of her wits that you ..."

But I retreated into my study to let them sort out for themselves who was to blame for losing Fr Duddleswell's enormous bunch of keys in his cassock pocket.

I settled down again and opened my breviary but I was in no mood for praying. I preferred that October morning to take stock of my career thus far at St Jude's.

Four crowded months had passed since I first presented myself at the rectory door to be greeted by Mrs Pring and the uncertain sound of Gilbert and Sullivan coming from Fr Duddleswell's hand-cranked gramophone. I was at that time, I recalled with a smile, as green and helpless as a pea straight from the pod.

By now I was used to hearing confessions and no longer feared I would forget the formula of absolution in the middle. Preaching, while not a pleasure, had ceased to be a torment. I enjoyed taking Holy Communion to the elderly and the bed-ridden, and they were always genuinely pleased to see me.

It wasn't so bad visiting people in their homes once I was inside. There was always a moment just before I knocked or rang when the devil put it into my heart to wonder whether I should call again some other day. I was particularly daunted by three old tenement buildings known locally as Stonehenge in the middle of my patch. They had no lights and no lifts. Most of the stone steps were chipped or broken and they smelled of carbolic or worse. Often there were no numbers on the doors. I had to take pot-luck, whisper "Come Holy Ghost," and hope to God I had come to the right place. It never mattered. Non-Catholics were invariably polite to "the cloth" and keen to redirect me to where lapsed Catholics were hiding out. Sometimes I was sure they were zealous in helping me find my lost sheep out of spite. I was relieved, I admit, whenever I received no answer. The Lord could not accuse me of not trying even if the results of my labors were negative.

Continuing the habit of years I exchanged letters with my mother every couple of weeks. The family were well. My salary was only £40 a year—Fr Duddleswell paid me for the first quarter in half-crowns—but this was supplemented by Mass stipends, which at five shillings a time and sometimes more brought in another £2 a week. There were other sources of income, too. At St Jude's there had recently been several weddings, a funeral, and a dozen baptisms. Fr Duddleswell had officiated at all of them but he had "shared out the proceeds," called stole-fees. He did not mention how he divided them, but my portion was so generous I never doubted that he gave me half. Board and lodging were free, and I was able for the first time in my life to send an occasional postal order to my younger brothers and sisters who were still at school. I missed them, especially on bank holidays when there was nothing for me to do and nowhere to go.

There were other gains besides my new-found affluence. I had my very own radio. Though it was an old three-valve model and crackled as if it were permanently on short-wave, it did enable me to listen to the news and find out what was happening in the world. In the seminary, I was not allowed a newspaper or magazine, except *The Catholic Herald*. I had read only half a dozen novels in my life. Their contents were far too trivial and worldly for one with his sights on eternal things.

The greatest gain at St Jude's was living alongside Fr Duddleswell and Mrs Pring. My parish priest, who claimed to be "as old as a bog mist," had taught me the value of discretion. "Open wide your heart, Father Neil," was his advice, "but fasten down the shutters of your mind. Should you turn your head inside-out in front of the good people, where is the use? 'Twill only worry and confuse them, and have they not enough complications in their lives already, like?" As for Mrs Pring, she was a staunch ally and showed in a hundred quiet ways she cared for me. Their altercations seldom involved me and the intensity of them, I sensed, was an index of their mutual regard.

I was even developing a fondness for urban life. After years of being surrounded by rolling hills, trees, tractors, and grazing cows, the town, particularly our district of Fairwater, had not initially appealed to me. It was by comparison noisy, dusty, and congested. Greys predominated instead of greens. The wide sweep of the sky was foreshortened and broken up by T.V. aerials and chimney tops. At any rate, I was now able to find my way around. I knew the names of the streets and was beginning to recognize some of the faces of those who walked them. In spite of the coolness creeping into the October air and the premature yellowing of the leaves on the city trees I was content.

Ahead of me stretched the calmest months of the Church's year. No Lenten fast. No long Holy Week services. Only Advent as we prepared for the coming of the Lord. Then Christmas itself, the season of peace and good will.

There was a rap on my door. "May the divil tear you from the hearse in front of all the funeral." Fr Duddleswell was not addressing me. He was concluding his conversation with Mrs Pring over the disappearance of his keys.

Flushed with what he took for victory, he laughed, "I have had quite enough of *her* babblement. That female would quarrel with her own two shins." He settled down to tell me how pleased he was to see me "coming out like a flower." To broaden the scope of my apostolate, he had arranged a christening for me on the following Sunday.

"Jimmy and Jeannie Dobbs are the parents, Father Neil. Good practicing Catholics. Ditto the godparents. Nothing could be easier. And by the by, Father Neil, one important consideration."

"Yes, Father?"

"Do not be so foolish as to leave your keys unchaperoned in this house. There is a lady tolerated here who has a propensity to conceal 'em in places no reasonable creature would pretend to look." His eye had a lost, far-away look. "Have I not just purchased her another vacuum cleaner, and she plays a trick on me like that." He shook his head in secret despair. "Ah, but it conflaberates me marvellously to see her standing idly, by nearly swallowing herself with a yawn."

Soon after he had gone, "conflaberated," I could hear him exclaim, "Will you stop acting the maggot, woman, and start fisting that broom around yon filthy floor." And Mrs Pring's stout reply: "I'll put your request on the long finger, Fr D."

I took my commission as a sign of Fr Duddleswell's growing confidence in me. I opened up my *Roman Ritual* to remind myself of my duties.

"Nothing could be easier," he had said, and on the face of it he was right. If only my previous experience of christening was not limited to pouring water over the head of a doll under the somnolent eye of the professor of moral theology in my last year at the seminary.

Canon Flynn had taught us that baptism is not valid if anything is used but "water for washing." I remembered his emphasis on that phrase. "Not liquids made up of water," he said, "which people do not normally use for washing. Not tea, therefore, nor coffee, neither beer nor lemonade."

I took it for granted that Fr Duddleswell did not allow such beverages in his font.

As Sunday afternoon approached, my chief concern was to pronounce the baptismal formula while actually pouring water over the head. Simultaneity of words and action was essential for validity. I kept wishing I had had more time to practice on that doll.

One thing I was determined to do: read the formula from the book. According to Canon Flynn, it was only too easy after a while to repeat in Latin the confessional form, "I absolve you" instead of the baptismal form, "I baptize you."

After Sunday lunch, Fr Duddleswell said, "Make sure you put all the details in the book: names of the child, parents, and godparents. And write legibly, Father Neil, not like Dr Daley making out a prescription for mumps."

These seemed matters of small consequence in the light of other disasters I could think of.

The christening was a relaxed family affair. Paul John Dobbs, three weeks old, was blue-eyed and as bald as a new

210

lamb of the Flock should be. I read the vital words "I baptize you in the name of the Father and of the Son and of the Holy Ghost" while pouring over him a liquid no Devil's Advocate would dare suggest was anything but Adam's ale. The baby did not cry at any stage of the ceremony, not even when I put "the salt of wisdom" on his tongue or poured autumnal water on his shiny head.

Afterwards, I filled in the baptism register in capitals. As I closed the book, Mr Pickles, the godfather, coughed and greased my palm with a pound note. I congratulated myself on the fact that everything had passed off better than I could have wished.

It was with a light heart that I accepted an invitation to the christening party at 1 Pimms Road, close by the railway junction.

The reception was as uncomplicated as the baptism itself. There was tea, cucumber sandwiches, and trifle. The new Christian was lying asleep in his cradle next to the settee. When after half an hour he awoke, Mrs Dobbs, a sturdy north country girl and former teacher, picked him up. She dipped her fingers in a square-shaped jar and started rubbing his head.

That was when my worries began.

I edged my way over to where Mrs Dobbs was sitting. "What are you doing?" I asked as casually as I could.

"Rubbing his scalp, Father. A trick my mother taught me."

"What with?"

"Vaseline. My mother swears it strengthens the roots."

I did not want to know what vaseline was supposed to do because of the sudden fear of what it had already done. Vaseline was waterproof. What if the baptismal water had not touched the baby's head at all? Trembling, I said, "Do you do that often, Mrs Dobbs?"

"Three times a day at least, Father."

"This morning, too?"

She nodded, tickled by my interest in the number of times she rubbed her child's head with vaseline. I swigged my tea, blindly shook a circle of hands, and said goodbye.

"Please come again soon, won't you, Father," said Mrs Dobbs. It was an invitation for which I had reason subsequently to be grateful.

I walked the sound-proof Sunday afternoon streets wrestling with the overwhelming problem posed by that vaseline. I was beginning to understand how Canon Flynn's national reputation as a moralist had been won. He had warned us repeatedly that many mothers saturate their babies' heads with creams, oils, lotions.

"Take care," he had said, "that the water flows over the child's scalp. Not merely the hair. Hair is composed of dead cells and is only doubtfully identifiable with the living child. See to it that there's no protective coating of cream on his head otherwise"—one of his rare jokes—"it might protect him from becoming a Christian."

The sacrament of baptism, I reflected, is a sign of washing. Unless the water *flows* and *washes* the body, there is no sacramental sign and so no cleansing of the soul. God has a right, I have to admit, to lay down certain requirements for salvation. His demands are not harsh but his ministers, especially after six years of preparation, have their part to play. What if I have sent away a pagan instead of a Christian from the font?

Madly I switched from self-pity to self-loathing and back. My mother used to say that when a baby cries at a christening it is only the devil going out of him. An old wives' tale. Still, how I wished Paul had screamed blue murder at the font.

Surely God was not so arbitrary or cruel as to deprive a child of the grace of baptism because a fond mother had spread a film of vaseline on his head? Yet I had heard of a child being killed on a level-crossing while his mother was pushing him to church to be christened. No Catholic theologian, as far as I knew, had ever suggested that the poor little mite could get to Heaven. The consensus was that the child was borne to Limbo, care of British Railways. Why, then, had the Church discarded the earliest and by far the safest method of baptism—immersion?

"Mighty pleased I am to see you taking the air, Father Neil."

It was Fr Duddleswell on a late afternoon stroll after his siesta. He was sporting the kind of floppy, broad-brimmed hat that artists wear. Would he be able to read the guilt written in capitals on my face?

"Hope I did not interrupt your meditation, like?"

I shook my head and agreed to walk with him to the embankment. Soon, with our backs to the line of trees, we were leaning on the black wall overlooking the rust-coloured waters of the Thames. Beyond, on the south side, were wharves and cranes and tall chimneys spewing out grey smoke. I brought the conversation round to baptism by handing over the stole-free for the christening. To accept any part of it would be to add crookedness to incompetence.

"How did it go this afternoon, Father Neil?" Before I could answer, he said, "And tell me, now, did you write all the details clearly in the register?"

I assured him of that. It set his mind at rest. How trivial the concerns and quiet the soul of the seasoned campaigner.

"Funny thing, Father," I began.

"What is that?"

"Baptism. Making a Christian with a few words and less than half a pint of water."

"Unless a man be born again of water and the Holy Ghost," he replied, quoting Jesus' words to Nicodemus. "John's Gospel, chapter three, verse five. Our Blessed Lord's disciples must all have been baptized, saving His holy Mother naturally who was conceived without original sin."

I put it to him that other Christians are not as careful as Catholics in administering the sacrament.

"The eastern Orthodox are," he insisted. "But I agree with you, not the Protestants. To start with, I do not think three-quarters of them believe in original sin. And—you will not credit this, mind—but it has come to me ears that our Anglican friend the Rev. Probble sometimes baptizes several babies at once. Sprinkles them. Not so much as a cat's lick. Well, you know how 'tis at the Asperges before High Mass. Not everyone is so fortunate as to get splashed in the eye. No matter. They are Christians already. Deprived of a few hundred days Indulgence they may be, but they can compensate for that by bowing their head at the Holy Name. But baptism, now, that is another kettle of fish altogether." His eyes swept over the Thames as though it were the Styx. "God alone knows how many innocent babes who die in infancy are deprived of the Beatific Vision because of the negligence of foreign clergymen."

I was not deriving any comfort from the conversation. "The river's high today," I said.

Undeterred, he continued, "If the water does not reach the body, where is the sacrament, Father Neil?"

I was too wounded to reply.

"D'you know," he went on, "I had not long ago a most untypical case." He paused to let a noisy barge go by. "There was this Spanish lass of seventeen summers came to me to get married. I told her: 'Write your parish priest in Barcelona, me darlin', for your baptism and confirmation certificates.' He sent back word of her confirmation but said all baptismal registers had been burned in the Civil War. I spoke to Bishop O'Reilly about her and he said, 'You will have to baptize her again conditionally to be on the safe side, like.' Well, God save us, Father Neil, I confides to meself, has not our microdot of a Bishop this time surpassed himself in caution. After all, the Señorita had received Holy Communion every Sunday for a score of years, had she not? But what d'you suppose, Father Neil?" I tried without success to keep my mind a blank. "Her mother owned up. Her daughter had been born just prior to the Red occupation. She was too terrified to have her baptized before and too negligent after."

"Baptism of desire," I suggested, clutching at a theological wisp too thin to be called a straw.

He agreed. "But think of the many graces and blessings she has been deprived of all her life. And what is more, her confirmation and all the Holy Communions were *invalid* because she was not even a baptized Christian."

Once more I tried to change the subject but failed.

"Give credit to the Bishop, Father Neil. Had we sailed ahead with the wedding without baptizing the Señorita, 'twould not have counted in the sight of God. Never would she have become a Señora and..."

I could see him visualizing a big brood of illegitimate Spanish babies filing by under the sad gaze of God the Almighty.

In the days that followed, my mind was preoccupied with the spiritual state of Paul John Dobbs. Why are souls invisible so you can't see what is going on in them? If I *had* failed in my first christening and if, God forbid, Paul died before the age of reason, he would be consigned to Limbo together with that unfortunate baby who was mowed down by a train.

Limbo, the Church teaches, is a place of perfect natural felicity. But it's not the same as Heaven where Paul's Catholic parents had every right to expect to find him when they eventually arrived. It was no consolation to me to know that my mistake would only be detected "on the other side."

The nights were terrible. I could not sleep. Inside my skull, at manic speed, I repeated a song from *Iolanthe* which, until then, I was not aware that I knew by heart.

> When you're lying awake with a dismal headache
> > And repose is tabooed by anxiety
> I conceive you may use any language you choose
> > To indulge in without impropriety
> For your brain is on fire, the bedclothes conspire
> > Of usual slumber to plunder you
> First your counterpane goes and uncovers your toes
> > And your sheet slips demurely from under you...

All the verses. In four seconds flat. At the same time, I kept telling myself that Paul was a perfectly healthy little boy. He was sure to survive to the age of seven and qualify for the baptism of desire. No Limbo for him, only the straight choice set before every grown-up soul of Heaven or Hell. On the debit side, I conceded he would be deprived of the Church's sacraments like Fr Duddleswell's Señorita. And there would be no intervention of the Bishop in his case to stop him becoming an unmarried husband and father.

Then came a night which I classified unhesitatingly as the worst of my life.

About one o'clock I took three sleeping tablets and drifted into a restless sleep. In my dream I saw Paul handsome and upright in his late teens. Not being a Señorita, he was able to enter a seminary. He was ordained a priest. It was invalid, of course. Due to my negligence he was still a pagan. I pictured him offering daily Mass, dispensing Communion, giving hundreds of absolutions—all of them invalid, too. I saw him anointing the dying. Many of these poor creatures, thinking quite reasonably, that Paul was a genuine priest, did not take the trouble to have sufficient contrition to merit final forgiveness of their sins. They ended up, surprised and aggrieved, in the wrong place where they cursed heatedly for ever and ever.

The irony was that the only sacrament Paul was able to administer validly was the one of which a film of vaseline had deprived him: baptism. Even laymen can baptize if they take proper care.

The depths were about to be plumbed. Paul, having been ordained, was consecrated bishop. Looking for all the world like Bishop O'Reilly, he handed on holy orders tirelessly, but his ordinations, unknown to anyone but God, did not "take." I saw in consequence hundreds of supposed priests dispensing hundreds of supposed sacraments year after year, century after century. In the diocese where Paul reigned there was a kind of huge, spiritual emptiness. No grace, no sacraments, no Christian hope. In that benighted place, the Catholic Church was no better off than the Church of England whose orders Leo XIII had solemnly declared in 1896 to be invalid.

I awoke in a sweat and with a fiercely pumping head, grateful that Paul had not gone on to become Pope. It was three o'clock. Certain that I would not sleep again that night, I stepped into my slippers and crept downstairs to the kitchen to make myself a cup of tea. While I was waiting for the kettle to boil, I thought I heard a click. In normal circumstances I would have had no difficulty in identifying it, but there was so much clamor inside my head I was not bothering about a tiny noise outside.

I was sitting at table about to sip my tea when I heard a car racing in the direction of the rectory. It screeched to a halt near the front door. From the hall came the sound of the bolts being hastily drawn and Fr Duddleswell's conspiratorial voice, "In there." Fast, heavy footfalls in the street, then in the hall. Next, the whole kitchen seemed suddenly to contract as it filled with uniformed men breathing heavily and mouthing obscenities to keep their spirits up.

As I sprang up, my right arm was gripped in a vice and pinioned behind my back. My head jerked back in a reflex action and thwacked my assailant somewhere about the face. He cried out in agony and released me. My relief was short-lived. Someone in front of me put the knee in, and I passed out.

I came round possibly a few seconds later in Mrs Pring's upholstered rocking chair. My eyes were watering, I felt sick, and I had difficulty in breathing.

Fr Duddleswell was pouring a cup of cold water over my bowed head and slapping my cheek. I was dimly aware that Mrs Pring, cold-creamed and curlered in her dressing gown, had joined a misty throng. She was assuring Fr Duddleswell that "poor Father Neil has been baptized already without you drenching him in my kitchen." She took over from him and placed smelling salts under my nose of such potency that they nearly lifted my head from my shoulders.

Gradually the haze began to clear. I made out two policemen. One was applying a cold compress to his colleague's eye. It was puffy and purple. I would have shown sympathy had I not been preoccupied with nausea and shooting pains in my infernal regions.

I heard Fr Duddleswell rambling on about new Hoovers and neighborhood thieves who did wicked things with them and Mrs Pring's obdurate tendency to mislay keys and to bolt the back door with a boiled carrot.

Mrs Pring soon set the room to rights and responded to Fr Duddleswell's request to "wet the tay" for all. She offered me three steaming cups in her three right hands. "You'll feel all the better, Father Neil, for pouring that down the red lane."

P.C. Winkworth, who had nearly bisected me, slowly undid the button of his tunic and took out a notebook. As he came into focus, I saw his cap was off. His straw hair stood on end, topping a brown furrowed face and a small red nose. His head looked like a pineapple with a cherry stuck on. Nodding towards Mrs Pring, he said to Fr Duddleswell, "Your Missis I take it, sir."

Fr Duddlewell swelled indignantly as he drew in his breath. "No, Constable, we only live together." He made haste to explain that Mrs Pring was his housekeeper and that while she had a good pair of shoulders underneath her head they did not so much as share an opinion or a tube of toothpaste.

"I see, sir. And your name, please, sir."

"Duddleswell. *Father* Duddleswell."

"Is that prefix some sort of title, sir?"

My parish priest explained carefully his central role in the community.

"And this young man, I take it, sir," the policeman said, indicating me, "is an associate of yours?"

"I have not me spectacles on me nose, Officer, but his features bear an uncanny resemblance to me curate."

"Am I to assume, sir," the policeman plodded on, "that you are not wanting to press charges?"

Fr Duddleswell looked at me sitting hunched up at the table clad in slippers and pajamas. He was obviously at a loss to know what he could charge me with except the misfortune of being his assistant. "No," he said generously. "If Father Neil is prepared to forget the incident, so am I."

"Well," went on P.C. Winkworth, "that makes it rather difficult for us, sir. You see, sir, Central Control logged your call. They ordered us to proceed here. They will also be able to ascertain from the state of P.C. Richards' eye that the young gentleman over there assaulted a police officer while resisting arrest."

It took my accuser ten minutes to accept that he had no legitimate cause to arrest a curate for sipping tea in his own kitchen even if he was responding to the invitation of the parish priest.

Eventually the two coppers left, one with head aloft dabbing at his eye. Mrs Pring thereupon started badgering Fr Duddleswell for not letting the curate make himself a cup of tea at night without dialling 999 and summoning the police. "Be careful, woman," he threatened, "for you are busy planting me with a mustard seed of wrath."

I slunk upstairs throbbing in more places than one. I was still miserable and yet, for no reason I could pin down, I found myself repeating the lines, "But the darkness has past, And it's daylight at last." As soon as my head hit the pillow, I fell into a dreamless sleep.

I awoke next morning at the usual time with a clear head and buoyant spirits, troubled only by a bruise below. I set about marshalling the facts.

It was not for me to turn my cranium inside out in front of the faithful. I could not go along to Mr and Mrs Dobbs and apologize for failing to baptize their infant. They had seen me do it. I could hardly expect them to appreciate the finer points of theology. Nor could I offer to rebaptize their son. That would be worse than a doctor re-inoculating a child because he had forgotten to put the serum in the first time.

"Poor Father Neil has been baptized already without you drenching him in my kitchen." Mrs Pring's words echoed in my mind. If *I* could be "re-baptized" in domestic surroundings, why not Paul John Dobbs? Fr Duddleswell had not scrupled to do that in the case of a little girl in Birmingham with far less justification than I now had. There was one important difference, of course. My baptism would be so private that even the parents themselves wouldn't know.

At breakfast, Fr Duddleswell tried to make light of "last evening's entertainment."

Mrs Pring brought him to a sharp halt with a special glower and went out.

"She will put a fat lip on her for a month of Sundays," he complained. "What can you expect of the unfair sex, Father Neil?" I smiled compliantly. "Always remember when arguing with a woman that conclusive evidence does not prove a thing." I promised to store away that pearl of wisdom. "I was but doing me duty as I saw it, like. No hard feelings?"

"No," I said, relieved that my problem was, in principle, resolved.

He squeezed my arm in gratitude. "May you live as long as a proverb, Father Neil."

On Thursday I went to Mrs Pring's kitchen for a morning cup of tea *and* to find out how long it takes a kettle of water to boil. I also picked a five-inch shrimpaste jar with a screw-on lid out of the dustbin.

As soon as Fr Duddleswell left for the day, I crept into his study and borrowed the keys to the baptistery.

In church there was an annoying stream of parishioners praying before the Blessed Sacrament. It was nearly an hour before I could unlock the baptistery gates and the padlock on the font without being seen. Begging the Lord's pardon, I filled my jar with oily water from the font. After lunch, I remained in my study until 2:30 praying that Mr Dobbs would be at work and Paul conveniently placed for christening.

"Please come in, Father," said Mrs Dobbs. "Surprised to see you so soon."

I was not sure whether this was a welcome or a rebuke for returning before my shadow was dry on the wall.

Paul was sleeping soundly in his cradle but to my dismay there was a neighbor present. Mrs Ivy Burns, a surly-looking creature, had not been invited to the christening. Her hair was tied up in a kerchief so it looked as if she was carrying a workman's lunch on her head. I got the impression she could jabber on all day.

To justify my visit I had bought Paul a christening gift. I handed Mrs Dobbs a paper bag with "Woolworths" in red on the outside.

Mrs Dobbs opened it up and took out a fire-engine. "Oh, you shouldn't have, Father."

"Bit young for it, ain't he?" croaked Mrs Burns, who was puffing away at her hand-rolled cigarette.

"It's for when he grows up," I said.

"Like a cup of tea, Father?" asked Mrs Dobbs kindly.

With Mrs Burns there my plan had misfired, and I was out of pocket for nothing. "No thank you. I've just had two large cups of coffee."

I am not by nature impolite, but it occurred to me that there was a way to get rid of the intruder: keep my mouth shut. Whenever I was addressed by either of the ladies I replied with a nod or a shake of the head while looking Ivy stolidly in the eyes. Something had to give. Mrs Burns surrendered and took her leave. I immediately came to life, wished her a very goodbye, and expressed the hope that our paths would cross again soon. Then I turned my attention to Paul's mother.

"Maybe I would, Mrs Dobbs."

"*Would*, Father?"

"I would like a cup of tea, after all."

"Good," she said. If she was puzzled by my strange behavior and sudden thirst she did not show it. "I'll join you. I'll put the kettle on."

I reckoned on having at least a minute while she was in the kitchen. As I stepped across to Paul's cradle I could hear Mrs Dobbs drawing water into the kettle. I had unscrewed the shrimpaste jar when Mrs Dobbs returned. I barely had time to thrust the jar into my left trouser pocket.

Mrs Dobbs, seeing me hovering and now cooing over her sleeping infant, came and stood beside me. In a whisper, she said, "Our pride and joy, Father."

"And rightly so," I returned, as I felt cold water streaming down my leg.

"We've been married a year now."

"Is he your first, then?" I asked, not immediately taking in what she had said and shaking my leg uneasily.

I bent down slightly over Paul's reclining figure and from there could see my black herring-bone trousers turning all glossy at the crotch and down one leg. I hoped my woollen sock would soak up the water. I didn't want Mrs Dobbs to have to tell her husband that the curate, besides insulting Ivy Burns, had relieved himself on the dining-room floor.

We stood there side by side gazing at Paul with widely differing emotions until a whistle from the kitchen signalled that the kettle was boiling.

"I'll make the tea, Father. Won't be long."

"Take as long as you like, Mrs Dobbs."

"Any biscuits?"

"Yes, lots, please."

"I'll bring the tin so you can help yourself."

My second and last chance. I took out the jar and was delighted to find it was still half-full. Bending down, I whiffed the faint baby-smell of ammonia. I rubbed a big patch of Paul's scalp with my handkerchief, then with unsteady hand poured what was left in the shrimpaste jar over it.

"*Paule, ego te baptizo* . . ." I managed to finish the formula but not before the new Christian gave irrefutable evidence that the devil had gone out of him. Never have I seen so much trouble on such a tiny face. So stupendous was the caterwauling he emitted that his mother, though weighed down with a large tea tray, came running.

Caught in that downward position I had no choice. I barely had a moment to wipe Paul's forehead, tuck the shrimpaste jar under the quilt, and take him in my arms. "I'm sorry, Mrs Dobbs," I said, "I must have disturbed him, so I picked him up."

Her surprise at seeing me grab and rock her pride and joy relaxed into a smile of approval at my evident fondness for him. "I'll put this tray down, Father, then I'll take him. He may be a bit wet and I don't want him to christen you." She blushed and apologized for her "slip of the tongue."

I handed Paul still bawling to his mother. He was transformed instantly into a whimpering bundle in her arms.

In essence, my mission was accomplished, but two problems remained. First, though the water spilt on Paul's bedding could easily be explained, I felt I ought to remove the shrimpaste jar. Only I or Ivy Burns could have put it there, and I couldn't see her taking the rap for me.

Second, I was sure Mrs Dobbs was bound to notice sooner or later the wet patch on my trousers, far too large for a month-old baby in water-proof pants to have made.

I would solve both problems at once. "Since you're holding the baby," I said, "why not let me pour?"

"That's very kind of you, Father."

I filled a cup, began to pass it to her, and "accidentally" spilt the contents on my vitals. "O my God!" I screamed, clutching myself immodestly in the spot where I was already wounded. Why hadn't I at least had the sense to put the milk in first?

My outburst roused Paul to fresh operatic heights. Mrs Dobbs, encircling him with one arm, proposed to fetch me a cloth from the kitchen.

In those precious seconds, through tears of pain, I retrieved the jar and returned it to my pocket.

Mrs Dobbs handed me a tea towel. I dabbed myself gently until the worst of the throbbing was over.

"Can I help in any way, Father?"

I said I didn't see how she could. She said she meant by calling a doctor or something.

"It's nothing, Mrs Dobbs, really. I'm maladroit, always doing careless things like this. I'm sure there won't even be a blister to speak of."

After we had mopped up, we sat down and quietly drank our tea.

"Biscuit, Father?"

There was no need to explain my reluctance to prolong my visit, but before I left I gave Paul my blessing and a light-hearted pat on his head for luck.

Ah, I murmured when I was in the street, who would have thought it was such a costly business turning pagans into Christians?

13

FEMME FATALE

I am no expert when it comes to jewelry but I couldn't help feeling that the rosary which the lady asked me to bless after Mass was strung with pearls. She thanked me in a quiet voice and handed me an envelope before threading her way through the emerging Sunday congregation. I watched her walk to a white Rolls Royce. As the chauffeur opened the door for her I glimpsed two white, well-groomed French poodles yapping excitedly on the rear seat.

I returned to my study before opening the envelope. It was pink, embossed, and scented. Inside was a £10 note.

Not knowing whether the reward for blessing a rosary was classed in the trade as a stole-fee, I put the matter to Fr Duddleswell. His immediate response was to rub his hands and say, "Miss Davenport is back."

Miss Davenport was the only child of a financier long dead. She had inherited everything and "everything," it appeared, was not a bad description of what she had inherited. The family business had continued to flourish because she took no interest in it. She was in the habit of passing each winter in a secluded Georgian house just over the border in the neighboring parish of All Saints. On the basis of past experience, her patronage of St Jude's was likely to be generous.

"We will have less difficulty paying our school's bill these next twelve months, Father Neil," Fr Duddleswell forecast, "provided we play our cards right. And for our part we can help this lady, too. Miss Davenport is—shall we say—a trifle whimsical. Promise me solemnly, now, that you will humor her."

Not knowing then the full nature of her eccentricities but liking the first of them I had met with, I gave him the assurance he sought. As to the money in the envelope, he said enigmatically that, all things considered, I was entitled to it this time.

That meeting on the church steps with Miss Davenport was the first of many. In the next two weeks, she appeared daily at Mass—always at my Mass, whether I was celebrating the 7:30 or 8:00. Afterwards, she came into the sacristy as I was unvesting to ask me to bless a medal or a picture of the Sacred Heart. Each time she handed me a pink scented envelope. Thoroughly embarrassed by now, I told her that the parish was very grateful for her support, and I would place her offering in the Poor Box.

I breathed again when no monetary reward followed the blessing of what looked like a jewel-encrusted dog-collar. Mrs Pring, though, had a wry comment when the local wine-merchant delivered a crate of half bottles of champagne to the rectory door marked "Urgent. For the attention of the Reverend Fr Boyd."

It was hard to escape the conclusion that Miss Davenport had taken a fancy to me. But how could I be sure? This might be one of the lady's whimsies which Fr Duddleswell had spoken about. When at Mass I turned round to face the congregation to say "*Dominus vobiscum*, The Lord be with you," my eyes were drawn to hers as if by a magnet. She seemed to glow with expectancy. She put me off my stride so much that I kept stumbling over the words of the Mass and losing my place in the Missal.

Until then, my sexual fantasies had taken the shape of being hotly pursued by dark and languorous females. They usually wore grass skirts, were garlanded with flowers, and had bare bosoms bumping up and down like bunches of grapes. Miss Davenport was hardly the kind of Judy whom Bishop O'Reilly had warned us against when he ordained us. She was less a temptation than a nuisance.

At a guess she was twenty-five years my senior. Fur-wrapped and affluent but flat-chested and not exactly beautiful. Her eyebrows, penciled thin and blue, gave a haloed appearance to those piercing brown eyes. There were lines on her forehead and down her neck, and her hair done up in a bun was streaked with grey. My conclusion was that it was silly and unfair to consider Miss Davenport some kind of *femme fatale* when, perhaps, she looked on me as a son.

True to my word, I handed over the envelopes to Fr Duddleswell who saw nothing incongruous in the scale of the offerings. His view was that if the good lady insisted on throwing her money around like snuff at a wake it was imperative that the right people should be there to gather it up. I was fast becoming a financial asset to St Jude's if nothing else.

One morning the telephone rang while Fr Duddleswell was giving me instructions for the day. He answered it, gagged the mouthpiece, and whispered, " 'Tis Miss Davenport for yourself, Father Neil."

She sounded distressed. Her pet canary was unwell. I asked her if she had called in a vet. Yes, a specialist from Harley Street was with him at this moment but what he really needed was a priest. I had so far spoken in ambiguous terms to spare Fr Duddleswell the bizarreness of the lady's conversation but there was no way to avoid asking, "You did say it's your *canary*, Miss Davenport?"

Fr Duddleswell was not in the slightest put out at hearing who was in need of my ministrations. "Tut, tut," he said softly, "poor little creature."

I advised Miss Davenport that if a Harley Street specialist was with him, her pet was in very capable hands. Fr Duddleswell signalled me to gag the receiver again before tapping my chest with his breviary and saying hoarsely, "Is it a cooking apple you have in there, you great Gazebo of a man?"

I gathered I was expected to accede to Miss Davenport's request. I momentarily rebelled and played one more card. "I'd be delighted to help, Miss Davenport"—Fr Duddleswell smirked—"but, you see, you live in All Saints' parish and really you ought to ask Monsignor Clarke to..."

Fr Duddleswell's shaky fist was promptly over the mouthpiece. "Jesus, Mary, and Joseph," he ground out, "tell the bloody lady you will bloody well be there in bloody double quick time."

I only hoped he had a sound-proofed hand. I relayed the message to Miss Davenport in milder terms and replaced the receiver.

All the time I was changing from cassock to jacket, walking down the stairs, putting on my bicycle clips, and wheeling out my bike, Fr Duddleswell was hovering over me, giving me a sermon on dropping once and for all this petty, trade union, demarcation-line mentality that was ruining the country and, instead, blessing the bloody canary and any other bloody thing necessary, as Jesus Himself would have done. I had never known him spit out so much blood.

I promised I would not disappoint the rich Miss Davenport and sped off as fast as two wheels would carry me.

The detached, white-pillared house was in a leafy square. It overlooked a small, fenced-in private park sparkling with well-watered grass on that bright October morning. I rested and padlocked my bicycle against the black wrought-iron railings next to a sign which said, "Le Casino."

A French maid wished me "Bonjour, mon père," and ushered me into the lounge where "Madame is anxiously attending you."

I was born an impressionist. I feel things but I do not always see them too clearly. I took in a Siamese cat sensually rubbing its side against heavy damask curtains. It was wearing the bejewelled collar I had blessed a few days before. I caught the distant barking of Miss Davenport's French poodles. I sensed I was in the presence of incongruous opulence. It reminded me of the set of a Molière play we had once put on at school.

Miss Davenport rose from her chesterfield where she had been reclining as she contemplated with damp eyes the canary in its gilded cage. With ringed hand, she set me beside her on the cool leather and took my hand. It was some time before she would give it back.

The symptom of the canary's sickness was that it refused every incitement to sing. "I have had him as a bosom companion," she murmured, "for quite six months, Fr Boyd, and never has he denied me this pleasure before."

"When did it...he..."

"Timmy is his name," she said, clasping my hand more tightly as though the name somehow bound us closer together.

"When did Timmy sing last, Miss Davenport?"

"Yesterday evening." She looked around her. "Did you not bring your vestments, Fr Boyd?" She explained that she was expecting me to pray for Timmy's recovery and give him my sacerdotal blessing.

Fortunately, I had taken Holy Communion to a sick person that morning before Mass and I still had a small stole, a bottle of holy water, and my *Ritual* in my pocket. Miss Davenport thanked me for coming prepared and reluctantly returned the hand she was holding to its owner.

I put on my stole, white side up, and thumbed rapidly through the *Ritual* in search of a suitable benediction. The closest parallel I could find in a hurry was the blessing of an airplane.

I raised my right hand over the little bird sitting sullenly on his perch and prepared to read the Latin formula.

"What is his name, Father?"

I was puzzled. "You just told me his name was Timmy, Miss Davenport. I'm not baptizing him..."

"No, he is baptized already, Father Boyd. I meant, what is Timmy's name in Latin so that I can recognize it when you utter it."

"*Timotheus.*" I was thankful that the canary had a simple

Christian name and that Miss Davenport's ignorance of Latin guaranteed she would not realize my prayer had been written with a weightier sky-traveller in mind. At random moments during the prayer, I slowed down to say "*Timotheus*" at which the kneeling Miss Davenport reverently bowed her head. At the end she said "Amen." Still no cheep from Timmy himself.

To complete the ceremony, I picked up the holy water sprinkler. It was simply a medicine bottle. The cork had been pierced to allow a few beads of water to escape when it was shaken over the sick. I aimed it at Timmy and began "*Benedicat te, Timotheus, omnipotens Deus...*" As I jerked the bottle, the cork flew out and a stream of water went in Timmy's eye. Before the blessing was finished, the canary was in full voice.

Miss Davenport was ecstatic at so sudden a cure. She sat down at her bureau twittering something about not needing to call in any longer that ineffectual "médecin" from Harley Street and writing out a check. She sealed it in a pink envelope and gave it to me "with boundless gratitude." "Do you love cats, too, Father Boyd?" was her final question.

"We dislike the same things," I replied diplomatically.

Outside the house, I was so incensed at being forced to make a fool of myself I tore up the envelope and stuffed the pieces in my back pocket. I cycled around town for half an hour, furious with Fr Duddleswell for casting me into the thin arms of a potty old girl merely to make a few extra bob for the coffers of St Jude's. When I had cooled down, I returned to the rectory.

Fr Duddleswell met me at the back door. "Miss Davenport rang," he said, "to make sure you returned..."

I wheeled my bike into the yard and, without a word, walked past him up to my study. The atmosphere between us was strained until the next day when he visited my room to make peace.

"D'you know your trouble in all this, Father Neil?" I played the silent innocent. He lifted his spectacles onto his forehead and licked his lips noisily. "You are a snob."

I stiffened at the unexpected rebuke.

He raised his "sermon fingers" at me, the first two on his right hand, and continued, "Now be truthful with me, Father Neil. Had an old age pensioner called you to her flat in Stonehenge to bless her canary that had fallen ill with laryngitis, would you have obliged?" I nodded. He removed his fingers from before my nose. "The rich are no different from the poor, Father Neil, except they have a lot more money, you follow?"

I apologized for sulking. Miss Davenport's distress at her canary's ailment was genuine enough. I should have sympathized more. Fr Duddleswell coughed and said he would be obliged if I gave him my signature. From his breast pocket he took out a check. "Mrs Pring found the pieces in your waste-paper basket when she was cleaning this morning, Father Neil. I have taken the liberty of pasting it together, like."

After I had signed "The Rev. Boyd" on the back, my resolution cracked. I turned it over to discover I had nearly thrown away twenty-five pounds.

When two days later, Miss Davenport begged me to bury her Siamese cat, Sleeky, who had been knocked over by a car, I went prepared and in a more charitable frame of mind. I took my black bag with me and on the journey, with each revolution of the pedal, I told myself that Miss Davenport was only a poor little old lady with a pile of money.

Sleekius was interred with almost military honors and his mistress's many tears. I promised her I would say a Requiem Mass for the deceased on condition I did not have to announce the intention publicly from the pulpit.

Back at St Jude's, Fr Duddleswell summed it up by saying that after my success with Timmy it was best for my reputation as a healer that Sleeky had been "killed beyond repair."

Apart from magnetizing my eyes at every *Dominus vobiscum*, Miss Davenport did not trouble me again for another week. Then she phoned one Friday morning at around 11:30. Fr Duddleswell had been in my study for ninety minutes talking trivialities until I wondered if he would ever leave. He was not normally so prodigal with his time.

Miss Davenport asked if I could be at "Le Casino" at eight. I was free but I consulted my diary while trying to conjure up an excuse to stay at home. Fr Duddleswell's grimaces left me in no doubt that it was my duty to humor the good lady. Having heard me say yes, he left before I had replaced the receiver.

At the evening meal, Fr Duddleswell seemed miles away. He was reminiscing about some obscure tribulations he had had to endure when he was a curate. Mrs Pring had cooked sausages and mash. In a fit of vacancy, Fr Duddleswell served me a single sausage. That was certainly not enough for one about to face the rigors of officiating at Miss Davenport's immediately afterwards. I asked for three more, buried them in a mound of mash and helped it down with a bottle of champagne. After that, plum pudding and custard. With a final flurry, I grimly downed two cups of Mrs Pring's tar-black tea.

"You are off, then, Father Neil? To Miss Davenport's is it?" I nodded. "The best of luck, lad," he said without his usual smile.

"Won't be long," I called after me hopefully as I rode off. How was I to know that at Miss Davenport's there awaited me something more simple and more terrible than anything I could have imagined?

At the front door of "Le Casino," the maid and the chauffeur, presumably the husband, were on the point of leaving. The maid curtseyed to Miss Davenport, kissed her hand and said, "*Encore*, Madame, my sincerest *condoléances*." Which member of the menagerie was dead now?

I walked in to find Madame attired not in black but in full evening dress.

In the hall, Miss Davenport monopolized my hand. The dining room door was open. Inside I could see the table tastefully dressed and lit by candlelight.

"I'm awfully sorry, Miss Davenport," I stammered, "if you're expecting guests I can come back tomorrow."

"Only you, Father."

O my God, I thought, do I have to dine with Miss Davenport by candlelight without any witnesses present? And with my stomach already crammed to capacity?

Only then did I grasp the significance of the hour: eight o'clock. Dinner! Damn!

"You do have an appetite, Father?" purred my regal-looking hostess.

"Usually, Miss Davenport." I was beginning to distinguish dangerous details in the semi-dark. Her low-cut dress, the pearl necklace, her hair brushing her shoulders and crowned with a kind of shimmering tiara. Taking my arm as well as my hand she propelled me to where the meal was waiting. Soft, intricate music was being played in the background.

I helped her sit before making my way to the other end and slumping down. I was surrounded by more cutlery and glass than I had ever had to deal with. Staring up at me malevolently were six large oysters bedded in crushed ice.

"You like oysters, Fr Boyd?"

Never having been that close to them before I was non-committal. "Is there anyone who doesn't, Miss Davenport?" I had no idea how to eat the blessed things, or were you supposed to drink them?

I took a long time unfolding the starched table-napkin while keeping a sharp look-out for which piece of silver she would select. A tiny fork. She squeezed a lemon over the oyster and made a little slicing movement with her fork. She picked up the shell and, as it were, tossed the contents down her throat.

My aim was never very good, and I was worried that oysters would not be companionable towards the *hors d'oeuvre* I had eaten with Fr Duddleswell. After the first throw I found my mouth full of a viscous substance like the raw white of an egg. It nearly made me vomit. My hostess's eyes were not yet accustomed to the light or she might have suspected something. I went on chewing surreptitiously behind my table-napkin till I managed to swallow.

In front of me was a Menu printed on parchment-paper in silver lettering. It read:

Oysters

Tournedos Bearnaise
Potatoes Lyonnaise
Tossed Green Salad with French Dressing

Tarte aux Abricots Bourdaloue

Cheese
Fruit

Coffee

To drink there was Château Haut-Brion (1918) and Haut-Peyraguey, and finally Cognac Courvoisier.

"Would you care to pour, Father?" Miss Davenport pointed to the wines. I was glad to do anything that afforded me some respite from another oyster.

As I rose, it occurred to me that I did not know which wine was which or the one to serve first. The white wine was on ice and the red on the side-board.

"Have you any preferences, Miss Davenport?"

"Yes, on these occasions, always Château Haut-Brion (1918)."

There was nothing for it. I chose the bottle resting on the ice. In the nick of time I read Haut-Peyraguey on the label. With considerable presence of mind, I half whispered, "What a splendid wine to follow, Miss Davenport."

"I am so pleased you know your Sauternes, Father," she said.

I picked up the red and put my napkin under it as if it were a Stradivarius. Approaching my hostess I found another distressing gap in my knowledge of etiquette. Into which glass should I pour the wine? Another hasty decision was forced on me with less fortunate results.

"That's the water glass, Father," said Miss Davenport,

touching my arm tenderly. She helped me by apologizing for the meagre light given by the candles.

Back at my place I looked down at the five-eyed monster on the platter in front of me. I noticed that the front of the Menu bore the initials D.D. and N.B.

"Fr Boyd," said Miss Davenport as I was about to tackle another oyster, "do you have a first name."

I put down my fork. "Yes, Miss Davenport."

"May I be let in on your little secret?" Since my initials were on the Menu and my full name was printed in capitals above my confessional, I did not mind revealing it.

"Neil? *Neil*." She ran it over her tongue appreciatively like wine. "Such an excellent vintage. It suits you. It *is* you. Now you have told me that your name is Neil, I could not conceive of you possessing any other name. I shall call my next Siamese 'Neil'—if it is a boy, of course." I acknowledged the compliment. "May I, *dare* I call you 'Neil'?"

"I don't think Fr Duddleswell..." I began as I aimed another oyster at my throat.

"Charles?" she said. I swallowed the oyster without difficulty. "Ah, Charles would not begrudge me such an innocent pleasure."

"Charles?" I managed to get out.

"I am Daisy."

"I'm sure you are, Miss Davenport."

"You see, dear Neil, I feel we have to be on Christian name terms if I am to confess to you the story of my love."

I stood up, seeing my first opportunity to escape that insupportable meal. "Miss Davenport, you are a Catholic and I am a priest."

"Daisy."

Less forcefully I repeated my objection preceding it with "Daisy."

"It is *because* you are a priest, Neil, that I can tell you without inhibitions of my love for..." I was about to stamp out when I heard the word "Henri."

"Henri. Monsieur le Comte. My first, my only love."

I sat down as though I had been shot. It was only my ear Miss Davenport was wanting to grab, after all. It meant I would have to see the meal through to the bitter end. Miss Davenport was destined to be my *femme fatale* in a way the moralists had not envisaged when they advised, "Never be alone with a woman, *Numquam solus cum sola.*"

As the meal progressed and the candle flame burned low I learned that Miss Davenport had met Monsieur le Comte in the Casino at Monte Carlo when she was seventeen. He was, hélas, a married man with a beautiful but boring wife, an ancient château on the Loire, and half a dozen children. It was a sad tale, and it moved me deeply.

Miss Davenport, having despatched her Tournedos Béarnaise touched her mouth with her napkin. "Rarely does it happen," she whispered reverentially, "that the perfect wine comes into being." As she fingered the stem of her glass, the candlelight played upon the ruby contents and from them flashed a star with the brilliancy of Bethlehem's. "Such marvellous blending of rain and sunlight is required, wind and soil, too, and perhaps the protecting curvature of some small hill. Celestial chemistry, Neil. Only such unique conditions can produce a Château-Haut-Brion (1918) or a genius like Bach— or a Monsieur le Comte."

Count Henri must have been a veritable bouquet of a man, handsome, high-principled, bronzed, most subtle in speech, and elegant in dress. The culture of his palate was evidenced in the meal before and within us. It was his favorite. It was the meal he had chosen to eat with Daisy the evening they said goodbye.

My pity was divided equally between Miss Davenport's past sorrows and my present predicament. Even as she related her sad "histoire" she remained the perfect hostess, urging me to eat this and drink that. My bladder was filled to overflowing.

I should have excused myself for a few moments and asked where the bathroom was. This, I felt quite reasonably, would have dampened her discourse. Afterwards, how could I return to my place as if nothing had happened, especially if the plumbing of the water closet was such that it left hissings and pipe reverberations? Like a fool, I decided to sit it out.

My eyes started to water with the discomfort and when the candlelight caught them in its glow Miss Davenport took it as the sign of sympathy and rapport.

"It was passionate but pure, Neil," she was saying. "Only one such as you committed to *la vie célibataire* could possibly comprehend my heartache and the subsequent solitude."

I did not know what time it was but it must have turned eleven o'clock, curfew hour at the rectory. What if Fr Duddleswell, not realizing I was out, had bolted the door?

The strain was now intolerable. "Miss Davenport." I changed to "Daisy" of my own accord to show the evening had not been wasted on me. "Daisy, I have a confession to make to you."

"Tell me, Neil." There was a touch of drama in her voice.

"I'm feeling ill, Daisy."

"Where, Neil?"

I did not want to put too fine a point upon it. "In my stomach. Frightfully, frightfully ill."

"Not the food, I hope?" she asked in some distress.

"I wasn't too well before I came, Miss Davenport. If you don't mind . . ."

"A cognac before you go. It is so good for an upset stomach, as Henri used to say."

To speed things up, I gulped down a small cognac, grabbed my hat from the hall and took my leave. I had the presence of mind to kiss her hand. "Daisy, adieu."

She was deeply moved and, fortunately for me, closed the door behind me immediately. I unchained my bicycle but was unable to lift my leg high enough to sit on the saddle. To avoid permanent injury I began to wheel my bike home. Until I had a flash of inspiration ignited by desperate need. I hailed a passing taxi.

The driver came to a halt, put his capped head out of the cab window, and asked in a puzzled tone, "Trouble, Rev.?"

"Deep trouble," I said.

236

"Puncture?"

"Almost."

"Want me to take the bike an' all?"

I had opened the back door and was already dragging my bicycle in after me. I thanked God for the sensible design of the London taxi.

"First time I've ever had a bike for a fare," called the driver good-naturedly over his shoulder. "Where to, Guv.?" I gave the address. "Roman Catholic, then, are you, Father?"

"Yes."

The driver relaxed his hand on the wheel and half turned round. "My old woman's a Catholic. Could you tell me something, Rev.?"

"I can't tell you a thing," I said, clasping myself where it hurt, "please get us home quick."

He slammed the glass partition between us with an "O-bleeding-kay, if that's the way you want it," and sped off through the city traffic like a maniac. Whenever he went through the red lights I gave him a special benediction. I prayed frantically that Fr Duddleswell had not bolted the door, otherwise I might have to pee against a lamp post.

The taxi jerked to a stop outside the rectory. The driver touched the clock and said, "And an extra threepence for your bleeding bike." I handed him a pound note and told him to keep the change. I was not prepared to wait for it. I hoped the liberality of the tip would soften his attitude to the leaders of his wife's religion.

The front door was already ajar and Fr Duddleswell stood there against the light in dressing gown and slippers. He must have heard the familiar ticking-over sound of the taxi. I expected a reprimand for being out after hours but nothing of the sort. He merely pointed. "Quick, up the wooden hill with you, Father Neil. The bathroom is free." I left my bicycle in his charge and heaved myself heavenwards.

Ah, such simple, unsung ecstasies. Such blessed relief. Never had life seemed so sweet, so very sweet.

Outside the bathroom Fr Duddleswell was waiting with a

bottle of milk of magnesia and a dessert spoon. I went with him into my study. "At your age, Father Neil, you have to be more careful that the Jordan does not burst its banks."

"She rang, then," I said, collapsing into a chair.

"Who, Miss Davenport?"

"Yes."

"No." I had swigged three spoonfuls of the medicine before it sank in that Fr Duddleswell knew my plight in some detail without being told.

"Monsieur le Comte," he said.

"You know about him?"

From his pocket he drew a dog-eared menu, a replica of the one on the table that evening except it was initialled D.D. and C.D.

"Charles," I exploded.

"We have all to go through it the once, Father Neil. I did meself and so did me two curates before you. Take your ease, and I will tell you about it."

He had known tonight was the night because of the date, October 13th, the anniversary of Daisy's final farewell to Henri. The incidents with the pets were part of the usual build-up to the banquet.

When I suggested that we should not make fools of ourselves for money, Fr Duddleswell looked hurt.

"'Tis true, Father Neil, that in a couple of days I will receive a cheque for £500 for the Schools' Fund as has happened a trinity of times before. But as God is me witness I did it all for Daisy."

It was news to me that anyone else had been involved but me.

He went on to explain that Miss Davenport had renounced her beloved rather than break up his marriage. She had acted in strict obedience to the Church's law on marriage and divorce. With her purchasing power she could have bought out any half-baked Frenchman. The meal I had just shared was, in his view, a kind of eucharistic memorial of the last supper when Daisy sacrificed herself for her faith.

238

"You believe her story?" I asked.

"To speak the truth, I have not the faintest idea whether it happened like that, or she imagined it. What matters is that 'tis real for her—you follow?—and the rich are especially worthy of a priest's consideration. You see, lad, they cannot take refuge in the ultimate human illusion that money is the cure of every form of ill."

I nodded, truly sorry for having misjudged both him and Daisy Davenport.

"One thing, Father," I said in a more sober tone. "You knew what was in store for me. Why did you let me eat that vast quantity of stodge beforehand?"

"Well, Father Neil, you had got so fractious over the mere blessing of a canary I thought you might opt out altogether, like. Besides, did I not try to let you off lightly by rationing you to a single sausage?" He stretched out his podgy hand in fellowship. "No hard feelings, lad?"

But this time I could not forgive him. I was lurching back to the bathroom on a more urgent errand.

14

FR DUDDLESWELL DRIVES UNDER THE INFLUENCE

Mrs Pring was serving breakfast in a new bottle-green dress and black patent leather shoes, a sure sign that today was her birthday.

I complimented her on her hair-do and presented her with a Parker pen. Fr Duddleswell's gifts were more exotic. The housekeeper's excitement grew as she rummaged in the carrier bag he had placed on the window ledge. A cameo-brooch, a microlite table-lamp for her bedside and, last, well wrapped up, a bottle of Gordon's gin.

"I don't know what to say," she got out.

"If I had known it needed but a little gift to render you speechless, woman," said Fr Duddleswell, "I would have practiced magnanimity towards you long ago."

I stood up and instinctively planted a kiss on Mrs Pring's plump cheek. That brought on the tears which Fr Duddleswell's remark was designed to check.

"Now Mrs Pring," he warned, "I will not have you behaving here like a Jew in Babylon, else I will give you the full of me mouth, your twenty-first birthday or no." I had never known him have such a blunt edge to his tongue. "Now, wash that Ash Wednesday mug of yours, will you not? And be ready, mind, when your daughter comes to fetch you."

At 9:30 a grey Morris Minor drew up at the back door. On hearing it, Fr Duddleswell bade me accompany him to the kitchen. Half a dozen cards were displayed on the mantel shelf and Mrs Pring was adding another from her daughter.

"Helen," cried Fr Duddleswell delightedly.

"Uncle Charlie," returned Helen, and she raced towards him with outstretched arms.

When the embrace was over, Fr Duddleswell introduced me to his "niece." Helen Phipps was in her early thirties, pretty, petite, and smartly dressed.

"Father Neil," said Fr Duddleswell, drawing himself up to his full five feet seven, "is this not the beautifulest colleen that ever set foot in St Jude's?" I did not say no. "Take that pair of sparkling eyes, now, those rosy lips. And those teeth on her, what are they if not Solomon's flock of even-shorn white sheep? Is she not living proof, Father Neil, that God Almighty can make a silk purse out of a sow's ear?"

"He's scrag end of mutton himself," said Mrs Pring, stifling her real emotions, "and he pretends he's fillet steak." A few more tears escaped and furrowed her cheek.

"Did you not hear me tell you," said Fr Duddleswell stamping his foot, "I will not have you dripping hot and cold in me kitchen."

"*My* kitchen," shouted back Mrs Pring, quite recovered all of a sudden, and Fr Duddleswell as his costliest birthday gift to her conceded the point. "'Tis worth more than double," he said, "so she takes her knuckles out of her eyes."

After a few more minutes banter and detailed instructions from Mrs Pring on how to heat up the stew for supper, Fr Duddleswell produced a two-pound box of chocolates for the three grandchildren. Then a sharp, "Be off with the both of you, and say a prayer to St Christopher, mind."

That day we lunched at the Clinton Hotel. Fr Duddleswell told me how Mrs Pring had been with him "the worst part of twenty years." It had not hit me before that Helen, whom I had met for the first time that morning, must have been with her mother when Mrs Pring "took up office."

Every time my parish priest spoke of Helen his eyes shone. As the meal wore on he was quite voluble in her praises. It could be his two half pints of ale had something to do with it.

After coffee, he asked if I were ready for home. I had drunk my usual couple of glasses of wine. "Certainly, Uncle Charlie," I said. I thought my impertinence may have affected him because it was with difficulty that he rose to his feet.

Though drowsy, I noticed in the car that he kept blinking furiously, and once he leaned over the wheel to rub the windshield with his sleeve as if it were misted up.

His erratic driving shook me out of my somnolence. I hung on to my seat with both hands and joined Mrs Pring and daughter in fervent prayers to St Christopher.

It was market day in the High Street. There Fr Duddleswell swerved and hit a greengrocer's stall. Fortunately, we had slowed to about five miles per hour, but the barrow collapsed instantly. Pyramids of apples, oranges, tomatoes and melons were tossed in all directions. Many burst and squelched under the tires of buses and cars.

Fr Duddleswell braked in a daze, his face ashen and his knuckles white. As he clutched the wheel, he was shaking visibly.

A noisy crowd was gathering and the stall-holder was cursing in colorful cockney as he tried to recover some of his fruit and vegetables.

Within thirty seconds, a police car was on the scene and out stepped the two constables who had invaded Mrs Pring's kitchen on the night I couldn't sleep.

P.C. Winkworth and P.C. Richards, approaching slowly from the front, recognized us immediately and exchanged a glance. Once more the senior of them started to take out his notebook.

He opened the door on Fr Duddleswell's side. "Would you care to step outside for a moment, sir, and show me your driver's licence?"

Fr Duddleswell heaved himself out and held on to the door to stop himself falling. "I'm not feeling..." he began.

P.C. Winkworth sniffed sardonically through his small red nose. "Been wetting your whistle, have you, sir?"

I leaned over and called out, "Only two halves of ale, Officer."

P.C. Richards, still sporting a black eye, poked his arm through the window and said roughly as he grabbed my shoulder, "When we want a statement from you, we'll ask for it, *sir*."

The stall-holder, his nerve restored, pushed to the front of the crowd. He saw for the first time that it was Fr Duddleswell who had done the damage. "Are you okay, Father?" he asked with concern.

"I am in no way wounded, thank you, Michael," said Fr Duddleswell, grateful, no doubt, that the stall-holder was one of the good people of his parish.

He summed up Fr Duddleswell's predicament in a flash, and, having no love for the law, he apologized for pushing his barrow too far into the road. "I might 'ave caused you two Fathers to be involved in a ruddy accident."

The two coppers took the hint, but P.C. Winkworth declared doggedly that they would have to run the older clergyman in on suspicion of being drunk while driving.

Since I couldn't drive, P.C. Richards radioed control for a breakdown van to tow our car to the police compound. Then we were driven to the station.

There again fortune smiled on us. The Sergeant on duty was Patrick O'Hara. He touched his forelock in salute as we approached his desk attended by his two junior colleagues.

The reception area, with its pale blue walls, was as inhospitable as a public lavatory. "I have not been to jail," muttered Fr Duddleswell, "since me last game of Monopoly."

"Drunk while driving," asserted Black Eye.

"Is that so, now?" said Sergeant O'Hara, peering over an enormous nose. "And which of the two reverend gentlemen would you be accusing of this heinous crime?"

"The short fat one," growled P.C. Winkworth, aware of forces at work here beyond his comprehension.

The Sergeant persuaded the two constables to leave the matter with him for a few minutes while they bought themselves a well-earned cup of tea. After they had gone with some reluctance, Sergeant O'Hara made no bones about it: when there was a conflict between the law and the Gospel, it was his duty as a policeman to uphold the Gospel.

"There is not a word of truth to it, Paddy," whispered Fr Duddleswell in a confessional tone of voice. "I came over queer, I am telling you, but not even a girl-child could become inebriated on one pint of diluted ale. Must have been something I ate."

Sergeant O'Hara broke the news to Fr Duddleswell that it was his duty to summon one of the doctors on their list. "What would you say, Father, to being examined by a Dr Daley?"

In ten minutes, Dr Daley arrived in bulk. Beads of perspiration stood out on a pink head bald but for a narrow circlet of white hair. His eyes were more bloodshot than usual. A cigarette was wedged in the corner of his mouth. The smell of whiskey preceded him as he moved in our direction humming for our benefit, "When constabulary duty's to be done, to be done."

Having listened with scant interest to the charge in the presence of the two constables, he asked the Sergeant to be allowed to examine the accused in the politeness of a cell.

The three of us sat round a table on which Dr Daley placed his black bag. "Now, Charles," he said, "I hear it rumoured you have been drowning the shamrock, like."

"A few sips of ale only, Donal. Barely enough to wet me tonsils."

"I cannot smell any alcohol on your breath, Charles, that's for sure," said Dr Daley, suppressing a burp.

"Donal," said Fr Duddleswell, "in all the years we have been acquainted, have you ever known me be guilty of foolishness?"

"Indeed I have not. I have confessed to you the same many a time," said Dr Daley choking, "and I have another assignation with you next Saturday night and all, when my hope is you will pity me as now I pity you." He sighed audibly and tapped his waistcoated tummy. "It shames me that when

I'm in my cups, my brogue betrayeth me, and I betray the Green." Another heave of his broad chest. "Sweet Jesus, but it is hard, Charles, mighty hard to mortify the meat." He slowly shook his head. "I have this thirst on me, you see, like a fire. It is stoked by quenching."

He went mawkishly on about his shame at allowing himself to become over the years "as round as a pickled onion and more entirely tonsured by time, Charles, than even yourself."

At length, he emerged from his reverie to assure Fr Duddleswell he would vouch for the innocence of one who had never raised his hand at any man, save in holy benediction. It was blasphemous to contemplate his reverence being brought before a hanging magistrate and having his licence endorsed or taken away.

Dr Daley opened his bag. A bottle clinked as he took out his stethoscope. Good, I thought, as he put it round his neck, at last the medical examination is about to begin. I was wrong. It had just ended. The doctor was walking briskly towards the door. He paused with his hand on the knob to ask, "And why, Charles, do you think these constables are endeavouring to smirch your excellent good name?"

Fr Duddleswell staggered to his feet. He explained that they had burst into our house one night without a warrant screaming obscenities and Father Neil had bravely blacked the eye of one before the other "kneed him in the unmentionables."

Dr Daley nodded sagely. "That clears that up, then." He flung the door open, pushed Fr Duddleswell ahead of him and proclaimed in the manner of Pontius Pilate, "Look at this man. I can find nothing to charge him with."

"But," protested Black Eye, "you haven't made him walk the gangplank yet."

"Nor have I, Constable," said Dr Daley. "Nor have I." He gestured to a thin white line parallel to the wall and indicated to Fr Duddleswell that he should walk carefully.

"Father Neil," whispered Fr Duddleswell in my ear, "I never had much of a talent for treading the straight and narrow."

I patted him on the back for luck and he followed the white line steadily enough until the end when he lurched to his right.

"There, what did we say?" called out Constable Winkworth, "he's drunk."

"He is as shober, shir," said Dr Daley, "as you or I. Watch me." He gave a dramatic slow-motion imitation of a high-wire performer that would have earned him half a dozen deaths.

Sergeant O'Hara was completely convinced. "Well, lads," he said kindly to the constables, "it seems as if we'll have to drop charges."

Outside, Dr Daley expressed himself satisfied that justice had been seen to be done. He told Fr Duddleswell he was probably suffering from a bilious attack. Nothing that a good dose of salts wouldn't cure. "If not," he said, "pay me a visit at my office."

He volunteered to give us a lift home but we preferred to walk and go on living. I phoned George Walker, a trusted parishioner, asking him to pick up Fr Duddleswell's car from the police compound and took "the drunk" home in a taxi.

At the rectory, Fr Duddleswell leaned on me as he went upstairs to his bedroom. When I left him, I heard him bumping into things. After that, silence.

He did not appear at tea, and as supper approached he banged on my wall. I found him propped up in bed. "Everything keeps spinning round, Father Neil, like a catherine wheel," he said, "till the world turns white as the skirt of a poached egg."

I ate the stew alone and waited anxiously for Mrs Pring's return. At ten o'clock she came in with Helen. She sensed that something was wrong and rushed upstairs, leaving me to chat awhile with Helen across the kitchen table.

It was easy to talk to Helen. She told me that when she was in her early teens, her mother couldn't make ends meet on a war-widow's pension. Jobs were hard to come by during and after the Depression. Fr Duddleswell had given her mother employment and both of them a roof over their head. "I never knew my father," she said simply, "so Uncle Charlie was a kind of father to me."

Helen had lived in rectories until she married Bill, a solicitor. "He had to give a good account of himself to Uncle Charlie, I can tell you," she laughed. "Uncle Charlie even pressured him into becoming a Catholic. He didn't want any mixed marriage for 'our Helen,' he used to say, and for once Mum agreed with him."

I felt sufficiently at ease to ask Helen why her mother and Fr Duddleswell were always at one another's throats. "That's his way of showing her affection without competing with my father," Helen replied. "Once he said to me, 'Helen, I only ridicule your mother so she realizes that in my eyes she is not beneath contempt.' It slipped out really, Father, but I think he was trying to say that if he was merely polite to her, as most priests are to their housekeepers, he would not be respecting her as she deserved."

It sounded to me more like an enigma than an explanation but just then Mrs Pring returned. "A real puzzle," she said. "He has no temperature and he's not vomiting, and yet he feels terribly sick and dizzy. It's either biliousness or food-poisoning."

At the Clinton Hotel, he had eaten pork fillet whereas I had chosen lamb cutlets. The pork may have been "off" but that was unlikely in view of the hotel's high standard of catering and the speed with which Fr Duddleswell had succumbed after lunch. Only time would tell what was really wrong with him.

For the next few days, I was Fr Duddleswell's constant companion. I assisted him at Mass. I made sure he didn't drop the chalice and I distributed Holy Communion for him.

"'Tis a strange thing, Father Neil," he said. "Me head turns round faster when I am lying down than when I am standing up." He was sleeping well enough provided he was propped up in bed, and his appetite was normal.

Mrs Pring decided that Fr D wasn't larking about this time and insisted that Dr Daley give him a thorough examination. This was arranged for eight P.M.

The doctor, smelling of peppermint, tapped and listened with his "cruel Siberian stethoscope on a tropical chest." He shone a torch into his patient's eyes and ears. Afterwards, he delivered his diagnosis in one word: "Labyrinthitis."

"It sounds," said Fr Duddleswell, "as though I have a horned minotaur prowling up and down inside me head."

Dr Daley explained that it was not his head that was the trouble. Labyrinthitis is a virus infection of the inner ear which interferes with the balance mechanism. "That's what I think anyhow," he concluded.

"Do you not know for sure, Donal?"

"Dogma is your own business, Charles. I'm but a poor relation in the guessing game."

In answer to how long it would last the doctor said, "Ah, it is not so easy to heal the sick as to forgive sins. It usually clears up in about ten days. Meanwhile, stay on the horizontal as much as possible. Don't drink or drive until you get the all-clear, and get yourself a walking stick. It'll lengthen the odds on you falling over arsy-varsy."

"I beg your pardon," I said, not sure if I had heard correctly.

"I said I do not want our beloved P.P. pirouetting in the street like a drunken ballerina and falling bang on his bum." My ears were in perfect working order.

The doctor prescribed tablets and promised to arrange for X-rays at the Sussex, one of the finest teaching hospitals in London, to verify his findings. "Top priority."

Three days later, Fr Duddleswell and I took a taxi to the Sussex. First, he was examined by Mr Taylor, a specialist who wore a kind of miner's lamp in the center of his forehead. Fr Duddleswell complained that he was "as noncommittal as a canon lawyer." After that, a nurse escorted us to a room where another white-coated gentleman made Fr Duddleswell lie on a bed and directed warm water from a nozzle into his ear.

Fr Duddleswell immediately noticed that pasted on the ceiling was a "lewd photograph." True enough, smiling down on us from on high was a picture of a young woman in a low-cut dress. Fr Duddleswell interrupted proceedings to demand an explanation for the strange location of such filth in a National Health Hospital.

The doctor said that injecting water into his ear would cause his head to spin and the picture would revolve wildly. His job was to time with a stop-watch how long it takes the patient to recover normal vision.

"Never," returned Fr Duddleswell, "while that hussy *in impuris naturalibus* is leering down at me." He closed his eyes firmly until they sent for a workman with a ladder to replace the pin-up with a picture of a Beefeater on duty outside the Tower of London.

Fr Duddleswell could only manage water in one ear. When the Beefeater finally came back into focus, he felt violently sick. "Me stomach's bid goodbye to its cage," he said looking green about the gills.

When he had recovered, I supported him downstairs to the X-ray room. "Take your clothes off, please, sir," said a West Indian nurse.

"I have not the slightest intention of peeling meself like a spud beneath the public gaze," retorted Fr Duddleswell, waving his stick at her. "'Tis an X-ray I am here for, not a Turkish bath."

According to the nurse, he only had to take off his spectacles, his upper garments as far as his undershirt, and to step out of his shoes.

Mumbling something about Soho and striptease and being seen in "the altogether" and not feeling like a human being at all without his clerical collar, he complied.

A doctor appeared and pointed to a kind of operating table. "Help your old dad up there," he said to me. "Oh, and by the way, get rid of that lucky charm he's wearing round his neck." Fr Duddleswell passionately kissed his miraculous medal and handed it into my custody.

Once on the horizontal, he was strapped down to prevent him moving his head while being X-rayed. Just before the pictures were taken he summoned me to him and said out of the corner of his mouth, "Tell me truly, Father Neil, d'you reckon I will make a tolerable Frankenstein?"

As he was putting his clothes back on, I realized something else was wrong with him. Not only was he unsteady on his feet, he was wriggling violently from side to side like a snake sloughing off its skin.

"What's the matter, Father?"

"'Tis the ultimate tragedy, Father Neil," he confided. "Me bloody collar stud has slipped down me back."

I encouraged him to keep wriggling and the stud was bound to reappear at the bottom of the trousers' leg. After three minutes of contortions it was clear my optimism was mistaken.

"I am afraid," he said through clenched teeth, "that the cursèd thing is stranded inside me Long Johns."

I looked at him in surprise. The weather was still far too mild to justify him taking to his winter woollies.

"I was not aiming under any circumstances—you follow, Father Neil?—to parade up and down this hospital like Adam before the Fall."

There was nothing for it but to locate the stud and work it downwards. I fingered it as far as his left calf, after which it would not budge. I asked the nurse if she could lend me a pair of surgical scissors. The only pair she had were the size of garden shears. I snipped a hole in the Long Johns and Fr Duddleswell was happy again. "Me curate has just removed a worrying little abscess, nurse," he explained.

As we were leaving, the nurse took me aside and advised me to go straight home and put the "poor old chap" to bed with a hot water bottle and a couple of aspirins.

"Father Neil," the poor old chap said to me the next morning, "*you* will have to do it." When I asked what, he replied that his imitation of Boris Karloff had gone far enough. Because he distrusted the shakiness of his head he was now sporting a five-day growth and "'tis against diocesan regulations to show a chin as tufted as a billy-goat's."

I offered to shave him with my electric razor but he

professed abhorrence of such new-fangled gadgetry. He would much rather use sand-paper.

He drew me to the bathroom and opened up the cabinet where he stored his shaving gear. Out came a long, black-handled, cut-throat razor, lethal-looking.

"I can't, Father," I stammered, "I'm maladroit, you know that."

"'Tis a scrubbish, mean man, so y'are, Father Neil." I acknowledged it. "A soft, wet potato." No description, I said, ever suited me better.

Mrs Pring overheard us and volunteered for the job. The equipment was set up in her kitchen. A Toby jug for the soap-mix was on the table and the leather strap hung from a hook on the door. "Keep stropping that razor, lad," Fr Duddleswell urged, "unless 'tis sharp, 'twill cut me to ribbons."

Mrs Pring sat him down on a straight-backed dining-room chair and draped a towel round his neck so that he looked like a criminal in the stocks. "I'll never have a better opportunity," she giggled. She removed his spectacles and asked him if he wished to be blindfolded. "Any last requests, Fr D? Burial? Cremation?" Then she lathered him to his eyes.

I handed her the razor. She rubbed the edge lightly against her left index finger. "Into Thy hands, O Lord," he prayed. She made a scything movement in the air and expressed satisfaction that now Father Neil had given her the tools, she would finish the job.

"He was led," intoned Fr Duddleswell, "like a lamb to the slaughter."

"And," took up Mrs Pring, "he opened not his mouth."

"Neither will *I*, woman, provided you do not wave that thing around like a crazy samurai."

"Close it," she warned, pointing the razor at his frothing mouth, and he obliged by closing his eyes, too.

For two minutes not a sound from Fr Duddleswell, only the crunch and scrape of the razor on his beard. "Not so much of your lip, please, Samson," rejoiced Mrs Pring, as she wiped the razor clean on a piece of tissue paper.

He only yelled once when she slightly opened up his chin. "Oh," cried Mrs Pring, "he's hemorrhaging. Father Neil, go fast and fetch Dr Daley to patch up his pimple."

Her last great moment came as she was finishing off his upper lip. "Alo-ong came a blackbird," she sang, "and—zip—pe-ecked off his nose."

Fr Duddleswell rose unsteadily and walked off without a word. "One thing, Father Neil," Mrs Pring said to me with a wink which had more worry than humor in it, "there's proof that you *can* get blood out of a stone."

Mrs Pring did not take her day off that week. It showed how anxious she was about him. She gave me an envelope containing a ten-shilling note "for a Mass for Fr D" and she confessed to saying not just the rosary but "the trimmings" as well for his recovery.

That evening I heard Fr Duddleswell groaning in his bedroom and went to see what was wrong. "You will never believe this, lad," he said, "but now I have the bloody toothache. Am I not stricken enough without fresh pains in me kneeders and grinders?"

Mrs Pring's hearing was very acute. She was at his side in an instant.

He turned a swollen cheek to me. "Am I all the while to have that bold woman on sentry duty at me door, Father Neil, staring at me with both ears?"

Mrs Pring declared she would call the dentist first thing in the morning and fix an appointment.

"If I am to die, Mrs Pring," he said, upright against the pillow, "what is the purpose of me suffering first in the dentist's chair?"

"Oh, Father," I blurted out, "surely you don't want to die with a toothache"—at which they both laughed heartily.

Mrs. Pring had her way and at eleven o'clock next morning Fr Duddleswell was in the "torturer's chair."

"Well, what is the verdict, Tom?" he said to the tall, thin, slightly cross-eyed dentist who had examined him. "Are you about to shove your road-digging equipment down me throat, then?"

Tom Read lowered his white mask, bit the inside of his lip, and shook his head. "It'll have to come out, Father."

"Never! 'Tis me best ivory by far, the last of me wisdom teeth."

"I'll give you an injection for it, Father."

"Maybe so, Tom," said Fr Duddleswell, eying the long syringe on the glass tabletop, "but what will you give me for the injection?"

As the young lady assistant prepared the instruments, Fr Duddleswell gave a brief survey of the course of his disintegration. Vertigo, being shaved by a woman, having to walk on his curate's arm or with the aid of a walking stick—and now the last worthwhile tooth in his head about to bite the dust.

I closed my eyes at the point where Fr Duddleswell seemed to be swallowing the dentist's fist.

On our return, Mrs Pring immediately noticed the blood on Fr Duddleswell's lips. "'Tis nothing," he said with merciful speed. "I have only parted company till resurrection day with one of me teeth."

Mrs Pring's rejoinder was instantaneous. "That's one less for your Reverence to gnash in the Fire."

He sat down and screwed his tongue into the blood-filled cavity before turning to me. "Father Neil, here am I, down on me luck like Job on his dunghill, and there is herself taunting me like Eliphaz the Temanite."

Mrs Pring offered him sixpence for the tooth. "If the mice don't want it," she said, "I can always leave it to the diocese as a first-class relic."

Fr Duddleswell did not appear to mind the fact that his "most valuable pair of scissors" no longer matched. I think it was because he was so relieved that the vertigo was disappearing. When he reclined in Tom Read's chair, he had expected his head to start whirling faster than a dentist's drill. Instead, he felt no ill-effects. "What is left of me," he prophesied, "is on the mend."

On the morning we returned to the Sussex to learn the results of his X-rays, Fr Duddleswell was in buoyant mood. He was sure he would be given a clean bill of health.

A stunning Korean nurse ushered us into a cubicle where we were asked to wait for Mr Taylor.

"Did you see that nurse, Father Neil?" he whistled. "She is wearing black stockings in mourningful anticipation of me decease. Some of them have such sweet faces on 'em they would turn me head any day of the week."

He went on to joke about the kind of funeral he looked forward to. A hearse drawn by six black horses. A solemn sung Requiem with the Bishop preaching a panegyric "packed with the most beauteous mendacities." Trembling hands lowering him gently into the narrow house. The clergy chanting *In Paradisum*, tongue-in-cheek, and after, while their tears rolled down their cheeks into their whiskey glasses, taking bets on who would be the next to go. And, of course, leading the procession in a black hairnet, old Mrs Pring.

That was when we became aware of Mr Taylor's voice drifting in from an inner room. He was talking on the phone in a somewhat tired voice like a judge. At that distance, I could only pick up snatches of his conversation but I distinctly made out, "Nice old chap... Good job there's not the complication of a wife and kids... No doubt about it... X-rays... Tumour on the brain... Yep, quite inoperable... Should see Christmas through with a bit of luck... No pain, no... Shall I tell him or will you?... Thanks, Doctor... I'll see you get all the..."

All this time, Fr Duddleswell's grip was tightening on my arm. There flashed through my mind the memory of an old lady I had once met in hospital when I was a student. She was dying and she kept describing how her head was in a whirl and she felt as if she was falling, falling from a great height.

The specialist entered and peered over the top of his half-moon spectacles. "The Reverend Charles Duddleswell?" He was obviously surprised to see us sitting there.

"Yes," I said.

As the specialist picked up the X-ray photographs, Fr Duddleswell sighed heavily, "I heard your prognosis."

"Prognosis?"

Fr Duddleswell said he didn't particularly want to leave

the discussing of such sorrowful topics to his old friend Dr Daley. Mr Taylor sat there stunned for a moment, as though trying to fathom the situation.

He burst out with a laugh. "I was gassing with a colleague on the phone, and it wasn't about you, Mr Duddleswell. The worst you've got is a flea in the ear, so to speak." He went on to explain that "virus" was a word used by the medical profession to cover up its almost total ignorance of the causes of many maladies. We were not interested.

A couple of minutes later, we shook hands with the doctor and went out, doing our best to support each other.

"Father Neil," Fr Duddleswell said, while we waited for the taxi, "that gentleman did not seem to realize that in the space of sixty seconds he had condemned me to death and reprieved me. Did you not hear him laugh?" After a few moments of reflection, "'Tis strange how sadness and hilarity grow from the same stem like roses and thorns."

Mrs Pring was waiting on the doorstep to check up on the efficacy of her Mass stipend. Her first sight of us could not have increased her hopes. We were both looking white and shaken as we stepped out of the taxi.

To Mrs Pring's inquiry, Fr Duddleswell replied with his usual delayed humour, "'Tis bad news, I am afraid." Before he could conclude with, "I am going to live," I was stooping down to pick the housekeeper off the floor. Fortunately, she had fallen without banging her head.

I carried her to Fr Duddleswell's study, settled her in a chair, and ran to the kitchen for a glass of water. When I got back, she was already regaining consciousness. She was saying, "O my head. Everything's spinning round and round."

Fr Duddleswell said he knew how she felt.

"I'll look after you, Father dear," she kept repeating, "I'll look after you."

Fr Duddleswell tried to break it gently to her that she might have a long and arduous job ahead.

"You *are* going to die, Father D?" she asked suspiciously, and she would not be fobbed off with another sip of water which was all he offered her for an answer.

I took the glass from him and stooped over Mrs Pring to make her drink, but she was so outraged at his deception that she knocked me sideways. As I lifted my head, I cracked it on the stone mantelpiece right in the tender spot which had blacked the policeman's eye. There was an explosion of white light inside my skull and I sank down slowly on the carpet. When I opened my eyes, there were the three of us in a circle, clasping our heads.

Fr Duddleswell held out his hands to us guiltily. "Ring-a-ring of roses?"

Mrs Pring pushed his hand aside. "You are a fraud," she cried. "Do you hear me, Father D?"

"Mrs P," he said, breathing heavily through his nose, "I could hear you in me deafest ear."

"A fraud. A fraud."

"Be careful, woman," he said menacingly, "or I will raise these hands to you with the fingers hid."

I had made my exit and bathed my bump in the bathroom a long while before the argument downstairs had ceased.

15

THE NOVEMBER BLUES

The sermon began, "'Twas fifteen hundred long years ago when Edwin King of the Anglo-Saxons was betwixt and between whether to receive the Christian missionaries into his kingdom."

The sermon was being delivered in my room. "At a banquet, one of the King's nobles arose and said, 'Sire, this life compared with the life to come reminds me of one of the winter feasts which you partake of with your generals and ministers of state.'"

The sermon was being given to me alone. By Mrs Pring. "'Imagine, me dear people,' says the nobleman to his King, 'the snowy cold without, the blazing hearth within. Driven by the storm, a tiny threadbare sparrow enters at one door and flies in a flurry of delight around the great hall before making his way out the other.'"

At this point, Mrs Pring's congregation was doubled. Fr Duddleswell entered as silent as a sparrow and stood at her elbow. "'No chill does that wee sparrow feel while he is with us, Sire. But short is his hour of warmth and contentment here. Then out flies he again into the raging tempest and the dreaded dark.'"

Here Mrs Pring raised her sermon fingers solemnly. "'Brief is man's life, Sire, as is the sparrow's.'" In chorus with the preacher, Fr Duddleswell declaimed, "'We are as ignorant of the state which preceded our life as of that which follows it.'"

As Mrs Pring tailed off in surprise, Fr Duddleswell continued quietly, "'Therefore do I feel, Sire, that if this new faith can give us more certainty than we now have, it deserves to be believed.'"

After a strange lull, Fr Duddleswell said, "'Tis a mighty fine sermon you preach, woman." There was not a trace of sarcasm in his voice.

Mrs Pring had forewarned me that as Mary's month of October was passing, Fr Duddleswell was due for his usual fit of the November blues. November is the month of prayer for the souls in Purgatory. The purple vestments, she maintained, darkened his soul like black frost on the window pane.

"'Twill be no ordinary November for me," he said out of her hearing. His recent experience at the hospital had, he swore, completely refashioned him. He had examined his conscience in so far as it would stand still long enough and learned a few home-truths about himself.

"Just being told you are going to die, Father Neil, is sufficient to kill you. And did I accept it? Indeed, I did not. No act of contrition. No *In Manus tuas, Domine. E contra*, me faith flew into fragments and there stood I knock-kneed and thrilled with fear. I could only picture meself stretched out like a sardine and carried on four black shoulders." He plucked three times at his breast like the strings of a double bass and sighed. "I always knew I was mortal, like, but not till that black day, that *dies irae*, did it so much as occur to me that I was going to die." I sensed that this was an oration it would be foolish of me to interrupt.

"There is worse to come, Father Neil. When the specialist told me someone else is doomed to die instead of me, I rejoiced like a heretic when the faggots went out. And though this unknown had no kith and kin to assist him through his last days I did not think even to ask for his name and address." When I said nothing, he added, "Not that they would have given them to me, mind."

He slowly rose and crossed to the fire. There he sank down on his haunches and picked up a lump of coal and said:

I sat on me hunkers
I looked through me peepers
I saw the dead buryin' the livin'

At this he dropped the coal onto the hungry flame. "In my case, Father Neil," he said arising, "growing old is like driving backwards down a long, dark tunnel. You think you are seeing further when you are only seeing less."

I stammered something about not judging oneself too harshly and leaning on the forgiveness of Christ, but he had not quite finished. He had decided that his life was "sodden with deviousness and uncharity." He apologized for his past misdeeds and assured me from his heart he was about to turn over a new leaf.

As October drew to its close, many other old leaves started to turn, and they tumbled in golden showers to the ground. The weather was chilly, and when I cycled on my early morning rounds to distribute Communion to the sick there was a mist sometimes high on the tower blocks and in the cul de sacs. Mrs Pring bustled about lighting fires before breakfast "to warm and content my two wee sparrows."

Fr Duddleswell kept his word. Whenever Mrs Pring tried to rile him, she found him lock-jawed. There he sat in a daunting silence. He gritted and bared his teeth in a passable imitation of a grinning skeleton.

"Ah, Father Neil," said Mrs Pring, "at least he died a happy death. Has his Reverence yet reached that driving-backwards-down-a-long-black-tunnel bit?"

He saved his remark for when she had left the room. "Women have the advantage over us, you see, Father Neil. They have an inexhaustible fund of ignorance to draw on." He meant this not as an insult but as a plain statement of fact.

I was the uncharitable one. I had cut back Mrs Rollings'

instructions to once a fortnight so that my wounds would have a chance to heal.

That Wednesday she came clutching a copy of *The Watchtower* which a Jehovah's Witness had put through her letter-box. My heart soared for a moment at the possibility of her embracing an alien faith and then crash-landed when she said she simply wanted me to answer "all their accusations against Catholics."

The magazine had gone to town on Indulgences. I explained to my only convert—forced on me by Fr Duddleswell—that after forgiveness there remains the punishment due to sins. An Indulgence is a remission of the punishment which a holy soul in Purgatory would otherwise have to suffer.

Where did this remission come from? From the infinite treasury of Christ's merits and those of his saints. Yes, Mrs Rollings, that's why the Pope grants so many Indulgences and, yes, Mrs Rollings, only Catholics out of all mankind are eligible for them. And the "days" in question, Mrs Rollings, refer to the days which the early Christians spent in harsh penitential exercises and which have been commuted in recent times to prayers and good works.

"So all these lies are true, then," she said. I asked her to list some of their calumnies so I might judge for myself.

"*The Watchtower* says," she answered, "that for a single Mass in San Francisco there was once an Indulgence attached of 32,310 years, 10 days, and 6 hours." I blinked in disbelief at the sheer crudity of the fabricated figures.

"Is that more or less than a plenary Indulgence, Father?" I confessed I had no idea.

She proceeded to read for my benefit how Spaniards at fivepence a person used to pay £200,000 a year to qualify for Indulgences and how the first plenary was given by the Pope to pious Crusaders for slaughtering the Turks.

I asked caustically if the author of the scurrilous article quoted any sources. "Yes, Father," she said, and mentioned *A History Of The Church* by a famous Jesuit historian.

I let her ramble on, hoping she would not notice my own

Papal Indulgence resplendent in its frame on the wall above her head. It entitled me to a plenary Indulgence at the moment of death provided I was in a state of grace, prayed for the Pope's intention, and uttered the holy name of Jesus. Dying is bound to be a busy time.

"By wearing a scapular of the Immaculate Conception," Mrs Rollings continued, "a Catholic can obtain 453 plenary Indulgences and lots of partial ones."

I could not let that pass. "Authorities, please," I demanded. She stumbled over the name, "Alphonsus... and something that looks like 'liquorice.'" "Liguori?" I said and spelt it. "That's right, Father."

St Alphonsus is a doctor of the Church but I did not tell her that. I made a resolution not to intervene again.

"The Pope in a Jubilee year grants not merely a plenary but a *most* plenary Indulgence." She paused and lifted her eyes from the page. "Why should Catholics need more than a plenary, Father?" I shook my head. "And if," she reasoned, "you can earn, say, a million days of Indulgences every twenty-four hours just by saying prayers, that's not very fair on the early Christians, is it?" I felt it was not for a curate to settle issues of that magnitude. "After all, Father, the early Christians had to scourge themselves for months on end for their pardon and Christians today only have to recite the rosary."

I only dimly heard her after that. Her theme was the folly of Catholics believing that souls, which are spiritual, can burn in Purgatory, the pluck of Martin Luther, and Pope Leo X rebuilding St Peter's in Rome on the proceeds of the sale of Indulgences.

Did I have to be condemned to death and reprieved like Fr Duddleswell before I could learn to love everyone?

At supper, I chanced to say I had been talking to Mrs Rollings about Indulgences. Fr Duddleswell congratulated me on preparing for November and asked if I had told her the story of Sixtus IV's visit to the Franciscan nuns at Foligno in 1476.

"No, Father Neil? Well, now, perhaps you did not realize yourself how the Pope gave the good sisters a plenary

Indulgence for the coming Feast of the Virgin. But the Holy Ghost moved him to give them something special." I was expecting the Pope to grant the nuns a most plenary Indulgence. "Pope Sixtus said, 'Sisters, I give you full immunity from your guilt *and* your punishment every time you go to confession.'"

"Fantastic," I said.

Fr Duddleswell smiled. "The Cardinals present had the same reaction, Father Neil. '*Every* time, Holy Father?' they gasped. His Holiness put his old hand to his heart and said, 'Yes, I give these lovely sisters everything I have, like.' And what then, Father Neil? The Cardinals all went down on their knees pleading, 'Us as well, Holy Father, us as well.' 'All right,' said His Holiness, 'you as well.'" Fr Duddleswell's eyes were glistening. "Such a tender tale," he said. "I love it, indeed I do."

I repeated one or two of the details Mrs Rollings had read from *The Watchtower*. Before I could quote the references, Fr Duddleswell had drawn in a deep breath and exhaled it to dismiss the Church's accusers in a single satisfying word: "Bigots!"

Halloween and the Feast of All Saints did nothing to lift his spirits. No more joyful songs from his gramophone. Even at Mass on All Saints' Day he preached about another sparrow that rubbed its beak upon a mountain top. Every thousand years another bird of the same family followed suit. "And when eventually, me dear people, that mighty heap was levelled to the ground, the first moment of eternity had scarcely begun."

On November 2nd, the Feast of All Souls, he revived. Up at the crack of dawn, he popped in and out of church, praying for the departed. He celebrated each of his three Requiem Masses on the trot with lugubrious glee, pausing only to point out to his congregations that if they recited six Paters, Aves, and Glorias and prayed for the Holy Father's intention, "a holy soul will obtain a plenary Indulgence and be freed forthwith from the pangs of Purgatory."

My Masses followed and after breakfast we spent the

morning freeing the dead, *toties quoties*, a soul a visit, so to speak. One gulp of fresh air at the church door was sufficient to mark off one visit from another. Owing to the speed with which Fr Duddleswell prayed, by my reckoning he helped two dozen more holy souls than I to freedom. Perhaps mine, I consoled myself, had been the greater sinners.

We were visiting the Blessed Sacrament after lunch when we spotted a shifty-looking character in a brown mackintosh reading the notices pinned to the church door.

"Take a close look at Pinky Weston," Fr Duddleswell whispered.

In the rectory he told me I had just seen my first Rapper. Someone who raps on doors to find out if the tenants have anything of value they are prepared to part with. Rappers are often ignoramuses which is why they mostly work in cahoots with antique dealers.

"I see," I said, though it was only through a glass darkly.

Rappers, he told me, peep through windows hoping to find a bargain. They team up with window-cleaners, interior decorators, meter readers—anyone who will give them a nod and a wink when they come across something that looks like an antique. It might be furniture, silver, pottery, or glass.

Pinky Weston had a special reason for reading the notices at the back of our church. A Requiem Mass alerts him to look up the deceased's address in the electoral register. He visits the house before the corpse is cold, hoping a destitute widow will part with an item of value for a pittance if only to pay for the funeral.

Fr Duddleswell reported the rumor that when Pinky's offer on, say, a piece of pottery is refused he sometimes fingers it and cracks it.

My surprise provoked Fr Duddleswell to say, "He cracks it expertly, apologizes for the little 'accident' and out of the kindness of his heart repeats his original offer. Most times, the owner says he can have it now and good riddance. Pinky takes it to his dealer who fixes it so you cannot see the join. Well what d'you say to that, Father Neil?"

"It's wrong, Father."

"God's holy Mother, lad, 'tis bloody facinorous, so 'tis."

"Very wrong," I said heatedly.

I expected to be sent back into church to release a few more holy souls, but the sight of Pinky Weston turned his attention to other matters. He invited me, instead, to accompany him by underground train to Portobello Road antique market.

Above the roar and rattle of the train he told me how their family house in Bath and later in Portobello Road had been full of beauty. "Full of it," he repeated with a yell. "Can you *hear* me?"

I nodded like an anxious duck.

I enjoyed the chatter and bustle of the cosmopolitan crowd in Portobello Road. Pigeons, like dun-colored Holy Ghosts, pecked away at scraps on the pavement. Chestnuts were being roasted on braziers. With Bonfire Night only three days off, children stood beside stuffed scarecrows piping out, "Penny for the Guy." We sifted through bric-a-brac on the stalls and flattened our noses against shop windows.

He taught me about Hepplewhite armchairs, when the Sheraton period was, and once he called out, "Look, Father Neil, a genuine Queen Anne chest of drawers dating from 1705." I, who couldn't tell whether a woman was twenty-five or thirty-five, was terribly impressed.

We were passing a shop pasted with notices "Under New Management" when a middle-aged couple emerged. The lady wore a bright, flowered dress and butterfly-winged glasses. She tossed her blue-rinsed head derisively at the remains of a chair in the window and called to her husband who had a camera round his neck, "Chuck, what a goddam load of junk."

"Ten pounds for that *thing*," said Chuck, tugging on his camera strap.

"What's that in dollars, honey?"

"A helluva lot," grunted Chuck. "Back home in New York, the garbage collectors would charge to take it away."

Fr Duddleswell seized my arm and dragged me after him.

Twenty yards further on, he released me and said, "Did you hear that, Father Neil?"

"Americans," I began, "coming over here and..."

"Shut your mouth. I mean, Father Neil, listen to what I am telling you. That 'thing' is a bloody Chippendale." I was about to say the chair was without a seat when I remembered that the Venus de Milo didn't have any arms and nobody seemed to mind. "Now, hear me, Father Neil, this is what we are about to do."

Five minutes later we were inside the shop admiring a statue, two and a half feet high, of the Madonna and Child.

"Would you suppose," said Fr Duddleswell in his preaching voice, "that Mrs Pring would like to have this?"

Before I could reply, a young assistant in jeans had pushed his hair out of his eyes to inquire if he could be of help.

After some sales patter about the statue's age, its haunting beauty, the beechwood of which it was carved, its Flemish origin, he said that for us the price was £250.

Fr Duddleswell blinked, removed his spectacles and breathed on them carefully like the risen Jesus on the apostles. He said, as he rubbed away the mist, that he thought the young gentleman had told him the statue was very old. A brand new one would surely be cheaper.

"How much did you want to spend on this lady, Guv?" the assistant sniffed.

"About five pounds," answered Fr Duddleswell, "maybe six."

"What's wrong with a fountain pen?" said the assistant before retiring to an inner room where he doubtless elaborated his suggestion to a young woman in slacks who was manicuring her nails.

We moved towards the door. Fr Duddleswell half opened it and called to the young man, "Could I perhaps have that old chair in the window for a fiver?"

The assistant, without looking up, said, "Ninety quid." I was thinking the Americans had got it wrong when the lad added, "But since it's opening day you can have it for nine."

Fr Duddleswell opened the door wider before asking me if Mrs Pring would care for that. "Could be," I said.

"You would not take six, I suppose?" asked Fr Duddleswell.

The young man wrenched his eyes away from his girl. "Seven pounds ten," he said, "and that's my final offer."

Grudgingly, Fr Duddleswell re-entered the shop. "Take a check?"

"Cash." And the deal was closed. "Sorry I can't wrap it," was the assistant's last audible irony.

Fr Duddleswell was in raptures. At breakneck speed, he sucked me in his wake until we reached *Duddleswell's*. Fred Dobie, the proprietor, greeted us with a smile. "Going that way?" he asked, pointing to the railway bridge where second-hand stuff was for sale. Then, "Good God, Fr Duddleswell, a Chippy."

Fr Duddleswell told him how he had acquired it and, after some hard bargaining, handed over the chair in exchange for fifty pounds. Cash.

"Now," said Fr Duddleswell to me, "I will buy you a cup of tay."

In the café, I insisted on paying for the teas and two doughnuts. He noticed that the chap at the counter had charged me tuppence too much and refused on principle to "waive the excess fare."

I ate and drank in silence while he tried to convince me that he had not diddled the vendor; talent in recognizing *objets d'art* is what the antique trade is all about. Portobello Road would close tomorrow if people did business in any other way. The chair did not even have a seat to it. Fred Dobie was likely congratulating himself this very minute on putting one over on *him*.

My silence was more telling than any counter-argument. Gradually, he was reduced to disconnected phrases like, "Turning over a new leaf," "no deviousness and no uncharity," "poor young things just starting out in the trade," and "on November 2nd when I should have been releasing holy souls."

His tea was untouched when he jumped up and marched out of the café. I followed him back to the shop. He told the startled young man what was what, wrote him out a check for £20 "to more or less split the difference," assuring him that his signature was genuine, and left.

The young man came running after him with the statue of the Madonna and Child. "I'm grateful, truly grateful," he said. "Please take this as a gift for your lady friend."

I was staggered at such generosity. "Virtue is rewarded," I crowed, when the young man was back inside his shop chatting up his girl.

"Do not be such a bloody fool, Father Neil," he snarled. "Nobody here gives you a handful of water for nothing."

"A fake, Father?"

He nodded. "At least 'twill never suffer from woodworm."

"Plaster?"

Another nod. "Woolworth's could not sell it for sixpence. Still, I reckon Mrs Pring will prefer it to a Chippendale that is as open as a navvy's toilet." He handed the statue to me as if it was more than his reputation was worth to be seen in its company.

In Pembroke Road, seeing a single leaf floating down from a sycamore tree he recited something about angel hosts that fall "Thick as autumnal leaves that strow the brooks/ In Vallombrosa."

His continuing purpose of amendment impressed me. If only it had not brought upon him another fit of the November blues.

On the way home it was all Ecclesiastes and Omar Khayyám. "Vanity of vanities" followed by "Alas that Spring should vanish with the Rose." The only interlude was when we stopped at a Games Shop in the High Street. Fr Duddleswell ordered five pounds worth of assorted fireworks to be delivered to the orphanage for Guy Fawkes Day, November 5th.

At the rectory door we were met by Mrs Pring. "I'm glad

you're back, Fr D. Someone just phoned to say Jack Dodson is sinking."

Fr Duddleswell snatched the statue from me, placed it in her arms, and rushed to collect the holy oils. Mrs Pring called out over the Virgin's crowned head that he should wear his overcoat against the cold, but he was already on his way. "Take care of the confessions for me, Father Neil, in case I should be late."

I did duty for him in the confessional and ate supper alone. My worries grew when curfew hour arrived and still no sign of him. At 11:15, Mrs Pring put a thermos flask in his study and retired for the night.

At nearly midnight, Fr Duddleswell came in panting furiously. He charged past me as I stood at the foot of the stairs saying, "Tell you about it later." I could hear him unbolting the church door.

In two minutes the bolts clanged to and he re-appeared. In his study he frantically unscrewed the top of the thermos flask and poured himself a cup of Ovaltine. He had taken one sip when the clock on his shelf chimed "the Mephistophelean hour." He put his drink down disappointedly. He could drink no more if he was to celebrate Mass the next morning.

I was concerned about him. He had not eaten or drunk a thing since lunch, and not even a drop of water would pass his lips until after his second Sunday Mass at ten o'clock.

I apologized for having ruined his tea. "'Tis of no consequence, Father Neil," he said gallantly. "This afternoon, you saved me from further deviousness and uncharity. I am much obliged to you."

I asked about Mr Dodson. "He passed over at 10:30." My parish priest looked tired and sad. "The leaves of life keep falling one by one.'" He rubbed his eyes beneath his spectacles. "I stayed to console the widow, like, on this her longest day. Ah, for her to be single-bedded after all these years. 'Tis enough to make an onion weep. No man at night to snug her and melt her with his breath." Then a thought cheered him up a bit. "Went off in style, though, did old Jack. It happened well to him. The last rites. He had it all, including the Papal Blessing. A very healthy death. Most likely he went straight home to God on angels' wings."

Since Mr Dodson had obtained a plenary Indulgence from the Pope, why had Fr Duddleswell rushed into the church before All Souls' Day was over to get him another?

He read me. "'Twas to make sure, like."

On Monday morning at ten, we set off together "to comfort the widow Dodson." On our walk, Fr Duddleswell expounded his views on Purgatory, the Catholics' half-way house to Heaven.

"The trouble with Protestant theologians, Father Neil, is they have no imagination. 'Tis their mistaken opinion that the bereaved like to think of their loved ones being taken immediately to Paradise."

My reaction must have put me among the Protestants. "When you lose someone you love," he explained, "you experience the overpowering need to comfort them. 'Tis hard indeed to picture the dead as blissfully content while you are still shattered and torn by the losing of them. There must be attunement betwixt living and dead, you follow? The Church's teaching on Purgatory takes account of this." His view was that when the sorrows of the bereaved ease off and they leave *their* Purgatory, then they are ready to feel that their dead have entered the joys of Heaven.

"What about the plenary Indulgence for the dead?" I asked.

"The faithful believe it, and they do not believe it," he said, which made the faithful seem as devious as himself.

The Dodsons lived in a "prefab," a single-story, factory-built house lowered into position almost in one piece.

Mrs Dodson, white-haired and almost worn away by time, was touched by our visit. "Come in, Fathers," she said, "while I make ye a cup of tea."

Fr Duddleswell took her right forearm, pressed it tightly, and simply said, "Mary."

Mrs Dodson put the kettle on the stove. While waiting for it to boil, she reminisced. Fifty-three years they had been together. God was good to let them see in the Gold.

"You'll never believe it, Fathers," she confided, "but when we wed, we couldn't afford a ring. So I went to the haberdasher's and bought myself a brass-curtain hook. One farthing it cost."

That hook had lasted fifty years when they bought each other fourteen karat gold rings. "His was engraved 'For my darling Jack' and mine has 'For my darling Mary.' I could have kept his, Fathers," she said, wiping away a tear, "but I thought it'd be nice if he wore it to Heaven."

"A wise fellow, your Jack, Mary," Fr Duddleswell put in hastily, "arranging to go on the most propitious day of the year, All Souls', when Purgatory is cleaned out."

"God's help is nearer than the door," she said. As she made the tea, she explained that out of their savings she was paying for a splendid funeral. "He didn't want to go owing nobody nothing, Fathers." The money even ran to a solid oak coffin.

"That's nice," I said for something to say.

We sat sipping our tea until Fr Duddleswell picked up a large, pitted silver pot from the sideboard. "How interesting," he said with a curious nostalgic smile, "how *very* interesting. Mary, did you know...?"

The doorbell interrupted him. Probably a neighbor calling to offer sympathy. When Mrs Dodson opened the door, we heard a simpering voice say, "Mrs Dodson?"

"Yes."

"I was a close friend of your husband's."

The caller's name was Philip Weston. "But friends of mine like your James call me Pinky."

Father Duddleswell confided to me that "that sharper must have the periscopic eyes of a toad."

Mrs Dodson had to admit that her Jack had never mentioned him, but she thanked him for the courtesy of his call.

"I used to have the odd drink with Jack in the local."

Mrs Dodson said it must have been a long time ago because he had been bed-ridden for the last ten years. Pinky Weston conceded it was a long time ago. "But you don't forget easy an old crony like Jack Dodson."

Mrs Dodson was unwilling to let Pinky in until Fr Duddleswell called out, "'Tis all right, Mary, we are just about to take our leave."

Pinky Weston's flat white face looked as if it were permanently pressed against a window-pane. Fr Duddleswell took no notice of him. Still with the pot in his hand, he said, "As I was telling you, Mary, I am very intrigued by this pot."

"My granma gave it me years ago," said Mary. "Her granny, I believe, gave it to her."

Fr Duddleswell smiled broadly. "That accounts for it, then. My own father, God rest him, had one like this. Elizabethan silver." When Mary expressed surprise at it being real silver, he said that the coating was worn off and she may not realize that antiques are often worth considerably less when they are re-silvered.

Patrick Duddleswell Senior had sold his for £95. "Mark you, Mary, 'twould be worth every penny of £200 were it up for sale today." He pointed to indentations on the lid. "There, it looks as if a fork has pressed down on the metal. Tiger marks."

It seemed to me that Fr Duddleswell had cleverly warned Mary not to part with a family treasure. Pinky Weston must also have known that if he swindled the old widow he would have to answer to the Church.

At the door, Fr Duddleswell said, "Keep in mind the old saying, Mary: 'The three most beautiful things in the world are a ship under sail, a tree in bloom, and a holy man on his death-bed." Mrs Dodson half smiled and half cried. "Oh, and by the way, Mary, which undertaker have you settled on?"

"Bottesford's," she said.

I apologized for making no contribution to the visit. "You are wrong," he returned. "You said but little but you said it well. Times there are, Father Neil, when words spoil meanings.

'Tis pitiful but when the deer of their woods has departed, what can you do but grasp them with kindness?"

He fell into a reverie, only coming out of it from time to time to utter the name "Bottesford." He clicked his fingers and a few minutes later we were on the doorstep of Bottesford's Funeral Parlour.

I had not seen the proprietor since he ran out of the church some weeks earlier. He was fat—Fr Duddleswell said his hand was too kind to his mouth—and he wore an atrocious ginger wig that did not blend at all well with the greying hair beneath. He had a nose that reminded me of Charles Laughton's Quasimodo in "The Hunchback of Notre Dame." The nostrils pointed skyward like a double-barrelled gun.

He was in the back room. We disturbed him while he was planing the lid of a coffin which rested on a carpenter's bench.

" 'Tis a sad day for the Dismal Trade when there is no funeral, Bottesford," said Fr Duddleswell.

The undertaker went on shuffling his plane back and forth. "People don't die to please me," he snapped.

Fr Duddleswell asked to be taken to the Chapel of Rest in order to pray over Mr Dodson. Mr Bottesford's attitude changed at once from defiance to anxiety. He insisted he would have to go first and prepare the Chapel. It would only take a few minutes, and in the meanwhile he invited us to take a seat.

When he went out, Fr Duddleswell seemed intent on taking something else. There was a large cabinet in the room full of small drawers. Fr Duddleswell opened up one after another until he came across the thing he was looking for. Whatever it was, he put it smartly in his pocket.

He gestured to the coffin nearing completion. "Look at the quality of that wood, Father Neil. Orange boxes banged together, nothing more. 'Twould not keep a corpse dry in an April shower. Not only does he fake his hair by putting a bird's nest upon his head, he also fakes coffins. What can you expect, Father Neil, of a man who makes a living out of death?"

Mr Bottesford returned puffing and blowing. He led us out and across a small grey courtyard into his Chapel of Rest.

It wasn't much more than a large garden shed. Black drapes from the war years kept out the light. In the center was a catafalque on which rested a superb oak coffin lit up at each corner by candles of yellow-ochre. No orange box in this case, I thought.

Fr Duddleswell suggested we all kneel for the *De Profundis*. "Out of the depths have I cried to Thee, O Lord," he began, "Lord, hear my voice," and Mr Bottesford and I joined forces with "Let Thine ear be attentive to the voice of my supplication."

When the prayer was over, Fr Duddleswell approached the catafalque. "I congratulate you, Bottesford," he whispered, "a most beautiful coffin."

"Casket," Mr Bottesford corrected him with the term favored by the trade.

Without warning, Fr Duddleswell hammered on the coffin lid with his fist. The effect in that confined space and wavering light was shattering. Mr Bottesford and I almost embraced each other in fright. Fr Duddleswell repeated his onslaught on the coffin from various angles. His recent preoccupation with death must have unhinged the old boy.

"Bottesford," he said threateningly, "'tis as hollow as is your heart. Where is he, tell me, now, this instant." Had the undertaker sold the body for the purposes of necromancy or scientific research? Mr Bottesford pointed to an object in shadow by the wall. "Bring a candle, Bottesford."

The undertaker pulled one of the huge candles out of its socket and carried it with quivering hand to where Fr Duddleswell was standing. "Take it off," he ordered, pointing to a tarpaulin covering something of indistinct shape.

I turned away almost expecting to see under it Jack Dodson's corpse. It was only a second coffin. It had on it a brass plate with Jack's name, his dates of birth and death, and R.I.P.

"An orange box," said Fr Duddleswell disgustedly, "masquerading as a coffin." Even by candlelight I could see that the coffin was neatly covered by a kind of wallpaper of oak design. Tear-filled eyes at a funeral might not notice it.

I was sickened by the undertaker's deceit but worse was to come. Fr Duddleswell said imperiously, "Take it off, Bottesford. The lid, unscrew it, Bottesford." No doubting his meaning this time.

"I can't," he said hoarsely.

"There is no need for an exhumation order, Bottesford. He is not buried yet."

Mr Bottesford's nerves were completely out of control. He bowed his head and the crackling candle flame shot up and singed his hair. Sparks flew and there was the odor of acrid fumes. He dropped the candle, tugged his wig off, and stamped on it.

Fr Duddleswell said, "'Tis but a foretaste of the cremation that the Lord has in store for you, Bottesford, if you do not alter the evil of your doings."

I couldn't help feeling sorry for him as he stood there in the macabre light, bald and trembling. But Fr Duddleswell was still not content. "'Tis not there is it, Bottesford?"

"He's in there all right, Father, I swear it. Please don't make me unscrew the lid."

"You know well enough, man, I said not *he* but *it* is not in there."

"I don't know what the hell you're spouting about," yelled Mr Bottesford, his spirit returning as he stooped to pick up his wig.

Fr Duddleswell put his hand in his pocket and pulled out a small object that gleamed in the candlelight. "The ring, Bottesford," he said, almost touching the undertaker's nose with it.

"You pinched it," whimpered Mr Bottesford, lifting his head like a dog.

"No, Bottesford, you are the miscreant who pinched it. Black you are without and black within. Father Neil is me witness that I found this ring inscribed 'To me darling Jack' in a drawer of your workroom. 'Twas not, I take it, the corpse that placed it there."

He made Bottesford promise on his "Catholic's honor" that the body would be transferred to the oak coffin—"casket" muttered Mr Bottesford—and the ring replaced on the finger.

We returned to the workshop. "Does the name Pinky Weston mean anything to you, Bottesford?"

It was evident to Fr Duddleswell that only the undertaker could have tipped off the Rapper, because no notice of Jack Dodson's death had been posted on the church door. He warned Bottesford that if Pinky Weston had swindled old Mary, he would get the bill. A final admonition: "Mend your devious ways, Bottesford, else I will see to it you no more box or heap the cold sod on parishioners of mine."

On the way home, I expressed disgust at Bottesford's goings-on. Fr Duddleswell, firm in his charitable resolve, did not entirely agree. "'Tis true that grave-digger would condiddle the chocolate out of a child's mouth." All the same, Bottesford performed the least loved of the corporal works of mercy, bedding down the dead.

"A man's profession is bound to set its mark on him, Father Neil, if you're still with me. 'Tis no laughing matter tailoring wooden suits and attending a hundred funerals a year. For that he needs a heart that cannot feel and a nose that cannot smell."

I reminded him of his words about Mr Bottesford making a living out of death. "And do not we with our Requiems, lad? After all, Bottesford is not Adam. He did not invent death. Indeed, by raising the cost of dying, he might even be said to discourage it."

Even when I mentioned the ring, Fr Duddleswell inclined to forgiveness. "'Tis easy to get hot under the round collar, Father Neil, but casting prejudice aside, to rob a cold ruin is not nearly so bad as robbing the living."

I was thoroughly irritated by his willingness to excuse the undertaker. "He robbed the living, too," I said. "He overcharged Mrs Dodson for the coffin"—"casket" he corrected me with a wink—"and nearly lost her that lovely silver pot."

Overcharging Mary, he agreed, was a different matter. No recently bereaved person likes haggling over the price of a funeral. It seems mean and a slur on the memory of the departed. "But, then Father Neil," he said smiling, "if I do not judge him too harshly for that even, d'you not think I owe him something?"

We were at tea when the doorbell rang. Mrs Pring announced that it was Mrs Dodson. In a flash, Fr Duddleswell was on his feet to invite her in. He took no heed of her protests. "Fetch Mary a cup, will you not, Mrs Pring? And, Mary dear, pity your poor feet and sit yourself down."

Mary's story was that Mr Weston had prevailed on her to part with her Elizabethan pot for £75 in crisp, new fivers.

"That's daylight robbery," I cried.

Fr Duddleswell told me to hear Mary out and not get so uppity for God Almighty's sake.

Mary looked crestfallen at my remark. "It's not as if my Jack had strong attachments to that pot, Fathers." She went on to praise Mr Weston's honesty. He had accidentally twisted one of the handles and didn't reduce his offer for all that.

Fr Duddleswell flashed at me a warning to itch where I could scratch. "Anyone in your position obviously has need of the money, Mary."

Mrs Dodson explained that Jack's illness took up so much of their savings "and we're—I'm—only an old-age pensioner." When the soil had settled on the grave she would now be able to afford a nice headstone.

Mary brightened up when Fr Duddleswell congratulated her on acting so wisely. All things considered, it was not a bad price. The pot *was* damaged. Pinky had to pass it on to a dealer who would want his rake-off, and selling to dealers is not always easy. Fashions change. Pinky took a risk in that there might not be a ready market for that kind of pot at this time.

"And now, Mary," Fr Duddleswell concluded, "tomorrow we will lay your darling man to rest. No more thistles where he lies, Mary, and prayers of yours will provide him with pillows of roses for his head. Ah," he sighed, "'tis nice to contemplate that when yourself gets to Heaven 'twill be a country where you are well acquainted."

He took twenty-five pounds out of his wallet saying, "'Tis your lucky day, Mary. Only Saturday last I rid meself of a perfectly useless chair and—would you believe it, now?—this is what I was paid for it." He thrust the money into Mary's hand before she could say no. "'Tis not for you, Mary, mind, 'tis for Jack. Towards his headstone, you follow?"

He led the widow to the door as if she were a queen. "Make sure, Mary, you order him a *beautiful* stone."

When he came back half-singing, "As leaves of the trees, such is the life of man," I tackled him with, "Father, don't try and excuse Mr Weston's rotten trick this time."

"Me soul detests it, Father Neil," he replied earnestly. "Would that I could poke me digit in his eye."

"Imagine cheating a dear old lady out of so much money."

"Abso-bloody-lutely, Father Neil, except that the pot was but a common or garden tea caddy worth less than half a dollar."

16

HELL AND
HIGH WATER

"It's a lonesome wash that there's not a man's shirt in," said Mrs Pring. My bedroom door was open and I could see her putting my clean linen in a drawer. I nodded, knowing that she was referring to the widow Dodson who had just gone home.

I offered her an opportunity for a chat. "Going to stoke up my fire, Mrs P?"

A couple of minutes later she was piling on the coals in my study. "At first when you're widowed," she puffed, as she knelt at the fireplace, "you can't believe it's true, or if it is true it can't be happening to *you*. It must be either a dream or someone in the War Office got the name and number wrong. Grief draws slowly like the morning fire."

She talked unemotionally about losing her husband. It was a long time ago. A whirlwind, war-time courtship. Love at first sight and she never wanted another.

One thing bothered her: she could not honestly remember the color of his eyes. "I know they were a sort of greeny brown, Father Neil, but I can't picture them, you see?" I pursed my lips and nodded.

"We were only married a couple of months," she went on, brushing the grate. "My Ted was much younger than you, of course." I was glad she did not see my surprised reaction to that. "I wrote to him straight away, soon as I knew, telling him that a little someone was on the way. But the letter came back with a batch of others in his effects. The only one unopened, it was. He was already gone, you..." She was still for a moment. "Two months after, the war was over. All the killing stopped." She paused again. "Thank God." I wanted to touch her on the shoulder, but I was too shy. "It meant my Helen was half-orphaned before she saw the light of a candle." She wiped her eyes on her sleeve because her hands had coal-dust on them. As she got up, she said, "I think people round here like talking to you, Father Neil." I blushed at the compliment. "You're a listening man."

The change of topic was abrupt. "At least *his* attack of the sullens"—she pointed below—"is over and he's back to abnormality."

I sat her down and told her how Fr Duddleswell had tricked Pinky Weston. I expected her to show some disapproval but, as usual when we were alone, she was not hard on him.

"He's as slippery as an eel's tail," she said, "but he never lied to the Rapper, did he, now? He only let him lie to himself." She blew a stray hair out of her eyes. "Ah, if only he was half as wicked as he thinks he is he'd be such a nice man. And much more fun to live with."

Through the floorboards, confirming Mrs Pring's view that Fr Duddleswell's November blues were over, came the strains of "The flowers that bloom in the Spring, tra la." Perhaps it was this song that caused Mrs Pring's *lapsus linguae*. She said, "He may be an old sour-puss outside but never mind him, inside he's full of the springs of joy." The song ceased suddenly when the telephone rang, and Fr Duddleswell took the call.

Mrs Pring was keen to know if I was really settled in St Jude's. In my reply I carefully avoided the word "settled." I said life was full of interest.

"Don't take too much notice of Fr D," she advised. As his steps sounded on the stairs, she stood up. "As you've probably guessed by now, his great weakness is the strength of his convictions."

There was a thump on the door. "Are you alone, Father Neil?" When I called out that only Mrs Pring was with me, he made as if to retrace his steps saying, "That giddy woman is too many for me altogether."

Mrs Pring opened the door and signalled to him that she was on the point of leaving. She was not offensive to him, maybe to reward him for his good work on behalf of widows.

His own uncharity and deviousness had returned full-blast. "I cannot understand why you associate with her, Father Neil," he barked. "In every other particular you are a commendable curate. D'you not know that herself would build a nest in your ear and twitter-twitter all the day long?"

"She was talking about her husband," I said.

That quietened him down. "'Tis always the young," he said, biting his lip, "who die in old men's wars." He settled into an armchair clutching a large tome. "As to the purpose of me visit."

First came a reminder of the next day's Clergy Conference on "Life After Death." Inter-denominational, it was to be held at St Luke's under the chairmanship of the Anglican incumbent, the Rev. Percival Probble. In addition to the three Anglican ministers, two Methodists and a Jewish Rabbi had agreed to take part. The true Church was to be represented by us two and Canon Mahoney, D.D. The Canon was Bishop O'Reilly's personal theologian. He had been deputed to keep us on the path of orthodoxy and answer all non-Catholic objections.

Fr Duddleswell handed me his tome, *The Mysteries of Christianity* by Matthias Scheeben, priced $7.50. "Hot from the States," he said. The author was the greatest nineteenth century German theologian. "I want you to mug up the passages on life after death, you follow? In case the Canon and meself are unable to cope, like." He was being funny, I think. "If the Protestants suggest we pray for reunion, we will do no such thing, you hear me? We are far too divided to pray with them for *that*."

The phone call had been from Mother Stephen, Superior

280

of the Convent. She had invited herself and Sister Perpetua, our sacristan, to the rectory in thirty minutes time. No reason had been given for the visit, but Fr Duddleswell needed no telling. It was the same every year. Mother Stephen wanted to cancel the fireworks display at the last moment. The pretext was usually the likelihood of damage to the convent's lawn or trees, or complaints from neighbors about the noise, or the good sisters having to keep the children in order when they should be reciting the divine office in chapel according to the rules of their holy Founder. "Be ready to buttress me should I begin to flag," he concluded.

On the dot of five, *Laudetur Jesus Christus* from Mother Stephen and *Semper laudetur*, "May Christ be always praised" from Fr Duddleswell. The Superior dismissed the offer of tea with a twitch of her bony hand.

"Fr Duddleswell, I have not come to ask you to cancel the fireworks display tomorrow evening." So the old man was mistaken. "No, Father, I have been obliged to cancel it myself already."

Fr Duddleswell inquired the reason. He was unruffled as if he were used to setbacks of this sort.

"Two-fold, Father." For first-fold, Mother Stephen had recently read a book on the Gunpowder Plot written by a convert to Catholicism. His thesis was that Guy Fawkes Day was a Protestant ruse to blacken Holy Mother Church. Guy Fawkes' attempt to blow up the Houses of Parliament in 1605 had been made a pretext to persecute Roman Catholics ever since.

"I should imagine, Mother," said Fr Duddleswell, "that had he succeeded, the whole country would have been beholden to him." The joke was lost on the black shroud seated opposite him.

Fr Duddleswell stated politely that the Bishop had appointed *him* defender of the faith in this area and he was perfectly satisfied with the theological propriety of burning a straw man on a bonfire. In fact, it was irrefutable proof of Catholicism, a proof not immediately evident to Mother

Stephen or to me. Protestants ridicule Catholics, he said, for making use of images in their religion, and here are the Protestants availing themselves of "Catholic methods of festivalizing." Before Mother Stephen could object he reminded her of the burning of heretics at autos dà fé, apart from Catholic belief in the retributive fires of Hell and Purgatory.

It convinced me that Guy Fawkes Day was a sound Catholic investment. Fr Duddleswell looked across at me as if to say, "One down and one to go."

Mother Stephen was already fumbling in the folds of her habit for her second argument. "This leaflet, Father," she said, "has been sent us by the Council. The police have cooperated with the fire brigade and the local hospitals to provide statistics of accidents to minors during last Guy Fawkes night." She read out figures. Five children under ten had burned their hands and sixteen under six had burned their legs, and so on. It was pretty grizzly.

Fr Duddleswell pretended to see no significance in the figures whatsoever.

"Fr Duddleswell, I have taken the liberty of going through the parcel of lethals you despatched to our convent. Crackers, rockets, smellies, smokies, catherine wheels—a whole arsenal of destruction."

Fr Duddleswell forced her to grind to a halt as he unfolded a leaflet taken from his inside pocket. He pressed out the creases noisily. "Police statistics, Mother, on the local children killed on the road in the last year, together with the number of accidents on the pedestrian crossings themselves." He smiled pityingly. "You are not proposing, Mother, that children should be forbidden to cross the roads?"

The Superior accused him of flippancy. Crossing the roads was a necessity, whereas she was about to prove that a fireworks display was not. He was already promising that he and I would set off the fireworks. "The only persons, Mother, in any danger are meself and me curate." He seemed confident that Mother Stephen would accept the display on such generous terms.

"Fr Duddleswell, you may set yourself alight or indulge in any other solitary pleasure on our convent lawn that brings you satisfaction. Our children will not be there to see it."

She was rising to her feet when Mrs Pring banged on the door and entered without an invitation. Fr Duddleswell was annoyed at being interrupted at this delicate stage in the negotiations.

Mrs Pring, clasping a copy of *The Universe*, was not in the least perturbed. "Father, I only wanted to ask you something about the display tomorrow evening." His face fell to below zero. "Are you using the Holy Father's blessing?"

Fr Duddleswell thawed instantly and met her inquiry with a quizzical smile.

"Last new year's eve," she explained, "the Pope blessed the fireworks and the children of Rome. A lovely prayer, as you remember, Father. Will you be using this"—she pointed to where the prayer was printed in capitals in the newspaper—"or the one in the Ritual?"

Fr Duddleswell assured her that of course he would be using the Holy Father's own blessing written specially for such occasions.

Mrs Pring departed to be followed soon by Mother Stephen. She had been faced with a straight choice: to obey God or Caesar. Sister Perpetua bowed out her defeated Superior before winking at us.

"Sister Perpetua," croaked Mother Stephen without turning round, "would you kindly regulate the movements of your eyelids in the manner of which our holy Founder would have approved."

Mrs Pring expressed delight that the poor little orphans would not be deprived of a rare chance to enjoy themselves, and Fr Duddleswell took the opportunity to relate his favorite tale about statistics.

In the west of Ireland, "in the dark days," a local deputation approached the visiting English Chief Secretary with statistics proving that they needed finance for the railway so they could send their produce to market. Next day, another deputation arrived with another sheaf of statistics proving conclusively that they needed food subsidies because not so much as a sprig of parsley would grow on their land. Fr Duddleswell laughed merrily before putting on his poshest English accent. "'Now, my good man,' said the Chief Secretary to the leader of the second deputation, 'yesterday's statistics prove the exact opposite of yours. How do you account for it?' 'So be it, your Honor,' says the leader of the second deputation, 'but y'see, yesterday's statistics were compiled for an entirely different purpose.'"

The rest of that evening I spent with Scheeben, reading about death, judgement, Heaven, and Hell.

After breakfast, Fr Duddleswell drove off to an unknown destination. He was back well in time to transport Canon Mahoney and me to the Vicarage.

In a committee room, we drank coffee before grouping around the table. The three Anglicans wore cassocks with capes, which we always held to be an affectation. Of the two Methodists, Sobb was bearded and Tinsey was clean-shaven. At the end of the table opposite Mr Probble sat Rabbi Epstein. He wore a broad-brimmed black hat on the back of his head, a bushy beard, and spectacles that covered the rest of his face. He was still in a frayed black satin overcoat and, for some undisclosed reason, he had another draped across his knees. He came from somewhere east of Dover.

The Rev. d'Arcy, the Senior Anglican curate, read a thirty-minute position paper on "Life after Death in the Old and New Testaments." It contained frequent references to *zoē aiōnios*, which at first I thought was a girl's name until it dawned on me that it was Greek for "eternal life." Mr d'Arcy had read Greats at Oxford, and his classical learning put most of what he said beyond my reach.

The first comment was made by Rabbi Epstein. Very politely he objected to the use of "the *Old* Testament." "You must remember well," he said in his broken English, "that for us it only is the Jewish Bibble. *You* call him old because you think your Bibble is newer. For us, the Jewish Bibble is always newest."

The Rev. d'Arcy apologized profusely for his careless use of terms "in present company."

"Thank you," said the Rabbi—his "th" was pronounced like a "z" in the Slavonic fashion. "Now where heaven is? I ask myself." Nobody round the table was anxious to help him answer his question. "Where God is, there heaven is." He tapped his outstretched fingers together as if applauding himself. "Heaven has not a place," he went on in a semi-mystical vein. "God is, as we say in Talmud '*ha-Geburah*, The Might.' He is the place where the world is. That is what we Jews think."

Canon Mahoney scratched his bald head and exchanged a glance with Fr Duddleswell which said it is not easy looking for the invisible wee folk in the pitch dark.

"We Jews," went on the Rabbi, his eyes so radiant it looked as if two lighted cigarettes had been sunk in the sockets, "we Jews believe passionately in *gehenna*, the pit of the fire." Fr Duddleswell nodded approval. "Also *Gan Eden*, the Garden of the Bliss and the Delight." The Canon and Fr Duddleswell both saw signs of hope in that. "In the pit of the fire," continued Rabbi Epstein, "the naughty boys go." I could see my two colleagues beginning to wonder what differences remained between ourselves and our Jewish brethren when the Rabbi said, "What more certain could be than that Jesus in the Garden of Delight is? He was a good Jew. But," he swung his head like a pendulum, "some of his followers, aaaah." That "ah" went down his throat like the last of the bathwater, in a noisy vortex, down the drain. Well, this was a curate's egg. The rest was all bad. "The *very* naughty boys sometimes spend a whole year in the pit of the fire before they enter the Paradise."

Everyone at the table disapproved of that and the Rabbi, not wishing to proselytize, said nothing after that except, "We Jews believe there are no ghettoes in Heaven and no pogroms in Hell."

The fat Rev. Pinkerton, puffing on his cigarette without ever removing it from his mouth, delivered his opinion on Hell. The fire was a symbol, like the worm that never dies and the teeth that gnash on endlessly, like Christ's command to pluck out your eye rather than let it look on wickedness.

Canon Mahoney, sucking his dead pipe, launched the counter-attack, ably supported by Fr Duddleswell. The Church has taught for nigh on two thousand years the reality of the fires of Hell and the eternity of the roasting prepared for those who die unrepentant. In this, the Church was simply reinforcing the teaching of our Blessed Lord who five times in the course of the Sermon on the Mount stressed the everlasting pains of the damned.

The Rev. Pinkerton stubbed out one cigarette and lit another before commenting caustically on the arbitrariness of the Catholic God. Why should He cut off one man's life immediately after mortal sin and another's immediately after he had repented of mortal sin?

Canon Mahoney handled that with ease. God in His divine fore-knowledge sees how both of them *would* behave whatever opportunities for repentance He offered them.

I was very glad the Canon was on my team. But, objected Fatty, did we really think God was so cruel as to punish eternally an evil deed done in time? Fr Duddleswell drily asked the Rev. Pinkerton if *he* expected to be *rewarded* eternally for some good deed he might do in time.

"Okay," wheezed Fatty, blowing out and filling the room with a pillar of cloud, "tell me how parents can possibly be happy knowing that their children are burning forever in Hell?"

"It is the very sweetness of divine justice," replied Canon Mahoney, "that will obliterate the pain, as will the vision of the beatific God."

Mr Probble was becoming increasingly agitated as the temperature of the discussion rose. He was smiling and murmuring words about keeping the ecumenical spirit alive and abiding by the Great Commandment to love one another.

Mr Tinsey, an alto, demanded to know if, in Catholic dogma, children were eligible for Hell. Fr Duddleswell replied that naturally they were, provided they had reached the age of reason.

"Which is?" peeped Mr Tinsey.

"Seven or thereabouts," answered Fr Duddleswell. Catching sight of Fatty almost swallowing his cigarette in a rage, he explained that Catholics respect the dignity of choice even among God's little ones.

Mr Tinsey remarked that "sevens" were not even old enough to play with fireworks.

The bearded Mr Sobb asked how fire could burn bodies *and* souls, and burn them forever without consuming them.

It was just the question I was hoping for. "May I?" I began.

"Certainly not," snapped Fr Duddleswell, turning to Canon Mahoney for the official answer to that conundrum.

"Let the lad say his piece, Charlie," the Canon said kindly.

I opened my Scheeben at page 693 and read in a trembling voice:

"Hell fire differs from natural fire in this respect, that its flame is not the result of a natural, chemical process, but is sustained by divine power and therefore does not dissolve the body which it envelops, but preserves it forever in the condition of burning agony."

I don't know if that answered the Methodists' objections; it certainly silenced them. It even seemed to precipitate the end of the Conference. There was only small talk after that.

We Catholic clergy repaired to the Clinton Hotel. The consensus was that there was no value in such conferences and the Canon would report this to the Bishop. Jews were as incomprehensible as a woman's tantrums. The Protestants, especially "that fat twerp," were so stubborn in their unbelief that there was little chance of converting them.

"You'd as soon convert a cock into a hen," suggested Fr Duddleswell.

Canon Mahoney peered moodily into his empty wine glass, proffered it to me to replenish, and sighed, "They went into a skid 400 years ago at the Reformation, Charlie, and they've been facing the wrong way ever since."

It was a matter of amazement to us that men of the cloth could doubt the everlasting flames when they were written large and clear in the Holy Book.

The Canon rolled the wine on his tongue and smoothed out a crease on his head. "No reverence have they, Charlie, for the Undebatables."

"'Tis the ultimate proof, Seamus," said Fr Duddleswell, downing his last drop of heavy wet, "that only the Catholic Church has the authority to keep the harsh truths of the faith alive in their pristine purity."

Mrs Pring accompanied us in the car to the orphanage. It was a clear, crisp, windless evening lit by moon and stars.

The Convent lawn, between bare trees, formed a kind of amphitheatre. My shoes were crunching acorns as we approached a huge bonfire built in a clearing with a Guy on top not easily distinguishable against the sky. Mother Stephen, for all her hesitations, had done us proud.

A few feet from the bonfire was a crate of empty milk bottles for the rockets and there were large flat stones for the crackers and the Roman candles.

A bell had been rung on our arrival and the children were parading in noisy expectation behind a rope at the opposite end of the lawn.

Fr Duddleswell crossed to greet them and they cheered. A group of them came up to me holding their right hands aloft and telling me their ages, $5\frac{1}{2}$, $6\frac{3}{4}$, and so on. A minute fellow in a dwarf's cap and Wellington boots trod on my toe to attract attention and crooked his finger to make me bend down. "A secret, Father. You won't tell?" I promised. "I'm two and four quarters," he whispered.

I patted him on the head. "Congratulations." He crooked his finger again. "Yes, son?"

"Can I have sixpence?" he asked.

As soon as the nuns were present I shone a torch onto Fr Duddleswell's paper to enable him to read the Holy Father's blessing. Two sisters brought forward the fireworks which had been stored in a tin tub. These, too, he blessed. While the children sang two verses of "Faith of our Fathers," he and I carried the tub towards the bonfire.

Fr Duddleswell wanted to begin spectacularly with a rocket. He put one in a bottle, lit the blue paper and we retreated to a safe distance. The rocket rose about two feet in the air and nose-dived into the fire. Groans and sarcastic applause from the children. Mother Stephen's voice could be heard above the din asking for more respect for "our parish priest."

He tried again. After using five or six matches, our parish priest could not so much as set the fuse alight. He bade me shine the torch on the fireworks. They were standing in at least eight inches of water. Sabotage.

Mother Stephen crunched her way solicitously across the grass. "Having trouble, Fr Duddleswell?"

"A temporary inconvenience, Mother, nothing more." He motioned to me to join him. We returned to the car to the groans and catcalls of the Lord's little darlings.

Fr Duddleswell opened the car boot. There was a box of fireworks even bigger than the first. "Never underestimate the opposition, Father Neil. As innocent as doves we must be, but as wise as serpents, besides."

The children adored the display. Oohs and ahs and spontaneous applause from them with the sisters dancing around as excitedly as anyone. Fr Duddleswell and I stuffed our pockets with "lethals" and ran here and there letting off rockets and jumping-crackers and the catherine wheels which we had pinned to the trunks of trees.

Mother Superior re-appeared out of the gloom with two sisters who were carrying an enormous iron grid on which were laid vast quantities of potatoes already half-baked. "With the compliments of the Convent, Fathers," she said.

We put the jacketed potatoes at the base of the bonfire and Fr Duddleswell waved to the children, held up a lighted match and applied it to the tinder. It flared up at once, illuminating the Guy who, I had to confess, looked very much like our parish priest. Black sacking did for a cassock. Its head was a kind of white soccer ball with spectacles inked on, and a few strands of a yellow mop were plastered over the top for hair.

Mother Stephen, who had remained in the vicinity, said

above the crackle and splutter of the fire, "The only authentic replica of *you*, Fr Duddleswell, at present in existence." Fr Duddleswell went closer to the fire to examine the insult. "I do agree with you, Father," his underestimated adversary went on. "There is something terribly Catholic about burning somebody in effigy."

Fr Duddleswell had approached too close to the blaze. The heat must have ignited the fireworks on his person for he suffered the same fate as Mr Bottesford. Smoke and sparks flew out of his right cassock pocket and loud rumblings were heard.

Mother Stephen and I had the same thought. I snatched the first box of fireworks out of the tub and we each took a handle and threw the contents over Fr Duddleswell. The fire on him was extinguished with a swish. He jumped up and down, damp, frightened, and miserable. The children roared more delightedly than ever as he gave a good imitation of the *Danse Macabre*, etched as he was against the red flames.

"Was I not branded like a steer, now, Father Neil?" In spite of the early hour, Fr Duddleswell was in pajamas and dressing-gown in front of the fire. Mrs Pring had brought us each a cup of cocoa. "'Tis a good job me foundations are firm, like." The same foundations were turned to the fire in the grate but not as close as before. "Next year, I have no doubts, I will appear in Mother Stephen's statistics with the under fives and under tens. Imagine, now. 'One under sixty with a burnt bum'."

I told him to have no regrets. Mother Stephen was so impressed with his performance she might demand a repeat next year.

"Ah, me one consolation in me hour of need was having a curate to stand by me come Hell or high water."

As I sipped my cocoa, it burned my lip. "Father," I said, referring back to the morning, "do you really think God will allow a son or daughter of His to burn in Hell for ever and ever?"

"In some cases," contributed Mrs Pring, indicating her

boss, "the Almighty has no other choice."

"But, Father, do you really believe that Scheeben stuff I read out at the Conference?" Fr Duddleswell puffed and blew and touched his scorched thigh. I persisted: "People, ordinary people like you and me and Mrs Pring?"

Fr Duddleswell looked at me witheringly. "Father Neil." A pause, a deep sigh and a new beginning. "Father Neil, Holy Mother Church bids us believe docilely in the reality of the eternal fires of Hell. Yet who but a raving lunatic would claim there is anybody there?"

17

ONE SINNER WHO WILL NOT REPENT

In early September, Fr Duddleswell had shown me how to make the rounds of St Jude's Junior School. It began in the playground before morning lessons. He crouched down to play a group of children at marbles. He cheated outrageously, kicking the marble in the right direction if his hand had "not dealt kindly" with him. He always won. Afterwards, he sold the losers their marbles back at a reduced rate and gave the proceeds to more needy children—"like Robin Hood, you follow?"

In each class it was the boy or girl who could answer three catechism questions in the shortest time without hesitations who received a silver threepenny piece. The winner had to go to the front of the class and fix it on his upturned nose. Failure to keep it there until he was back at his place meant Fr Duddleswell confiscated it on the spot.

He was convinced of the value of *The Penny Catechism*. It had served the Church well since Victorian times. It contained, in a brief and eloquent form, the main tenets of the Catholic faith. The child may not grasp all its subtleties at once, but in the years ahead, with maturity, would come recognition and guidance. Remembrance was guaranteed by the sheer music of the words.

"God made me to know him," he recited for my benefit,

"to love him and to serve him in this world, and to be happy with him forever in the next." He dared me to suggest that Shakespeare himself ever penned more memorable lines than those.

I started with the best of intentions on Monday morning, armed with two hundred assorted marbles from Fr Duddleswell's collection in a canvas bag. Unfortunately, I was no great shakes at marbles and worse still at cheating. I made little contact with the children because I lost every one of my marbles in the first twenty minutes.

In Class Five—the nines to tens—the form teacher was a charming, fair-haired Mrs Hughes. Her class knew their religion so well I could hardly make up my mind which of them could repeat the catechism fastest. Eventually I decided that a dark-haired girl in the back row had pipped the rest at the post. I signalled to her to come to the front for her reward. Mrs Hughes whispered to me, "That's Esther, Father."

"Esther," I said, giving her a silver threepenny piece in her grubby little hand, "I hope you will always know your faith as well as you do today. And may it stand you in good stead throughout your life."

There was a stunned silence in the class. I thought the other children did not agree with my verdict or were jealous.

When Esther had returned to her place nodding to right and left—with her tongue out, I suspected—Mrs Hughes whispered again, "Esther is Jewish, Father."

Out of the corner of my mouth, I whispered back, "Are there any other non-Catholics, Mrs Hughes?"

"Only one, Father."

"Would you point to whoever it is?"

Mrs Hughes gently stabbed herself with her finger. "I'm a Methodist," she said.

During that Christmas term I grew to like Mrs Hughes' class best of all. They were disciplined and yet alive and full of fun. The top class became so surly and disagreeable they refused to answer any of my questions even for sixpence. Not wanting to see them caned for a lack of interest in the religion of love, I was reduced to asking Mr Bullimore, the form teacher, to get them to write out their questions and put them in a box to which I alone had the key. I promised the children anonymity. Some of the questions were obscene, some merely abusive. Most were illiterate.

One contribution read: "If its a *free* cuntry why do I have to go to school eh? *and* drink milk. call *that* a free cuntry eh?" Another provided me with a piece of unwanted domestic information: "In our hous we call dad Mosis cos he gives us 10 comandments evry day befour brekfirst." Another was a plain affirmation: "I don't like going to school bicause there's nothing to do when you get there except learn lots of things I don't wanner know. Another thing if they put old Bully on the telly I would switch him off before he came on."

Interestingly enough, only the obscene ones were signed. No doubt with someone else's name.

On the morning after Fr Duddleswell had been "burnt in more than effigy," I entered Mrs Hughes' class hoping for a taste of sanity. The children were their usual enthusiastic selves. Before I could finish any of my November questions on death, judgment, Hell, and Heaven, they were bouncing their bottoms on their benches with vibrating arms outstretched and calling "Please, Father; please, Father."

When I had adjudged Philip in the front row to be the winner, I asked them a few more unscripted questions. "I don't suppose any boy or girl here has ever been to a funeral?"

Philip, of course, had been to everything. "Please, Father. I went to a terrific funeral once."

"Really, Philip?"

"Yes, Father. I saw these four dead men carrying a big box."

Up leaped Robert, his hand in the air. "Last year our granny came and died with us, Father." Before I could offer him my condolences, he added joyfully, "But we made sure she was dead before they planted her."

Lucy Mary had more melancholy tidings. "When Susy my

rabbit died and went to Heaven, Father," she murmured, "she left her carrot behind."

Even this news did not dampen the youngsters' spirits for long. Mark said, "Please, Father, our granma died and went to Heaven and everyone's pleased but not granma."

Frank, a fat boy in long trousers, turned the tables on me by asking, "My gran said when she gets to Heaven she'll pray for us. What makes her so sure, Father?" I said I could not answer that because I didn't know his gran.

"You must know her, Father," insisted Frank, "she wears glasses and brown shoes."

"Mrs Phipps, Father," said Sean breathlessly, "Mrs Phipps who lives next door is dead, but dad says there's nothing else wrong with her."

I assured Sean his dad would not have said it if it wasn't true.

Sean had an afterthought. "She's moved now, Father."

To stem the tide a bit, I asked them what happens to people when they die. "In your own words, please, children."

Patricia, who looked like a little owl, spoke up for the rest of the class. "If their soul's white they go to Heaven, if it's black they go to Hell, and if it's got measles they go to Purgatory till it clears up."

I glanced at Mrs Hughes to inquire if she was trying to undermine Catholic teaching on life after death. She shrugged her shoulders to disclaim any responsibility for these heterodox opinions.

That was when I glimpsed Jimmy Baxter sitting at his desk to my right with tears running down his cheeks. It struck me that Jimmy, one of the brightest in the class, had not contributed anything that morning.

Ken piped up from the back row next to Esther. "When my granpa went to Heaven, Father, he was very, very old so I don't s'ppose he'll last there long, will he?" I was too distracted by Jimmy's tears to reply to that or to correct Judy who called out, "Stupid! In Heaven everybody's made of stainless steel, aren't they, Father?"

"Please, Father," shouted Dean, the terror of the class, "when you go to Hell can you take your dog with you?"

"Certainly not," I said, still looking at Jimmy Baxter out of the corner of my eye.

"Mine likes it in front of the fire, Father."

Mrs Hughes called a halt by telling the children to get on with their sums. It gave me the chance to ask her what was the matter with Jimmy. She referred me to the headmistress.

Miss Bumple, of uncertain age, had been teaching long before systematic training had been devised for teachers. She was an amiable eccentric. Somewhere in her long campaign, she had been decorated with a cauliflower ear, the only one I had ever seen on a woman. She still wore an earring in it. Her mother had had her ears pierced when she was a baby, and it wasn't like Miss Bumple "to waste the holes."

Her eyebrows were white but her short-cut hair was dyed an unnatural black. Fr Duddleswell had given me the clue to her vocabulary which consisted basically of permutations of the one word "egregious." "Egregious" for Miss Bumple meant "normal." "Highly egregious" meant "entertaining." "Exceedingly egregious" meant "very funny." "Excessively egregious" meant "intolerable," "beyond a joke."

For all her strangeness, Miss Bumple, according to Fr Duddleswell, was entirely trustworthy. Whatever you said to her in confidence went in one of her ears and was corked by the other.

On this November 6th, the "head," dressed in her usual tweeds, was in her jumble-sale of an office surrounded by cups and trophies that looked gold until closer inspection revealed them to be of tarnished silver.

Taking a big pull on her cheroot, she rose to greet me. "Fr Boyd," she exhaled all over me with gusto, "*delighted.*" When she spoke she tightened her cheek muscles and pursed her lips as if she were about to blow a trumpet. Her voice, with an East London edge to it, was both musical and compelling. She grabbed my hand and almost wrenched my arm out of its socket.

I told her I was worried about Jimmy Baxter. "Dearie me," she said, "that is not exceedingly egregious." Jimmy's grandfather, Mr Bingley, had been poorly for some time and now was proper poorly. Jimmy was very attached to him. Since his dad had died, Jimmy had been brought up by his grandfather.

When I offered to help, Miss Bumple surprised me by her insistence that I was no use in this instance. Jimmy was simply frightened that because his grandfather did not believe in God and never went to church he would go to Hell when he died.

"If, Fr Boyd, you tell children there is a Hell and that unrepentant sinners go there," trumpeted Miss Bumple, "they are bound to draw their own conclusions. Mr Bingley, you see, is a lapsed Catholic. This makes the matter"—she loosed a huge current of smoke—"excessively egregious."

I returned to the rectory in an unhappy frame of mind. Mrs Pring informed me that "the rooster" was in the garage. I found him lying on an old rug underneath his car. When I hailed him, he slid out and eyed me from the ground. He had on a Churchillian boiler-suit; his face and hands were covered in oil.

Bingly, J.J., he told me, had once been a model Catholic. His misfortune was, at the age of twenty-five, to marry a girl who turned out to be a whore. She had walked out on him after only three months in favor of a Russian sailor. After ten years, J.J. had divorced her and married again outside the Church. His second wife was a Catholic, too. It was the great sorrow of her life that she was barred from the sacraments. J.J. took a more truculent line. He repudiated the harshness of the Church's teaching, renounced his faith in God and joined the ranks of the Friday meat-eaters. He even became a paid-up member of the Communist Party. Maureen, his wife, had insisted all the same in bringing up the two girls as Catholics. The elder of the two, Janice, was Jimmy's mother.

I remembered that Mr Bingley was a widower. "Hadn't that made a difference?"

"Only for the worse, Father Neil. I anointed Maureen and buried her meself. J.J. would not attend her funeral. It made him even more bitter to learn that now his woman was taken from him he was free to return to the Church. He would *not*. If his wife was deprived of the sacraments throughout their marriage, so would he be till his dying day. And I believe he is unshaken in his resolve. He is one sinner who will not repent."

When he saw my eagerness to help he let me go to the hospital with the warning not to be disappointed if I did not succeed. "J.J. is as loggerheaded a fellow you are ever likely to meet."

Jimmy's mother was by her father's bed at the end of a long ward. From a distance I could see them chatting. Mrs Baxter was tucking in the bedclothes and patting the pillow. When she caught sight of me, I thought I saw both pleasure and apprehension on her face.

I introduced myself. Mr Bingley was high up in the bed with his long white hair trailing on the pillow. His skin was taut over his face as though it were covered with a white stocking. And he stared right through me.

It was an unnerving experience. Nothing I said made any impression on him. Not a smile nor the blink of an eyelid. As far as he was concerned I did not exist.

I spoke to Mrs Baxter. "Would you leave us for a few moments, please?" Mrs Baxter immediately rose and went out. I explained very simply to the old man why I had come. Not for his sake but for Jimmy's. I told him about my visit to the school and Jimmy's tears.

He could have been carved out of granite. After a couple of minutes, I gave up, murmured "God bless you," and joined Mrs Baxter in the corridor. She was crying. She knew her father hadn't long left. Jimmy, she said, would never get over it if her father died without confessing his sins so he could go to Heaven with granma.

With nurses passing to and fro nearby, I explained as best I could that only God knows what goes on in a man's heart. Someone could receive the sacraments and still be a bad man. Another could refuse the sacraments and still be humble and acceptable to God like the publican in Jesus' lovely parable.

It consoled her a little. "But how can I explain that to a nine-year old, Father?" she asked. "Jimmy keeps saying granpa commits a mortal sin every Sunday and Holyday by not attending Mass and I say it's not a new mortal sin each time, Jimmy." She looked up at me to inquire whether or not she was propounding heresy. "It's not a lot of mortal sins, is it, Father?" I didn't reply. "Isn't it just one? A big one, perhaps? But just one?" She was pleading with me for a merciful reply.

"Once is enough," I said hedging. I followed it with the only answer that would fit the situation, slightly modified from *The Confessions of St Augustine*. "It's impossible for Mr Bingley to perish when his little grandson is crying for him."

Mrs Baxter said, "Father, even if God is good to my father and he goes to Heaven, you won't be able to bury him with mum, will you?" I was not sure what Fr Duddleswell would say to that. "It hurts, Father, the thought that dad won't be buried by a priest and they'll be separated in death after all their years together here."

"Why don't you put that to your father, Mrs Baxter?"

"I have. He says my mum is only dust and ashes now, and there'll be no separation because after death there's nothing."

Fortunately, the ward sister was in her office. She confided to me that Mr Bingley was not expected to last more than a day or two. He could go any time. The drugs were very effective in taking away the pain and occasional whiffs of oxygen perked him up, but there wasn't any long-term hope.

I reported on my visit to Fr Duddleswell. He was surprised to learn that the end was near. He slipped out of his boiler-suit and went to clean up. After that, I expected him to race off to the hospital but he made no move. He went into the church to pray. After a quick lunch, he did not take his siesta but returned to the church and stayed there until tea time on his knees. After tea, he proclaimed that at last he was spiritually ready "to have a go at J.J."

Jimmy was with his mother at Mr Bingley's bedside. We were hesitant about breaking up a family group that would soon be dissolved by a sterner hand. I could not help admiring the old fellow for the strength of his convictions.

Fr Duddleswell went into the ward and soon Jimmy and his mother kissed Mr Bingley and came to join me. From afar, we saw Fr Duddleswell earnestly talking to Mr Bingley who treated him as he had earlier treated me. I could feel mother and child next to me grow tense with disappointment at the total absence of response.

Then Fr Duddleswell bent over and whispered something in Mr Bingley's ear. From then on, it was like watching someone on the receiving end of one of Jesus' instant miracles. The patient immediately sat up and spoke. Fr Duddleswell listened intently and bent over him again, at which Mr Bingley became quite voluble. We couldn't make out what was being said, but he and Fr Duddleswell were deep in conversation. Fr Duddleswell brought it to an end by raising his hand high above the patient's head and bringing it down so sharply that had it landed it might have despatched him aloft straight away. We relaxed. It was only the first part of a huge blessing.

The Baxters' tears turned into tears of joy. Fr Duddleswell returned like a conquering hero. Jimmy spoke in secret to his mother, and she gave him a silver threepenny piece which Jimmy fixed on Fr Duddleswell's nose. He couldn't keep it there and when it fell to the floor Jimmy pocketed it.

"Well, now," said Fr Duddleswell warmly, "you can both be content, like. I have done everything for him in me power. You can safely leave the rest to the Almighty."

Mrs Baxter wanted to know if her father could now be buried in her mother's grave. Fr Duddleswell told her to ask Jimmy, and Jimmy said of course he could because he was a Catholic again.

On the way home, Fr Duddleswell said buoyantly, "*Nil desperandum*, Father Neil. Never give up, like."

His long vigil before the Blessed Sacrament had paid off. I confessed I thought there was no chance of the old chap repenting. I had never seen anyone so hardened against the grace of God.

Fr Duddleswell recalled a phrase from a curious French writer, Charles Péguy, a Catholic who could not bring himself to believe in Hell. "'The appalling strangeness of the mercy of God,' Father Neil. An apt description of the case in question, would you not say?"

I said I presumed he would return later and clean up, so to speak, by giving Mr Bingley extreme unction, viaticum, and the Papal Blessing.

"To be perfectly honest with you, Father Neil, 'twas not entirely as it seemed." What had caused Mr Bingley to sit up was Fr Duddleswell whispering in his ear, "J.J., you have been a bloody fool all your life, and you will be a bloody fool to the bitter end."

I was astonished. God's mercy *must* be appallingly strange if abuse can bring a lost sheep back to the fold when kindness fails. "What did he actually say to that, Father?"

"He cast dreadful aspersions on the honor of me mother, Father Neil. Then 'twas"—my parish priest was blushing— "then 'twas I bent down again and . . . I bit his ear, God forgive me."

"But at what point did he *repent*, Father?"

"Did not St Peter, the Prince of the Apostles himself sever Malchus' ear completely with a sword in the Garden?"

I repeated my question.

"Did I ever say to you he repented, now? Did he not swear at me and I at him? And did he not threaten to do unspeakable things to me if I did not sling my hook? That was when I nearly brought me fist crashing down on his head. Only the appalling strangeness of God's mercy sweetened me fury and transformed me blow into a benediction."

"That was all?"

"Almost, Father Neil. His last solemn words uttered in me hearing were 'Sod off.' And that, me dear boy, is a euphemism, like."

Fr Duddleswell and I were chatting about finance in his study next morning at ten when Mrs Pring ushered in Mrs

Baxter. Her eyes were shining with joy and grief.

"He passed over in the night, Fathers."

We signed ourselves. Fr Duddleswell said, "May he rest in peace," and squeezed her arm.

Mrs Baxter expressed relief and gratitude that at least her father had made his peace with God. She had already telephoned the undertaker, and Jimmy had rushed off to school to tell Mrs Hughes the good news.

As she was leaving, Mrs Baxter said, "It's a real case of between the stirrup and the ground, isn't it, Fathers?"

Fr Duddleswell kissed her hand. "God's mercy, Janice, is fathomless." She slipped him a five pound note for a Requiem Mass. "Heaven be in your road," he said.

Afterwards, he held the fiver up. "Father Neil, it pays to be kind to the dying, does it not?"

I was more concerned to know how a professed atheist and card-carrying Communist was eligible for a Catholic burial.

He winked at me like a schoolboy. "Father Neil, did I not tell you before that to please a child I would, in full regalia, bury a hedgehog or a tin mouse. I have no quarrel with the dead."

When I tried reasoning theologically, he stopped me. "That rabbi at the conference had something, Father Neil. No ghettos in Heaven, no pogroms in Hell. Somehow I feel that in the Hereafter we shall all of us be model Catholics."

He walked over to the crucifix on the wall and gazed up at it as though he were St Francis expecting the Crucified to talk to him. "Tell me truly, now, Father Neil, was I right or wrong?"

I'm not God. I couldn't settle the matter of his conscience for him.

"The way I look at it, Father Neil, is this. Old J.J. made his daughter and grandson sad enough while he was alive without adding to their misery after his death." Reflecting on Jimmy's tears I savored the truth of that. "J.J.," went on Fr Duddleswell, "was a kind enough man, kinder than was life to him, you follow? Deep in his heart, at a level neither you nor I could hope to reach, he was ever a Catholic and the dear Lord grasped him there with kindness."

I said plainly that I agreed with him.

He flared up in anger at that. "You have no business agreeing with me, you young whipper-snapper. I came to me uncanonical views only after years of blood, sweat, toil, and tears. You are not entitled to such views until you have suffered likewise. *Agree* with me, indeed!"

I waited till he had simmered down. He picked up the five pound note again. "D'you know what, Father Neil? Whatever malignities he uttered against me mother, I am going to send J.J. the most expensive wreath in the shop. Whether he likes it or not." He smiled his dolphin smile. "After all, 'tis not every day I lay to rest a corpse with me teeth marks on his ear."

18

MY FIRST
MIRACLE

Fr Duddleswell, having convinced himself that I was now "settled" at St Jude's and was keen to do hospital work, announced his intention of appointing me official chaplain at the Kenworthy General. I had stepped in for him on his days off but it was a sign of his growing confidence in me that I was to have full responsibility for 400 beds.

"'Twill be an entertaining experience for you," he promised. "You will be surprised how the wickedest folk will be calling out for you immediately God horizontalizes them."

His advice was very practical. I had to register in the Chaplain's Office the chief details about the Catholics, especially whether the patient was married or not. "Mind you, Father Neil, I counsel you not to put that question to the women in maternity." In his experience, it was often less embarrassing to ask them for the name and address of their next of kin.

He forbade me to light candles when baptizing an infant in an oxygen tent, otherwise a premature death would follow hard on a premature birth. "The poor mother, you see, might not take too kindly to the speed with which her baby went to God." Another thing," he said with a twinkle in his eye, "do not bite too many ears, like."

His main concern was my relationship to the Matron, Miss Norah Bottomly. "An extremely funny woman, Father Neil."

"A great sense of humor?"

"None at all. Nevertheless she is in every sense the biggest thing in the K.G. Like the mercy of God itself, pressed down and running over. Not that she has much in there," he said, tapping his temple. "There is less to her than meets the eye, that's for sure. Finally, let me warn you, Father Neil, that Matron is a model of rectitude, the sort that puts a premium on wrongitude."

Matron was in her high-ceilinged office on the ground floor. Not a pen or piece of paper or stick of furniture was out of place. Miss Norah Bottomly—that was the name on the door—looked as though she had been laundered and starched inside her dark blue uniform.

Her hand was as smooth and hard as a statue's. "Be seated, please, Fr Boyd."

Matron's sentences mostly began with "We in the Kenworthy General" or "Our policy is." It was like being addressed personally by a Papal Encyclical. Every nook and cranny of the hospital was, as it were, a valley in Wales. In a most chilling voice, Matron said, "You will find a warm welcome in every ward, Fr Boyd."

Perched on the edge of my chair, I kept nodding at appropriate moments with "Thank you, Matron. Thank you. Thank you very much."

Every word and gesture of this formidable lady was intended to impress on me that, in whatever Church I had been ordained, in the Kenworthy General she was High Priestess.

"In conclusion, Fr Boyd, may I be permitted to say this? For as long as you remain strictly within the province of caring for souls, there will be between us nothing but the most unbounded harmony, cooperation, and good will. Now you may go."

I scooped myself up and bowed and scraped my way to the door.

From the first I enjoyed my work at the K.G. As Fr Duddleswell had forecast, Catholics who had lapsed from the Church for twenty years and more were keen to see me. This may have been due to the strangeness and boredom of hospital life or the sense of being nearer to God the nearer they were to surgery.

Twice a week, I chatted with the patients individually, heard their confessions behind curtains that could not be relied on to keep out the draught and, in the early mornings, took them Holy Communion.

In Prince Albert Ward, a man's ward on the third floor, I came across Nurse Owen. I had met her before on my occasional visits, and I had seen more of her at the Bathing Beauty Contest in the summer. I learned that she was a Catholic. I instantly felt that there was a very spiritual and loving atmosphere in Prince Albert Ward.

Lying in the second bed on the left was an African. I asked Nurse Owen if he was a Catholic because from childhood I had heard stories of white missionaries baptizing black people from morning till night until their arms ached.

Mr. Bwani was not "one of us" but a Muslim from the Gold Coast. Something drew me to Mr Bwani, maybe my pity for him being a Muslim. I knew little about Islam beyond its ambivalent attitude towards the flesh. It forbade the eating of pork not only on Fridays, as in Catholicism, but throughout life, while it permitted polygamy. I was pleased if puzzled that Muslims are reputed to have a tender devotion to the Virgin Mary.

I stuck my right hand in my jacket pocket and blessed Mr Bwani from afar, praying for his welfare, bodily and spiritual. I don't know if it helped him any but I was aware of two big eyes peeping over the sheets like a bunker and following me along the line of beds. My impression was that he needed me.

On my second visit I was introduced to the sister in charge of Prince Albert Ward. Sister Dunne was as spectacularly thin as Matron was robust. Even the staff called her "Old Barbed Wire."

I also spoke to Dr Spinks. He had nodded to me before, this time he was keen to deepen our acquaintance. Winking at me, he drew me into sister's office and closed the door. "It's okay," he said, "Old Barbed Wire won't be on duty for another hour. Spinks is the name, Jeremy Spinks. Senior House

Officer." He rubbed his right hand down his white coat as if to rid himself of microbes before seizing mine. I took an instant dislike to him.

"I'm Fr Boyd." I was already beginning to feel exposed without my title. "Fr Duddleswell's assistant."

Dr Spinks, in his late twenties, tough-looking, tanned with a close-cropped head, went into a eulogy on Fr Duddleswell. Talk about a super bloke. Talk about his reputation with the locals who still remember him fire-watching every night of the Blitz. Talk about the guts of the guy, risking his life time after time to rescue families trapped in blazing buildings.

I had to admit this was the first I had heard of it.

Dr Spinks was sitting on sister's desk, his legs dangling below his white coat. For some reason he was trying to intimidate me and doing rather well. He suddenly turned on me. To get straight to the point, there was something I could do to help. "Fr Boyd, we have an African patient on our hands."

"Mr Bwani?"

"Come on board, Father," he said urgently. "I need your help to cure him."

I felt a wild surge of apprehension. "I'd like to, Doctor, but I know very little about medicine. You see, we barely touched on it in our moral theology when I was a student."

Dr Spinks swivelled off the desk and stood over me. "It's a problem of the mind."

I really hate people who glue you with their eyes. "I'm not very good at psychology either," I rushed to say, "especially black people's psychology." I thought I had better come clean. "To be frank, I've never actually spoken to a black man."

Dr Spinks tried soothing me. It wasn't exactly formal psychology I was needed for. A bit of horse-sense would be enough.

"What's the matter with him, Doctor?"

"He's dying."

"Poor man," I gasped. "What of?"

"Nothing."

I stood up to make him understand I thought he was having me on. He pressed me down, gently but firmly, until my pants touched the chair. "It's no leg-pull, please believe me, Fr Boyd. Mr Bwani is not a dedicated Muslim. He is riddled with superstition. And he's dying because he is utterly convinced that he's going to die."

Mr Bwani was a member of a Gold Coast community which had settled in Colborne, West London. They had brought their own witchdoctor with them. This medicine man was hired to put spells on his compatriots. If a chap wanted a house or a bicycle or someone else's wife, he called him in, paid a fee, and the witchdoctor went to work.

When I had heard Dr Spinks out, I expressed scepticism of such superstitions, but he was adamant. When in the Navy, he told me, he had come across someone in sick bay who was stoned out of his mind because a witchdoctor had put a spell on him. "In fact," he said, "two perfectly healthy patients of mine who'd been cursed actually ended up in Davy Jones's locker." I had no idea of the effect of fear on people brought up in the bush.

"Now, Mr Bwani, Father. He's convinced that this witchdoctor has poisoned his blood. It's beginning to boil. When it has boiled long enough, he's going to die." I continued sitting there listening to this nonsense because Dr Spinks gave me no choice. "Unfortunately, Fr Boyd, when Bwani was admitted, the nurse took his blood pressure. Normal routine, you understand. But it was the worst thing she could have done in the circumstances. He felt the blood build up in his arm and, as he put it, he heard it bubbling."

The doctor moved away, confident no one could be a sceptic after that. "Since then," he said, "Bwani hasn't stirred from his bed. He won't talk or touch his grub, and he can't sleep. He's lost nearly twenty pounds in two weeks."

"I'd like to help," I said, preparing to make a quick get-away.

"Good," he said. "I knew you wouldn't let him down."

I did not like his hectoring tone. "I'll say the rosary for him."

"That's not enough."

I promised to offer Mass for Mr Bwani, privately, of course, because he was an infidel.

Dr Spinks impressed on me that I was required to help Bwani back to health, not pray for his conversion or cast devils out of him with the sign of the cross. But now that I was on my feet, I was less daunted. "I'm sorry, Doctor," I said, mindful of Matron's warning. "I'm here to save souls not lives. That's *your* job."

Dr Spinks went red in the face. Talk about a Good Samaritan. Talk about that good guy Duddleswell rushing into burning buildings. "Think he felt guilty," he threw at me, "because he wasn't a fireman? Talk about this crazy religion lark that stops you saving someone's life when only you can do it."

I challenged him to prove that only I was able to help Mr Bwani.

"Father," he said, "you must have seen those eyes following you up and down the ward. He looks on you as a white witchdoctor."

I heatedly repudiated such a ridiculous title.

"I didn't say you *are* one," he explained, "only that he thinks you are. As far as he's concerned, you're the only one who might be powerful enough to break the spell he's under." The whole matter, I felt, was moving now along humanistic lines. "Father," he said, "I don't doubt that prayer works wonders in the long run, but we're short of time. Bwani could be in the morgue in a couple of weeks." His manner became menacing. "You and I have got to use medicine."

"No," I said with alarm.

"Unorthodox medicine."

"Doctor, I don't like unorthodox *anything*."

In a final burst of exasperation, he asked, "Father, are you going to help me or aren't you?"

I refused to be brow-beaten. "Maybe," I said.

Seeing he was making no headway, he invited me to the staff canteen. We bought ourselves coffee and joined Nurse Owen who was sitting alone drinking tea. If this was part of a prearranged plan I had no objections. After all, she was a Catholic.

Nurse Owen confirmed Dr Spinks' story. She felt personally responsible because she was the one who had taken

Mr Bwani's blood pressure when the trouble began. "I could think of no more fitting role for a priest, Father," she said, her eyelids fluttering attractively. "Jesus was a priest, wasn't he? And He went all over Palestine healing the sick."

Jesus Himself might have had second thoughts with someone like Miss Bottomly around. "That's true," I agreed.

Dr Spinks saw the opportunity to open his plan. In every ward, next to the Sister's office, there was an amenity room usually reserved for the more serious cases. Bwani could be placed in there for observation. All I had to do was don my brightest Mass vestments and utter incantations over him. When I requested further elaboration, he mentioned incense, burnt feathers, chickens' blood, and foreign-sounding formulas. It had to look authentic. He couldn't guarantee this would work but certainly nothing else would.

I had had a bellyfull. I thanked him for the coffee and took my leave. I made one promise: I would mention the matter to Fr Duddleswell. That was safe enough. I already knew his enlightened views on superstitious and ungodly practices.

Fr Duddleswell heard me out with intense amusement. I was relieved to hear him deride Dr Spinks' proposals. I said, "If Mr Bwani's going to die, Father, we'll have to accept it as God's will."

"God's will, Father Neil?" he smiled. "God's *will?* Let me tell you this, lad. If the will of God were done on earth as 'tis in Heaven 'twould lead to an impossible state of affairs."

He was opposed to the doctor's plan because he did not approve of voodoo and black magic, yet might there not be another less objectionable path to the same end? He left me in Limbo for twenty-four hours while he pondered. Then:

"Father Neil, is there any reason why you should not heal this African gentleman with a perfectly straightforward miracle?"

I thought Fr Duddleswell's plan scarcely less bizarre than the doctor's. Someone seeming to be seriously injured is to be planted in the amenity room alongside Mr Bwani. The nurse calls me in to cure him—not so difficult, since there is nothing wrong with him in the first place. Mr Bwani is so impressed, he is open to the suggestion of a cure in his own case.

I had a terrible vision of Miss Bottomly discovering my misdeeds. "But, Father, remember the Matron," I said apprehensively, "I assume..."

He cut across me. "Father Neil, you would be well advised to leave assumptions to the Blessed Virgin. Let me do the worrying, will you not? Was I not already several years a priest when you were still smoking your dummy?"

Certain aspects of his plan still puzzled me. "What kind of serious injury did you have in mind?" I asked.

"Why not a compound fracture—say, a leg broken in a couple of places? The leg will look very fine when 'tis splinted and wrapped."

I protested with my usual vigor. I was not going to lie by claiming a man's leg is broken if it isn't.

Fr Duddleswell put on his offended air. "I was suggesting no more, Father Neil, than that you should say the patient's leg bends congenitally in two places." Seeing me still puzzled: "At the knee and ankle, you follow?" I followed though I had no wish to. "You simply enter the room, sprinkle your patient who has a... bent leg with holy water..."

"*Holy* water, Father?"

"Secular water, if you prefer, straight from the pump, and *Miracolo*! Much to Mr Bwani's astonishment, his partner in misfortune takes up his bed and walks."

"Who does, Father?"

"Your patient."

"But who *is* my patient?"

"Father Neil, this is your miracle, is it not? You can surely find some discreet parishioner to assist you in this charitable enterprise? A quick change into pajamas and he will soon be restored to health, you can guarantee that."

Fr Duddleswell asked for a few days grace to "cogitate me plan further, like." In the meantime, I was to set about finding a candidate for a Lourdes-like miracle.

It was becoming clear to me that things were going to become worse before they got even worse.

"Hello, Archie. Glad to find you at home."

"'Ello, Father." Archie was pleased to see me. "Come up the apples and pears." As we ascended the stairs past the fat landlady who had let me in, Archie said, "Got another job for me, then, 'ave yer, Father?"

I told him there was no one better qualified for what I had in mind.

Archie shared a dingy, second-floor flat with the retired accountant Peregrine Worsley. Peregrine was seated comfortably, his shirt sleeves rolled up, reading *The Sporting Times*. He carefully folded his paper, removed his bifocals, and rose to greet me. "Delighted, sir, to make your acquaintance." When I reminded him that we had met before he said, "Ah, yes, sir, but I meant informally, out of hours, for a *tête à tête*."

Now I knew Peregrine was not the irreproachable citizen I once took him for, I liked him a lot.

"A pint of pig's ear, Father?" asked Archie.

"Not for me, thank you." I explained at length the purpose of my visit.

"What a set up," whistled Peregrine at the end of it, and Archie said, "Cripes, what a con-man you'd 'ave made, Father." I did not turn down the undeserved compliment. "'Course," went on Archie, "I wouldn't dream of lyin'."

I said I honestly hadn't meant it to be a lie but that if he felt it was a problem...

Archie cut in, "No, 'taint no problem, Father. I did break one of me clothes pegs uncommon severe, not four years past."

I was relieved that the way was clear for us to deceive Mr Bwani without any hint of a lie.

Archie had been making a dash from prison. He was just over a twenty-foot wall when the rope snapped "and so did me bleedin' leg."

After begging my pardon, he went on, "I was laid up for six weeks with one leg in the air like a blinkin' can-can dancer." Archie paused reflectively. "Funny thin', Father. That's the only time ever I got remission for good conduct."

Much to Archie's disgust, Peregrine wanted to talk terms. "As to 'the actual,' young sir, how much remuneration will he be entitled to, should we manage to pull off this daring escapade?" I suggested a fiver. "For each of us?" asked Peregrine. I nodded. "Done," concluded Peregrine, bringing down his paper on his knee like an auctioneer's hammer.

Archie coughed apologetically. "Manners," he said, putting his hand to his mouth. "Am I s'pposed to wear pajamas for this job, Father?"

"Only for a few minutes, Archie. I promise you there'll be no embarrassment."

" 'Taint that I mind taking off me trousers round the 'ouses in public, Father. But, straight up, I've not 'ad a pair of pajamas since I was a kid in Borstal."

Fr Duddleswell was developing his plan in ways that boded ill for my future. He came home one day bearing a number of boxes and jars with strange symbols and a book which he had borrowed from the municipal library. I was unfortunate enough to notice that it had "Elementary Chemistry" in the title.

He went immediately to his bedroom and locked himself in. For three days, he spent all his spare time there. From the cracks in the door emerged thick vapors, evil odors, the sound of bubbling, and an occasional bang.

Before supper on Wednesday, Mrs Pring warned me that Fr D was sporting his antlers. He had obviously done something "tragic to his few head whiskers." He must have been trying to invent a lotion either to make them grow or to dye the grey hairs.

Fr Duddleswell came down to eat in his biretta. The hair below it was a bright green. Neither Mrs Pring nor I made any reference to it during a subdued meal. When it was over, he monopolized the bathroom till bedtime.

Next morning, he announced that he had made all the necessary arrangements with Dr Spinks on the telephone. Thursday, being Old Barbed Wire's day off, was D-Day. He communicated "the further refinements of me plan," and it would have been ungenerous of me not to admit that they were brilliant. But I had lived with him long enough by this time to know that he always had more up his sleeve than his elbow. When I showed reluctance to go through with it without being party to all the facts, he reprimanded me sharply. "Deep is the rumble of a bull in a strange pen," he said inconsequentially.

"Right, Father," I said, "you win. I'll do it next week."

"Next week, lad?" he said with scorn. "Next *week*? You will be doing it the day before tomorrow."

We walked under a dappled sky to the Kenworthy General. I was carrying a new pair of pajamas in a paper bag. In the lobby we teamed up with Dr Spinks who had already introduced himself to Peregrine and Archie.

On the stroke of ten we sneaked into Sister Dunne's office. Nurse Owen, having seen to it that the walking patients were in the day-room, was in the amenity room fussing over Mr Bwani.

Archie, without a blink, changed into my best pajamas. They were several sizes too big for him but he was like a boy scout donning his first uniform. "Can I keep 'em after, Father?"

"Sure, Archie," I whispered, hinting that he should keep his voice down.

Dr Spinks asked Archie to sit on a chair and he started to cut off the left leg of the pajamas with scissors.

"Tell me, Doc," moaned Archie, a pearl in each eye. "'Ave you got to do that?"

"Sorry, chum. When the bandages are removed, I want Mr Bwani to see *these*." He traced with his finger where Archie's leg showed signs of a nasty accident. Archie acquiesced, then settled down on a trolly from the operating theater while the Doctor splinted and bandaged his leg. "Pity I can't put it in plaster," he grinned, "but this is the best I can do in the time."

"It's only a game, Doc," said Archie.

Dr Spinks was saying that on the contrary it was a matter of life and death when he saw that Archie was eyeing his colleague. Peregrine, standing aloof with his hat on and leaning on his rolled umbrella, began to phip-phip like a sparrow. He took off his bowler with a flourish and advanced with a wallet in his hand. "Archie's quite right, Doctor. A child's prank." Dr Spinks thrust the wallet into his back pocket without a word and went on bandaging.

"Father Neil," muttered Fr Duddleswell, "I commend you

for your talent in casting such an *admirable* pair."

At 10:15, Nurse Owen appeared and took charge of the trolly on which Archie was lying flat out. Peregrine, once more his serene self, put his bowler hat under his arm, adjusted his spectacles, and prepared to accompany the bier. He touched Nurse Owen's shoulder, "No tears, please, my dear."

Fr Duddleswell said, "You stay here, Father Neil, you are not required yet."

Through the partition I could hear Peregrine and Archie talking in an exaggerated tone as though rehearsing for a Christmas concert in Wormwood Scrubs. They were determined to earn their money.

"Does it hurt, Mr Lee?" I could just make out Nurse Owen's gentle voice.

"Doctor," exclaimed Peregrine, "has his leg been *broken*?" It was melodramatic but Mr Bwani, cowering under his blanket, might appreciate it.

Dr Spinks replied that a leg broken in two places as was Mr Lee's normally takes months to heal. With that, Doctor and Nurse joined me in Sister's office from where we heard Peregrine bidding adieu.

Archie said, "I'm goin' to call in a real doctor."

"A specialist, you mean?"

"A *real* doctor," repeated Archie.

"Well, so long, old chappie," drawled Peregrine. "See you in a few months time if not before." He came into the office and whispered in my ear that, in his considered opinion, his faultless performance entitled him to a tenner. When I refused, he went off in a huff. A few seconds later, a hand appeared round the door and stayed there palm upwards until I had put a fiver in it. It closed, turned over, and waved goodbye with a wag of the index finger.

I heard Archie ask, "Been in 'ere long, then, 'ave yer, mate?" No audible response from Mr Bwani. Suddenly Archie burst out, "Goo-er, me bleedin' leg. Just like that tea-leaf of a doctor to tie the bandages too tight. I'm losing all the circulation in me blood. 'Ell, said the Duchess.'" Then more calmly: "What's yer name, mate?"

Mr Bwani, perhaps out of compassion for the state of

Archie's blood, must have mentioned his name. "Bwani," cried Archie. "You're not Irish, I s'ppose. A joke, mate, no offence. Dunno about you, but ever since I was a kid I've 'ad the mockers on me, grasp me meaning?"

"Yessir."

"Nurse," shouted Archie, "I want my priest, do you 'ear?" More softly: "Bwani boy, I've got a priest that'll shift me out of 'ere quicker'n you can say Man Friday. No 'arm meant, mate."

"Yessir? Really, sir?" Mr Bwani was becoming garrulous.

When Archie went on to say that I work miracles every morning before breakfast, it distressed me that, after a promising start, he should resort to telling lies.

"Yeah," went on Archie. In church 'e conversations with Gawd and brings 'Im down to earth on a little stone. You b'lieve that, Bwani boy?" Archie was keeping strictly within the bounds of truth, after all.

"Nurse," bawled Archie again, "get me Fr Boyd."

I took a deep breath and prepared to play the star role. Fr Duddleswell restrained me. "No hurry," he said. "Give them another thirty minutes together. We do not want to break up a beautiful friendship, like."

The interval was filled with Archie's virtual monologue in praise of his priest, punctuated by screams for the same to be sent for at once. Finally, Nurse Owen led me in.

"Thank Gawd you've come, Father," cried Archie.

Mr Bwani, his face glum as a pickled walnut, was half-raised on his pillow. That seemed a good omen but I took no notice of him. "What's up, Archie?" I asked.

"Me leg's been broke, Father, and me life's got the mulligrubs. You are Gawd's man, Father, so please 'elp me."

I bade Archie put his trust in me, drew out my Roman Ritual and started reciting Latin prayers. I went through the baptismal ceremony and the blessing of a pregnant woman, followed by the thanksgiving for a safe delivery.

"Nurse," I said, "hand me the water." I sprinkled Archie with it. Some spattered Mr Bwani who promptly dived under the sheet. I was relieved to see him reappear immediately. At all costs, he must not miss the next bit of the show.

"Nurse," I ordered, "remove this man's bandages. He is healed."

I saw amazement in Mr Bwani's eyes. He lifted himself up to get a clearer view of Archie's hairy leg.

"Me smeller and snitch," said Archie touching his nose, "tells me I'm as good as new. Just the odd scar where the fractures was."

"Stand up, Archie Lee," I commanded.

He stood up, shakily because the bandages really had interfered with his circulation. It added realism. "I can walk again, Father," Archie proclaimed ecstatically. He knelt down to kiss my feet. "'Ow can I ever thank yer enough, Father?"

I acted the cad. "By keeping the commandments, Archie, and by attending Mass on Sundays and Holydays. Will you promise me that, Archie?"

"Tell you what, Father," said Archie, taken aback. "I'll give it a lot of thought."

The three of us left the amenity room. I judged it best not to speak to Mr Bwani. The first move would have to come from him.

Archie got dressed, and I paid him his fiver. As he was leaving, he said, "We're a smashing team, Father. Any time you wanner work another miracle, send for Archie."

I gave him my word and watched him amble off with his precious pair of one-legged pajamas tucked under his arm.

Nurse Owen returned to the amenity room to remake Archie's bed. I distinctly heard Mr Bwani say, "Nurse, I want to see heem."

"Who, Mr Bwani?"

"The prist. May I see heem? Pliz, Nurse."

Fr Duddleswell rubbed his hands. " 'Tis taking," he said, "but do not be too anxious to perform your miracles, Father Neil. Let us go home to lunch and at three o'clock this afternoon he should be nice and ripe for a cure."

"Hand Fr Boyd the syringe, Nurse." Dr Spinks was about to rehearse in detail Fr Duddleswell's method of healing Mr Bwani. "You'll need first to draw out a drop of blood."

I saw the vengeful gleam in his eye. "Whose?" I asked.

"Before you take a blood sample from Bwani, Fr Boyd, you'll have to take one of your own."

"Can't *you* do it, Doctor?"

"Afraid not, chum. It's vital that you draw out some of your own blood in Bwani's presence."

"Father Neil," put in Fr Duddleswell, "will you please stop moaning like a seal. Cannot you see that you have to obtain Mr Bwani's total confidence? You are the witchdoctor, not Dr Spinks nor anyone else. So take a sample, and I will tell you what to do with it." When I recoiled, he asked cruelly, "Did not Jesus shed his blood for you?"

"No, Father," I corrected him, "other people shed it for him."

Fr Duddleswell was in no mood for splitting hairs. "Get on with it, now," he threatened.

Nurse Owen tied a piece of rubber tubing round my upper arm, rubbed the crook of my arm with a small disinfecting pad, and said, "Choose the biggest vein, Father."

I asked if I could sit down. Nurse Owen brought me a chair and patted my shoulder. It gave me the strength I needed. I dug the needle in. She put a glass to my lips and I drank a few drops before raising the top of the syringe with my thumb and drawing up a fraction of blood. It was like being asked to operate on myself.

"A bit more," urged the prodigal Dr Spinks, "you've lots to spare." I drew out another half an inch, and he was satisfied.

I extracted the needle. Nurse Owen swabbed the tiny puncture and wiped my brow with a cool, damp cloth. "You're so brave, Father," she said, and it seemed then all worthwhile.

Dr Spinks poured the remains of my glass into the saucer and added my blood to it, tinting the water. "Right," he said, "battle stations."

I accompanied the Nurse to the amenity room. "Now, Mr Bwani, I believe you wanted to see me."

He indicated that he would like to whisper in my ear. He said, "Mr Priest, sir, my witchdoctor curse me, and I go dying."

I nodded gravely. "I believe you, Mr Bwani."

His face lit up with joy at having found at last a healer who did not ridicule his plight as so much jungle nonsense. "Mr Prist, I want you pliz to uncurse me. My blood, she boil. Terrible hot already, Mr Prist, sir."

"Powerful curse, Mr Bwani. Power-*ful*."

"Yessir, yes-*sir*."

The tray which Nurse Owen was carrying held a medicine glass, two saucers and a syringe. I gingerly fingered the syringe and took another sample of my blood from the identical hole. I emptied the contents on to the liquid in the first saucer and turned it red. "Now, Mr Bwani," I said, "it's your turn."

He eagerly stretched out his arm. He did not flinch as I dug the needle in, but at the sight of his own blood rising in the syringe he shuddered violently.

I pressed out the contents on to the liquid in the second saucer. Even I was staggered at the way it started to froth and bubble and smoke. Hydrogen peroxide is potent and evil-smelling stuff.

Mr Bwani's eyes popped, his mouth gaped like a frog's, and he fell back stiffly on his pillow. I thought he was dead and wondered how Matron would react to the news. Nurse Owen, unperturbed, raised Mr Bwani up and tried to coax him back to consciousness.

"Mr Bwani," I said, slapping his face. At the fifth attempt, he heard me. "Mr Bwani, heap plenty trouble here."

"Plenny trouble," he managed to gasp.

"Powerful medicine of black witchdoctor. Power-*ful*." He attempted to voice his agreement, but no words came. "Me much more power-*ful*," I said, continuing to give as good an imitation of a Red Indian chief as I could. "Me put bigger spell still. You want?"

He wanted all right. Out came the Ritual and more Latin. I sprinkled him with water and made an impressive sign of the cross over him. Then I handed him the strong sedative in the medicine glass. As he relapsed into sleep I kept up the prayers, adding more promises to complete his recovery as soon as he came round. "When you awake, Mr Bwani, no more hot blood. You be cured. No more curse." My voice helped hypnotize him. "Sleep, sleep, Mr Bwani." He slept and snored mightily.

Dr Spinks had prepared about twenty ice-packs. We put

them in the bed around Mr Bwani. Within twenty minutes his face whitened and his teeth started chattering. I was worried that he might get pneumonia or frostbite. The Doctor said this would help convince him that his blood had stopped boiling.

As he began to come to, we took away the ice-packs and brought in another tray. When everyone else had withdrawn, I patted Mr Bwani on the cheek. "Awake, Mr Bwani, awake. Blood no boil no more."

He kept repeating something like "Bloody cold." When I had interpreted it I said, "Yes, Mr Bwani, blood cold, very cold."

Soon he was restored to teeth-chattering consciousness. Once again, the trick with the syringe, his arm only. This time, his blood tinted the water without causing the slightest tremor on its surface.

Mr Bwani beamed. "Curse fineeshed, Mr Prist. You are my father, my brother, my mother, my seester!"

Within a few days, Mr Bwani had put on weight and was completely well. Since he was to be discharged the following Thursday I was able to visit him undisturbed by Old Barbed Wire. I made him a present of a syringe and told him that should the witchdoctor curse him again he need not worry. My blessing was permanent like an injection against polio. He would be able to prove it easily. "Take saucer of water and put in drop of blood. Not too much, leave some in arm, savvy?"

Mr Bwani proclaimed, "You are my father, my brother, my mother, my seester."

These and many other relatives and friends, all gaily clad, were waiting for him in the vestibule. As soon as they saw him they broke into song. Mr Bwani made me anxious by telling the crowd that his recovery was due entirely to the white witchdoctor, at which they broke into loud applause.

When they left, I was about to go home myself when the fat Anglican curate from St Luke's, the Rev. Pinkerton, passed me puffing on a cigarette. "There's a missive for you from Norah in the Chaplain's Office," he said. "I'll pray for you, old boy."

This was the first note I had received from Matron. It was

headed: "Ref: Prince Albert Ward" and contained a brief injunction to appear before her that very day at twelve o'clock.

The next hour was spent in anguish and recriminations. The Bwani affair was bound to leak out, I was a fool not to realize that. Was it a criminal offence, I wondered, to practice medicine without qualifying as a doctor? Would Bishop O'Reilly haul me up and ask me to justify my extraordinary methods of evangelization?

I did not regret what I had done because I had saved a man's life. I regretted terribly what I had done for less elevated motives. One thing was clear: I would not implicate Nurse Owen in any way.

When I met Matron, she did not look any more severe than I had remembered her to be. "It's about what happened in Prince Albert Ward, Fr Boyd."

"I think I can explain, Matron," I blurted out, not knowing what on earth I would say once I started.

"There is nothing to *explain*, Fr Boyd. This letter says it all." She put on her pince-nez and addressed me over them as though I were a refractory audience. "It is from a retired chartered accountant."

Hell, I thought. So Peregrine has informed on me just because I wouldn't pay him an extra five quid. Iscariot!

Matron read the letter. It stated in three or four tortuous sentences that Fr Boyd had proved himself a marvellous chaplain when his friend Archibald Lee had been a patient in Prince Albert Ward. He had not only helped Archibald spiritually but also financially when he was down on his luck. He begged Matron to thank Fr Boyd personally for his ministrations.

"Really, Matron," I stammered with relief, "there is no need..."

"Indeed there is not, Fr Boyd," and she proceeded to lecture me in a booming voice on the fact that she had sternly warned me in our first encounter to restrict myself to the religious sphere.

I have never seen a bittern, but she looked like one.

"What you do with your money outside these walls, Fr Boyd, is entirely your concern. But here in the Kenworthy

General we leave financial matters to the Lady Almoner." She stressed that this was the last instance of indiscipline she would tolerate in her Junior House Chaplain. I was dismissed.

It was Purgatory, but I had been expecting Hell.

At the rectory, Fr Duddleswell asked if I had seen the black man safely off the premises. I said yes.

"Ah," he complained, "when medical science was powerless you prevented him dying by utilizing all the resources of the faith, and doubtless you did not receive so much as a Mass stipend."

I confirmed that the miracle was free on the National Health. I did not say I was worse off to the tune of ten pounds and a new pair of pajamas. He was himself a witness to the fact that I had shed blood for the cause.

Fr Duddleswell screwed up his eyes. "Did he ask to become a Catholic, like?"

"No," I said.

"Imagine that, now, Father Neil. You pull him back from the edge of the grave, and he remains an infidel." For a few moments he pondered the inexpressible sadness of a priest's life. "Bloody heavens, Father Neil," he exploded at last, "what will you have to do to make your own first convert—raise the dead?"

19

A THIEF IN
THE PARISH

"As a seamstress, Father Neil, she is without equal." Fr Duddleswell was pointing proudly at the patch on his cassock around his previously charred right pocket.

"Magnificent," I said, surprised at this rare paean of praise for Mrs Pring.

"'Tis true, indeed. Once she puts reins on a needle, she is off at a gallop." He stroked the patch as if it were a piece of mosaic he was pressing into place. "Scarce of resources in the brain-box she may be, but she could mend spiders' webs and sew a feather back on a bird."

Mrs Pring, the evening before, had taken a more detached view of her accomplishments. "This is the last time, the very last. I'll not patch his patches no more, not no more."

I suspected that Fr Duddleswell had not invited me into his study to admire Mrs Pring's handiwork, and I was right. "Father Neil," he said, "there is a shortage of you as there is a glut of me." I blinked, then stared. "You are beginning to look, lad, as if you were me cheese ration for the week." I sighed voicelessly. It encouraged him to say more emphatically, "We cannot have you and me doing a Laurel and Hardy on the parish, you follow? No two ways about it," he went on in a biblical vein, "you must increase and I must decrease. The lady housekeeper suggests to me that, alas, poor brother, you need a rest. In brief, you may be heading for a breakdown."

So that was what he was wriggling towards. I insisted I had never felt better in my life.

"Breakdowns in people as in motor cars, Father Neil, can be very sudden, like. And when an Englishman goes to pieces, 'tis my experience he does so with panache, like a sliced loaf."

Mrs Pring had reported to him that in a few days time it was my parents' twenty-fifth wedding anniversary. The day after that was my twenty-fourth birthday. "I don't know, Father Neil, but that you need a holiday. So go home, now, and spend a couple of days in helping your dear ones celebrate."

Celebrations were not the outstanding feature of our home. We lived happily in Hertfordshire, in the town of Clover Hill, thirty miles north of London. My father was a greengrocer. To the locals, "Boyds" was the "corner shop" which a tall, thin, cloth-capped gentleman, slightly deaf and with a grey brush moustache, kept open at all hours.

He had not ever altered in my memory, my father. His habit was to sit sideways at table, invariably with his cap on. He preferred eating with a spoon. He even managed bacon and eggs with a spoon.

He was gruff and of few words. He sometimes shouted at his six children, of which I was the eldest, but he never laid a finger on us in anger, of which he had little, or in affection, of which he had much. I admired him. More than that, I loved that silent, stubborn man.

Old corduroy trousers under a brown overall. In winter, a sack round his middle and khaki woollen mittens from which protruded raw fingers with nails permanently broken and packed with dirt from shoveling potatoes.

My father never had an assistant in his shop which was really the converted front room of our house. He couldn't afford an assistant, he said, not with eight mouths to feed. At five o'clock most mornings, rain or shine, he would be off to market or a nearby farm in his old Austin van. Often at night he would be working in the dark "out the back," shelling peas. He had a talent for buying up sackfuls of peas with sticky pods which no one else wanted, shelling the peas into a bucket and selling them by the pint. The thumb of his right hand, I recall, was nearly always swollen.

We were not exactly the potato-less poor, but economies were his specialty, a kind of art form. He never smoke or drank or drove the van except on business. He never went to the cinema or read a book, and he only turned on the radio for the news, a habit he picked up during the war. Our holidays were walks to a lovely wooded park three miles away on dad's half-days where we picnicked when the weather was fine. Our clothes were second-hand and hand-ons. It was a case of first up, best dressed. Dad made us use the paper wrapped round oranges for toilet paper.

On Friday nights, dad took out his orders on a black three-wheeled carrier bike. For an hour or two, one of the children was made to "mind the shop" and see that no customers duped him into letting them have food on tick when dad had blacklisted them for not paying their bills.

My father never tried to teach us anything, though he had learned a lot since he finished his schooling at thirteen. If a fuse blew or a tire punctured or a window was smashed, it was he who mended it—and in secret. He had the unassailable pride of the uneducated man. His children might attend the grammar school and the convent—intellectuals, he called us—but in his house he did all the fixing. He was the boss.

In fact, he was nothing of the sort. It was my mother who made all the major decisions about our schooling and our religion and about my being sent away to the junior seminary. An inexhaustible fund of affection, she was what our seminary professors called one of the "simple faithful." Her faith was as unquestioning as a child's. It was her faith that saw me through the difficult times in the major seminary, especially the first two years. That was when I studied philosophy which was as intelligible to me as Chinese.

My mother was fond of calling to mind her own childhood. Her father was often without work, and her mother had to stand at a washtub in a laundry from eight in the morning till eight at night for a shilling a day. "Yet," my mother said, "we were happier in those days. Mind you, I wouldn't want them to return." That was a paradox I could never resolve, for we were happy, too, though we had little enough of the things of the world.

I used to spend my Christmas and summer vacations at home. I was especially close to the youngest of the family, my two sisters, Meg and Jenny. After I was ordained, mum wanted brother Bob, my junior by two years and a trainee accountant, to give up his attic bedroom to me. She said I needed a quiet room at the top where I could be alone to pray and say my Office. I preferred to share with Bob, and at nights we talked into the early hours about past, present, and future.

Mum now asked me to say grace before and after meals. One look from her made the boss take off his cap in a rare display of his white hairs.

The silver wedding anniversary fell on a Sunday. I presided at a solemn sung Mass in the parish church at eleven o'clock. My parents had a special prie-dieu and chair on the sanctuary. Both were in new clothes bought off the peg. Mother had a trim red hat. Father wore a three piece suit *and* a new pair of mittens.

When I turned round after the Gospel to read a blessing over them it was those mittens that made me choke. Not mother's love for us, their joint protection of us, but those mittens and everything they stood for: the lack of opportunity in his life, the long, unbroken, indistinguishable hours, his endurance of ice and cold and grime and dirt without a murmur to us. I gave my nose a big blow to get a grip on myself. I managed to hold out. Just.

When I returned to St Jude's after our celebration I was tired but full of joy and gratitude at belonging to such a close-knit family.

The parish was "in a state of chassis."

"It all began yesterday with the washed Chinese carpet." Fr Duddleswell pointed grimly to the bare boards in front of the Lady Altar. Lord Mitchin, our richest parishioner, had donated it together with a Persian rug on the sanctuary which had also been stolen. "Worth £500 the pair, I'd say, Father Neil. I do not know what we are going to do."

He had called in the police but they were not interested in petty theft. They could not be expected, in any case, to put a round-the-clock watch on every church in the district.

Fr Duddleswell complained that he was not getting the protection he was entitled to as a taxpayer. The first suggestion of the police was that he should lock up the church outside of services.

"But, Father Neil, we do not want a one-day-a-week church, do we, now? The good people of the parish would not be able to pray in front of the Blessed Sacrament. Think of the indulgences they would lose."

The police next proposed that we should take out anything that moves—carpets, statues, candlesticks, vases, the lot. "They have no appreciation of the fact that we are *Catholics*, Father Neil. Can our folk be expected to pray without the customary aids to devotion? Indeed they cannot." He refused to turn his beautiful church into a bare Protestant meeting hall. "Who do these Bobbies think they are, Father Neil, Henry VIII?"

It appeared the police had no idea who the thief was. It could be a tramp, a gang of kids, a regular criminal." In other words, they have as many clues to our thief's identity," he said, "as to that of Jack the Ripper. We can but pray that the thief, whoever he is, turns his attentions elsewhere."

But the anonymous thief retained his preference for St Jude's. Next day, he struck again. He walked off with a pair of silver candlesticks from the Sacred Heart Altar.

"Where is it going to end?" moaned Fr Duddleswell, when, after lunch, we witnessed the results of the latest depredations.

He knelt down before the life-size statue of the Sacred Heart, saying, "Let us say a prayer for the criminal, Father Neil." And he proceeded to gabble, "Hail Mary, full of grace...pray for us sinners...at the hour of our death, Amen." All this before my knees could touch the floor.

I made a token sign of the cross to show willingness.

"What's next, Father?" I asked.

"Doubtless, soon he will be breaking into the boxes."

This prophecy, too, was fulfilled. That very evening. There were a number of boxes at the back of the church to catch the offerings of the faithful. Boxes for the Poor, the Holy Souls, Catholic Newspapers, Candles, Peter's Pence, and Catholic Truth Society pamphlets. The thief showed the catholicity of his tastes. "He has prized the lid off every one," roared Fr Duddleswell, his temper in full bloom.

I examined the locks and lids and suggested that the thief had used a screwdriver.

Fr Duddleswell said, "We are dealing with a blasphemer, are we not, Father Neil? Not only does he rob the poor and the Holy Father himself, he even breaks open boxes containing money meant for the Holy Souls. And that is a problem on its own."

I asked him what he meant.

"If the thief stole five shillings from the Holy Souls' Box," he explained, "that is the price of a Mass stipend, and we ought to say a Mass for the donors' intentions."

I agreed. It would be terrible if a Holy Soul remained one minute longer in Purgatory's cleansing fires than was strictly necessary because the Mass he was entitled to had not been celebrated. "I'll offer a Requiem tomorrow, Father."

"Ah, there, your heart is in the right place, Father Neil. I would offer the same meself but for the fact that I have already promised Janet Murphy to say Mass in the morning for her cat. She is having an operation. A hysterectomy. And she will be lonely, you follow?"

Finding this information highly ambiguous, I said I quite understood he couldn't disappoint Mrs Murphy or her cat.

A locksmith was called in. For £3, he mended the boxes and put a heavy padlock on each. "That's the best I can do, sirs," he said, already hinting that his best might not be good enough.

And so it proved. The thief's screwdriver managed once more to prize open the boxes without touching the padlocks. This time he had also broken the lock on the baptistery and stolen the casket with the small silver phials of holy oils used for baptisms and anointing the dying.

Fr Duddleswell was crestfallen. It would cost him another £3 to replace the oil stocks and then he'd have to go to the Cathedral to beg for a re-fill. "Pray to the Holy Mother," he counselled me, "that no one decides to die on us, Father Neil, before a fresh supply of holy oil arrives."

If that were to happen, I could see myself offering another free Mass for the repose of a brand new Holy Soul.

"God help us, Father Neil, but this thief is a thorn in me eye. He is spoiling me sweet repose and putting the whole of the parish through the mincer." He decided to draw up a list of watchers to keep an eye on things "as we did during the war, like."

We were to ask for volunteers on Sunday but in the meanwhile we would have to take turns ourselves.

"Just you and me?" I asked, wondering whether I could survive vigils of several hours at a stretch. And Sunday was five days away.

"Mrs Pring will be only too glad to help, that's for sure," he said. "She has a nose sharper than a briar and more eyes than a fisherman's net. Besides," he added loudly, "she would far sooner park her bum on a bench than lick this house with a broom."

Out in the hall, Mrs Pring started up a kind of boating chant. "Hewing and drawing, cooking and frying, rubbing and scrubbing, washing and drying."

Fr Duddleswell muttered, "The voice of the turtle is heard in our land. By the law of averages she was bound sooner or later to blunder into poesie."

After Mrs Pring had sung her song a few times, she moaned, "I'm just a beast of burden, I am. A beast of burden."

"Well, Father Neil," Fr Duddleswell confided to me, "she is not Balaam's ass that spoke but once, that's for sure."

No sooner was Fr Duddleswell's scheme put into operation than I realized its futility. For security reasons, he kept the door leading from the sacristy to the church permanently locked and barred. Whenever a watcher started to open it from the sacristy side, a thief would have half a minute to make his getaway. Another thing, the watcher had to sit or kneel in the benches in front of the boxes so that any prospective thief would see immediately if anyone was on guard.

It was very embarrassing having to turn around whenever a worshipper dropped into church. The faithful resent being spied on by the clergy at their devotions.

Once I tried sitting in the dark of my confessional. Mrs Betty Ryder, President of the Legion of Mary, spied me. She came in and poured out her very fluid soul. After a forty-minute drenching, I chose to sit a couple of rows from the back relying on my ears to warn me if anything out of the ordinary happened.

On Wednesday I ate a big lunch, and Fr Duddleswell left me to keep watch while he took his siesta. I must have dozed off because when he came, red-eyed from sleep, to relieve me at 5:30, not only had the Poor Box been broken into but all the candles had been pinched.

"He must be an indigent eskimo," observed Fr Duddleswell, when he had made an inventory of our losses, "but what the mischief came over you, lad?"

I apologized profusely. The thief had been in my grasp, and I had let him go.

Fr Duddleswell scratched his forehead and acknowledged the improbability of the thief being so stupid as to return that day. He was wrong. The rest of the boxes were emptied before supper.

"Father Neil, when the bait is worth more than the fish, 'tis time to stop fishing." After that, he refused to have the boxes mended any more.

I determined to make amends for my unplanned siesta. After supper, I called on Archie Lee, who, as ever, was delighted to see me. From a clothes line by the fireplace hung my pair of pajamas.

"Sorry Peregrine's out, Father. 'E's gone to Bedford to see 'is old auntie. She's been taken ill." Anxious not to be caught out in a lie, he told me this was a code for Perry being at the races. Perry's gambling was the reason he was always broke. He kept back one fiver to wrap round pieces of newspaper and stuffed the lot in his wallet for his sack-Archie campaigns. "Sometimes," complained Archie, "Perry goes to the gee-gees and leaves me working in a shop all bleedin' day."

I told Archie I had come to see *him*.

"Another 'orspital job, Father?" said Archie eagerly, rolling up his pajamas and hiding them under his pillow.

I explained what had been going on in church and said I wanted his help in finding out who the culprit was.

He smiled. "No trouble there, Father."

"Not you and Peregrine?" Archie was shocked at the suggestion after he had proved his honesty in so many ways. "But," I said after an apology, "I thought you said you *knew*."

"Right," said Archie. "I'm surprised the fuzz don't. Most like, they do but they ain't lettin' on." He explained that every thief is a sort of craftsman with his own little trade-marks. "The marks in this case," he said, "is clear as 'is autograph. 'Cept the bloke in question can't write."

"Will you tell *me* who he is."

"I might," said Archie cannily, "and then I might not."

"I can't raise much cash this time, Archie. That hospital job cleaned me out."

"It ain't the bread, Father, I just don't wanner grass on one of me old mates. It don't do to shop one of yer own kind."

I said I fully understood his sense of honor.

"Right, *right*," reflected Archie, who approved of that way of putting it. "Also, this bloke is one of us."

"A con-man?"

"You've been and gawn an' done it again," Archie said reproachfully. "I mean 'e's an 'oly Roman, like you an' me."

"That makes it worse."

"That makes it better—for 'im, I mean," said Archie. 'E knows 'is way round the church, where all the goodies is, when the boxes is fattest with the lolly an' that type of thin'."

When I assured him we didn't want to have the thief

arrested, Archie relaxed. I knew that when Fr Duddleswell heard the thief was a Catholic, he would want to save him from himself, redeem him, reform him.

"'E'll never manage that, Father."

"Well, at least *stop* him."

"Even that'll take some doing," said Archie. "This gaffer's been pilfering from churches since 'e were six." It had started when he went to Sunday school. The boxes were crammed after the morning Masses, and he developed the habit from there. "Went from strength to strength, see?" I nodded. "'E don't mean no 'arm by it. Knows no different. 'Ow else would 'e eat, tell me that?"

"Either he goes out of business or we do," I said.

"Bad as that, is it?"

"If I promise we won't 'shop' him, Archie, or disclose who put us on to him, will you tell me who he is ... for old time's sake?" I was so excited at the prospect of finding the culprit I was not above a bit of blackmail. Archie hesitated. "I give you my word that he'll come to no harm, Archie, and we'll do our best to see he gets a chance in life. Like you," I added.

"Ah," sighed Archie. "If only 'e'd go straight like me and Perry. 'E's never 'ad our chance, 'as 'e? And 'e's about as bright in the 'ead as a star by day."

"This might be his last opportunity, then."

"It's Bud Norton," burst out Archie.

"Where does he live?"

"'E don't live nowhere. Or, rather, 'e lives everywhere, but not somewhere."

"No fixed abode."

"That's what I just said, didn't I? You'd as easy find a wisp of smoke from yesterday's fire."

I was thinking we would have to catch Bud Norton in the act, after all, when Archie asked if Bud had taken more than money.

"Yes, the silver stocks containing the holy oils."

"Wicked," said Archie. "You'll 'ave to get on 'im before 'e breaks open yer tabernacle. Anythin' else?" I told him the rest. Archie frowned and said, "Wanner know where to get 'em?"

I could hardly believe my luck. "You mean you know where Bud Norton keeps his stolen goods?"

"'E don't keep 'em. 'E passes 'em on to a bloke name of Pedlow in Larkin Street." Larkin Street was off the Kings Road in Chelsea. "Pedlow buys up everythin' from Bud for a bleedin' song. Real bent, 'e is, and as genuine as a sea-breeze off a snail-stall."

"I'll keep mum, Archie, I said, touching the side of my nose, "you can trust Fr Boyd. Oh, *yes*."

Next morning, after breakfast, while Mrs Pring was keeping watch, I took a bus to the Kings Road. Larkin Street had a narrow entrance and was deep in shadow. The only shop in the street was *Pedlow and Son, Furniture Dealers, Est. 1881.*

In the very front row of the window display were our two candlesticks. A notice on them said, "Priceless Silverware, £35 the pair." I couldn't see the carpets.

Now I was at the shop, my nerve failed me. There was no sign of an assistant. What if he turned out to be a typical example of the criminal classes and brutally assaulted me?

I plucked up courage, prayed to the Holy Ghost, and went in. An old-fashioned bell fixed on top of the door tinkled, and I was assailed by the odor of old furniture, mildew and cold stale air.

A white-faced man, about five feet two inches tall, shuffled in from a back room in carpet slippers. He hadn't a hair on his head. A pair of rimless spectacles gave him the appearance of a near-sighted egg. He wore, in striking contrast to his face, a black corduroy jacket set off by a drooping black cravat.

Seeing my clerical collar, he broke into a smile. "James Pedlow, at your service, sir."

"I've come for the candlesticks in the window."

"You have admirable taste I *can* see, sir, and an eagle's eye for a bargain, *if* I might say so." He had a habit of accenting unexpected words. "Where else *in* London," he continued, "could you pick up a pair of antique silver candlesticks *like* that for only £35?"

"I haven't come to buy them, only to claim them," I said.

"I beg *your* pardon, sir," said Mr Pedlow, taking one sharp shuffle backwards.

I told him I had come to claim them because they were stolen from our church. His demeanour instantly altered. "What's your *little* game, then, eh?"

"Game?"

"What are you, a cop?"

"Do I look like one?"

He lifted his spectacles onto his forehead and ran his eye up all six feet and more of me. "As a *matter* of fact, you do. *Are* you in plain clothes or something?"

Fingering my clerical collar, I replied that I was in my normal uniform.

"You must be a con-man, then," he said.

What twisted minds these crooks have, I thought. "I happen to be a Roman Catholic priest, Mr Pedlow. No," I added, to forestall a further question, "this is not a front."

When he demanded to see identification I realized that I hadn't any except for my name inscribed on my miraculous medal. I didn't think that would do.

"Have you a visiting card?"

"I have only just been appointed to St Jude's, and I've not had one printed yet."

"A driving license perhaps?"

"I ride a bicycle."

"A check book?"

"I haven't got a bank account."

This must have been the crushing proof that I was a Catholic priest. He cracked. Like Humpty Dumpty, he was never the same again. "Well, sir," he said, bracing himself, "that's *as* may be. But that gives you no entitlement to claim my candlesticks as your own. I purchased them in good faith *on* the open market."

I felt my star was in the ascendant. "You did no such thing," I affirmed, "you received them from Bud Norton."

He cowered in my shadow like a naughty schoolboy. "That's the first time in twenty years Bud's grassed on me."

"He didn't," I said. "I got a tip-off." Those Hollywood gangster movies were proving useful.

"An enemy has done this," he said, sounding quite biblical to my ears.

"It doesn't matter who did it, it's done," I cried, "and I demand my candlesticks back, otherwise I'll prosecute you for theft."

"Theft!" exclaimed Mr Pedlow, riled by the word. "Theft! I have never stolen anything in my life."

"To receive or retain what you know belongs to another is as much theft as if you had taken it yourself. Whoever steals through another is himself a thief." Moral theology had its uses, too.

Mr Pedlow appeared to think I was quoting from a law book. "How can you prove they belong to you?" he asked more respectfully.

Time for my trump card. "Here," I said, pulling out a picture from my inside pocket, "is a photo of those candlesticks in the place Bud Norton stole them from: the Sacred Heart Altar."

He didn't even bother to look. "They're yours," he said miserably.

My triumph could not have been more complete if I had pulled a gun on him. "Do you want me to call the cops?" I thundered, revelling in my role of bully-boy.

"What's up?" he asked timorously. "Didn't you hear me say they're yours?"

"The carpets. I want them back, too."

"Which ones, sir?"

"Chinese and Persian."

"Come with me, sir," he said with a gesture of defeat.

I followed him into the back room and searched a tall pile of carpets till I found the two belonging to St Jude's. "Finally," I said greedily, "where are the candles?"

"I don't stock candles."

That jogged my memory. "Forget the candles." I could afford to be generous. "Where are the stocks with the holy oils?"

He knew exactly what I meant. He crossed to a cupboard and drew out the casket with the three silver phials. As if despairing of mankind, I asked, "What possible use could anyone have found for these?"

"They would have made such nice snuff boxes," he whimpered.

I struggled with the stolen goods up to the Kings Road where I stopped a taxi. As luck would have it, out of the hundreds of cabbies in London, it had to be the one who had taken me and my bike home in less happy circumstances. He took one look at my haul of furniture and said, "Don't tell me, St. Jude's."

When Fr Duddleswell saw his precious possessions, he raised his eyes to heaven, saying, "*Magnificat anima mea Dominum.*" Then in a more earthly tone: "So you tracked him down, Father Neil?"

"It's useful having one or two contacts in the underworld, Father." I proceeded to tell him the whole story, adding a spice of drama here and there, but leaving out the thief's name. "That," I said, "is a professional secret."

"You cannot even tell me his initials?" I shook my head.

He didn't press the point. Once he knew the thief was an R.C. he felt a special responsibility towards him. Besides, to take him to court would only bring Holy Mother Church into disrepute.

"Shall I take the carpets and candlesticks into the church, Father?" I asked. It seemed clear to me that if the thief were to see them there, he would know we were on to him and leave us in peace.

Fr Duddleswell didn't agree. On past evidence, the thief was quite capable of stealing them and offering them again to the Chelsea fence. He had devised his own method of stopping the thief's tricks. "Come with me, Father Neil, and I will show you something that escaped me notice before."

In the church, Mrs Pring was keeping solitary vigil. He put her on guard outside so that the burglar would not be tempted to enter and went up ahead of me into the organ loft.

"Well, Father Neil, we never thought to keep a lookout up here, did we?"

The loft overhangs the back of the church. "But this is no use," I said, peering over the wooden balustrade. "We've no view of the boxes from here." This was why we had discounted the place as a watchtower in the first place.

Fr Duddleswell drew my attention to the back of the loft. "Look down there." In the floorboards was a crack half an inch thick. "Here," he said, "we can see without being seen."

I made the point that by the time we clattered down the spiral stairs the thief would be further away than the Houses of Parliament.

"Ah, to be sure. But since he is a Catholic, Father Neil, we are not aiming to nab him. Only reform him. And," he said mysteriously, "we will accomplish that without laying a finger on his person, without so much as letting him set eyes on us."

He outlined his plan. In our parish, lived Paul J. Bentley, a radio actor in the BBC drama company. The idea was to get him to put a "message" on tape. When the thief appeared, we would play this message very loudly from our hiding-place in the loft.

Within twenty-four hours, the recording was in our hands. In Fr Duddleswell's study it sounded stupendous. A BBC engineer had added a sinister echo effect.

Fr Duddleswell was to have the tape recorder all warmed up, and when Bud Norton came in, I was to give a signal. He only needed to release the pause button, and Bud would get the message.

Next morning at eleven, after we had been watching for an hour, an elderly, balding gentleman in a black overcoat appeared. He sank to his knees in silent prayer for fully five minutes. I had seen enough of life lately not to be taken in by pious attitudes. When he rose, looked around him furtively to see no one was looking and crossed to the Poor Box, I gave Fr Duddleswell the agreed signal. The recorder gave out at full blast:

"THIEVES WHO ARE UNREPENTANT WILL PER-ISH... PERISH... PERISH..."

The natural echo of the building intensified the ghostly echo on the tape. It chilled me to the marrow. Fr Duddleswell pressed the pause button down, and we kept quite still, scarcely daring to breathe.

Below, there was no sound. Puzzled by the silence, I peeped through the crack in the floorboards to find that the thief had returned to his place and was once more lost in contemplation. His conversion must have been as sudden as St Paul's. I beckoned Fr Duddleswell to me. He tiptoed across and put his eye to the crack.

"Holy Jesus," he whispered, putting a shaky finger to his lips. "'Tis Lord Mitchin himself. Deaf as a trumpet. He cannot be wearing his hearing-aid today."

"Lucky for us," I whispered.

"*Deo* bloody *gratias*," he said, signing himself.

When after a quarter of an hour, Lord Mitchin left, Fr Duddleswell wound the tape back. I asked him if we should go on with it.

"How else, Father Neil, are we to recover one of Christ's lost sheep, tell me that, now?"

I went back to my post, and Fr Duddleswell bent down, his finger poised to release the button. There was a clatter of feet. This time, when I looked through the chink in the floor, there was this shabby, shifty-looking character. Bud Norton for sure. An army great-coat reached to his ankles. Beneath it was a pair of shoes without toecaps and with string for laces. On his hands he wore a pair of khaki mittens.

Bud made no pretence of praying. He simply stood there, his face raised and his body arched like a squirrel's, listening. I saw his grimy bald head, his grizzled face, his red-rimmed, watery eyes. My heart, in a mad gallop, went out to him. It was the mittens that did it.

Until this moment, Bud Norton had been a shadow among shadows, a thief, a nuisance, a name stirred half-jokingly into conversations. Now here he was, a common, shameless, pitiable vagrant who walked the streets in toeless shoes by day and slept where he could at nights. "As bright in the 'ead as a star by day," as Archie in his mercy put it, and as much soft flesh and warm blood as Fr Duddleswell or I.

Bud went over to the Poor Box. In his hand appeared a

338

rusty screwdriver. Out of the corner of my eye, I saw Fr Duddleswell grow tense as he waited for my signal. It was cowardly of me, but I gave it.

The ugly sound from the tape-recorder reverberated round the church. Bud stood there paralyzed.

"Once more?" Fr Duddleswell mouthed in my direction.

I nodded and the next message must have gone right to the heart of poor, old Bud Norton.

"THOU SHALT NOT STEAL...STEAL... STEAL..."

I saw Bud start and shiver, and I heard him say in a hoarse whisper, "Godalmighty!" Then something which, together with his mittens, broke me up: he genuflected. The next moment, he was gone.

In the organ loft, we both stayed motionless for a while. I closed my eyes, only opening them when I felt Fr Duddleswell's hand on my shoulder.

"Get up, lad," he said gently. "I feel the same as you. 'Tis a dangerous game, playing God, to be sure, even to put a stop to a man's thieving." He stood up. "I only barked so I would not have to bite. But I should have devised another scheme."

Fr Duddleswell was at last able to have the locks on the boxes fixed permanently. Together we combed the district looking for Bud for three days till late in the evening. We called in at the local bunk house and the Salvation Army Hostel. One old lodger, reeking of methylated spirits, claimed to have seen Bud three days before but not since. "Imagine," said Fr Duddleswell, "no one has so much as heard a taste of him."

It was cold and wintering early. The Lord had started to shake his salt shaker over the nights and mornings. I was wobbly on my feet as if I was heading for a bout of 'flu, and Fr Duddleswell confessed to feeling "as wretched as a Christmas without snow."

We were forced to conclude that Bud had moved away. In a last desperate effort at atonement I persuaded Fr Duddleswell to come with me to Archie Lee's. Archie was eating lunch alone. He pointed to his poached eggs on toast. "Adam and Eve on a raft," he said, laughing.

When I put Archie in the picture, he asked what day it was. I said it was Saturday. No, he wanted to know the day of the month. November 30th.

"And what's the hour?" asked Archie.

In exasperation, I said, "12:45."

"Then," said Archie glumly, "I can't 'elp yer, 'cept to tell you 'e could be an 'undred miles away by now." The only predictable thing about Bud Norton was that he only stayed one month in any district. On the last day of the month, before midday, he was off. "By tonight," said Archie, "'e could be in Land's End or John O' Groats."

That was that. Fr Duddleswell shook Archie's hand papering the palm with a pound note, and we walked slowly home to St Jude's.

Before we went into the rectory, Fr Duddleswell suggested we pray for Bud in front of the Blessed Sacrament. Neither of us could have guessed when the whole miserable business began how overjoyed we would be to find that for the last time the boxes had been rifled.

20

SEX BOWS ITS
LOVELY HEAD

During the night I could hear awful howls and screams. In a
daze, I kept asking myself if it was the wind, or had a huge dog
been let loose in the alley? It occurred to me that I might be
responsible for the noise, but that was impossible; I was in no
pain.

I was a tall tree which a lumberjack felled with a single
stroke of the axe and lifted up in one hand and felled again.
Each time I hit the ground my body shook and threatened to
disintegrate.

I was dreaming, and in my dream I was by the sea and the
racket I had heard was the wind and waves pounding the shore.
There was salt spray on my face and lips, and I slipped on the
rocks and fell into black waters and was drowning.

The room was an orange split down the middle. Red,
molten light was shaken on to my eyeballs. Fr Duddleswell, a
total stranger in his dressing gown. Mrs Pring in spectral
curlers and hairnet. The pugnacious smell of whiskey and Dr
Daley with a halo like a blister round his entire head was
wheezing something about pneumonia and hospital.

I desperately wanted to help whoever was ill but I could
not shake myself awake. I was still drowning, slowly but surely.
The river-bed of my throat was as narrow and clogged as a
capillary tube.

Now I was on my back in a hammock. There were fireflies

in the night sky, and a long white liquid road stretched up to the moon.

"A hundred and two, Father."

Was I as old as that? Nurse Owen had not aged, and here was I all of a sudden one hundred and two.

"It's going down, Father," Nurse Owen said. And so was I, coughing my dry cough, and going down, down, down, into the waters.

Dr Daley, half-drunk, was still a good diagnostician. I had pneumonia. I came round in the amenity room where I had cured but failed to convert Mr Bwani.

For a few days I had terrible pains in the chest and a fever. Nurse Owen sweetened every aspect of my discomfort. Ever by my side, she soothed my brow, took my temperature, and held my wrist to try to catch up with my racing pulse. I fervently wished Archie had not walked off with my best pair of pajamas.

When I could breathe more deeply again, there followed days of bewildering happiness. Nurse Owen was giving me more of her time, I was convinced, than I was entitled to as a mere patient. The amenity room made it possible for us to talk in a quiet, natural way, mostly about our work.

On her day off, when I did not see her, the hours limped along like wounded grasshoppers. Feeling sorry for myself, I reflected that I had passed my life in entirely male-dominated surroundings since I was fourteen. That was when I entered the junior seminary. My mother and sisters apart, women had only walked on the horizon of my world. I had never taken a girl to the cinema, or been to a dance. I went to my last party at the age of twelve.

I had no female friends of any sort. Yes, I was chaplain to the Legion of Mary. Most members were pop-eyed, middle-aged ladies who talked world without end about "true Marian devotion."

I was welcomed as a polite, anonymous stranger at many a hearth. But to no one could I allow myself the luxury of saying who I was. To them I was Melchizedek: no father or mother or brothers or sisters or antecedents. Worse, no present feelings and no future hopes.

"Give me, good Lord," I prayed each night with Lacordaire, "a heart of flesh for charity and a heart of steel for chastity." Outside the amenity room, I felt my life was becoming steelier and lonelier every day.

When Fr Duddleswell and Mrs Pring visited me, bearing gifts like the Magi, I kept saying I was very keen to return to work. Mrs Pring arranged the chrysanthemums while Fr Duddleswell opened up the get-well cards while he swallowed my grapes. "By the time you leave here, Father Neil," he said, his mouth full of purple mush, "provided they do not starve your plate, like, your shadow should be considerably fatter."

How could I tell this quaint, benign couple that in the center of my being I never wanted to quit the Kenworthy General?

Fr Duddleswell suggested I be transferred to the private hospital run by nuns where the sick clergy of the diocese were usually treated. I would not hear of him being put to any inconvenience. Nor did I want to convalesce in a rest home by the sea, also run by the good sisters.

After that, no further attempts were made to evict me from Paradise.

Once or twice I asked myself if that strange flutter in the region of my stomach when Nurse Owen held my hand was the stirrings of love. I put it out of my mind. Fr Duddleswell was bringing me Holy Communion every morning at first light, and I was keen to be worthy of the Lord's coming.

Such bliss could not last. The dark day came when the doctor signed my discharge. I was "free" to go home. It was more like a sentence of perpetual banishment.

Half an hour before Fr Duddleswell came to collect me, Nurse Owen appeared and shyly thanked me for being a model patient.

"I'm very grateful, Nurse," I said, "for *everything*." She shrugged and smiled as if to say it was all in the course of duty. "Anyway, Nurse, I'll see you around the ward before long."

However, long would be too long.

She left to attend to a fat Greek boy named Nicos who had developed a fever after having his appendix out. Happy, happy Nicos.

For a few days, Fr Duddleswell "adamantinely" refused to let me loose on the parish. During my enforced confinement I tried to sort out my ambiguous relationship with Nurse Owen. Was her shyness really coyness or was it respect for the priesthood? What did I feel for her? Did she feel anything for me? With such questioning, the mornings no longer came before my head hit the pillow at night. Hours pretended they were months. I was afraid to go into the kitchen at night for tea in case the police should invade the place.

Nothing had been resolved by the time I resumed my chaplaincy work. All I knew was I wanted to talk to Nurse Owen privately from time to time. I would ask her if she was of the same mind.

I walked up the staircase to Prince Albert Ward with a thumping head. Fortunately, she was alone in Sister's office writing up her reports.

"Hello, Nurse." I smiled nervously.

She beamed back at me. "Fr Boyd, how nice to see you up and about."

I judged her welcome to be more than friendly. She was aglow. If I did not say quickly what I had prepared to say I would never say it.

"Nurse Owen."

"Yes, Father?"

"Nurse, I feel really indebted to you for all you have done for me." She cast her lovely brown eyes downwards, without a word. "I was wondering, Nurse, if I might ask you a personal question."

The Holy Ghost must have been on my side at that moment. I saw she was wearing a diamond ring. I pointed to it stricken but smiling bravely.

"Yes, Jeremy . . . that is, Dr Spinks, has asked me to marry him. We became engaged last Saturday." She began twirling the thing round her finger in front of me. "I shouldn't be wearing it really while I'm on duty, Father, but it is still such a novelty."

"Congratulations," I said, commiserating with myself. With all the lucidity of mind keen pain can bring I added, "As I was saying, Nurse, I want to give you a box of chocolates, and I'd like to know the sort you like best."

"Oh, Black Magic are my favorites."

"You are sure you didn't mind me asking?" I added confusedly.

"Not in the least."

"Fine, well, Nurse, if you'll allow me, I'll bring you ... and Dr Spinks ... a pound box of Black Magic next time I pass this way."

I left the Kenworthy General without attending to a single patient.

I was hurt. I was humiliated. I was angry. At first I wondered why she had gone out of her way to be so nice to me. What made *her* think she could be nice to me? Soon I realized I was being stupid. Why should Nurse Owen single me out for an uncharacteristic attack of nastiness?

Guilt waxed in me as anger waned. I started to blame myself. I knew that if I wasn't careful I'd blame myself too much and accuse myself of impure thoughts and desires. If that happened, I would find myself in the altogether murkier realm of mortal sin which, as I had told Mrs Rollings, required confession—number and species. It was wiser to forget the whole affair.

But my conscience gave me no peace. What if I was no longer in a state of grace and making things worse by celebrating Mass and administering the sacraments when I needed absolution myself?

I had to get if off my chest. I did not want to trouble my normal confessor at the Cathedral who knew me for my laziness, exaggerations, and impatience. I chose to pop along instead to a nearby Jesuit House of Studies and confess to a priest who did not know me from Adam.

One morning at ten o'clock, I screwed up my courage and

rang the bell. A Brother with a club foot opened the door. "Come for confession, Father?" Was guilt written so large on my face that a total stranger could read it at once? "No one here at the moment, save Fr Strood. An American, Father. But I dare say if you're in a hurry." I said I was. "Second floor, Room 12, then. There's no phone in his room so you'll just have to go on up."

I knocked on Room 12 and was greeted by a loud, drawling, "Come in, please." The voice was Jimmy Cagney in a friendly mood.

I opened the door only to recoil in horror. There in the middle of the room was a crew-cut, middle-aged gentleman clad only in the briefest of blue underpants. He was holding a towel but not for protection.

"I'm sorry to disturb you," I said.

"What makes you think you're disturbing *me*? I was about to freshen up, that's all." Sensing my embarrassment, he added, "I *am* wearing my fig-leaf."

"I was looking for a priest," I stammered, "for confession."

"That's okay, Father, you've found one. I'd be glad to oblige." He promptly collapsed on to a chair, put the towel round his neck like a stole and motioned to me to kneel beside him. "Ready?" he said. "Shoot."

I told him it was four days since my last confession. "Great, Father," he smiled, "glad to know you frequent the sacrament. Now, what's on your mind?"

I explained as best I could my feelings toward the Nurse who had looked after me, first of tenderness and lately of bitterness.

"Gee," he said, tugging on the ends of his towel and then scratching his hairy chest. "I've been hospitalized three times in seven years, and I've fallen in love with my nurse *every* time, can you imagine? *Different* ones at that. I guess I'm just *promiscuous*." He paused as if contemplating the pretty faces of all the nurses whose hands he had been through. "Plan to see her again, Father?"

I answered that I was bound to see her on my rounds but

she had become engaged to a doctor. "That's probably what made me so sore," I admitted.

"I *read* you, Father. Anything else?" I hadn't prepared anything else. "Okay, Father, tell the good Lord you're sorry for all the sins of your past life. For your penance, I want you to pray that your nurse friend will be very happy." Through two or three camel-like yawns, he gave me absolution.

As I stood up, he grabbed me by the hand and squeezed it till it hurt. "Frank Strood from Jersey City," he said, grinning from ear to ear. "And you, do you have a name, too?" I wasn't used to shaking hands with underpanted Jesuits, but I told him who I was. "Great to meet you, Neil. See you again, I hope."

"Thank you, Father," I said, retreating to the door. I was afraid that if I didn't get out in a hurry he might want to confess his promiscuities to me. "You've been extremely helpful, Father."

He waved the towel after me like a handkerchief. "Think nothing of it. Bye now, Neil. Bye."

"Here are the chocolates, Nurse. Sorry I didn't remember them before." Lies. I had thought of nothing but her and her chocolates for days.

She thanked me, adding out of politeness, "I'd forgotten all about them Father."

With a bitterness that surprised me, I thought, "I bet you did."

To prove to her and myself that I had no designs on her I had bought her a half pound box of Cadbury's Milk Tray. She seemed pleased all the same as she clutched them to her breast.

"Father," she said, "I was wondering if you could possibly help me"—oh, yes—"help *us*"—oh, no. "Jeremy and I are planning to marry next Spring." Remembering the confessor's admonition I wished her every happiness.

She had been told that Jeremy had to have three or four instructions before marriage.

"He's not a Catholic, then, I take it, Nurse?"

"Jeremy's not anything." It staggered me that a beautiful, devout, apparently intelligent Catholic should contemplate giving herself away to a self-confessed pagan. "It helps, doesn't it, Father," she asked eagerly, "him not believing in anything?"

"I suppose so," I replied. "It means he won't object to the children being Catholics."

Her rose-like face rushed into bloom at the mention of children. I explained that non-Catholics had to sign in advance a promise that all children born of the union will be baptized and brought up in the Catholic faith. This seemed to upset her.

"Look, Nurse, he's not likely to raise any objections, is he? You made the point yourself that he hasn't any faith."

"No, Father, but he does have very strong convictions."

Blind prejudice, I thought, and nothing more. I said, "Presumably, he'll want you to follow your conscience?"

"What about *his* conscience? What if he wants...any children born of the union...to decide for themselves when they're old enough?"

"Awkward," I said unsympathetically.

Nurse Owen looked irresistible as she clutched her small box of chocolates to her heaving bosom. "That's why I was looking to you for help, Father. Could you have a meal with us?"

This was rubbing salt in the wound. "When's best for you, Nurse?" She mentioned Friday evening at eight. My diary was blank on that day, but a streak of perversity made me say, "Sorry I can't make that evening. The Friday after is all right."

She was so grateful and so quintessentially nice that if I'd had the talent I would have kicked my own backside. By eating at her place I would at least be spared having to share the bill. I was beginning to think that curates don't get paid nearly enough for all they have to suffer.

"Flat 6A, Flood Court," she said. "I share with a secretary. She goes out Friday evenings, so we can have a quiet meal, just the three of us."

The prospect of instructing Dr Spinks on the rights and duties of marriage made me nervous. He had seen sex in the raw; I had only met it in Brown's four volumes of *Moral Theology*. There all the spicy bits had been put into Latin, presumably so that inquisitive layfolk could not read it. Unfortunately, I was never very good at Latin.

Apart from Brown, there were only two ways we seminarists had been formally instructed on sex.

One was when Canon Flynn, our Professor, called us up two by two to his dais in the lecture room. This was in our fifth year. Spread out on his desk was a battered old tome with two sectional drawings, suitably distanced, of the respective anatomies. The text was in French, the parts were listed in Latin. To cap it all, sectional drawings, even of cars and airplanes, never meant anything to me.

The Canon darted here and there with his long pencil, taking care not to touch the page. He hurriedly gave the names and functions of various arcane organs which Brown had referred to in a lump as *membra minus honesta*.

"Any questions?"

There were never any questions. The chief point of seminary training was that you should know all the answers and none of the questions. It was all over in forty-five seconds.

In our sixth and final year, any gaps in our knowledge of sex and procreation were to be filled by Father Head, a Scottish priest who had been a surgeon before his ordination.

He turned out to be the leanest, most highly-strung individual I have ever seen. He stood at the blackboard from which he had hung enormous charts, red-faced and quivering, and proceeded to describe the act of intercourse as if it were a torrid, North African tank battle between Rommel and Montgomery.

I remember Jimmy Farrelly, the wag of the year, declaring afterwards, "Jesus! I still can't figure out who won."

I was in dire need of help when I went to Fr Duddleswell's study. He was engrossed in a tabloid newspaper which he bought regularly "for Mrs Pring." He looked up at me and tutted: "Father Neil, newspapers these days. 'Tis all bosoms and et ceteras. Cast your eye over this."

The picture in the center-spread was of a pretty girl in a nothing dress. The caption was "Thigh Priestess." He was at a loss to know why the media chose to advertise those parts of the human person so devoid of interest that previous generations had refrained from showing them at all.

"Seen one, seen 'em all," he said. "Like elbows. D'you not think, Father Neil, that sex is a bit like the aroma of coffee? It promises far more than it can possibly deliver."

I decided to take his word for it and nodded agreement.

He asked, "Be honest, now, can you imagine any sane individual getting titillation from the likes of *this*?"

"No, Father," I gulped, amazed at what age does to a man. I told him I had a mixed marriage arranged for the new year and wanted to know how to go about it.

He went across to his filing cabinet for the forms. The most important was the dispensation form for disparity of cult. The non-Catholic had to sign, promising never to interfere with the faith of the Catholic partner and to allow the children to be brought up in the true faith.

I told him the bride was a nurse and the groom a non-Catholic doctor from the K.G. "Well, Father Neil," he said, "be sure to put him right about birth control, divorce, abortion, and things of that sort." I was particularly to stress the Church's teaching on contraception. Sex is not a child's plaything. It is "a most marvellous mechanism for the manufacture of children." In this, men as far apart as Gandhi and Bernard Shaw were in agreement with the Church. "Birth control" usually meant no birth and no control.

I asked whether the dispensation was granted easily. "No trouble these days," he replied, "provided there's a reason for the marriage. Is the girl pregnant, for instance?"

"I shouldn't think so," I said, biting my lip to hide my indignation.

"Better check, Father Neil. Pregnancy is by far the most acceptable of the canonical reasons. Then there is *firmum propositum nubendi*, a firm determination to marry."

I acknowledged grudgingly that she had that. "What I mean," he explained, "is, would she marry in the Register Office if the Church refused her a dispensation?" I said I guessed not because she's a pious Catholic. "If we are not careful," he winked mischievously, "she will prove to be too pious and we will find *no* canonical pretext for marrying her off. Is she *super-adulta*, now?"

"What is 'over-age,' Father?"

"Twenty-four. Any girl above that is reckoned to have distinctly reduced chances of marrying. That is why the Church allows a dispensation, especially if she has a face like an old boot in the bargain."

Seeing I was stunned at what constituted advanced years in a woman, he explained that the law was made with Latin ladies, fed on a diet of spaghetti Bolognese, in mind. "They are mostly blown like autumn roses before our own women are in bud, you follow? But if canon law works to our advantage in this instance, why complain?"

I said that the girl in question couldn't be more than twenty-two and was not really ugly, so I supposed, almost joyfully, that was the end of it.

"Nothing of the sort, Father Neil," he came back, dashing my last hope. "The matter is exceedingly simple. Do not forward the application for a dispensation till the last minute and plead *omnia parata*. You tell the Chancellor of the diocese that 'everything is ready' for the wedding, and it would cause a ripe issue if at this late hour 'twere to be called off."

I put it to him that canon lawyers would find a loophole to let Satan have a holiday from Hell.

"Father Neil, the Church has all the loving deviousness of a mother, if you're still with me." I had to make sure the forms were filled in but not dated. If I reminded him to countersign them four days before the wedding, he would pass them on to the Chancellor himself. "And warn that young Medic, mind, I want no hanky-panky over birth control."

With polished shoes and brushed suit I rat-tatted on the door of Flat 5A. Nurse Owen, her long red hair cascading on to her shoulders, answered my knock clad in a long cherry-coloured dress. I admired the propriety of its high neckline.

Spinks was a mess in sandals, jeans, and open-necked shirt. The only bosom on show was his.

"Jerry it is," he said in a friendly tone. Since he already

knew my name I shook his hand in silence. "Glad Sarah could persuade you to come."

Sarah. Sarah Owen. What a lovely name.

"Our paths have hardly crossed," Dr Spinks went on, "since you cured that chap from the Gold Coast."

He actually had a small bald patch on top, the size of a florin. What was Sarah up to, hitching herself to a prematurely balding pagan? The Church really shouldn't be so liberal with her dispensations.

"Talk to Father, Jeremy," urged Sarah, "while I put the finishing touches to the meal."

When she went to the kitchen, Dr Spinks said, "Beer?"

"No thanks."

"Sherry?" I shook my head. "You *will* have a glass of wine with your meal?"

"Please."

He looked relieved that I had some weaknesses. "Tricky business, Fr Boyd, putting down the anchor."

It was in his favor that he had addressed me correctly. "I'm sure," I said.

A black hole yawned in the conversation. He asked me if I would like a record put on. I tried to shake myself out of my boorish mood and failed. "Not particularly."

Sarah must have had her ear pinned to the door. She returned and thrust a plate in front of me. "Have a crisp, Father. And here's the cheese dip." One glance at Dr Spinks told him, no records tonight.

"Marriage is a sacrament, isn't it, Father?" she said. "Jeremy is ever so keen to know what that means, aren't you, Jeremy?"

I was happy to be on home ground. I replied that it is a sacrament provided both partners are baptized.

"You *have* been baptized, haven't you, Jeremy?"

Dr Spinks said "Yes, love," but he had repudiated all that when he was twelve. I insisted that if he had been baptized, he was in some marginal sense a Christian, and if he married another Christian it would be a sacrament.

"Whether I like it or not?"

"Yes," I said aloud, and inwardly, "whether you damn well like it or not." He asked what follows from that. "To begin with," I answered, "when the marriage has been consummated there's no possibility of a divorce."

"Consummated?" He spoke it plainly as a four-syllable word. "Just once?" I nodded. "Bloody hell," he laughed, winking at Sarah, "only once *after* we're married, and it's till death us do part."

Sarah turned the color of her dress and retreated into the kitchen. Was he such a swine as to cast aspersions on his fiancée's honor?

Through avocado pear, plaice and chips, and apple pie it was sex and marriage. Dr Spinks was against everything the Church stood for on moral issues. He argued the reasonableness of abortion if the prognosis is that the baby's likely to be born deformed or the mother's life is in danger. Likewise in cases of rape.

I did not care to pursue this topic over fish and chips, but I made my position clear. God infuses the soul at conception and so the child in the womb has all the rights of a human being.

For him, talk about "murdering embryos" was mere rhetoric. The Church's teaching on birth control was "plain daft." "I've been researching into women's periods," he announced to Sarah's discomfort. "I've had the nurses at the K.G. and half the girls from the Teachers' Training College keeping charts and thermometer checks."

Sarah stood up to remove the dirty dishes. "Cheese and biscuits to follow."

"I even asked Norah if she'd care to take part," Dr Spinks went on. "Just to flatter her, of course."

The conclusion of his survey was that women are about as reliable as the English weather. My experience of Sarah had taught me that already.

"Did you know, Father," he confided in a boozy stage-whisper, "Sarah is one of my menstrual girls?" He roared with laughter and overturned his glass of Beaujolais. "Her cycles are so irregular, I call her 'Penny-Farthing.' One is thirty-three days, the next is eighteen." My right hand was volunteering to punch his nose.

He started dabbing up the wine with his table napkin. "Just my luck to be marrying the most inconsistent girl in the whole bloody troupe. Her only safe-period will be from fifty-five to ninety." He chuckled at his own joke. "I tell you this in strictest confidence. If, as your Church seems to want, I'm limited to every inconceivable opportunity, I might as well become one of the *castrati* in the heavenly choir." He dug me in the ribs. "Like you, old pal."

I should not have come. There was always the risk of this detestable chumminess.

"Safe-period," Dr Spinks mocked. "I heard your Church was against sex before marriage but denying it to a randy fellow *after* marriage is bloody ridiculous. Encourages infidelity." Without respite: "And why should a celibate presume to instruct me on sex. It's as lunatic as allowing only orphans to be marriage counsellors."

I was about to push his face in when the key turned in the lock. Sarah rushed in from the kitchen crying, "Oh, no!"

A young woman was at the head of eight or nine dishevelled youngsters. All were loaded down with tins, bottles, and French loaves.

"Debbie," said Sarah, wringing her hands, "you told me you were at Jane's for the evening."

"We were, Sarah darling, but her parents returned unexpectedly from Sunderland. Puritans the pair of them. They even lock up the beds while they're away."

Sarah introduced me to her flatmate. "Debbie Shackles, Fr Boyd."

"He's cute," said Debbie, pursing her lips in a lewd fashion. "Shake."

A tousle-haired lad, looking like a pearly king in a black leather jacket sewn with silver buttons, caught sight of me. "Sarah," he rejoiced, "you didn't tell us you were having a fancy-dress."

Someone put on a jazz record and several started to bob and weave. Johnny, the lad who imagined I was all dressed up, pointed to where a girl had parked herself on the floor and was gazing blankly like a guru into space. "Rebecca Sacks, Reverend. She's high."

"I'm Roman Catholic," I said.

"Care for a puff?" Johnny asked, after exhaling meticulously.

"No thanks, I don't smoke."

"Sticking to cigarettes, eh?"

I went across to Rebecca and tried to shake her hand. It felt broken. "Fr Boyd," I said.

"Tweet-tweet." She flapped her arms pathetically.

"My!" yelled Johnny from across the room. "You've really made a hit with Becky, man. Stay with it, and she's a regular communicant."

Sarah took my arm and steered me towards the door. "Father," she said, "I'm terribly sorry about this."

"Don't apologize," I shouted above the din.

As she let me out, Sarah was saying, "You will come again, won't you, Father? If you talk to Jeremy long enough, he's bound to come round to our way of thinking."

I was still licking my wounds next morning when the phone rang. A raucous voice: "Jack Hately, here. My wife needs to be anointed. Come quick, Father."

The phone went dead before I could ask the caller for his address. I rushed down to Fr Duddleswell's study. He wasn't there. I raced to the kitchen to ask Mrs Pring if she could decipher the call.

Calmly, without raising her eyes from her ironing, she said, "The Hatelys? Yes. They're on Fr D's side of the parish." Mrs Hately had been seriously ill for years, and Fr Duddleswell anointed her every month to be on the safe side.

"I'd better go along all the same, Mrs P."

"Wouldn't if I were you. Fr D'll be back within the hour, and he'll go himself."

"You're *not* me," I retorted, "and I'm going."

"Suit yourself," said Mrs Pring with a toss of her head. "3 Springfield Road."

I cycled there at speed. Effects of bombing were still to be seen in the battered buildings and vacant housing lots.

Number 3 was now the end house. Hardly a house. It was a basement, its outer wall buttressed by wooden beams sunk into the ground.

I knocked three or four times, louder and louder, until a woman's voice cried out, "Jack, a visitor, a *visitor*!" and an old chap beyond the biblical span hobbled to the door. He had a loud, hollow voice. "Is Fr Duddles away? You'll have to do, then."

Behind him, propped up on a large, brass bed was his wife, her yellowy-white hair splayed across a discolored pillow. Desolation. Water dripping into a pitted zinc basin, shelves in disarray, greasy stove, an ancient iron bath-tub, the pervasive smell of an old person's untended sick room.

"You the new curate?" Mrs Hately enquired hoarsely. "I can see all the girls falling for you." She was a flirt. "You're easy on the eye. Much nicer'n my Jack." I looked at Jack and marvelled at the minuteness of the compliment. "I keep telling Jack, I do so admire men with thick, wavy hair."

Her bald-headed Jack nodded and smiled inanely. Only a deaf man could have absorbed so many insults without protest.

I asked Mrs Hately about her health. "Haven't been well for centuries," she replied.

"There, there," boomed Jack in what was meant to be a soothing tone.

"First my arthritis, Father, and now"—indicating the faulty organ—"my heart."

"There, there, me darlin'."

I took out the holy oils. "Fr Duddles," she said, "anointed me last week."

"There, there," sounded the drum.

"Oh, shut up, Jack, won't you?" she yelled at him. He smiled until he saw her grimacing. "The anointing don't help ' me none," she croaked. "I'm a condemned building. Jack's done it. He'll be the death of me." Jack smiled slyly and toothlessly from the far side of the room. "The Church is taking my Jack away from me."

What did she mean? What possible use would the Church find for dear old Jack?

"He's just longing for me to drain away and die, Father. So's he can return to the bosom of Holy Mother Church."

Jack or Mrs Hately or both must have been married before. That made their present marriage invalid in the Church's eyes. If Mrs Hately died, Jack would be free to return to the sacraments.

I jumped to Jack's defence but she was not listening. "Been together more'n forty years," she moaned, "and now he wants rid of me. The cold, damp sod for me, the warm bosom of Holy Mother Church for him." She had evidently played this part before.

Jack stepped across to me and exploded in my ear. "Care for a nice cup of tea, Father?" My gesture of acceptance could not have been demonstrative enough. "P'raps another time, then," he said.

The scene was so dismal, so Dickensian, I couldn't wait to get out. "You're not in any pain, Mrs Hately?" I said, preparing to leave.

"Never in anything else." After a gesture of disgust in Jack's direction, she turned her face to the black and peeling wall.

"There, there," cried Jack. He sat quite still, the tears pouring down his cheeks. "There, there, me love, me precious." Her back was iced against him. "I'm never going to leave you, me dearest, never."

I moved nearer to his wife to give her my blessing. There was no thawing of the little iceberg in the bed, so I blessed her from behind. With a large, scaly fist, Jack signed himself.

When I left the room that was a house he was still crying, and a deaf old woman was resolutely turned towards the wall.

"Mrs Pring informs me that you went to the Hatelys, Father Neil." I was at my desk preparing Sunday's sermon. Fr Duddleswell said, "You were not to know, lad."

"That they are living in sin?"

He looked startled and wanted to know what I meant. I said I had worked it out that there must have been a previous marriage and divorce, as in the case of Mr Bingley.

"Nothing of the sort," sighed Fr Duddleswell, sinking into

a chair. "Steel yourself, lad, while I tell you the whole unsavory tale." I was in no mood for the facts of life. "You see," he said, secretively, "not to put too fine a point on it, Jack Hately is a priest."

It was my turn to look startled.

"Now do not take it too hard, Father Neil. These things happen, if you're still with me." He outlined the story.

Jack Hately, now eighty-three, left the priesthood in his late thirties and married Betty, "his partner," in the Register Office. There had been two children. The first appeared "far too soon" after they married. Both had emigrated to Australia.

Jack had been faithful to Betty according to his lights. He had worked hard as a postman and was not long retired when a landmine during the war sliced off the top two stories of his house. They had lived in the basement ever since.

Old Jack never went to church. He probably couldn't see the point because he and Betty were excommunicated, and he was bitter as well. When an Indian Bishop came to St Jude's to appeal for money, Fr Duddleswell took him to see the Hatelys. He couldn't converse with Jack who was already deafer than a pillar-box, but as he was leaving, the Bishop knelt down. Jack gathered he was asking *him* for his blessing. "Well, strike a light, Father Neil. Old Jack had not seen the inside of a church for more than forty years, and here was a coffee-colored Bishop kneeling at his feet, begging his blessing."

Jack started going to Mass again. He couldn't receive Holy Communion, of course. Mrs Hately could because she was in danger of death, and Catholics are entitled to lots of things in danger of death. Then eighteen months ago Jack came to the rectory to say he wanted to apply to Rome to have his excommunication lifted. This explained Mrs Hately's fear that the Church was going to take Jack away from her. She was doubly upset at the moment because Fr Duddleswell had received word from Bishop's House that Rome had at last replied to Jack's appeal.

"Tomorrow," said Fr Duddleswell, "I am off to see the Vicar General to hear what Rome has decreed."

As soon as he returned from Bishop's House next day at 11:30, he called for a cup of coffee—"the strongest the handle will take, Mrs Pring, if you please."

After that, he took a large white envelope from his briefcase and drew out of it a Latin document footed by a big red seal. The gist of it was that the excommunication could be lifted provided Jack and Betty swore solemnly to live henceforward as "brother and sister."

Fr Duddleswell slapped the document like a naughty child. "According to this, Father Neil, should there be one sexual lapse on Jack's part, he will re-incur all past censures, and we will have to start the long judicial process all over again."

"That's inhuman," I gasped.

"But very wise, very *worldly* wise, would you not say, Father Neil? Mother Church realizes only too well that the flesh is weak."

I protested. "Father, Jack's eighty-three. His flesh is far too feeble to be weak." But I had to admit that at his age and with his wife a permanent invalid, their living together as brother and sister was not too harsh an imposition.

Fr Duddleswell guessed that what would upset Betty Hately most was a condition laid down by the Vicar General. To ensure that Rome's terms were carried out to the letter, he personally decreed that Jack and Betty had to sleep in separate rooms. "When I told him, Father Neil, that they only have one room, he insisted that at least Jack and Betty should have separate beds."

"Poor old sods," I said.

Fr Duddleswell did not reprimand me, but he said quietly and firmly as if to silence insubordination, "Jack is a priest, you follow, Father Neil? He may die soon, and the V.G. wishes him to die in his own bed not in hers."

I did not accompany Fr Duddleswell when he briefed the Hatelys on Rome's decision. He came back, not too dispirited, to report that the old lady had sung her usual lament and started once more to outstare the wall. She had cheered up, though, when she learned that Jack was not about to leave home after all.

"Now, Father Neil, there is the little matter of a pair of single beds."

At Franklin's Store, Fr Duddleswell went into a huddle with the manager of the bedding department. It was a slack period, and the manager agreed to two divan beds being delivered immediately.

We were at 3 Springfield Road half an hour later when the van arrived. The delivery men screwed on the legs and, to my surprise, joined the divans together to make one double bed.

Fr Duddleswell winked at me. "Father Neil," he joked, "in me seminary days we used to say, beware of bulls and canon lawyers. They have minds like razors, you see, as sharp and as narrow. Better to let 'em have their own way, don't y'think?"

Jack Hately was delighted to have the best of both worlds: to sleep next to his wife and yet have a bed of his own. He lay down on it, sat on it, and bumped up and down on it.

As we were leaving, Fr Duddleswell slipped Jack a fiver which he pocketed out of sight of his arthritic mate. Then we drove off.

On the homeward journey, I said I thought it would be more merciful of the Church to dispense priests like Jack from the vow of celibacy if they wish to marry.

To my surprise, Fr Duddleswell was vehemently opposed to the idea. "Merciful?" he exclaimed. "Merciful? To whom, Father Neil? Tell me that, now. Is not the Church's first concern for the majority of priests who do not give up the Latin to run off with women? And are not those who stay confirmed in their vow by the Church's firmness in never granting dispensations?" He whistled through clenched teeth. "Priests who are tempted to wed in the Register Office are mightily dissuaded by the knowledge that they will never be able to marry in the sight of God or offer a woman the blessing of a Christian home."

It seemed to me that Jack must have felt as lonely as a sparrow on a roof top when he teamed up with Betty. "What about special cases?" I asked.

360

"Father Neil, believe you me, *all* cases are special. The strength of our Church lies in the fact that her rules are bent for nobody. She will no more allow a divorced barmaid to remarry than King Henry VIII. She will no more dispense a priest one year in the ministry than one who is middle-aged with a dozen illegitimate children to his discredit. Everybody, priest and layman alike, knows exactly where he stands."

He went on to give me a sharp lesson on the value of celibacy. In the seminary, we had learned that priests do not marry so that, freed from domestic ties, they can look after their people day and night. Fr Duddleswell had an altogether broader vision.

For him, a priest is "no tin cock on a church steeple." The whole system of Catholicism, its ethic, its creed, and its discipline, rests on priestly celibacy. It is celibacy that gives the priest moral authority to teach unpalatable truths. He may be out of touch in many things, but none of his congregation ever doubts that he has freely made an enormous sacrifice for their sake. He has the *right* to hand on the tough Catholic teaching on birth control, abortion, divorce, and homosexuality because he is a sign of Jesus, lonely and crucified, in their midst. "In the priest, Father Neil, sex bows its lovely head to something lovelier: self-sacrifice."

I had had recent experience of what he meant.

"Furthermore, Father Neil," he said peering through the windscreen as if he were gazing at some impossibly hideous futuristic vision, "should the Church ever relax her discipline on celibacy, the whole pack of cards will come tumbling down. Even bishops will be found making exceptions in 'special cases' to birth control and divorce. The good sisters, seeing the laxity of the clergy, will themselves leave their convents like flocks of migrating birds. And in the end, we will have Catholics advocating euthanasia for babies born handicapped and for old people who are incurably ill or a burden on the community." He was silent for a few moments before adding, "Merciful, he says. *Merciful.*"

We had reached the garage gates. I prepared to jump out and open up for him, but he touched my arm. "One more thing to further your education, lad." I looked at him wondering what next. "The Vicar General said that Bishop O'Reilly wants me to persuade Betty to retire to an old folks' home. She will be well looked after there, and he will foot all the bills."

"And old Jack?" I said, shocked at the prospect for one so near the grave.

He leaned his forearms on the wheel. "The Bishop would like him to go into the Dogs' House." This was the clergy's name for the Monastery of St Michael's, a kind of reformatory for naughty priests. "The Bishop's idea, Father Neil, is that Jack should end his days there. After a few months, Rome might be prevailed on to let the Prodigal say Mass again. That way, he could die with dignity."

However impressive the principle of celibacy, this was too much for my stomach. "Father," I burst out angrily, "Mrs Hately's old and infirm and in constant pain. *I* think Jack has a duty to stay with her as long as she lives."

"Whatever the Bishop says?"

I didn't hesitate. "Yes, whatever the Bishop says."

Fr Duddleswell looked at me with wrath all over his face. "Young man," he snapped, "have you no regard for the wishes of your Superior and father in God? Get out with you and open that gate." I rose but before I could slam the door on him, he leaned over and said, "I tell you this, Father Neil. If old Jack should ever leave his Missis after all these years, I will knock his bloody block off."

21

THE SEASON
OF GOOD WILL

Fr Duddleswell told me at breakfast of his decision to invite the Rev. Percival Probble, the Anglican Vicar, and "his good lady" to tea.

"He is convinced, you see, that at the summer swimming gala he saved me from a watery grave." I could not deny it. "I have no wish to disabuse him and so injure his self-esteem."

Mrs Pring put the dishes down with a clatter which showed what she thought of serving a clergyman's wife at our table.

Fr Duddleswell was looking for support. "What do *you* think, lad?" Honesty compelled me to say that Mrs Pring's opinion should be taken into consideration. What I meant was that she was, in a sense, our good lady, and she never ate with us.

"Well, then," said Fr Duddleswell, "that makes a slender majority of one to two in me favor." He obviously did not count votes, he weighed them. When Mrs Pring walked off in a huff, he said, "That will muffle her clapper for a while."

The prospect of tea with a married cleric reminded him of the time he had been on a pilgrimage to Rome before the war. In his hotel just off the Veneto was an Anglican bishop who was well and truly "conjugally matrimonified." "Now, Father Neil, the waiters in the restaurant were so flabbergasted that the Bishop, *il Vescovo,* should have a family that they called his wife *la Vescova* and the kiddies *i Vescovini*." He was shaking with mirth.

"Did they?"

My dry response quenched his ebullience. "I suppose, Father Neil, you would have to know Italian to appreciate the finer points of the joke." I kept silent to tease him further. "It seemed strange to them, you follow? that a man in a Roman collar would have a wife and bambini."

"Why strange?"

He said lamely, "They were not used to it."

"Is something 'strange,' Father, simply because an Italian waiter in an Italian restaurant in Italian Italy is not 'used' to it?" He must have thought a little divil had got into me that morning. "Didn't you tell them, Father, that St Peter who emigrated to Italy had a mother-in-law and so presumably a 'good lady' of his own?"

He was in rapid retreat. "I did not think of it, like."

"More's the pity," I said, sucking in the air like soup. "Those Italian waiters would have been very droll on the topic, I'm sure. Imagine, now, the first *Papa* having a *Papava* and, who knows? even a few *Papavini*?"

He slid off the end of the conversation by rising to his feet and saying his Grace after meal in a single movement. "I've fixed tay for tomorrow at four. Sharp. And, remember, Father Neil," he bawled, "'tis the season of good will to all." He slammed the door behind him.

Mrs Probble over tea reinforced every argument I had ever heard in favor of celibacy. Obese and topped by a plumed hat of Royal Ascot dimensions, she was one long verbalized stream of consciousness.

When the Vicar managed to edge in a word and attributed Christ's prayer, "That they may be one" to Luke instead of John, Mrs Probble squawked at him, "Husband, I *told* you to leave the theology to me."

She was intrigued to know how we made so much money each year on our bazaar. She herself toiled like a Trojan to make a success of St Luke's Garden Fête with the most meagre results. "How *do* you manage it, Fr Duddleswell?" She pronounced it "Duddle-swell."

My parish priest explained to "Mrs Prob-bull" that we Catholic priests have more numerous female helpers than Solomon himself. Their womanly hearts are touched by our masculine ineptitude to rally round without our needing to ask.

Mrs Probble seemed to contemplate for an instant the possibility that she was a liability to her husband and not the huge asset she had always presumed. "Is that how you explain it?" she said.

"Now, it can hardly be sex-appeal, can it, Mrs Prob-bull?"

"Evidently not," replied the Vicar's good lady haughtily. If she replied less haughtily than she might have done, it was because she had a favor to ask for her husband. On the last Sunday before Christmas, St Luke's was to have a visitation from the Anglican Bishop of the diocese. A social gathering had been organized to greet him in St Luke's Church Hall. Fr Duddleswell must know that Anglicans, for all their deeply held Christian beliefs, were not so good at "attending" as Roman Catholics. And what Mrs Probble wanted to ask—as did the Rev. Probble, of course—was, "Would Fr Duddleswell, in the spirit of the season, bring some of his own flock to swell the numbers?"

As the request unfolded, I could see Fr Duddleswell's good will being stretched to its limits. He disliked intensely the ascription of episcopacy to a "doubtfully baptized Anglican layman." He also loathed the idea of any remotely religious association with those "Church of England cuckoos who threw us out of our nest."

The Rev. Probble, sensitive to Fr Duddleswell's religious scruples, assured him that they were cancelling Evensong. It was to be a simple "fraternal" gathering with beer laid on for those who wanted it. Fr Duddleswell's Benediction of the Blessed Sacrament was at 5:30, which would enable him to bring as many of St Jude's congregation to St Luke's at six o'clock as had a mind to come.

Fr Duddleswell listened in silence as the Vicar explained

that to have three Anglican clergy present and only the usual twenty to thirty of their parishioners would not create a very fortunate impression on "Bishop Pontin"—another wince from my parish priest.

It was Mrs Probble who let the cat out of the bag. "It will so help Percival's preferment, you see, Fr Duddleswell"—she pronounced his name this time with meticulous accuracy.

The Rev. Probble was man enough to admit that he had his eye on a Cathedral canonry, "but far be it from me, Father, to ask you to violate your Catholic conscience." It was a good pay-off line.

Fr Duddleswell eyed me to see if I was voting with him, but I stayed disenfranchized. "You promise me, Vicar, no Evensong?"

The Vicar gave his word and made things easier by pointing out that our co-religionist, Mr Albert Appleby the Mayor, had graciously accepted his invitation to meet the Bishop.

When the Vicar and his wife had left, Fr Duddleswell tried to make light of his defeat. "I am not one to renege on me debts," he said, "when there is no matter of principle involved." Then changing the subject with a rueful laugh: "Such is the 'felicity of unbounded domesticity.'"

His laughter became less forced when I replied, "The Vicar, now, he is a regular Duke of Plaza-Toro and no mistake."

Preparations for Christmas began in earnest. Paper chains and bells were hung in the hall and the dining room. Dangling from the ceiling above Fr Duddleswell's chair "in hope forlorn" was a sprig of mistletoe. The large plaster figures for the crib were taken down from the organ loft and given their annual dusting.

Mrs Pring was stirring silver threepenny pieces into the Christmas cake mix, as thick as cement in an enormous bowl. I heard Fr Duddleswell tell her that he would provide the turkey.

The carols on the radio attuned our minds to the peace and good will of the festive season. I had even arranged for Mrs

Rollings to be received into the Church on Christmas Eve. She was not ready for it and never would be but at least, with Christmas over, I could begin the new year without the prospect of meeting her every couple of weeks.

The mood started to change on Fr Duddleswell's last day off before Christmas. In the afternoon, Mrs Pring went to Siddenhall to visit her daughter. Being at a loose end, I donned an old roller-knecked pullover and gum boots and puttered around in the garden. The weather had turned mild, and I put in a spot of digging with the garden fork. I was well stationed to hear the telephone and the front doorbell.

It was the side-doorbell that rang about 3:15 just as dusk was coming on. Standing there were two sturdy, clean-cut young men in dark suits. At first, I thought they were policemen in plain clothes. One of them put his foot in the door while the other thrust a huge open book in front of my nose. It was too black to see but I smelled it was a Bible. Having only a garden tool in my hand I was at a disadvantage.

"May we come in, Brother?" said Brother Frank, the Bible-bearer, in an American accent, pushing past me. I did not like being addressed below my rank, but what could I do?

They carried me with them into Mrs Pring's kitchen and deposited me in a chair at the table. Brother Frank and Brother Hank sat down opposite me and told me that they represented the Church of Christ Shepherd.

Was I a Christian? A Catholic, gee. Well, they wanted to tell me there and then that in their eyes nobody was beyond the mercy of God.

They had a beautiful message for me personally from Jesus if only my eyes were not blind and my ears not deaf.

There followed a long but speedy history of "the fastest growing religious movement in the history of this planet." I would be relieved to know that their beautiful Founder, the divine Father Shepherd from Scranton, Pennsylvania, had no hang-ups about sex, indeed he positively encouraged the exercise of "all these beautiful faculties," and they could prove his assertions from this beautiful and holy Book.

Now to the nitty-gritty. In the Church of Christ Shepherd,

every member had to freely contribute the biblical tithe of his salary. "So how much do *you* earn, Brother?" asked Brother Hank of the protruding foot.

I was so surprised at being allowed to speak I couldn't get the words out. After further encouragement, I said, "Forty pounds a year."

"Are you on welfare, Brother?" said Brother Frank.

"No, I'm a Roman Catholic priest."

"Jesus Christ!" they exclaimed in chorus. I instinctively bowed my head, followed them as they raced to the door and bolted it after them. They couldn't have made a quicker exit had I admitted to being a leper.

In the morning, Mrs Pring took me aside. "Any visitors yesterday, Father Neil?"

I said that two religious cranks had tried to convert me. "Why?"

"Because," she whispered, "the clock on my mantelpiece went missing."

I apologized and promised I would buy her another for Christmas. She wouldn't hear of it. It had never worked and was purely ornamental. If she raked around in the garden, she said, she would probably find it there. At least, they hadn't stolen the Hoover.

I thanked her for not telling on me to Fr D. In my heart, I could not be sure the young men had taken the clock. I hadn't seen them take it, and they seemed sincere. What made me furious was their vicious method of evangelization. They muscled in, took over your castle, and brought out the worst in you. I was glad Catholics did not browbeat people like that.

Later, above the cooing of pigeons, I heard Fr Duddleswell talking to Billy Buzzle the Bookie across the garden fence. "Seeing 'tis the season of good will," Father Duddleswell said as he tossed Pontius, Billy's black labrador, an enormous bone. Billy was maintaining that two of our flock had knocked on his door the afternoon before and tried to convert him. Fr Duddleswell replied that none of his parishioners was stupid enough to attempt any such impossible thing.

"They had Irish brogues, and they wanted to sell me a

Bible," said Billy. This was proof for Fr Duddleswell that they were none of his. Orangemen at worst. Catholics rely on the teaching authority of the Church and do not go in for Bible-hawking.

"Anyway, Fr O'Duddleswell," said Billy, "they didn't succeed. I persuaded them instead to put £5 at 10 to 1 on Twinkletoes in the 3:30 at Plumpton. It came in last."

He asked Fr Duddleswell if he would care for a little wager himself. It was already snowing in Scotland, Yorkshire, and North Wales. Billy would bet £5 even money that it would snow in Fairwater in the next three days. Fr Duddleswell said that whatever the forecast his rheumatics told him the opposite. The final terms agreed were these: If it snowed within three days, Fr Duddleswell would pay out £5. If it didn't, Billy would give Fr Duddleswell a ten-foot Christmas tree for the church and a fifteen pound turkey.

A large round thrush alighted on the fence in time to see the two men, in the spirit of the season, shake hands on it.

My mood darkened further when Mrs Rollings came for her final instruction prior to her reception. I had run through the ceremony with her including the mechanics of confession when she burst out, "I don't know how to say this, Father." She found a way to tell me that, while she accepted without argument the Catholic doctrine on Hell, Indulgences, Papal Infallibility, the Real Presence of Christ in the Blessed Sacrament and the Virgin-birth, she could not agree with the teaching on birth control.

If she had broken the news to me three months before I would have rejoiced. I had not wanted her in the first place, but to lose her after all that agony was hurtful and humiliating. With hindsight, it was naïve of me not to realize that something was wrong with her marriage when she had twins of eight and no more children.

I had to be true to my convictions. There could be no compromise on a matter of principle, and I had no intention of browbeating her in the manner of those phoney evangelists.

We shook hands on the doorstep and said our last goodbye. I would not have believed it possible, but there were tears in her eyes as she left. And there were pangs in my heart, too.

I told Fr Duddleswell the bad news at the first opportunity. He treated it as a huge joke. As far as he was concerned there was no question of me losing my first scalp. He paid tribute to my long-suffering.

I wanted to know how he could take it so lightly.

"Well, you see, Father Neil, in ethical matters I am far more concerned that she practices what the Church preaches than gives it her full-hearted consent. I have already assured the Bishop that she will be a model Catholic, at least in that respect."

It was a mystery to me how he expected Mrs Rollings to practice what she did not believe in.

"To tell the truth," he said, "'twould be a needless expense on her part to contravene the Church's law and 'twould require the operation of the Angel Gabriel for her to conceive again." He explained that "the necessary equipment" had been taken from her after the twins were born.

He immediately got on the phone to the baker. "Wilf," he said, "get your woman over here on Christmas Eve at eight A.M. sharp. Fr Boyd will do the drowning himself."

Fr Duddleswell's rheumatics proved an accurate barometer. A tall Christmas tree was duly delivered to the church and a turkey to the rectory with a terse note attached to its neck: "To the luck of the Irish." Fr Duddleswell pinched his arm and prophesied that God would not whiten the world before Christmas Day itself.

On the evening of Sunday 22nd, Fr Duddleswell conducted a short Benediction with the three standard hymns, *O Salutaris*, *Tantum Ergo* and *Adoremus*. The hundred or so present were reinforced by members of the Legion of Mary, the Saint Vincent de Paul Society, and the Union of Catholic Mothers, as well as various unattached parishioners who had heard rumors of free Anglican beer.

By 5:45, Fr Duddleswell and I led our well-muffled army through the streets of Fairwater singing carols. A thoughtful

370

Irishman, Paddy Feeney, took a collection from the passers-by on our way. There must have been two hundred of us.

In ten minutes we were in the warm climate of St Luke's Church Hall. The Anglican clergy and their wives and about twenty parishioners were waiting to greet us. On the stroke of six, the Mayor arrived and, soon, Bishop Pontin, modestly dressed by Catholic standards in a black suit with a clerical collar above a purple stock.

The Rev. Probble introduced Fr Duddleswell and me to the Bishop, adding barely coherent comments on the excellence of inter-Church relationships in Fairwater.

The Bishop, speaking Oxford English, thanked Fr Duddleswell for bringing along "one or two" of his parishioners.

"Or three or four, sir," replied Fr Duddleswell.

After thirty minutes of eating and drinking in small groups, the Vicar clapped his hands at a signal from Mrs Probble to announce that the fraternal meeting would have to close until the Carol Concert in the church was over.

Fr Duddleswell, who had no idea it was going to begin, was furious at the deception practiced upon him by his opposite number. The Mayor, forewarned no doubt, took him by the shoulder. "Don't be upset, Farver," he whispered. "It's Mrs Probble's doing. No 'arm. I'm attending it myself."

"Well may you, Bert, but I have no official position to maintain, d'you hear? To enter that mausoleum would be tantamount to *communicatio in sacris*. 'Twould be to desecrate all within me that is holy." He gritted his teeth. "I am withdrawing meself, me curate, and me entire flock."

"Farver, Farver," pleaded Mr Appleby, "you can't do that in the season of good will." He argued that if angels could sing hymns for Jewish shepherds, there was nothing to stop Catholics singing a few carols for the conversion of Protestants. "Besides, Farver," he said, "I am officially deputing you to act in this civil function. You can give out the food parcels to the old-age pensioners." A bus-load of them were at that very moment stepping down and trooping into the church.

That seemed to pacify Fr Duddleswell's conscience.

Before the Vicar invited him to accompany the Bishop to the vestry, I saw Mayor Appleby slip Fr Duddleswell his own small mother of pearl rosary.

We were into the third carol before Fr Duddleswell appeared. In spite of the disguise, there was no doubting the fact that it *was* he dressed as Father Christmas. At least he wasn't required to sing with us—and the beard hid his blushes.

He told me afterwards that his being cheated in earnest was all made worthwhile by the Bishop remarking to the Rev. and Mrs Probble in his hearing: "Percy, my dear fellow, I do congratulate you on having so many devout Irishmen in your congregation."

Just before eight o'clock next morning, Mrs Rollings appeared white-faced in the sacristy as I was preparing to vest. She was clutching a Catholic Truth Society pamphlet in which was printed the ceremony for the reception of a convert. She was worried that in the part about "abjuring heresies" she would have to denounce totally her former religious upbringing and all its errors.

"I can't say it, Father," she sniffled.

I tried a different approach. "All right, Mrs Rollings," I said sarcastically, "if you can't say it, try whispering it."

Instead of slapping my face, she brightened up immediately. "It won't be so bad like that, will it, Father?"—and she returned to the front bench to join her family.

Everything went well until her confession. I led her down the church to the confessional. Before I could stop her she had gone into my side and closed the door. It took some time to sort it out and get her kneeling on the prie-dieu in her proper place. She was muttering something about the "number and species of all my mortal sins."

Fr Duddleswell's opinion was that there are basically two types of female penitents. Those that suffer verbally from either diarrhea or constipation. "The latter sort," he had said, "need a liberal laxative of kindness."

Mrs Rollings was of the latter sort when it came to confessing her sins, and I was running out of kindness. The confession took fully twenty minutes. I did not know if she had got everything off her chest. If it was still a bit grimy, I consoled myself with the thought that that was her responsibility not mine.

When it came to the conditional baptism, I longed for the return of the ancient practice of three-fold total immersion. After all, I had a strong right arm.

Of course, I was sorry for my wicked thoughts afterwards when I saw the joy on the faces of the Rollings' family. The nominal head of it took me aside when Mass was over. "Fr Boyd, since my wife started her instructions, she is a different person."

"So am I, Mr Rollings," I said.

All dismal reflections were banished by the approach of Christmas and the birth of Christ. Ever since I was a child, the highlight for me has been Midnight Mass.

The church looked gorgeous with its flowers and potted-plants, the lights and decorations on the Christmas tree, and the crib with the babe in the manger.

Some strong men of the parish had been deputed to bring a couple of hundred extra stacking chairs from Tipton Hall and to keep out the drunks. Fr Duddleswell and I, clad in cassock and biretta, began by greeting the parishioners as they trooped in smiling.

The Rollings family was there and old Jack Hately and Mrs Dodson and Dr Daley and Lord Mitchin and Mr Appleby with his wife. To my great joy, Archie and Peregrine arrived early and sat in the front row. It hurt me that Fr Duddleswell should tell me to make sure "that fine pair keep their hands out of the till."

Mr Bottesford, the undertaker, sneaked in and sat at the back like a publican. Mother Stephen led a representation from the Convent. Even Billy Buzzle put in a brief appearance to cast his eye over his Christmas tree. "Tell you what, Fr O'Duddleswell," he said, "I'd willingly swop my takings for yours tonight." There was bound to be a congregation of five hundred.

We spent the last quarter of an hour before Mass hearing

confessions. When I opened my box to go to the sacristy, who should I see but Nurse Owen with Spinks, the abortionist, in tow. "Herod come to worship the Lord," I thought. I could have sworn that his bald patch was now as big as a half crown.

Fr Duddleswell was to sing the Mass and preach while I assisted him. Already the church was bursting at the seams. In the loft, the choir was in full voice. "*Adeste fideles*" and then "Silent Night, Holy Night." "Ah, 'tis enough," I said, as I helped Fr Duddleswell struggle into his white vestments, "to turn your taps on."

The sermon, full of theatrical gestures, was superb. It was received in utter silence. For his text he chose St Paul's words: "Christ, though rich, became poor to enrich us with his poverty."

He began by calling attention to the Christmas tree, "donated by a devout parishioner." That tree was the most Christian of all our symbols. Did not the first Adam eat from a tree in disobedience to God? And did not the second Adam, Jesus, eat the bitter fruit of another tree out of obedience to God His Father? Legend has it that the cross of Calvary was planted in the very spot where once grew the tree of the knowledge of good and evil.

Was not the Christmas tree itself the signal proof of God's power to bring life out of death? Here it was, green wood in the deadness of the year. Like a Child born of a Virgin Mother. Like resurrection following upon Calvary's death when our Lord and Saviour Jesus Christ flew on His wooden bird to God the Father.

God, according to Fr Duddleswell, is deviousness carried to infinity. He quoted Crashaw's lines on the birth of Christ:

> Welcome all wonders in one sight!
> Eternity shut in a span,
> Summer in winter, day in night,
> Heaven in earth and God in man.

Jesus forsook his eternity to enter time. He gave up His infinite riches to become poor for us and to enrich us with his poverty. He forsook the bosom of His Father for birth in a cave. None of this could have happened had not God humbled Himself to become as a child in order to enter the Kingdom of Man. God planned it so that Mary the Virgin would be her Maker's maker and her Father's mother.

And what is the meaning of all this?

"That we, me dear people, should ourselves forsake guile to merit the blessing God gives to the weak and foolish of the world. That we should forsake our love of earthly riches for the sake of the spiritual blessings brought to us in abundance by the poor little Babe of Bethlehem."

Throughout the recitation of the Creed that followed the sermon, the congregation was rustling through pockets and purses to forsake some of their money. The Christmas offering, the most generous of the year, is by tradition the personal gift of Catholics to their priests. As the collection was being harvested, I glimpsed it out of the corner of my eye. I could only marvel at the sight of the notes mounting in a dozen plates borne by the parish jury of twelve just men. I was already contemplating buying Meg and Jenny a bicycle each.

So eloquent was the sermon, so beautiful the singing, that for the first time I could remember there was no mass exodus of parishioners as soon as the celebrant gave the last blessing.

Fr Duddleswell and I put on our birettas prior to leaving the sanctuary. He handed me the precious tabernacle key saying, "Put this in the safe, Father Neil, and then join me in the porch."

Within a minute, I had locked the key away and, having removed my cotta, joined him at the church door to wish the congregation a happy Christmas as they threaded between us.

When we were left alone, Fr Duddleswell locked the front door, and we retired to the sacristy where he unvested. "Ah, Father Neil," he said, "the old saying is true: the Christmas midnight Mass equals twenty-one Masses."

He was the first to notice that there was something disturbing about the collection plates. They contained only silver and the usual assortment of brass with Irish pennies predominating. The notes, the checks, and the envelopes specially designed to hold the offering of a whole family had disappeared.

My heart experienced a great pang when I saw what the loss of the money meant to him. He seemed so vulnerable at that moment. "There must have been nigh on £300 in notes," he gulped. "Have you any idea where the divil it can be, Father Neil?"

Half-jokingly I said, "Search me, Father," and turned my cassock pockets inside out to reveal nothing but a bunch of keys. As an afterthought, I asked, "This is serious, isn't it, Father? You're not having me on?"

He did not hear me. He was muttering something about cash being the only thing not covered by the insurance. He opened the door leading to the house and asked Mrs Pring if she had taken the big money into the rectory for protection. I heard Mrs Pring deny stridently that in all these years she had laid one finger on his filthy lucre.

I helped him search the vestment drawers and cupboards. We looked into the confessional and he even rummaged in the straw of the crib. Not a smell of it.

"Father Neil," he sighed in desperation. "I want you to dial 999 and get the police here immediately."

When I returned a couple of minutes later, the lights in the church were ablaze. I saw him turf the baby Jesus out of his crib in case the thief had temporarily hidden the loot there.

We unbolted the front door and stood there waiting for the police. "Did they give you any indication when they would arrive, Father Neil?"

I said no. The police prided themselves on answering any emergency call in any part of London within three minutes but, of course, this *was* Christmas Eve.

Fr Duddleswell's glasses were steaming, and he was thumping his arms diagonally against his shoulders to stop himself from shivering.

Outside the church, the scene was one of perfect peace. In the windows of houses across the road, the lights of Christmas trees were winking off and on. Smoke from chimneys was ascending like incense to heaven. In that mild winter, a few rose

376

bushes, caught in the shaft of light from the church, could be seen still bearing flowers.

As we waited, he went crazily through the suspects. Archie and Peregrine he accused first. I defended them stoutly. Peregrine was capable of anything, but surely Fr Duddleswell remembered how Archie had made him give the doctor back his wallet.

He turned his ire on Billy Buzzle. In revenge for losing his bet, Billy could have climbed the fence, got in through our back door, and slipped into the sacristy after the collection. Even Fr Duddleswell discounted this theory. Billy Buzzle, he admitted, was far too crooked to stoop to straightforward theft.

Bottesford, now, what about Bottesford? He certainly had a score to settle. Another ludicrous suggestion. He was a rich man and found it far less hazardous robbing the dead than the living.

Still no sign of the infernal police. He sent me to look in the confessionals again. I reported that I'd had no luck.

"Father," I said, "isn't it more likely that the thief is someone without any criminal record who found all that money lying around too great a temptation?"

"One thing, lad," he said—"Oh, where are these bloody police? When they arrive there will be no Silent bloody Night, Holy bloody Night around here. And they will probably send that brute who biffed you under the counter." He was now able to pick up the thread of his thought. "One thing, I promise you, lad. *You* will not go short. I will make it up to you."

"Please, Father, no," I replied staunchly. "If Jesus became poor for..."

He interrupted me. "You cannot sole your shoes on £40 a year without your fair share of the Christmas offering, you follow? Neither can I, come to that. Oh, where in heaven's bloody name are the police?"

Mrs Pring addressed us over our shoulders. "Isn't it about time you two men came in from the cold?"

Fr Duddleswell pulled his biretta more firmly down on his head. "This is man's work, woman, and we are awaiting the police."

Mrs Pring said, "They're not coming."

"They are delayed, woman, but they will be here any hour now." Mrs Pring was adamant that they were not coming. He turned to me. "Father Neil, did you not phone them?"

I carefully removed my biretta and smartly turned it upside down so as not to lose any of the precious collection of notes, checks and envelopes.

He sat down on the cold step, rubbed his eyes inside his glasses, puffed, and rubbed his eyes again. Then he sprang up as if to box my ears.

I took one step backwards. "Now, remember, Father Charles, 'tis the season of good will."

Mrs Pring roared with laughter. He silenced her by giving her a mistletoe peck on the forehead and wishing her a merry Christmas.

"Lock up, Fathers," she said in a snuffly voice. "I've boiled the kettle, and there's an Abishag waiting for each of you in your beds."

We stayed there together for a few moments longer looking out on the quiet scene. In the light of the streetlamps, we saw the first snow of the winter fall. A large flake settled on my eyelash till I blinked it away.

"Ah, Father Neil," said Fr Duddleswell serenely, "are they not the only pure white doves this sordid city sees?" I nodded, half asleep now. Suddenly he turned on me. "I have something else I have been meaning to say to you." I didn't think he would let me off that lightly.

He stretched up his arms and embraced me. "Merry Christmas to you, Neil."

"Merry Christmas, Father," I said.